Lenge 6 9th
_5:15_

WHITE WOMEN'S RIGHTS

WHITE
WOMEN'S
RIGHTS

The Racial Origins
of Feminism
in the United States

LOUISE MICHELE NEWMAN

New York • Oxford

Oxford University Press

1999

Oxford University Press

Oxford   New York
Athens   Auckland   Bangkok   Bogotá   Buenos Aires   Calcutta
Cape Town   Chennai   Dar es Salaam   Delhi   Florence   Hong Kong   Istanbul
Karachi   Kuala Lumpur   Madrid   Melbourne   Mexico City   Mumbai
Nairobi   Paris   São Paulo   Singapore   Taipei   Toyko   Toronto   Warsaw

and associated companies in
Berlin   Ibadan

Published by Oxford University Press, Inc.
198 Madison Avenue, New York, New York 10016

Oxford is a registered trademark of Oxford University Press

Library of Congress Cataloging-in-Publication Data
Newman, Louise Michele.
White women's rights : the racial origins of feminism in the United States /
Louise Michele Newman.
p.   cm.
Includes bibliographical references and index.
ISBN 0-19-508692-9; ISBN 0-19-512466-9 (pbk.)
1. Feminism—United States—History.   2. Women's rights—United
States—History.   3. Racism—United States—History.   4. White
women—United States—Social conditions.   5. Minority women—United
States—Social conditions.   I. Title.
HQ1410.N475   1998
97-53286

1 3 5 7 9 8 6 4 2

Printed in the United States of America
on acid-free paper

Acknowledgments

I BEGAN THIS BOOK as a graduate student in the American Civilization and History programs at Brown University over a decade ago, and my greatest debts are to the faculty and graduate students there who befriended and supported me while I was writing my dissertation. Most important, I want to thank Professor Mari Jo Buhle for the extraordinarily generous and incisive criticism she gave me year after year, draft after draft, and for the unobtrusive way she provided for all my academic needs. I also benefitted greatly from the careful readings of Professors Jack Thomas, James Patterson, and Mary Gluck, each of whom contributed substantially to my development as a historian. In addition, I would like to express my appreciation to Naomi Lamoreaux, who encouraged me at a crucial stage in the formulation of the topic, and to Tony Molho, whose compassion sustained me at a critical juncture. I also benefitted immensely from the discussions held by the Pembroke Seminar, under the direction of Karen Newman and Elizabeth Weed. Moreover, a number of scholars outside my graduate institution treated me with great kindness and respect, bolstering me when I was feeling discouraged. I am especially grateful to Hazel Carby for her expansive commentary at my first professional conference; to Nancy Hewitt for validating my work at a very early stage; and to Gina Morantz-Sanchez for adopting me as one of her graduate students, even though she already had plenty of her own. Finally, I had the unbelievable good fortune to be surrounded by a remarkable community of vibrant young scholars, whose work has been the inspiration of my own. To these friends and colleagues, I offer my love and gratitude: Kevin Gaines, Matt Jacobson, Gail Bederman, Bob McMichael, Lyde Cullen Sizer, Todd Gernes, Linda Grasso, Oscar Campomanes, Ann duCille, Tricia Rose, Suzanne Kolm, Lou Roberts, Elizabeth Francis, Ruth Feldstein, Lauri Umansky, Donna Penn, Michael Topp, Yardena Rand, Harry Williams,

Bruce Dorsey, Roseanne Camacho, Jim Cullen, Krista Comer, Jane Gerhard, Jessica Shubow, Bill Hart, Joanne Melish, Nan Boyd, and Melani McAlister.

I also would like to express my gratitude to my former colleagues at Harvard University, who welcomed me into their community and expressed genuine interest in my work, especially Liz Muther, Jan Thaddeus, Chris Appy, Jim Engell, Pat Palmieri, Meredith McGill, John Norman, Bob Lamb, Mark Dolan, and Laurence de Looze; and to my current colleagues at the University of Florida who have taken me under their wing and challenged me in many ways: Bob McMahon, David Colburn, Ron Formisano, Bert Wyatt-Brown, Bob Zieger, David Chalmers, Jeff Adler, and Tom Gallant. Special thanks to Susan Kent, Carol Lansing, Maria Todorova, Betty Smocovitis, Sue Rosser, Elizabeth Langland, Pat Miller, Jeff Needell, Eldon Turner, and Maureen Turim for their loving mentorship and helpful criticism of my work. I also would like to acknowledge Kathryn Burns, Fitz Brundage, Fred Corney, Jay Tribby, Mark Thurner, Sheryl Kroen, and Alice Freifeld, colleagues-in-arms, for their sincere enjoyment of my work and to thank them, as well as Arun Agrawal and Rebecca Karl, for the exquisite pleasure of their intellectual company. Finally, I want to express my deep appreciation to Betty Smocovitis, Matt Jacobson, and Rebecca Karl for their thorough perusal of my manuscript. Betty saved me from many embarrassing errors, Rebecca compelled me to fill in (some of) the logical gaps, and Matt assured me that the manuscript was ready for publication. There is no question that this book would have been much the worse without their interventions.

In addition, I feel a great debt of gratitude to Marcia Dambry of Harvard's History and Literature program, Sybil Mazor of Brown's American Civilization program, and Betty Corwine and Kimberly Yocum of the University of Florida's History Department, for taking such good care of me, far in excess of what our professional relationship requires. I have also been blessed to have had many wonderful students, and I am truly grateful for their interest and support. I want especially to thank Andrew Chancey, James Wilson, Matthew Franks, Carol Giardina, James Thompson, Andrew Frank, Lisa Tendrich Frank, Wendy Beauchamp, Julian Chambliss, Donna Jacklosky, Adam Lifshey, Rebecca Walkowitz, James Forman, Jr., Jace Anderson, Ben Wizner, Ryan Schneider, and Linda LeCraw.

Scholars can not do good work without great librarians, and I have been fortunate to have had the assistance of some of the best. Elizabeth Coogan and Beth Beretta-Wendt in the interlibrary loan division of Brown's John D. Rockefeller library worked tirelessly to furnish many crucial sources. Karen Lamoree, during her tenure as the Farnharn archivist in the Hay Library, shared with me many of her discoveries of previously unknown materials. John Van Hook at the University of Florida has proven to be a resource beyond measure. Moreover, I will be forever grateful to the American Council of Learned Societies for believing in this project enough to grant me a year-long fellowship, and to the University of Florida for providing financial assistance in the summer of 1994 and release time from teaching in 1995–96.

I would also like to express my respect and gratitude to the staff at Oxford University Press. In particular, I want to thank my editor Thomas LeBien, who has had faith in me from the start; Susan Ferber and Robert Milks, who have taken care of all the nagging details with extraordinary patience and grace; and my copyeditor, Martha Ramsey, whose dedication to perfection has made this a much better book.

Finally, I want to thank my family and friends who have stood by me these many years: my mother, Marsha Newman, who did everything she could to ease the pain of writing; Barbara Walzer, who taught me how to read the past in physical objects; Matt Jacobson, whose inimitable mix of humor, compassion, and understanding sustained me at the end; Gina Morantz-Sanchez who read (and liked) every word I wrote; and Kevin Gaines, who believed in me and appreciated the value of my work, long before I did.

Contents

WHITE WOMEN'S RIGHTS

Introduction

Woman's Rights, Race, and Imperialism

> If rethinking the historical contours of Western racial [and femi-
> nist] discourse matters as a political project, it is not as a mani-
> festation of an other truth that has previously been denied, but as
> a vehicle for shifting the frame of reference in such a way that
> the present can emerge as somehow less familiar, less natural in
> its categories, its political delineations and its epistemological
> foundations.
>
> Robyn Wiegman, *American Anatomies* (1995)

IN THE SPRING OF 1888, the renowned suffragist Elizabeth Cady Stanton (1815–1902), at age seventy-three, presided over an international gathering of women. The meeting was held in part to commemorate the fortieth anniversary of the Seneca Falls Convention of 1848, the first organized meeting of woman's rights activists in the United States. This was a joyous occasion, a time of celebration and renewed commitment, an opportunity for younger members to pay tribute to older pioneers. Lucy Stone (1818–1893), Susan B. Anthony (1820–1906), and Julia Ward Howe (1819–1910) all occupied places of honor on the stage. Alongside them sat Frederick Douglass, famous ex-slave, abolitionist, and elder statesman, a longstanding supporter of woman's rights. Invited by Anthony to say a few words, Douglass expressed his pleasure at seeing Stanton chair such an extraordinary gathering, alluding to how great a change in public reception had occurred since the 1848 convention. Then Anthony singled out of the audience a black Philadelphian, Robert Purvis, for special mention: "Let us hear from the one man who was willing to wait without a vote for twenty years, if need be, that his wife and daughter might vote with him."[1]

Anthony was acknowledging the support that these prominent black men, Douglass and Purvis, had lent to the woman's movement over the past three decades. Yet her words of welcome and praise also concealed mixed feelings about the way in which woman's rights had become subordinated to civil rights in this era. The issue to which Anthony referred when she spoke of Purvis as "the one man who was willing to wait" was Purvis's opposition, some twenty years earlier, to the Fourteenth and Fifteenth Amendments. These amendments had recognized freed male slaves as citizens and provided sanctions against states that excluded African American men from the franchise. But they had made no such provisions for the suffrage of black or white women. In voicing his opposition to the proposed amendments, Purvis had taken an unusual stand among African Americans, most of whom supported the amendments as a first, although incomplete, step to full racial equality.

Anthony's own decision to oppose these amendments was also a poignant one. She had been an ardent abolitionist in the 1840s and 1850s and had called for the emancipation and enfranchisement of enslaved men and women. Yet, at a moment of celebration thirty years later, Anthony could not help registering the lingering anger she felt over what she and other suffragists called the Republicans' betrayal of women. Suffragists had actively supported the Republican party during the Civil War and had expected to be rewarded with the franchise afterward. But this had not happened. Despite the growing visibility and influence of the woman's movement in the 1870s and 1880s, woman suffrage still had not been granted.

In Anthony's mind, Purvis's opposition to the Fourteenth and Fifteenth Amendments contrasted starkly with Douglass's support, and she harbored continuing resentment. Several years earlier, in 1884, Anthony had refused to support publicly Douglass's second marriage, to Helen Pitts, a white woman, telling reporters, "I have but one question, that of equality between the sexes—that of the races has no place on our platform."[2] When Stanton, Anthony's dearest friend and longtime associate, was considering a statement supporting Douglass's marriage, Anthony importuned her not to do so: "I do hope you won't put your foot into the Douglass question, the intermarriage of Races! Only to think of how Douglass threw the principle of Equality of political right to women—overboard—in '69 & all along—saying himself first and you afterwards! If there were no other reason—you should now let him carry his own burden if he has voluntarily risked such."[3] This remark, made in private and in obvious pique, nonetheless signals the extent to which racial tension between white and black activists lasted for decades and was a crucial part of the context in which the white woman's movement defined its own interests in the postbellum period. Anthony's comment serves as a tragic reminder that the possibility for interracial cooperation between the struggles for civil rights and woman's rights was diminished in the 1870s and 1880s by white women's feelings that a great injustice had been done them when black men received the franchise ahead of them.[4]

Moreover, Anthony's statement to reporters that interracial marriage was a race question and so outside the purview of her suffrage organization was motivated, in part, by a desire to avoid the controversy that interracial marriage raised for a white public. Anthony did not want to consider whether the marriage of Helen Pitts, a white woman, to Frederick Douglass, a black man, might also be deemed relevant to white women's right to marry at their own discretion. Acknowledging privately to Stanton that Douglass "may be right & general feeling wrong," Anthony was nonetheless determined to keep white women's struggle for the franchise separate from this other concern.[5] More than just a strategy to keep the woman's movement focused on a single issue, Anthony's efforts to avoid this particular controversy reveal how white activists worked to develop specific relationships among race, gender, and equality: that is, to establish the white woman as the primary definer and beneficiary of woman's rights at a time when the country was growing increasingly hostile toward attempts to redress the political, social, and economic injustices to which African Americans were subjected. White women's expressions of resentment over the enfranchisement of black men and these women's subsequent decision to keep the movement clear of "race" questions were part of a larger post-Reconstruction retreat from support of racial justice.

On the other hand, expressions of sympathy for the enslaved, which was at the crux of white abolitionist ideology in the antebellum period, had continuing resonance for the white woman's movement in the postbellum period. In the 1840s and 1850s, white female abolitionists had emphasized the similarities between their own oppressed status as wives and daughters under patriarchy and the debased condition of "the Negro" under slavery. White women, the argument went, could empathize with enslaved peoples because they, as women, experienced a similar oppression due to their sex. White female abolitionists urged white women to engage in political activity on the slave's behalf: to remonstrate with their own family members, to raise money, to sign petitions, and so forth—in fulfillment of their Christian responsibility to remedy the injustice of slavery.

However, new realities had to be addressed as a result of emancipation (1863–1865) and the ratification of the Fourteenth and Fifteenth Amendments (1868–1870). Legal recognition of black male citizenship meant that white women could no longer claim a shared political status (disenfranchisement) with black men. White women's social identities had to be reconstituted to reflect the changing relationship of "woman" and "the Negro." Where antebellum suffrage ideology often emphasized a common victimhood, postbellum suffrage ideology stressed white women's racial-cultural superiority to newly enfranchised male constituencies—not just black men, but also naturalized immigrant men. "Think of Patrick and Sambo and Hans and Yung Tung," Stanton proclaimed in 1869, "who do not know the difference between a monarchy and a republic, who can not read the Declaration of Independence or Webster's spelling-book, making laws for Lucretia Mott, Ernestine L. Rose and Anna E. Dickinson."[6] From Stanton's perspective, the proposed Fourteenth and Fifteenth Amendments threatened to introduce a new gender-based hierarchy that overlooked distinctions of education, virtue, and refinement, qualities that Stanton believed existed in greater degree and preponderance in white women because of the more advanced development of their race. "If the Fifteenth article of [the] Constitutional amendment ever gets ratified . . . it will have one good effect," Stanton declared, her anger and pain palpable. "Woman will then know with what power she has to contend. It will be male versus female the land over. All manhood will vote not because of intelligence, patriotism, property or white skin, but because it is male, not female."[7]

Anthony refrained from discussing her feelings of anger and resentment in public and overcame them sufficiently to form political associations with African American leaders, including Ida B.Wells (1862–1931), Booker T. Washington, and Frances W. Harper (1825–1911).[8] Indeed, upon their deaths, Anthony and Stanton were remembered by African American reformers as devoted friends of the race.[9] Perhaps focusing on the earlier days and conveniently forgetting the later tensions, Robert H. Terrell, a black justice of the municipal court in Washington, D.C., would recall having heard in his boyhood, just after the Civil War ended, that Stanton, Anthony, and Julia Ward Howe had "devoted all their efforts toward obtaining the ballot for the Negro, even to the neglect of their own dearly cherished cause."[10] During the renewed suffrage battles of the 1910s, Terrell argued that it was the duty of "every man with Negro blood in his veins" to support woman suffrage, as a way of paying back a debt to those white women who had supported abolition and black male suffrage.[11]

In the decades from 1870 to 1920, however, despite moments of interracial cooperation, the woman's movement remained largely segregated.[12] Many white leaders dismissed the concerns of black women—such as miscegenation, interracial rape, lynching, and their admittance to the all-women cars on the Pullman trains—as "race questions," irrelevant to the woman movement's foremost goal of "political equality of women." For instance, Alice Paul, president of the National Woman's Party, refused to allow Addie Hunton, a black field secretary for the NAACP, to address the National Woman's Party in 1921 about the disenfranchisement of southern black women, because Paul considered it more appropriate for this problem to be taken up by a racial rather than a feminist organization.[13] The refusal of white reformers to address black women's specific experiences of gender oppression meant that the white woman's movement would remain mostly white, even when individual women of color were invited to become members of white-dominated women's groups.

Anthony's way to respond to the political complexities of black women's intersecting oppressions of race, class, and gender was to slot black women into norms and roles delineated for white women. In 1900, for example, she urged the National Negro Race Conference to "include women of color," arguing that ever since the Fourteenth and Fifteenth Amendments recognized black men as citizens, "from that hour [on] the colored wife owed service to a husband instead of to a slave-owner, so that legally she simply exchanged a white master for a colored one who controlled her earnings, her children and her person."[14] Anthony was adopting the decades-old argument that white women had used to articulate their criticism of patriarchy, an argument they created in the 1840s to validate their own sense of subjection to husbands by comparing their suffering to that of slaves. Black women, however, rarely formulated such arguments in expressing their resistance to political oppression, since they generally considered black men their allies and protectors against a racist culture. Most black women supported the Fourteenth and Fifteenth Amendments, which they considered advantageous to the black race as a whole and thus to themselves, even though their own rights to citizenship went unaffirmed.

Instead, black women protested the ways in which white culture sexualized and victimized them, exposing the unstated but implicit racism in the ideology of true womanhood, which stigmatized women of color as incapable of chastity, purity, and moral virtue.[15] Finding that white women's organizations often refused to take action on their behalf, black women formed national organizations of their own, such as the National Association of Colored Women and National Council of Negro Women, in which they worked to gain for themselves the respect, safety, and physical freedom that society routinely accorded white middle-class women.[16]

The woman's movement was never entirely segregated, however, and dialogues between white women and women of color took place in public forums. In May 1893, for example, six black women addressed the delegates at the World's Congress of Representative Women, a mostly white convention that assembled as part of the Columbian Exposition in Chicago, and spoke to the ways that African American women were struggling to redress racialized forms of gender oppression. Yet, as Hazel Carby reminds us, "the fact that six black women . . . addressed the World's Congress was not the result of a practice of sisterhood . . . but part of a discourse of exoticism. . . . Black Americans were included in a highly selective manner as part of exhibits with other ethnic groups which reinforced conventional racist attitudes of the American imagination."[17] Carby's perspective is not merely the wisdom of hindsight. White visitors to the Chicago Exposition were acutely sensitive to this discourse of racial exoticism that linked blackness with primitivism and used such moments to define and position themselves in relation to primitive peoples in an ongoing process of national identity formation. One white woman wrote home:

> [After seeing] man in his primitive state . . . black, half-clad, flat-headed, big-nosed, protruding lips, a perfect type of brutality and heathenizm [sic] . . . it occurs to you— why—you are the only race not "on exhibition—" & the whole exhibition is evidently for you—& you are the crowning glory of it all. You are [aware] how vastly superior is the light of our Christian civilization to the dark and semi-darkness of other lands, how our race in intellect stands towering above other races, & how grateful one feels that their [sic] lot has been cast in such an enlightened clime—& not in the lands that have got it all yet to go through before they catch up."[18]

White women in the movement formulated their views on equality in the context of such highly charged debates on race and were acutely sensitive to the racial dimensions and implications of their ideologies and practices. Proclamations of white racial superiority were everywhere around them, justified in lynchings, performed in minstrel shows, and celebrated in fairs and expositions. It is not surprising, then, that white activists had a heightened racial consciousness of themselves as civilized women, contributing to and reinforcing dominant religious, scientific, and cultural ideologies that attributed to them unique moral and political roles on the basis of this identity. Blending religious conviction (the ideal of Christian evangelical benevolence) with science (social evolutionary theories) and political ideology (progressivism), white proponents of woman's rights helped create new roles for themselves that explicitly maintained the racial hierarchies that were based on the presumption that Anglo-American Protestants were culturally, as well as biologically, superior to other peoples. By 1900, as Joan Jacobs Brumberg has demonstrated, white women had become fully conversant with the newly emerging languages of evolution and ethnology and had developed "an entire vocabulary that implied the degradation of [nonwhite, nonwestern] women: zenanas and harems; the seraglio and the bagnio, female infanticide and suttee, concubinage and polygamy; bride sale; foot-binding and ear and nose boring, consecrated prostitution and sacrifice; bastinado; child marriage and slavery."[19]

Like other white reformers, white woman's rights activists measured the (lack of) "social progress" of non-white races in terms of their (lack of) conformity to Anglo-American Protestant middle-class gender relations. One of the most profound ironies of this history, then, is that at the very moment that the white woman's movement was engaged in a vigorous critique of patriarchal gender relations, it also called for the introduction of patriarchy into those cultures deemed "inferior" precisely because these cultures did not manifest these gender practices. White leaders' critique of the cult of domesticity—as too restrictive and oppressive when applied to themselves—went hand in hand with their defense of domesticity as necessary for the "advancement" of "primitive" women.

The implications of this paradox were far-reaching in U.S. society and race relations. First, it limited the critiques white women could offer of the racism and sexism within their own culture because in the end they had to acknowledge that patriarchy had been key to their own racial advancement. Second, white women's belief in their own race-specific trait of moral superiority permitted them to view other cultures with condescension, if not outright disrespect, enabling a Sinophile like Donaldina Cameron, for example (who spent most of her adulthood living happily among the Chinese women she "rescued" from prostitution in San Francisco), to lament that "the Chinese themselves will never abolish the hateful practice of buying and selling their women like so much merchandise, it is born in their blood, bred in their bone and sanctioned by the government of their native land."[20] Such reasoning made it possible for white women to overlook the ways in which white culture was implicated within the systems of oppression that governed the lives of nonwhite women. White women often scapegoated the purportedly less enlightened men of "primitive" cultures as the worse perpetrators of abuse, when the problems were much more complex. (In the Chinese case, U.S. immigration law made it difficult for Chinese men to bring their wives and families to this country, and states forbade intermarriage between Chinese men and white women.)

Most significantly, white women's use of this discourse to empower themselves as central players in civilization-work during the late nineteenth century helped consolidate an imperialist rhetoric that delegitimized dissent from nonwhite and non-Christian women. Civilization-work encompassed all activities intended to "elevate" a "lower race," including converting "savages" to Christianity, "Americanizing" immigrants in settlement houses, "uplifting" Negroes for the Freedmen's Bureau, and "bringing civilization" to Indians on reservations. (See fig. 1-1 in chapter 1.) Although white women frequently expressed feelings of sympathy and solidarity with non-white, non-Christian others, these pronouncements also served to increase their own authority, both in relation to other groups of women, who had to uphold Christianity as a superior religion in order to gain access to the sisterhood, and in relation to white men, who were slowly having to acknowledge white women's claims to greater effectiveness in civilization-work.

The evolutionist discourse of civilization also had profound significance for women of color, who had to demonstrate that they too were "true women" (pious, virtuous, genteel, refined, soft-spoken, well-dressed) in order to certify that their race already was or could soon become civilized. Black women reformers offered themselves as models of black womanhood to prove to white racists that there was nothing inherently inferior about the black race. Josephine St. Pierre Ruffin, a leader in the National

Association of Colored Women, declared, "Too long have we been silent under unjust and unholy charges [that black women are immoral and unchaste]. We cannot expect to have them removed until we disprove them through *ourselves*. . . . Now with an army of organized women standing for purity and mental worth, we in ourselves deny the charge."[21]

As the personal and political struggles of Anna Julia Cooper, Ida B. Wells, and Mary Church Terrell suggest, civilization, racial progress, and woman's protection within the home were interconnected in ways that made it impossible for black women to repudiate altogether the prevailing ideologies of the cult of domesticity and true womanhood. Like their white counterparts, black women reformers also used evolutionist discourses of civilization to justify their own social activism. They asserted their duty to "elevate" and "uplift" the masses of black women, upholding the values of domesticity, chastity, temperance, and piety that the white middle classes considered to be evidence of a civilized race.[22] Olivia Davidson (Booker T. Washington's second wife) declared, "We cannot too seriously consider the question of the moral uplifting of our women, for it is of national importance to us. It is with our women that the purity and safety of our families rest, and what the families are, the race will be."[23]

Black women's desire for and advocacy of bourgeois respectability, which mandated conformity to the norms of patriarchy, was not so much evidence of their class conservatism, however, as it was of their commitment to taking responsibility for racial uplift. Racial uplift entailed self-help, racial solidarity with black men (rather than criticism of them), temperance, thrift, chastity, social purity, as well as acceptance of patriarchal authority.[24] As this list suggests, there was some commonality of goals between black and white woman's movements, particularly with regard to temperance, purity and suffrage. But these common commitments were not sufficient to override the social and political divisions between black and white women that derived from the material differences in their lives and that were exacerbated by nineteenth-century discourses.

Ideologically and materially, theories of social evolution raised specific problems for African American women that were not present for white middle-class women. How could black women stay at home and have husbands support them, when the conditions of their lives required that they contribute to family income? How could they maintain the submissiveness and sexual purity demanded of the "true woman" when white men could rape black women at will? How could black women take part in a white woman's movement that believed in the myth of the black male rapist and persistently declared that blacks were mired in animalism? Evolutionist theories helped placate white women who were dissatisfied with their own social roles by suggesting that they were much better off than were African American (and Asian American and Native American) women in their own cultures. But evolutionist discourses called into question the status of black women, who had to devote their efforts to proving that blacks were as civilized as whites.

In sum, evolutionist discourses limited and prescribed the social positions, political ideologies, and utopian visions of "Negro" and "Anglo-Saxon" women in very different ways. White women's determination to transcend the limits of the domestic sphere, which they accomplished by proclaiming themselves central to civilizing missions, enabled them to imbue themselves with social authority at a time when their access to more formal, public, institutional forms of power was severely circumscribed. Black women's analogous claims that they too were central to their race's social progress meant that they had to disavow their cultural past, adopt patriarchal gender norms, and celebrate white cultural practices. The strictures of social evolution required that black women ascribe to that which white women were beginning to reject (domesticity, protection, patriarchy). In the end, the argument that black women might also act as civilizers (or uplifters) of the more "lowly" among their race, as Kevin Gaines has argued, "implicitly faulted African Americans for their lowly status" and "replicated the dehumanizing logic of racism."[25]

This book, then, begins by exploring the particular precepts of evolutionist theories concerning social progress, woman's nature, and racial difference that Anglo-American Protestant women used to empower themselves. Although Anglo-Protestant elites often argued that physical differences (especially in reproductive organs, psychology, and mental functioning) distinguished "man" from "woman," they did not think that men of different races shared the same masculine nature, or that women of different races shared the same feminine nature. Rather they believed that different races were gendered in different ways, or that gender was race-specific. White woman's rights activists thought of themselves as widely different from white men in sexual terms yet fundamentally similar to white men in racial-cultural terms. They believed that "primitive" men and women exhibited far fewer sexual differences between them than did "civilized" men and women. Sex differences both accounted for, and were the product of, the development of higher civilizations; to eradicate sexual differences between civilized men and women would mean the de-evolution of civilization back into a less advanced society.

In other words, evolutionist discourses specified that the sexual differences between (white) women and (white) men were both the cause and effect of bourgeois patriarchal gender practices and the key to white racial advancement. (White) women's physical frailty, emotional sensitivity, and moral superiority were presumed to be the evolutionary consequences of those patriarchal practices that characterized middle-class gender relations among (white) Christians: (white) men purportedly shielded (white) women from hard labor, protected them in a domestic sphere, and loved and cared for them within patriarchal, nuclear families. In 1875, the young physician and labor reformer Azel Ames succinctly summed up the significance of evolution for woman's status when he proclaimed that "[woman] has been, in all time, man's companion and helper . . . degraded with the savage, lightened in her burdens and raised to higher dignities with each step of man's advance."[26] Evolutionist theories construed the social condition of the (white) woman as both a measure and consequence of the advanced development of her race within the superior Christian civilization of the United States.

I have used parenthetical modifiers here, and will do so throughout this book, to signal how nineteenth-century discourses used universalizing language to make generalizations about the "race," "woman," or "man," while intending these generalizations to apply only to people of Anglo-Saxon (or Euro-Protestant) descent. Nine-teenth-century discourses conflated race, class, culture, religion, and geographic origin, so that "Anglo-Saxon," "American," "white," "civilized," "Caucasian," "Chris-tian," and "Protestant" frequently served as interchangeable terms, with each of these categories encompassing the others.[27] I have chosen the term "white" as a convenient abbreviation, but I am using it in the nineteenth-century sense to refer to those Amer-icans of European descent who in this period were designated as members of the white middle class.

In addition to delineating class and racial boundaries, social-Darwinian thinking also proscribed religious hierarchies. Catholicism, although recognized as part of the Christian tradition, was considered to be less evolutionarily advanced than Protes-tantism.[28] For example, throughout the nineteenth century, the subordinate and im-poverished economic status of Irish Catholics as laborers in the United States testified to their cultural-racial-evolutionary inferiority. Later, at the end of the nineteenth century, when Irish Catholics gained political power in urban areas like New York and Boston, their supposed antirepublican forms of municipal government, purported susceptibility to bribery, and alleged close associations with organized crime, offered further evidence of their status as a not-quite-civilized race. Social evolutionary theory also reinforced dominant beliefs that Jews (Hebrews) were a heathen race, but here interesting exceptions were made for those wealthy Jewish Americans who could trace their ancestry in the United States back to the eighteenth century, and who thereby presumably had benefited from their contact with the civilizing influence of Christian culture. Upper-class Jews who could establish the requisite social pedigrees were granted their own legitimate forms of "civilized" culture and history.

In general, then, social evolutionary discourses in the late nineteenth century treated race as a stable, although not entirely inflexible, biological *and* cultural entity. A person was born with his or her race predetermined by ancestry, and the conse-quences of this inheritance was of great import. To be identified as a member of a spe-cific race (Anglo-Saxon or white; black, Negro, or African; Hebrew; Italian; Celt or Irish; Slav; Chinese; Indian; Malay; etc.) designated the individual as an inheritor of specific cultural and religious practices. For the individual, little could be done to transcend this racial identity in his or her lifetime, although education and upbring-ing could temper the original racial inheritance. Yet within a generation or two, for Euro-Americans at least, the cumulative effects of climate, geography, education, up-bringing and acculturation could dramatically "improve" or "advance" a race. In fact, in less than a century, the racial identities of certain Euro-American groups would be entirely redefined. In the 1890s, for example, the Irish and Italian Catholics, as well as Jews of East European origin, were each considered separate races, distinct from Anglo-Saxon Protestants, and definitely not white. But by the mid–twentieth century, the descendants of these groups were assimilated as part of a newly defined white race and were reclassified as "Caucasians."[29]

As historian Anne McClintock has pointed out in relation to Britain, nineteenth-century discourses used race, class, and gender as analogies for one another: "the rhetoric of race was used to invent distinctions between what we would now call *classes,"* while "the rhetoric of *gender* was used to make increasingly refined distinctions among the different races," and "the rhetoric of *class* was used to inscribe minute and subtle distinctions between other *races*."[30] In other words, the Zulu male could be termed the gentleman of the black race; the white race figured as the male of the species, and the urban poor likened to savages. (White) women were considered inherently less advanced than (white) men, akin to black peoples, primitives, and apes. In the words of the famous French psychologist Gustave Le Bon, "All psychologists who have studied the intelligence of women, as well as poets and novelists, recognize today that they represent the most inferior forms of human evolution and that they are closer to children and savages than to an adult, civilized man."[31]

Out of such ideological frameworks specific questions arose for white reformers. How much room was there for transcendence of or escape from these evolutionary categories? Could individuals of specific races, classes, and sexes be modified by education and upbringing to such an extent that they would then transmit to their own offspring racial-cultural-sexual traits that were different from those they had inherited from their parents? Northern Europeans, who had had a Protestant tradition in their native homelands before emigrating to the United States, had proven their capacity for "Americanization," but what about the Irish and Italian Catholics, or East European Jews? Were Africans, Indians, Filipinos, and Chinese similarly civilizable? If so, what might be done to accelerate the evolution of these purportedly lower races? How could they be assimilated into, without slowing down, the evolution of white Christian civilization? Specifically, what should be done to reform Native American men who had multiple wives and refused to give up their "savage" practices? Would permitting the immigration of Chinese women help instill Christianity among Chinese men, or would the increased numbers of Chinese women merely accelerate the propagation of a heathen race? By way of answering these questions, Anglo-Protestant women forged a new identity for themselves as experts on racial questions and "protectors" of vulnerable peoples (See fig. I-1).

With the best of intentions and in the name of "sisterhood," white women urged each other to enlarge their sympathies and expand their understandings of the "woman question" so as to be able to address the various social, economic, and political circumstances of nonwhite and non-elite groups of women. As part of their civilizing mission, white women organized their own separate organizations to pressure the U.S. government to change its Indian policies and outlaw lynching. They also created home missions and settlement houses to introduce patriarchal domesticity to other races and "Americanize" immigrants. For example, in 1874, Presbyterian women organized a Chinese Mission Home in San Francisco as a refuge for Chinese prostitutes.[32] In 1886 a branch of the National Woman's Christian Temperance Union (NWCTU) established the Colorado Cottage Home to care for unwed mothers in Denver. That same year, Angie Newman founded the Industrial Christian Home in Salt Lake City for Mormon women who wanted to leave polygamous marriages.[33] Jane Addams established the first settlement house for immigrants in Chicago in 1889, creating an organizational model that would soon be adopted in other urban areas.

Much suffering was alleviated by these efforts, and many success stories could be

FIGURE I-1 Racial uplift and the supplicant slave. Lincoln Centennial Souvenir. Postcard, 1909. White women appropriated and transformed the ideology depicted here—of a white male liberator—into an ideology of the white female civilizer during the second half of the nineteenth century.

told of individual women who received higher educations, became able to support themselves, left abusive marriages, or escaped prostitution to lead much happier lives. One might suppose that such successes would have led white women to question their belief in their own imputed racial and class superiority, as nonwhite and working-class women demonstrated that they could be as intelligent, virtuous, chaste, pure, religious, and home-loving as white middle-class women. But these individual successes only proved to white women that their faith in social evolutionary processes was justified—that such processes did have the power to advance women of "lower" races and classes. White women continued to base their own resistance to patriarchy and to protest their exclusion from the franchise on the grounds that they were effective civilizers, every bit the equals of white men because of a shared evolutionary history.

On the one hand, evolutionist discourses enabled the United States to subsume that which was problematic and contested—white middle-class women's emergence as public actors—within a utilitarian ideology of white racial progress. On the other hand, the multiple ways in which white woman's rights activists made use of evolutionist racism—in their responses to scientific and medical literature, in their travel writing and ethnographies, in their fiction, poetry, essays, and letters—assisted the United States in carving out an identity as an imperial nation in an age of empire, allaying the nation's doubts about its rightful place in the "civilized" world. Colonialism took shape around the Victorian invention of patriarchal domesticity, as the middle-class home became a space for the display of imperial spectacle.[34] Imperialism, in turn, suffused domesticity and woman's rights ideology with ideas about evolutionary progress and white racial superiority. Anglo-American female activists proudly took credit for the importance of the domestic sphere (even as they critiqued it as too restrictive), using it as a locus from which to demand an expansion in political rights for themselves.

Woman's Rights and Imperialism

From 1870 to 1920, the period encompassed by this study, U.S. society was undergoing massive and unprecedented social and economic changes that were sparked by the Civil War, a cataclysmic event that left deep scars in the country's collective consciousness. Articles appearing in such periodicals as the *National American Review, Nation, Atlantic Monthly*, and *Harper's* depict a nation struggling to overcome political divisions between north and south, economic divisions between capital and labor, and racial divisions between whites and blacks, native-born and immigrant, Anglo, European, African, and Indian. Although political reconstruction of the South formally ended in 1877, the North remained focused on the "Southern Question" and worried that the South might regain its political ascendancy over New England by creating a political alliance with the West. Whites throughout the country remained obsessed with the Negro Question, arguing over what to do about the ever-growing numbers of lynchings and incidents of vigilante violence. Growing concern with the "woman question"—that is, white women's increased visibility in the public sphere and their demands that they be granted equal political rights with white men—occurred simultaneously with these other developments. Observers at the time linked these various phenomena, viewing the drop in white women's fertility in relation to the demographic increase in the populations of non-white peoples. They drew connections between what they interpreted as white women's refusal to have babies and an increase in the availability of higher education for women, between demands for suffrage, mounting immigration, and continuing pressure on urban wages.

By the late 1890s, the country also found itself faced with the question of whether it should colonize Cuba, Guam, and the Philippines. The Spanish-Cuban-Filipino-American War of 1898–1902 precipitated vociferous debates about the United States' decision to annex the Philippines. These debates revolved around the question of whether assimilationist policies that had been created in the years immediately following the Civil War to deal with Negroes, Indians, the Chinese, and other immigrant groups residing within the United States would be effective in addressing the situation of "primitives" residing in the tropical climates of foreign lands. Those opposed to annexation argued that assuming the government of foreign territories was in violation of the Monroe Doctrine and went against democratic principles, especially the principle of government by consent[35] and that benign forms of colonization would be ineffective and harsher forms too brutal to have the desired effect of "uplifting" savages.[36] Opponents of annexation often invoked the domestic "Negro problem" to warn the United States against embarking on the "deluded" mission of trying to assimilate *foreign* "primitives." The outlook of Mrs. Jefferson Davis was characteristic:

> [T]he President probably has cogent reasons for conquering and retaining the Philippines. For my own part, however, I cannot see why we should add several millions of negroes to our population when we already have eight millions [of them] in the United States. The problem of how best to govern *these* and promote their welfare we have not yet solved. . . . The question is, What are we going to do with these additional millions of negroes? Civilize them?[37]

Other anti-imperialists, like Carl Schurz, believed that assimilation had been partly successful at home, but they doubted that assimilationist policies would succeed if implemented abroad: not only would Anglo-Saxons fail to "civilize" the primitives of the Philippines, but in the process of trying, it was feared that whites would lose their own distinctive racial traits, as the enervating effects of the climate would be too great for Anglo-Saxons to withstand. The Protestant work ethic would disintegrate; adherence to democratic principles would deteriorate; and, most worrisome for anti-imperialists like Schurz, bourgeois Victorian sexual morality and gender relations would dissipate.[38]

To make an overseas civilizing mission both theoretically possible and politically appealing, certain reconceptualizations of white men's roles in the evolution of civilization needed to take place. The supposed superior adaptability of the Anglo-Saxon male, previously understood as an advantageous trait in a so-called "empty" American wilderness, was considered a drawback when it came to colonizing what were recognized to be fully inhabited foreign lands. The adaptability of the Anglo-Saxon male and the inflexibility of the primitive other had to be partly reversed for imperialism to make sense. Anglo-Saxon civilizers had to be able to retain their whiteness, while primitives had to be able to modify their blackness, for the spread of white civilization to occur. White men either had to resist the temptations toward miscegenation (which they clearly had not done in the U.S. South) or if they succumbed, then somehow it had to be shown that an increase in a mixed-race population would not jeopardize the future development of white civilization. (See fig. I-2.)

Important theoretical developments occurred from the late 1880s through the 1910s that addressed these concerns. First, social theorists like Edward Ross and Thorstein Veblen reconceptualized racial and sexual traits in new evolutionary terms, with the result that the Anglo-Saxon male colonialist was no longer seen as *so* adaptable as to be in danger of losing his racial distinctiveness while residing in the tropics.

A Test of Discipline

FIGURE I-2 Sexual dangers of U.S. colonialism. A Test of Disipline. Postcard, c. early 1900s. For anti-imperialists, one of the greatest dangers of colonizing primitives was the threat of miscegenation.

Second, white women, who previously had been seen by evolutionists like Charles Darwin and Herbert Spencer as inferior to white men—and thus held responsible for retarding the progress of white civilization—were suddenly transformed by theorists like Lester Ward, Otis Mason, and Charlotte Perkins Gilman into "racial conservators." White women now supposedly provided the racial stability that ensured the nation's future "racial progress," so the country could proceed with its imperial projects. This theoretical redefining of white women's role meant that white men were more free to cross the color line sexually, without there being any risk of white racial degeneration, as long as white women kept having adequate numbers of white offspring. Any decline in white women's fertility, however, was interpreted as a tremendous social problem, leading to "race suicide." (See figure 1-1 in chapter 1.) Miscegenation between white women and black men was deemed to be so threatening to whites' racial future that many whites found it inconceivable that white women would voluntarily have sex with black men. White women's traditional role as "mothers of the race" along with their new role as conservators of the race made them crucially important to the successful carrying out of U.S. colonial projects.

Woman's Rights Historiography

This study is part of a thirty-year tradition in women's history scholarship that has concerned itself with the ways in which white women have responded to and manipulated racial ideologies in their quest for gender equality. Ever since the publication of Aileen Kraditor's *The Ideas of the Woman Suffrage Movement* in 1965 and Ellen DuBois's *Feminism and Suffrage* in 1978, women's historians have understood that beliefs in white superiority profoundly shaped the arguments and strategies of white leaders in the suffrage movement. Kraditor argued that as the (white) suffrage movement transformed itself from a "visionary movement [an outgrowth of northern abolition] . . . to a practical cause with a real chance for success," white suffragists relinquished earlier arguments based on concepts of natural rights and justice and adopted new ones based on "expediency" (how woman suffrage would benefit society).[39] As part of this transformation, Kraditor claimed, northern white suffragists, who were increasingly concerned about immigrant and labor problems, united with southern white suffragists, who worried about the Negro problem—to argue that enfranchising women would strengthen white middle-class values (because "better" classes of women would vote in much larger numbers than "worse" classes of women and men combined). As Suzanne Lebsock has observed, "Kraditor's characterization of the white suffragists has had a great deal of staying power."[40] Many scholars, both white and black, have followed in Kraditor's stead, criticizing white suffragists for excluding women of color from their organizations and for exploiting racist arguments.[41]

Yet, where Kraditor argued that the white suffrage movement slowly gave up its "egalitarian" (her term) arguments, other narratives depict a movement that became increasingly more expansive, not just in membership but in its ability to encompass the differing views of various constituencies. As Nancy Cott perceptively notes, "the gathering force of the woman [suffrage] movement had by the early twentieth century encouraged into voice women who spoke out . . . about disfranchisement explicitly informed by [their own] racial, political, or economic loyalties. . . . The vote appealed instrumentally to different subgroups [black women, white Southern women, socialist women, trade union women] for various reasons, while they had their common disenfranchisement to unite them."[42]

Seemingly at odds, Kraditor's and Cott's perspectives are not as contradictory as they might first appear. White suffragists throughout the nineteenth century expressed views that repeatedly affirmed their belief in white racial superiority; yet other groups engaged in antiracist politics envisioned that the vote might help their cause as well. Racial and class divisions among women were not overcome by the suffrage movement, they were merely subsumed, momentarily, within the common goal of suffrage (as they are today subsumed in "right to choice" arguments), even as white racism and middle-class paternalism rose to their full expression.

My narrative about postbellum suffragism, presented in chapter 2, has different emphases from the Kraditor school, even though I agree with the crucial underlying point—that both suffragism and antisuffragism were fundamentally racialized and racist discourses. The work of Nancy Cott has opened up a way to question Kraditor's sense that egalitarian arguments were gradually replaced by expedient ones, or that nonracist claims about universal rights gave way to racist attempts to buttress white supremacy. As Cott has argued, it was not simply a question of one rhetorical strategy substituting for another: "nineteenth-century women protesting against male dominance . . . did not choose to argue simply on the basis of women's human character (that is, likeness to men) or simply on the basis of women's unique sexual character (that is, difference from men). Women voiced these two kinds of arguments in the same breath."[43] In other words, arguments about expediency and the political benefits of maintaining woman's sphere (which were racialized) coexisted throughout the suffrage debates with arguments about natural rights and equality (which were also racialized—more on this hereafter). From 1848 to 1920, the white woman movement affirmed (white) women's racial similarity to (white) men because of the conviction that white women drew on the same evolutionary and racial heritage as white men. Yet, at the same time, white suffragists affirmed (white) women's sexual difference from (white) men because they believed sexual differences formed the bedrock of whites' civilization. This "functional ambiguity," as Cott describes the tension, was not so ambiguous at the time: social evolutionary discourses specified quite plainly that white women were both fundamentally similar to white men (because of "race") and fundamentally different from white men (because of "sex").

In addition, Jean Fagan Yellin's research compels us to assess the ideology of northern abolitionist-suffragists more critically than Kraditor did.[44] The so-called egalitarian arguments of many abolitionist-suffragists demanded that citizenship should not be restricted solely on racial grounds, but white abolitionists still believed that the white race was "higher" and that whites currently manifested a superiority to blacks in character, morality, intelligence, and civilization. It was just that blacks and other racial inferiors could be "elevated" or "uplifted"—if freed and treated properly, educated, Christianized, and granted citizenship. In this regard, the abolitionist-suffragists were not very different from postbellum suffragists; indeed they were often literally the same people. Perhaps the abolitionists more frequently evoked metaphors of space (high/low) while later suffragists preferred metaphors of time (backward, forward, progress); but there is a great deal of overlap and continuity between the two. Social evolution did not fundamentally change abolitionists' previous understandings of race, gender, and citizenship. Older abolitionist-suffragists, like Stanton, merely took up the new discourse when social evolutionary theories offered them an explanation of *why* blacks and Indians were "inferior races" and more "backward" than whites and Europeans, who were "superior races" and more "advanced."

Consequently, my narrative begins with the perspective that citizenship in this country was (and still is) racialized and gendered at its core. Instead of trying to see how woman's rights advocates went wrong—how an egalitarian movement became a racist one—I explore the ideological and political strategies that various white women reformers used at different times to assert the citizenship rights of groups (themselves and others) whom they believed did (or did not) manifest the attributes of the normative white male citizen. My hope is that this approach will help us come to a better understanding of how discourses of race and gender still inform discourses of equality and citizenship (and vice versa).

In the 1980s, work by black scholars made white feminists even more aware of the dangers of composing narratives that took the experiences of white middle-class women as the norm and treated black and working-class women solely as tokens, marginal figures, or victims.[45] In 1987, Hazel Carby protested that attempts on the part of white feminist literary critics and historians to recover a "lost sisterhood" left uninterrogated the ways in which white women's ideologies operated as "sites of racial and class struggle," enabling white women to "negotiate their subordinate role in relation to patriarchy."[46] In recent years, a burgeoning literature has emerged in which scholars are re-examining the history and current operations of white racial formations. Gail Bederman, Tracey Boisseau, Ruth Frankenberg, Jane Hunter, Carolyn Karcher, Peggy Pascoe, Laura Wexler, and Jean Fagan Yellin, among many others, have looked anew at white women's use of and embeddedness within the racial discourses of abolitionism, benevolence, suffragism, missionary ideology, civilization, imperialism, progressivism, and feminism.[47] David Roediger, Noel Ignatiev, and Matthew Jacobson have examined how various ethnic and working-class groups worked to create white identities for themselves to compensate for their exclusion from economic, political, and social forms of power.[48] This book draws heavily from this new historiography, as well as from the rich theoretical insights of scholars working in anthropology, cultural studies, critical legal studies, and British colonialism.[49]

Argument and Goals

In the most general sense, I argue that imperialism provided an important discourse for white elite women who developed new identities for themselves as missionaries, explorers, educators, and ethnographers as they staked out new realms of possibility and political power against the tight constraints of Victorian gender norms. White women in the late nineteenth century were engaged in a struggle for a positive female identity in a deeply misogynistic society: they articulated new arguments about race and gender to assert themselves as the political, social, and racial equals of white men. By offering themselves as the epitome of social evolutionary development, they were also trying, simultaneously, if paradoxically, to articulate an egalitarian vision, one that could be inclusive of women of color and that envisioned "lower races" as their potential equals *in the future*. They hoped that assimilation would lead eventually to full racial equality, and they believed that nonwhite women would want to follow them down this road. They did not see assimilation as a form of racism, for they were convinced, as were many black elites in this period, that assimilation was vastly preferable to racist notions of fixed biological difference. In their minds, assimilation denoted a social vision that encompassed both a melding of peoples *and* a firm sense of hierarchy—an invitation to Others to participate (as almost-but-not-quite Anglos) in the body politic. Early feminist theory as articulated by Charlotte Perkins Gilman and Mary Roberts Coolidge grew out of and bolstered the "civilizing missions" of the nineteenth century, was firmly grounded in social evolution theory's stipulations about white racial supremacy, and defended cultural assimilation as a means of promoting the equality of nonwhite peoples.

My goal, to echo Robyn Wiegman, is to shift our frame of reference so that we become more sensitive to the ways in which contemporary discourses continue to draw on their assimilationist legacies. Most important, I hope to shake up what I see as a lingering complacency in egalitarian liberalism as an effective means of addressing issues of racial, gender, and class inequalities. Claims about the egalitarian goals of feminist politics (in the nineteenth century as well as now) reflect a common confusion about racism, sexism, and classism that needs to be exposed: too often, it is posited that nonracist (nonsexist, nonclassist) behavior requires a purposeful overlooking—a notseeing—of difference, even when the consequences of such not-seeing lead to the maintenance of structures of oppression. (Think of the white liberals who proudly exclaimed, "Oh, I never thought of him/her as black" as if this constituted evidence of an enlightened racial consciousness.) The same confusion operates in well-intentioned "feminist" claims that sexual equality is best achieved by treating men and women the same. The national romance with colorblindness, and its corollary, gender sameness, is a fundamentally misguided strategy (metaphorically, a two-headed ostrich with both heads in the sand)—an ineffective way to address the real discursive effects of social hierarchies intricately structured along the multiple axes of race, class, gender. The favored approach of the U.S. legal system in questions of legal equality—treating similarly situated individuals similarly—works only when individuals are indeed similarly situated. But what if they are differently situated? In the context of American political culture in which power is already aligned along gendered, racialized, and class lines, people of different races, classes, and genders are always already situated differently. To assert "sameness" is to purposefully ignore the material and ideological effects that race (gender, class, sexuality) have had in creating oppression, inequity, and injustice.

This book, then, has four specific goals: first, to analyze how evolutionary constructions of racial progress and sexual difference were central to the ways in which white women activists in the late nineteenth and early twentieth centuries conceptualized woman's rights and sexual equality; second, to examine how white women in the progressive era anchored their political activism to this ideological foundation, creating new forms of public authority for themselves that emanated from their understandings of their unique roles as civilizers of racially inferior peoples; third, to explain how feminism developed out of this earlier discourse as a racialized theory of gender oppression. In this regard, I examine feminism's connection to two related contexts: first, to the United States' efforts to assimilate Native Americans, African Americans, and the Chinese at home, and second, to the country's struggle to assert itself as an imperial power abroad. Finally, this book shows how ongoing discussions about and among U.S. feminists today remain indebted to these earlier conceptions from the late nineteenth century of gender and sexual difference as *the* defining features of "advanced" or "civilized" nations.

This study is arranged in three sections. Chapters 1 and 2 explore the developments in evolutionist theories and national politics of the 1870s and 1880s that provided the intellectual underpinnings for white women's racialized views of sexual equality. Chapters 3, 4, and 5 explore how white women modified and made use of social evolutionary discourses in several different contexts: in the debates over "sex in education" and "sex in industry" with the physicians Edward Clarke and Azel Ames, respectively, during the 1870s; in the Indian reform movement of the 1880s; and in the popular response to May French-Sheldon's safari in East Africa in the early 1890s. Chapters 6 and 7 turn to the emergence of feminist theory in the early twentieth century. Chapter 6 explores how Charlotte Perkins Gilman and Mary Roberts Smith Coolidge, two self-proclaimed feminists, managed to remove "sexual difference" as the defining factor in the evolutionary hierarchy of races, while still maintaining that Anglo-Protestant women were the best civilizers of racial inferiors by virtue of their special evolutionary history. The final chapter examines how this paradigm was slowly transformed in the 1920s and 1930s by analyzing how Margaret Mead successfully challenged the Victorian idea of evolutionary assimilation, yet was not able to relinquish the cultural ethnocentrism that celebrated the United States as a superior nation on the basis of its gender ideologies.

The dangers of such an approach are formidable. Because of its focus on the racism *within feminism,* this study may be taken as mitigating, if not rendering invisible, "worse" forms of racism in the culture at large and of aiding an ongoing conservative backlash against the women's movement. My hope, however, is that this recasting of the history of woman's rights might give us more insight into how and why the legacies of evolutionary feminism continue to endure and perhaps might even help us to imagine new departures. While it may be unsettling to look at our past in this way, it is critical that we acknowledge the inheritance bequeathed to us by these early feminists—for we are all caught in the webs of race and patriarchy, just as they were.

1

Evolution, Woman's Rights, and Civilizing Missions

It matters not whether we regard the history of the remotest past or the diverse civilizations of the present, the emancipation and exaltation of women are the synonym of progress.

Otis T. Mason, *Woman's Share in Primitive Culture*, 1894

A s THEY LOOKED BACK over recent decades, contemporary observers of the 1890s recognized this period in U.S. history as "the Era of Woman"—a time when women's organizations proliferated and the country seemed especially focused on women's issues and women's rights. Richard T. Ely, director of the School of Economics, Political Science, and History at the University of Wisconsin, declared, "Our age may properly be called the Era of Woman, because everything which affects her receives consideration quite unknown in past centuries."[1] Commentators at the time were impressed with the recent "progress" of woman, her increased visibility in public and political affairs, her entry into colleges and universities, and her commitment to social reform. Those in sympathy with the woman's movement viewed these changes in woman's status as the manifestation of evolutionary progress, a sign that the civilization of the United States was equal to the higher civilizations of Europe and far superior to the primitive cultures of Asia and Africa. In the words of Joseph Rodes Buchanan, a professor of physiology, medicine, and anthropology, "sustained womanhood is a Western condition, as degraded womanhood is the Oriental condition. . . . The darkness that rests upon Asia and the midnight that enshrouds Africa, where woman has no rights . . . have their appointed time to pass away in the illumination of which the American Republic is the destined centre."[2]

For Buchanan, as for many others, social evolution theory provided the framework and language through which changes in woman's sphere were interpreted. Demands for woman's rights arose simultaneously with the spread of evolutionist ideas about racial development, sexual difference, and social progress. For prescient observers, it was not merely coincidental that the woman's movement had grown to unprecedented heights in the 1880s, at precisely the same moment that politicians, businessmen, educators, and scientists were all promulgating the "survival of the fittest" and laissez-faire principles of social Darwinism.[3] Rather, it was evolutionist theories that made possible new social and political roles for white women as "civilizers" of the race, strengthening longstanding beliefs in (white) women's moral superiority. Moreover, the emergence of a strong imperialist sentiment, the effort to establish the United States as an empire, and the extension of missions, both domestically and abroad, fundamentally influenced the direction and content of white feminist thought in the late nineteenth and early twentieth centuries. For contemporaries like Buchanan, the rise in the woman's movement could not be understood apart from these other developments. As Buchanan articulated the relationship, the woman question was more than a question of woman's rights; it was "a national question, a race question, a world question."[4]

In other words, the simultaneous development of two ideologies, woman's rights and social Darwinism, accompanied and made possible white women's entry into the public sphere, at a time when new corporate and monopolistic forms of capitalism were creating vast differences in wealth between an educated white managerial class and an impoverished (often immigrant and nonwhite) working class. Social-Darwinian theories encouraged and enabled the development of ideologies concerning white middle-class women's emancipation that emphasized (white) women's specific role as the "conservators of race traits" and the "civilizers" of racial and class inferiors. The Anglo-Saxon Protestant woman's self-proclaimed burden at the turn of the century was to help her nation in rescuing these so-called primitive and working-class peoples from stagnation and decay, to protect them from the violent abuses of the U.S. government (and primitive and working-class women from the supposed abuses of their men), and to assimilate evolutionary inferiors into a more advanced Christian civilization. White women who participated in domestic and foreign missionary societies, in the local, national, and world temperance movements, in the settlement house movement, in the international peace movement—in any of the organized white woman's movements at the turn of the century—built their institutions on the premise that they, as Anglo-Saxon Protestant women, were the best conveyors of advanced civilization. Supporters of the women's settlement house movement could be quite candid about the relations this ideology produced between themselves and the objects of their civilizing efforts. Katharine Coman, a professor at Wellesley College, observed, "A settlement is a colony planted in a strange land by immigrants from a superior civilization. . . . Hull House has become a potent force in the civilizing of the great city wilderness where it was planted."[5]

Ideas about evolution, woman's rights, and civilizing missions were widely disseminated in the culture through what historian Anne McClintock has termed commodity racism, which took the form of advertising, photography, national expositions, and museums, and converted "the narratives of imperial Progress into mass-produced *consumer spectacles.*"[6] Commodity racism occurred not only on a grand scale, for example in the Midway portion of the Chicago Exposition in 1893 and in the ape exhibits of the New York Museum of Natural History, but also filtered down into popular and material culture in a more mundane way, on trade cards that promoters used to advertise household goods such as soap, cereals, and sewing machines.[7] Idealized notions about how evolution would led to racial assimilation and racial progress were even disseminated through children's toys, as a puzzle of the United States, manufactured by McLoughlin Brothers in New York, probably sometime in the 1880s, suggests. (See fig. 1-1.)

On the box cover of the McLoughlin puzzle are two metaphorical figures, the white woman as civilizer, and the unassimilated primitive. In the center, demanding the viewer's attention, is a goddess-like woman seated in a forest setting, clothed in a white flowing robe, a royal blue sash draped around her shoulders. At her side is a diminutive figure, childlike in form, though with a countenance too knowing for a child, yet too naive for an adult. This childish figure, outfitted in a short skirt, with pretty moccasins on its dainty feet and a single feather in its long, flowing hair, represents a quintessential, sexually undifferentiated Indian—although the bare breasts and the bow and arrows strewn along the ground reveal this to be a nonthreatening male Indian. The woman is pointing at a map in a book held open in her lap. Following her gaze, the Indian is also looking at the book, and his posture, more than the unreadable expression of his face, suggests that he is open to, if not exactly eager for, the instruction about to be dispensed.[8]

The colors of the woman's dress—white and royal blue—connote her sexual purity and aristocratic heritage, signifying that she represents not only the best of idealized womanhood, but also the white civilized race. Her red headdress (recalling the headgear of Joan of Arc) completes the tricolor scheme of red, white, and blue. This female figure is a national icon, a symbol for the United States, the embodiment of the nation's Christian duty to educate Indians. The masculine strength and ferocity of a savage warrior has been replaced by an ineffectual, cartoonlike Indian whose bow and arrows are heedlessly left strewn about like those of a white child interrupted at play. This Indian figure, physically immature and absurdly small, poses no threat to the civilizing mission.

The box cover embodies several cultural meanings. Most explicitly, it represents a marketing strategy directed at white families desiring to educate their children in national geography. The image encourages an identification between the white child, for whom this puzzle was intended, and the Indian child depicted on the cover. Yet the cover also narrates in an unintentionally ironic, but nonetheless poignantly accurate way, the story of how civilization-woman-nation descends upon the Indian-man-child, saying in effect: "Now that you've been denied your former way of life, and can only play at being Indian, let me teach you some geography in accordance with our remapping of a wilderness that once was yours." Because the woman-nation is making an effort to teach the Indian man-child, the assumption here is that the primitive *is* assimilable into U.S. civilization. In the context of the late nineteenth century, this idealized woman and still-to-be-assimilated Indian encapsulated a progressive view of race relations that derived from an evolutionist conviction that races could change and progress: primitives could be turned into the civilized. The educational programs at Hampton and Carlisle Institutes were institutional manifestations of the same ideology.

FIGURE 1-1 Civilizing mission of white women. Dissected Map, United States. Puzzle Box Cover, c. mid-1800s. As white women became the symbolic representatives and upholders of civilization, white activists employed this ideology to carve out new social and political roles for white women as civilization-workers.

AS HISTORIAN CYNTHIA RUSSETT has observed, the rise of an evolutionary science focused on sexual difference was a response "to the particular historical moment in which [Anglo-Saxon Protestant middle-class] women were asserting new claims to a life beyond the domestic hearth."[9] Although organized forms of women's resistance to patriarchy can be traced back to the Seneca Falls Convention of 1848, where Lucretia Mott and Elizabeth Cady Stanton convened a gathering of approximately two-hundred women and forty men to discuss white women's grievances, the woman's movement increased its numbers dramatically after the Civil War and became even more vocal in espousing woman's right to personal autonomy, self-government, and economic independence.[10] According to one contemporary observer in 1892:

> The last twenty years have seen the definitive term "Woman's" prefixed to more societies than have been designated by that distinction in the world's history previously. . . . Woman's Home and Foreign Missionary Societies, Woman's Christian Temperance Union, Woman's Suffrage Association, Woman's Protective Agencies, Woman's Relief Corps, Woman's National Indian Association, Woman's Press Clubs, National Association for the Advancement of Women, King's Daughters, Deaconness Societies, Daughters of the Revolution, and lastly the Lady Managers . . . besides all the local societies for women, literary social, esthetic, philanthropic, professional, educational, industrial, hygienic and dress reform.[11]

Historians believe that this postbellum explosion in women's organizing was precipitated by the radicalizing influence of the Civil War, which brought women into public view in record numbers—a breakdown temporarily at least in the rigid ideology of separate spheres. As historian Catherine Clinton has written, "the [Civil] war brought changes of staggering proportion. Most were changes in degree: public arenas in which women had only token representation before the war were brimming with women during wartime."[12] For example, increasing numbers of women found employment in northern factories. In 1860, 270,000 women worked in the textile, shoe, clothing, and printing industries, but the war created one hundred thousand new jobs. Northern white women also got posts with the Union government (nearly five hundred women were employed by the U.S. government by 1865), and roughly three thousand women became army nurses. The most important women's organization to come out of the war was the Sanitary Commission (later renamed the Red Cross), which raised millions of dollars to furnish supplies to soldiers, widows, and orphans, and helped train nurses for work in hospitals and on battlefields.[13]

In the mid-1860s, immediately following the war, an additional four thousand northern white women went south to help set up schools for the Freedmen's Bureau. Some of these women were widows; others had been too young to marry before the war. In 1870, the Harvard paleontologist Nathaniel Shaler would write contemptuously of the "northern woman who toils her life away [in the South Seas Islands off the coast of South Carolina] under the delusion that she can fight all Africa with a spelling-book and multiplication-table."[14] (See fig. 1-2.) But in 1885, Alice Fletcher, suffragist and leader of the Women's National Indian Association, would credit these women with having successfully brought civilization to the Negro:

FIGURE 1-2 Off to civilize the primitive. If They'll Only Be Good. Political cartoon, *Puck* (January 31, 1900). Caption underneath reads: "Uncle Sam—You have seen what my sons can do in battle;—now see what my daughters can do in peace." The stereotypical representations of the white women (Irish matron, Old Maid, Prissy Schoolteacher, Innocent Debutante, and the Benevolent Nurse) suggest that the cartoonist found the woman's movement's involvement in imperialism ludicrous.

> An army of [self-]sacrificing Northern missionaries, with Bible in one hand and spelling books in the other, scarcely waiting for the smoke [of] battle to scatter, followed in the march of the Union army, sought the freedmen, extended the help which they so much needed, but which the poverty and temper of the South at that time could not afford. Northern benevolence then and since has planted over $25,000,000 in this Southland, and has furnished an army of her best men and women to assist the negro in his dire necessity."[15]

Most of these women had returned north by the late 1870s, but a few made their homes in the South and became involved in political activism, agitating for state funding for black schools, pressing black land claims, and supporting black male suffrage.[16]

Although the temporary shortage in manpower caused by the war created new economic opportunities for white middle-class women, the Civil War also fundamentally altered many of these women's sense of their rightful place in the world. Many women who had been used to having male providers were now deprived of them—some only momentarily while the war lasted, others permanently. In the Civil War 620,000 soldiers died (roughly 9 percent of the total white male population aged eighteen to forty-five), a number almost equal to the total number of deaths sustained in all the rest of the nation's wars combined (680,000).[17] After the war, the decline in marriageable men prompted many young white women to pursue careers. Contemporaries estimated that roughly three-hundred thousand (white) women sought wage employment who might otherwise not have entered the paid labor force.[18] By the 1880s, two-thirds of public school teachers nationwide were women; in 1892 this proportion had increased even further, to five-sixths.[19] At the end of the nineteenth century, white middle-class women also dominated office work (they were only 3.3 percent of office workers in 1870 but 75 percent in 1900); two-thirds of the stenographers and typists were young single white women between the ages of fifteen and twenty-five, the majority living at home with their parents.[20] Furthermore, during this period, white women demanded and received access to institutions of higher learning so that they could receive the appropriate training for the more lucrative and prestigious "male" professions of law, ministry, college teaching, and medicine.

Married white women also became more visible in public arenas: they joined church groups and missionary societies, they took part in charity work and benevolent associations, and they even assumed appointive positions in local and state governments, serving on school boards, state sanitary commissions, and so forth. Collectively, these developments represented extraordinary, unprecedented change in white middle-class women's social roles, necessitating a new ideology about womanhood and woman's rights.

Equally relevant for specific articulations of woman's rights in this period was the country's continued inability to address and resolve racial conflicts. Ongoing immigration and urbanization in the 1870s and 1880s transformed neighborhoods, schools, towns, and local cultures. As increased contact between different racial, ethnic, and national groups became a fundamental feature of urban life in the late nineteenth century, many white elites grew more fearful that their way of life would disappear. Immigration from southeastern Europe fundamentally altered the demographic structure of the Euro-American population; new immigrants brought with them their religions (Catholicism, Judaism) and different cultural practices. Urbanization meant that the older and familiar forms of maintaining social order, which had depended on the local authority of town ministers and governors, had to be replaced with urban bureaucracies, police forces, and social welfare organizations. Reconstruction's enfranchisement of newly freed black male slaves compelled whites everywhere to rethink their fundamental convictions about race and citizenship. Native Americans continued to wage battle against the U.S. government, and career soldiers were redeployed after the Civil War to help subjugate Indian tribes. Thousands of unmarried Chinese men emigrated to western states to help build railroads during the Civil War and then came into conflict with whites when they stayed on to work as miners, farm laborers, and cannery workers.

All of these developments fueled tensions, mistrust, and violence among Anglo-Saxons and other racial groups. At such vulnerable moments, Anglo-Saxon elites found in the concept of social evolution a reassurance that the changes occurring before their eyes would be orderly and predictable. David Starr Jordan, president of Stanford University, explained that evolution "as a science . . . [was] the study of changing beings acted upon by unchanging laws."[21] Evolutionist theories buttressed whites' flagging confidence that the fittest would survive and appealed to those elites who felt uneasy about the challenges to their social authority and political power that were coming from new alliances of industrial workers and farmers (Farmers' Alliances), from potential coalitions between free blacks and poor whites (Populism), from the Catholic Church, and from evangelical white women (the woman's movement). Anxious about their future and fearful of racial equality in its myriad aspects—integration as well as miscegenation—many whites looked to evolutionist theories to help them understand the relationships among race, sexual difference, and civilization—to reassure themselves that their own culture would prevail.[22] Evolutionist treatises dealing with such issues found a ready market among intellectuals. An editor for *Harper's New Monthly Magazine* remarked in 1874 that the "origin of race" was of "greater interest to the student than almost any other problem."[23]

From 1870 to 1920, then, as historians Nancy Leys Stepan and Sander Gilman have observed, evolutionary science "became both more specialized and authoritative as a cultural resource and language of interpretation" for understanding biological and cultural differences.[24] At the same time, evolutionist theories grew more popular and more familiar to masses of Americans. One journalist reported that "evolutionists [have gained a] hold upon the thinking world; and they will not be answered, if ever, until they shall find an opponent as studious of life and as unflinching in reporting its testimonies as are Darwin, Lyell, Lubbock, and Tylor."[25]

Influential texts for laying out foundational principles of evolution and social evolutionary theory were Charles Darwin's *On the Origin of Species* (1859) and *Descent of Man* (1871), and Herbert Spencer's *The Principles of Biology* (1864) and *Social Statics* (1865). Spencer developed his own theories concurrently with Darwin, coining the term "survival of the fittest" in *The Principles of Biology*.[26] While Darwin continued to emphasize the idea that adaptive changes occurred fortuitously, Spencer gave his version a sharply teleological cast, asserting that evolutionary changes occurred so as to produce social and racial progress, leading to ever higher and more advanced civilizations and races.[27] It was Spencer's versions, even more than Darwin's, that drew American interest, in part because Anglo-Saxon elites were interested in using evolutionist theories to forecast social development for the future. In 1872 Edward Livingston Youmans founded a new journal, *Popular Science Monthly,* to help disseminate Spencer's work, and by the 1880s the United States had become, in historian Richard Hofstadter's well-known phrase, the Darwinian country.[28]

As a theory that linked biology and culture, social evolutionary theories connected societal change with individual change, equated advanced civilizations with white racial superiority, and anchored both of these in sexual difference. Social evolutionary theories also introduced the theoretical possibility that sexual and racial differences could change over time—and change as a result of individual and social actions. In the United States, these theories offered support both to those who were arguing that racial inferiors could be quickly civilized through assimilationist programs as well as to those who were opposed to government intervention in political affairs. In other words, social evolutionary theories purported to predict progress, but they also delineated the limits of human agency, specifying the point at which social reform could no longer be expected to be effective. Always, there were white elites who resisted the idea that evolution implied progress or were skeptical that careful selection of mates would produce superior offspring (the basis of eugenic theories in this period). For example, Louis Agassiz, a Harvard scientist, objected to the principle of the survival of the fittest. He wrote, "The whole subject of inheritance is exceedingly intricate, working often in a seemingly capricious and fitful way. Qualities, both good and bad are dropped as well as acquired, and the process ends sometimes in the degradation of the type and the survival of the unfit."[29] So while evolutionary processes seemingly had brought about current manifestations of (white racial) superiority, further evolutionary development might bring about racial degeneration. Because social devolution was always a theoretical possibility, white elites felt that they had to be particularly careful about the activities of white women, precisely because they began to hold this group responsible for the development of new race-and-sex traits, which, via Lamarckian processes, could be transmitted to offspring and become part of "the race's" future inheritance.[30]

Darwin's fourth edition of On the Origin of Species appeared in 1871, along with the newly written Descent of Man. These works along with books by other evolutionists, like Alfred Russel Wallace's Contributions to the Theory of Natural Selection, Edward Tylor's Primitive Culture, Henry Lewis Morgan's Ancient Society, and John Lubbock's Origin of Civilization and the Primitive Condition of Man, were widely read among U.S. intellectuals in the 1870s, causing one reviewer to comment that the "doctrine of evolution," "what is now known as 'Darwinism,'" had won over even those "eminent students of science who claim to be orthodox."[31] White women also read these treatises, in particular Darwin's Descent of Man and Spencer's "Psychology of the Sexes," but with increasing consternation, because of the seeming disparagement of white women as evolutionary inferiors to white men.[32]

As historians Sue Rosser and Charlotte Hogsett have explained, Darwin accounted for variations among individuals (and races) by stressing two types of struggles: in the first type of struggle [natural selection], he said, "males . . . drive away or kill their [inferior] rivals, the females remaining passive." In the second type of sexual struggle [sexual selection], females "no longer remain passive, but select the more agreeable partners."[33] According to these strictures, males who beat out their rivals or were deemed more attractive by females gained the opportunity to mate, thus passing on their own advantageous characteristics to offspring. In other words, evolution was largely driven by the males of the species, whose competitive or attractive qualities made them successful in outliving and outreproducing others with less adaptive traits.

Theoretically, according to Spencer, sexual differences were considered the evolutionary products of the social functions of each sex.[34] Change the functions of each sex. (make primitive women homemakers, for example) and their sexual differences would change, with the newly acquired sexual traits being passed on to offspring. Both Darwin and Spencer speculated that traits acquired early in the life of an individual, particularly physical attributes such as size and strength, were acquired through natural selection and were transmitted to both sexes through the law of equal transmission but were manifested only in one sex. Characteristics that appeared later in life—such as intelligence and reason—were supposedly acquired through sexual selection and transmitted only to the offspring of the same sex, according to the laws of partial inheritance. Men passed on male forms of intelligence to sons; women passed on female forms of intuition to daughters.[35]

Men's intellectual superiority was never doubted by male evolutionists—although woman's rights activists would repeatedly challenge this evolutionary assumption.[36] Spencer offered the explanation that women's brain remained less developed than men's because of "a somewhat earlier arrest of individual evolution in women than in men; necessitated by the reservation of vital power to meet the cost of reproduction."[37] Spencer assumed that all women, but especially women of the higher races, needed more "vital power" than men to carry on the biological functions of reproduction, and that this vital power could not be used to sustain intellectual growth without risking severe injury to the female reproductive system. Women who attended college would have to draw on vital power in pursuing their educations, and this in turn would deprive them of the necessary energy to reproduce (thus supposedly accounting for the lower birth rates of college-educated women). Edward H. Clarke and G. Stanley Hall, influential educators in the 1870s and 1880s, adhered to this view, cautioning women that if they attended institutions of higher learning intended for men, they would subject themselves to great physiological dangers, resulting in the worst case in infertility and death.[38]

Following these social-Darwinian precepts, biologists and social scientists often believed that there was less variability among Anglo-Protestant women than among Anglo-Protestant men—these women as a group clustered around an average type, with few excelling in any particular way.[39] This average type of woman exhibited certain characteristics that were also common among "primitives" or "lower races": irrational and slow thinking, intuitive or instinctual approaches to knowledge, religiosity, emotionality, and so forth. The more advanced mental functions—imagination and reason—were presumed to be characteristic of the more highly evolved brains of civilized men.[40] The terminology is revealing: "woman" was used to mean an Anglo-Protestant woman; "lower races" or "primitives" were used without reference to gender because the theory presupposed that there were no significant sexual differences among primitives.

What was new and destabilizing about evolutionist theories in relation to earlier ideologies about race and gender, however, was the idea of the potential for racial and sexual differences to change over time. Prior to the 1870s, the philosophical and theological traditions that white elites had drawn on to explain sexual and racial differences to themselves had emphasized the permanency, universality, and naturalness of sexual and racial differences. According to the earlier traditions, sexual and racial differences were attributed to the "laws of Nature" or the "laws of God"—interchangeable terms, as God was the ultimate Creator, Nature being his handmaiden. Woman's nature, in other words, was determined by God on the day of creation, and like all of God's work was considered complete, perfect, and unalterable.[41]

The cult of true womanhood, as historian Barbara Welter has termed this endur-ing ideology, which lasted into the late nineteenth century, had both descriptive and prescriptive elements embedded in it, specifying that woman's nature was character-ized by four essential attributes: purity, piety, domesticity, and submissiveness.[42] As a prescriptive category, woman's nature established the cultural boundaries of what was considered "normal" for a woman and set forth an ideal by which all groups of women were judged and to which they were supposed to adhere. As a descriptive category, it characterized the daily pursuits of millions of white middle-class married women who spent their lives cultivating these feminine attributes. The most radical of white thinkers at the time, women like Lydia Maria Child for example, believed that women of other racial groups shared these same intrinsic qualities, even though they might not yet be manifested in behavior and appearance.

Nonetheless, white woman's rights advocates in the 1830s and 1840s found this ide-ology of woman's nature constraining and argued for an enlargement of woman's sphere—for the need and value of (white) women assuming public roles. They be-lieved in the possibility that their own womanly nature, although God-given, could change over time. Although they did not yet have access to evolutionist notions of change, woman's rights activists in the antebellum period distinguished between *woman's inherent nature* and current manifestations of *women's present natures*, agreeing that the former was God-given and unalterable but asserting that it had not yet been at-tained by most women. As Lucretia Mott, the Quaker abolitionist and woman's rights reformer, declared in 1850, men had wrongly equated the "present position" of woman with the "original state" designed for woman:

> We would admit all the difference, that our great and beneficent Creator has made, in the relation of man and woman, nor would we seek to disturb this relation; but we deny that the present position of woman is her true sphere of usefulness. . . . True, nature has made a difference in [woman's] configuration, her physical strength, her voice, etc.—and we ask no change, we are satisfied with nature. But how has neglect and mismanagement increased this difference! It is our duty to develop these natural powers by suitable exercise, so that they may be strengthened "by reason of use."[43]

In Mott's formulation, certain deficiencies in woman's character had been height-ened and magnified because of unfair restrictions, societal conventions, and lack of use. What was "natural," were not those qualities or characteristics that were cur-rently being exhibited by women but the qualities or characteristics that God had made available to women even though they were not yet manifest in woman's nature. One reason that evolutionist theories would later prove so attractive to woman's rights activists was because they reinforced this notion that new attributes could emerge. It was even possible to conceptualize how, given appropriate activities, women would develop in ways that would diminish apparent sexual differences. At a time of laissez faire in social and political affairs, these woman's rights activists were re-questing the deregulation of woman's nature so that it could approach the ideal of God's design.

During the antebellum period, most white advocates of woman's rights were evangelical Protestants or Quakers, and they spoke out of a theological conception of womanhood. Their religious beliefs asserted the universality of womanly qualities and made it possible for adherents to argue that all women—despite racial, ethnic, class, or other differences—shared, or could potentially share, a common womanhood. Most antebellum advocates of woman's rights acknowledged that differences existed between (white) men and women, but they believed that these differences (white women's smaller physical size and lesser muscular strength, for example) were relatively insignificant and not relevant for deciding whether to grant (white) women political equality with (white) men. Sarah Grimké, a well-known southern abolitionist and proponent of woman's rights in the late 1830s and 1840s, for example, argued that the original, God-given differences—as opposed to the manifest ones—were so insubstantial in fact that they would not deter (white) women from extending their activities outside the home.

White male conservatives vehemently disagreed, going so far as to declare that since (white) women could not financially support themselves or others and could not protect themselves or fight in wars, they could not be equal citizens with (white) men and should not be allowed to vote or take part in political activities. Patriarchal families and republican forms of government (in which white men represented white women) had developed in accordance with natural sexual differences: strong, intelligent, courageous (white) men had been assigned by God the duty and responsibility for providing for and protecting weak, emotional, and vulnerable (white) women. Consequently, white women had been assigned to their own, separate sphere, where they were loved and cherished, protected from the brutal day-to-day struggles of mankind.

By the 1860s, white advocates of woman's rights routinely argued that opponents were substituting their own convictions about woman's nature for the ideal created by God. What God created would withstand all human efforts to alter it. What man falsely conceived as woman's nature would break down as women expanded their sphere of activities. "If you want to know what is the true sphere of man or woman," Reverend Samuel Longfellow, a supporter of woman's rights, preached to the already converted audience at the Tenth National Woman's Rights Convention in May 1860, "just leave the man or the woman alone, and the natural law and the divine law, which can not be broken, and which are as sure in the moral and human world as they are in the external world, will settle the matter."[44] Abba Goold Woolson, New England reformer and author of *Woman in American Society,* observed, "It is an amusing inconsistency which never seems to have struck them [opponents of woman's rights]. If this limitation of [woman's] powers to any one sphere be Nature's provision [and not theirs] . . . why should there be need of so many precautions to keep her from the higher walks of service and learning from which she has been debarred?"[45] The suffragist Elizabeth Cady Stanton made the same point with deliberate irony: "If God has assigned a sphere to man and one to woman, we claim the right ourselves to judge of His design in reference to us, and we accord to man the same privilege."[46]

Although evolutionist theories encroached heavily on preexisting theological and philosophical discourses, in some ways they were compatible and continuous with

these earlier traditions. With even more emphasis than the theological and philosophical viewpoints that preceded it, evolutionist theories linked sexual differences
with racial progress. "Civilized" races were differentiated from "primitive" races according to the specific sexual traits and gender roles that characterized the white middle classes. As historian Gail Bederman has argued, civilization itself was understood
in the 1880s as a biologically transmissible racial trait—so far exhibited only by the
more advanced white races.[47] In 1897, William I. Thomas, a social scientist at the University of Chicago, specified with utmost clarity the concept of the evolutionary connection between sexual difference and racial progress: "The less civilized the race the
less is the physical difference of the sexes."[48] Or to put the same relationship another
way around: the more civilized the race, the more the men and women of that race
had to differ from one another.

Evolutionist theories also helped support the longstanding belief that (white or
civilized) men and women were naturally, inherently different and strengthened the
longstanding Christian conviction that civilized countries treated women better than
uncivilized societies, a mainstay of Christian missionary practice for at least two centuries. Within the context of empire-building, Christian doctrine held that women
were best off in Christian (civilized) societies because those societies operated in accordance with "the law of love." Evolutionist theories were used to argue that, as a result
of Christian love, civilized women had changed physically, mentally, and morally to
become more delicate, intelligent, moral, chaste, and refined than women of "lower
races" because they had been protected and cherished by civilized Christian men.[49]

Theories of evolution thus gave scientific backing to missionary and women's
movements long underway, further encouraging large numbers of women, most of
them white and middle class, to assume responsibility for bringing Christianity, civilization, and citizenship to peoples whom they considered their evolutionary and
racial inferiors. In the early part of the nineteenth century, the job of civilizing "primitives" had fallen mostly to white men—most often trained ministers (albeit frequently accompanied by their wives) who were sent to the field to convert the heathen. Only eleven single women served as foreign missionaries in the antebellum
period.[50] The Civil War marked a watershed for white women's involvement in both
the home and foreign missionary movements. In this period, as social Darwinism sat-
urated the ideological atmosphere, the number of single women serving as foreign
missionaries rose into the thousands, and the movement attracted the support of millions of women. Between 1868 and 1873, as historian Joan Jacobs Brumberg explains,
"foreign missions were, among women at least, a veritable growth industry."[51]
Women in each of the major American Protestant evangelical denominations separated from the "parent boards" of male directors to form their own foreign mission
organizations under female leadership. The numbers of the women's auxiliary sections among the Presbyterians alone expanded from 100 in 1870 to 10,869 in 1909.[52]

Generally, antebellum women's rights activists used the terms "woman's nature"
and "woman's sphere" in the universal singular, as if the concept applied equally to all
groups of women—poor as well as rich, Christian as well as non-Christian, native
born as well as foreign born, black as well as white. While they might not have be-

lieved in black equality, white woman's rights activists generally opposed slavery, and they regularly compared "woman's status" (the women here were also assumed to be white) to the "Negro's" (assumed to be men), leaving out of these comparisons altogether the specific experiences and conditions of black women, both free and enslaved.[53] Yet elite white women's analysis of the woman question did not go unchallenged: throughout the antebellum and postbellum periods, women of color struggled for recognition and inclusion in white women's reform movements and successfully articulated alternative discourses of womanhood.[54] As Hazel Carby has argued, Anna Julia Cooper, Frances Ellen Watkins Harper, Fannie Jackson Coppin, and Ida B. Wells, among many others, fought to establish their own public presence in the nineteenth century, finding themselves in a highly contradictory position: both a part of and excluded from the dominant discourse of white women's politics.[55]

For white women activists, black women activists served both as a promise that it would be possible to advance the black race and as an indication that the supposed physical constraints of womanhood that immobilized white women could be overcome. For example, the white Ohioan abolitionist-suffragist Frances Matilde Gage saw in Sojourner Truth a physical reminder that women were not necessarily a weaker sex—that they did do equal work with men and thus were deserving of equal political rights. Gage's fictionalized account of Sojourner Truth's extemporaneous speech at a women's rights convention Gage presided over in 1851 (published twelve years later in the New York *Independent* in 1863) emphasized how Truth was able to quiet a restive audience by her sheer physical presence: "every eye was fixed on this almost Amazon form, which stood nearly six feet high, head erect, and eye piercing the upper air like one in a dream. At her first word there was a profound hush."[56] In Gage's retelling, Truth gave a hostile white audience the following dressing-down:

> "Well, chillen, whar dar's so much racket dar must be som'ting out o' kilter. I tink dat, 'twixt the niggers of de South and de women at de Norf, all a-talking 'bout rights, de white men will be in a fix pretty soon. But what's all this here talking 'bout? Dat man over dar say dat woman needs to be helped into carriages, and lifted over ditches, and to have de best place eberywhar. Nobody eber helps me into carriages, or ober mudpuddles, or gives me any best place;" and, raising herself to her full height and her voice to a pitch like rolling thunder, she asked, "And ar'n't I a woman? Look at me. Look at my arm," and she bared her right arm to the shoulder, showing its tremendous muscular power. "I have plowed and planted and gathered into barns, and no man could head me—and ar'n't I a woman? I could work as much and eat as much as a man, (when I could get it,) and bear de lash as well—and ar'n't I a woman? I have borne thirteen chillen, and seen 'em mos' all sold off into slavery, and when I cried out with a mother's grief, none but Jesus heard—and ar'n't I a woman?"[57]

Historian Nell Painter argues that Gage made up the dialect and drew on slave imagery (in the image of Truth baring her arm and the allusion to her children being sold at the auction block) in order to make Truth into a black folk hero who transcended the physical and psychological limitations of ordinary white womanhood. Painter also argues that by making up the phrase "Ar'n't I a Woman?" and having Truth reiterate it four times, Gage both highlighted and erased the specificity of slave women's experiences, invoking white beliefs in black racial difference—Truth's size, strength, and outspokenness—to respond to opponents of woman's rights who were asserting that (white) women's need for men's physical protection and support was a legitimate justification of their exclusion from the franchise.[58]

Gage's account played on crucial ambiguities and confusions in whites' understandings of womanhood. If God had created one universal woman's nature, how had such extraordinary differences (extraordinary in the eyes of white elites in this period) developed among different races of women? If all human beings were descendants of Adam and Eve's union, as recounted in Genesis, how had racial differences developed? Could climate and geography have had such a profound impact in producing sexual differences among the different races? What about the impact of culture and history?

White elites drew on social evolutionary theories to help them resolve these kinds of conundrums—both to compose more satisfying accounts of how racial and sexual differences developed in a relatively short time and to express optimism about the country's continuing attempts to assimilate its racial primitives. Despite the awe they felt at Sojourner Truth's size and strength, white women reformers continued to believe that social and racial progress lay in infusing sexual differences into sexually homogeneous races by making primitive women more delicate, more passive, more subservient, and more feminine. (Primitive men were deemed sufficiently masculine, although too violently sexualized, and still lacking advanced forms of male intelligence and emotional restraint.)

With the enfranchisement of black men and the naturalization of immigrant men, fears of "the race" becoming "overcivilized" or "degenerating," of (white) men becoming "effeminate," or of whites being "tainted" by the black race abounded. Despite the optimistic assumptions about progress that were present in most social-Darwinian descriptions of evolution, many white elites feared that there was no guarantee that white racial progress was an inevitable outcome of evolution.[59] Social evolution seemed to have produced white racial superiority so far, but whites were concerned about their racial future. They feared that the United States could regress from civilization into barbarism or savagery. Such occurrences had happened in the past—the so-called dark ages and the Middle Ages were understood as times of such cultural regression.

Indeed, resistance to woman's rights increased whenever fears of white masculine decline were heightened. White men's concern that white women were becoming "desexed" and "unwomanly" was a projection of their own anxiety about racial-sexual devolution. Women at the time understood that this was what was at the bottom of white men's antagonism to woman's rights. Sarah Grand, a woman's rights advocate, declared, "True womanliness is not in danger. The trouble is not because [white] women are [becoming] mannish but because [white] men grow ever more effeminate. . . . [W]e are accused of aping men in order to conceal the side from which the contrast should evidently be drawn."[60]

Thus social reformers who were attending to problems of racial assimilation in the second half of the nineteenth century became obsessed with issues of heredity, miscegenation, and the transmission of racial traits. Mary Lowe Dickinson and Lydia Maria

Child reflected on these issues in their novels *Among the Thorns* (1880) and *A Romance of the Republic* (1867), respectively, works whose central female heroines are initially unaware of their black parentage and so grow up constructing themselves as white.[61]

The novels relate what befalls these heroines as adults when they and others learn that they have black ancestry. Essentially, their white husbands and lovers are unable to keep their vows of love and loyalty, despite the fact that these women embody to the fullest extent possible the virtues of true womanhood (piety, chastity, domesticity, submissiveness). Thus, the women experience an immediate and irreversible decline in economic and social status, ending up single, isolated, and impoverished. The plots unfold as tragedies, the authors offering critiques of a white male racism that prejudges these women on the basis of racial affiliation rather than character. For the authors, this type of white racism is irrational and unfounded: the blackness of these characters is simply a label placed on them because in every significant way—appearance, behavior, upbringing, culture, outlook—these women appear white and act civilized.[62]

Dickinson's and Child's remonstrances notwithstanding, the primacy of color over character was the point from which white elites in the age of evolution could never escape. Implicit but never directly explored in these novels was white men's unarticulable fear of being deceived by white-looking wives into propagating a black race. While Child and Dickinson do not allow this possibility to arise in their fiction (the marriages are terminated before reproduction occurs), a postcard from the turn of the century graphically speaks to this concern. (See fig. 1-3.) In this image, a white couple have come to an alienist's office, the husband seeking recourse because his wife has just had a black child. Although no explanation is offered textually, the image itself allows for two possibilities: either the wife has committed adultery with a black man, or one of the partners has black ancestry and has been passing, knowingly or not, for white. Over the past several years, white viewers to whom I have shown this postcard generally bring up the first possibility and interpret the (white) woman's tears as admission of guilt over her adultery. Black viewers frequently raise the second alternative, explaining the (black) woman's tears in terms of her alarm and shame caused by the exposure of her undisclosed black racial heritage. None of the viewers I have encountered initially suppose that the white-looking man might actually be black, although when I raise this as a possibility, all have acknowledged that the text allows for such a reading. What the postcard reveals about the late nineteenth and early twentieth centuries, I believe, is white men's fear that they could not fully control the process of racial reproduction, a fear that was endemic in the period from 1870 to 1920, and which fundamentally colored (pun intended) the debates over woman's rights and race suicide. Interestingly, most of my several hundred viewers, regardless of race or gender, continue to hold the woman responsible for the birth of the black baby, a fact that I think reflects more than our ongoing cultural assumption that women's primary role is reproductive. My (admittedly unscientific) survey suggests to me that the effects of evolutionist discourse, which held white women accountable for racial development, are still in evidence a century later, even though the late nineteenth-century assignation of the woman as "conservator of the race" has long been forgotten.

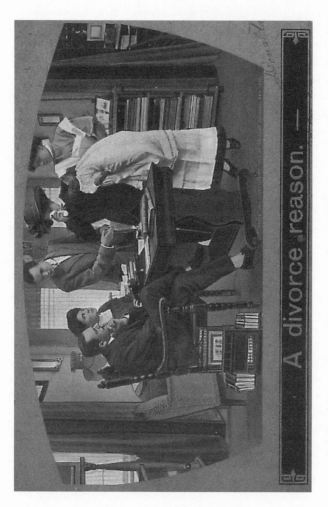

FIGURE 1-3 Racial Purity. A Divorce Reason. Postcard, c. early 1900s. Ensuring racial purity was presumed to be the responsibility and obligation of white women—intercourse between white women and black men was stigmatized as deeply shameful for the woman and grounds for lynching the man. In contrast, interracial sexual liasions between white men and black women were tolerated by whites, who attributed these relationships to the unchaste and predatory nature of black women.

White Women's Responses to Evolutionist Theories: Evolving a New Woman without Endangering the Race

> When, therefore Mr. Spencer argues that women are inferior to men because their development must be earlier arrested by reproductive functions, and Mr. Darwin claims that males have evolved muscle and brains superior to females, and entailed, their pre-eminent qualities chiefly on their male descendants, these conclusions need not be accepted without question, even by their own school of evolutionists.
>
> Antoinette Brown Blackwell,
> *The Sexes throughout Nature,* 1875

The theoretical linkage of the "advancement of civilization," "racial progress," and the "intensification of sexual difference" in dominant evolutionist theories deriving from Spencer's initial formulations had a profound effect on how white woman's rights activists formulated their own claims to sexual equality in the postbellum period. At one level, the effects can be seen in the type of discourse and language that woman's rights activists developed. Religious claims about women's moral superiority were no longer sufficient; it became impossible to argue for a change in woman's sphere without first thinking the argument through in evolutionist terms. Science had to be used to counter science, or, as cultural historians Stepan and Gilman have argued, "[t]he outcome was a narrowing of the cultural space within which, and the cultural forms by which, the claims of biological determinism could be effectively challenged."[63]

Earlier in the century, white Protestant women had been able to invoke their superior moral character as Christian women to justify their demands for the franchise. Now they also had to prove that voting would not be detrimental to their health, reduce their fertility, or interfere with their social responsibilities as wives and mothers. Women like suffragist Elizabeth Cady Stanton and the Boston reformer Abba Woolson, who were past college age when evolutionism became the craze in the 1880s, kept up with these theoretical developments by reading journals and newspapers and responded with their own articles and books to explain why the expansion of woman's sphere would not endanger the Anglo-Saxon race. Younger women who went to the newly established women's colleges in the 1880s gained the necessary scientific expertise and authority by taking courses in biology and the social sciences that they would later use to mount an effective challenge to evolutionist precepts about woman's nature in the early twentieth century.[64]

In the 1880s and 1890s, though, white women were extremely careful to show that their demands, if met, would not jeopardize the sexual differences on which their racial supremacy and Christian civilization were based. Instead, white woman's rights activists argued that their sexual differences, the sign and measure of their civilized status, constituted the proof that they shared in the racial superiority of the white race. Their sexual differences, rather than barring them from political and social equality with white men, they argued, should be seen as the predominant justification for their equal treatment.

Elite white women strengthened evolutionists' stipulation that whites were a superior race because it gave them a theoretical foundation on which to stake their own race-specific claims to sexual equality. While male evolutionists continued to disparage "woman" by comparing her to the "Negro," "slave," "African," and "lower races," white women's appropriation of theories of evolution resisted these comparisons and instead emphasized the racial commonalities between white women and white men. White women's first move was to insist that sexual differentiation need not necessarily imply sexual inequality; Antoinette Brown Blackwell argued, "It is the central theory of the present volume that the sexes in each species of being . . . are always true equivalents—equals but not identicals in development."[65]

Basically, white women's responses can be divided into two main categories. One category of responses tried to downplay sexual difference by taking what evolutionists said were "male" traits and showing that these were also possible for (civilized) women. "The fact that all human creatures are the subject of environment and of hereditary conditions," Lizzie Holmes wrote in 1898, "signifies that [the white] woman is no exception. There is every reason to suppose, that under like conditions with men, women would develop in a manner as men do."[66] Holmes tried to universalize as "human" the qualities that most evolutionists deemed were "masculine." Tentatively, and with a great deal of hesitation, she moved away from sexual difference in the direction of sexual identity.[67]

This was an unusual position for white women to adopt in the 1880s and 1890s, although some women boldly began to assert that "qualities which deserve to survive to the next dawning, should be equally developed in both men and women fitting for a time when sex is to be obliterated."[68] Its rarity was due, at least in part, to the problem of asserting sexual identity between man and woman without threatening the foundation of white superiority. In the hands of U.S. commentators, theories of evolution offered explanations for how changes in human nature had occurred. Yet white women were hesitant to argue for encouraging further change in woman's nature, even as they were strongly demanding alterations in women's social roles. This was a tricky business—a logical contradiction, given that Spencer had posited that alterations in woman's sphere would bring about changes in woman's nature. As they moved toward advocating that women could potentially become more like men, white women knew they were threatening the hierarchy of sexual difference on which white civilization was based. Thus they had to find ways to reassure themselves that increasing the similarity of activities performed by themselves and (white) men would not bring about racial degeneration or undermine their own racialized conceptions of themselves as belonging to a superior race and civilization.

This theoretical problem was not resolved definitively until Charlotte Perkins Gilman found a way to dismiss sexual difference as an "archaic" trait in the early 1900s. Until then, a common response among white women was to accept the need for white women's sexual difference but call for a reassessment of white women's role in reproduction and mothering. For example, suffragist Ora Brashere wrote in 1902, "Judging by the best ethical standards of humanity, those qualities corresponding to mental and moral forces which were bequeathed by the female are to be ranked higher than the predominant propensities of the male." Brashere considered man's love for society, his conceptions of right and wrong, and his conscience an "extension of [woman's] maternal love." Without the "influence of female instincts, males would never have risen beyond an overmastering desire for sex-gratification."[69] This strategy demanded a revaluation of the sexual traits (emotionalism, intuition, moral sensitivity, selflessness, altruism) and the social duties (childrearing, homemaking, schoolteaching) that were customarily associated with middle-class white women and that were devalued by white men. Brashere's strategy depended on making these female traits central to civilization itself, more than just a useful supplement to white men's rationality, intelligence, and proficiency with technology. Instead of denying that "female instincts" were inherent in white women, Brashere and others responded that feminine qualities ought to be more highly valued for their centrality to the white race and to U.S. society as a whole in its competition for international status and power. After a careful reading of the *Descent of Man*, another white woman's rights advocate, Eliza B. Gamble, reported that she "became impressed with the belief that the theory of evolution . . . furnishes much evidence going to show that the female among all the orders of life, man included, represents a *higher* stage of development than the male." For Gamble, Darwin's theories also offered a refutation of "theological dogmatism," in which "man . . . regarded himself as an infinitely superior being."[70]

Sometimes the two approaches—woman's sexual differences can be eliminated without racial degeneration, and woman's sexual differences, revalued in positive terms, are crucial for racial progress—existed side by side within the same text in an uneasy but not entirely contradictory fashion. For example, Frances Emily White (1832–1903), who graduated from the Woman's Medical College in Philadelphia in 1872 at the age of forty and was a professor of physiology and hygiene at her alma mater from 1876 to 1903, criticized evolutionary accounts for overemphasizing (white) women's sexual differences from (white) men. But her arguments for "woman's" potential to become more like "man" were full of qualifications. On the one hand, she believed that evolution involved changing sexual roles. On the other hand, she wanted to keep some of womanly nature unchangeable. She brought these antithetical points together by arguing that since evolution was a theory about progressive change, woman's sphere should be allowed to evolve, but she also claimed that evolution would not produce any undesirable social effects for civilization because, (white) woman's inherent mental and physical traits would act as a natural boundary for an expanding woman's sphere.[71]

This ambiguity or tension within White's arguments derives from the intellectual difficulties that elite white women, well schooled in evolutionary science but still operating within an older discourse of woman's rights rhetoric, encountered as they tried to wrest evolutionist theory away from social conservatives who were using it to restrict white women to a narrowly defined sphere of homemaking and childrearing.[72] White was struggling with what she feared might be two irreconcilable goals: one was to obtain recognition of a "higher character of womanhood," which, by the precepts of civilization and evolution, meant increasing sexual differences. Another was to expand "woman's sphere" to encompass professional opportunities, which was not only a longstanding demand of the woman's rights movement but also a personal objective of White's (that she had indeed fulfilled). If society refashioned woman's sphere to become more like man's, then women themselves might become more like men (lowering, not raising, women's character). White never resolved this dilemma. She remained fearful that an expansion in woman's sphere would jeopardize womanly character and diminish the civilized status accorded to white middle-class womanhood.[73]

As the case of Frances White reveals, white women used evolutionist precepts to challenge the confining boundaries of the culturally prescribed "woman's sphere," but they were equally intent upon preserving traditional notions concerning "womanly nature." For White, the key to (white) woman's own racial progress was a separate sphere of development in order to allow the development of her particular racial-sexual differences—those traits specific to her own race-sex. White women remained committed to maintaining woman's separate sphere, all the while demanding its enlargement, so as not to jeopardize white racial superiority.

Evolutionist Theory, Racial Difference, and U.S. Imperialism in the Age of Empire

Evolutionist theories did more than offer ways to differentiate white women from white men; they also made possible a whole range of cultural distinctions: between "civilized" and "primitive" women, between women of the "West" and women of the "Orient," and between "Christian" and "heathen" women. The greater power of the West was not just symbolized by the status of its women but was understood to be a direct consequence of its superior (patriarchal) gender system. Similarly, the powerlessness of the Orient was construed as the result of an inferior and perverted gender system. For the ruling elite of the United States in the late nineteenth century, sexual difference, race, and national power were all causally connected.

As I have shown, the mental-psychological traits associated with the most "advanced" women, such as emotionalism, spirituality, and sexual chastity, were considered the evolutionary consequences of these women's treatment by (civilized, Christian) men, qualities that were passed on from generation to generation through the racial inheritance of acquired sexual traits. The primitive woman, on the other hand, was presumed to lack the sexual differentiation and moral development of the civilized woman, due to her centuries-long exploitation by the men of her own race. Whether the "primitive" woman was embodied in the white imagination as the Indian squaw, an Oriental harem girl, or an African savage, she became the physical yardstick by which white women in the United States measured their own moral status, social progress, and racial development.

From the perspective of liberal white elites, the overarching problem of the 1880s was to create a homogeneous Christian community out of the discrete racial-cultural groups of people who were lodged at different stages in the evolutionary hierarchy.

The challenge was to assist evolutionary inferiors, especially those residing within the United States, to advance more rapidly, so that they could be more quickly assimilated into the supposedly more advanced civilization of Anglo-American and European whites. Acculturation of the primitive—at least through assimilation—was far from assured. (See figs. 1-4–1-6)

Perceptions of the difficulty of assimilating purportedly "inferior" peoples at home led many assimilationists to turn to eugenics, including immigration restriction and other forms of social control, to contain and limit interracial contact—to "protect" the country from the "racial" "degeneration" that "hordes of foreigners" and "unassimilable" blacks signified for those who identified themselves as part of "civilized" Anglo-Saxon culture. Although eugenics had its intellectual basis in the work of Francis Galton—a cousin of Darwin who published his own theoretical works beginning in the 1860s—eugenics as a social movement began to flourish in the United States in the last two decades of the nineteenth century and continued to attract supporters into the 1920s. Eugenicists, like their philosophical opponents, the social-Darwinists, also adhered to Lamarckian laws of inheritance (despite the rediscovery of Mendel's theory of genetic inheritance in 1900) and discussed the transmission of racial and

FIGURE 1-4 Assimilation far from assured. I Strive for a Higher Positon. Postcard, c. early 1900s. This image mocks political efforts to assimilate blacks into the civilization of whites, representing African Americans as monkeys still residing in the jungle. Despite the accoutrements of civilization (Victorian dress) and the seeming conformity to Victorian gender relations (male chivalry), the cartoonist upholds whites' belief in the inherent inferiority of African Americans. The slogan, "I strive for a higher position," which echoed the rallying cry of the woman's movement in this period, indicates how closely the two struggles were connected in the minds of contemporaries, with the juxtaposition of slogan and image implying that (white) women's sruggle to obtain gender equality was as absurdly problematic as African Americans' struggle to obtain racial equality.

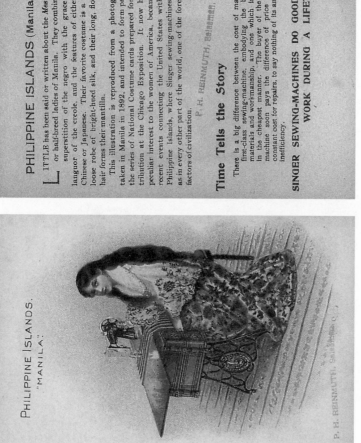

PHILIPPINE ISLANDS (Manila).

LITTLE has been said or written about the *Mestizos*, or half-breed ladies of Manila. They combine the superstition of the negro with the grace and languor of the creole, and the features of either the Chinese or Japanese. Their favorite costume is a long, loose robe of bright-hued silk, and their long, flowing hair forms their mantilla.

This illustration is reproduced from a photograph taken in Manila in 1892, and intended to form part of the series of National Costume cards prepared for distribution at the Chicago Exposition. It now has a peculiar interest to the women of America, because of recent events connecting the United States with the Philippine Islands, where Singer sewing-machines are, as in every other part of the world, one of the foremost factors of civilization.

P. H. REINMUTH, Salesman.

Time Tells the Story

There is a big difference between the cost of making a first-class sewing-machine, embodying the best of materials and workmanship, and one which is made in the cheapest manner. The buyer of the cheap machine soon pays the difference of price in the constant cost for repairs, to say nothing of its annoying inefficiency.

SINGER SEWING-MACHINES DO GOOD WORK DURING A LIFETIME

FIGURE 1-5 Assimilation in progress. Philippine Islands, Manila, and text appearing on back of trade card. Singer Sewing Machine, Trade card distributed at the Chicago World's Fair, 1893. Singer marketed its sewing machines worldwide by asserting itself as "one of the foremost factors in civilization." The obvious purpose of the machine was to clothe the naked. Covering the body, especially the female body, was deemed the first step in advancing a society from primitivism to civilization.

44

FIGURE 1-6 Assimilation achieved. Typical Manila girl and her uncivilized sister, Philippines. Postcard, c. 1902.

sexual traits in terms of the biological transmission of acquired characteristics. However, in opposition to the laissez-faire principles of social-Darwinists, eugenicists advocated governmental intervention in social processes in a variety of ways: immigration
restriction laws, antimiscegenation laws, birth control practices, and so forth. All these
policies were intended to control the reproduction of so-called "inferior" groups in
order to promote "racial progress" (of whites). The comments of historian George W.
Stocking, Jr. regarding the eugenics movement in Great Britain also apply to the
movement in the United States; he writes that eugenics was the "product of a period
when traditional liberalism, threatened by forces of democracy and collectivism at
home, and by those of nationalism and militarism abroad, was no longer the optimistic creed it had once been. . . . [E]ugenics was an attempt to compensate for the
failure of natural selection to operate under the social conditions of advanced civilization."[74] As early as 1887, commentators argued forcefully that there "should be shut
out, [all those] who belong to a civilization essentially lower than our own."[75] To ig-
nore the "problem" that these uncivilized represented or to let social-Darwinian laws
(survival of the fittest) operate without any governmental intervention was to risk
permitting U.S. society to fracture along the fissures of cultural and racial difference.

Despite the threat that racial differences signified for white elites in this period,
many reformers remained hopeful that the cultural incorporation of others into the
United States' Christian civilization was possible and could take place quickly if sufficient attention were brought to the cause. Yet in the minds of some white Christian
civilizers, mistakes had been made in the past and should be avoided in the future. To
have enfranchised blacks during Reconstruction before they were fully civilized
seemed to some northern whites in the 1880s to have put the cart before the horse.
They laid the blame for the failure of Reconstruction not on national or state governments or even on individual blacks themselves but on the primitive evolutionary state
in which blacks were still mired as a race. Other whites, however, including the liberal
Ohioan President Garfield, believed that "the emancipated race [had] already made remarkable progress" and thought that the educational programs implemented as part
of Reconstruction's industrial training for blacks should serve as a model for other
"primitive" groups.[76]

In this period, most whites referred to blacks living in the United States as "Negroes" or as "Africans," depending on how "civilized" the particular group of blacks
appeared to them. (Lighter skin color, European dress and hairstyles, and the assumption of middle-class values all signified evolutionary advancement.) Whites thought of
themselves either as "Europeans" or "Americans" and believed that they had greater
"adaptiveness" or racial flexibility than Africans.[77] Hundreds of pages in the popular
press were devoted to the question of whether Africans could be assimilated, given
their supposed greater resistance to climate, geography, and environment. These kinds
of debates took place in relation to other racial groups as well: Indians were seen as
even more resistant to civilization than Africans (and their right to U.S. citizenship
was delayed until 1924). The Chinese threatened evolution's racial hierarchies sufficiently for whites to pass special antimiscegenation and immigration restriction laws
forbidding their intermarriage with whites and making it impossible for Chinese la-

borers to bring their wives and families to the United States until after World War II. The Chinese Exclusion Act of 1882 made certain exemptions for travelers, students, merchants, and their families, but even so, in 1900 the overall sex ratio for Chinese living in the United States was nineteen men to every one woman; and for foreign-born Chinese residents, it was more than thirty-six to one.[78]

Although evolutionist theories opened up a way to conceive of how lower races could become more like higher races (and racial difference eliminated or transcended), many whites doubted whether so-called primitive groups had developed the evolutionary capacity for adaptation and learning. They were not convinced that education would produce new racial traits that would then be inherited by the next generation, and they questioned whether evolutionary processes worked in exactly the same way for blacks, Indians, and the Chinese as they had for the English, Germans, French, and Scandinavians. Moreover, northern white elites in particular were worried by the miscegenation that had already taken place between the black and white races in the South during slavery and feared that black racial progress was predicated on white racial degeneration. Out of these concerns, many white intellectuals, social scientists, and political leaders went to great lengths to make sure that the kind of race-mixing that had produced a significant interracial population in the South would never occur in the North.

The views of two prominent U.S. social scientists, Nathaniel Southgate Shaler (1841–1906) and Lester F. Ward (1841–1913), can serve to illustrate how evolution was used in different ways to articulate and alleviate these fears. Shaler, writing in the 1870s, as the United States was struggling with the politics of Reconstruction, used evolutionist theory as a justification for why Reconstruction did not work and should be dropped. For Shaler, blacks fell outside the laws of evolution and were highly resistant to change. Hence assimilationist processes, such as education, seemed ineffective to Shaler, a waste of time and resources. He subscribed to laissez-faire doctrines (it was best for governments not to interfere with nature) and was convinced that the laws of evolution would eventually result in the elimination of blacks as a race, yet he still felt it necessary to suggest that the government scatter blacks over the United States to prevent them from becoming too much of a burden on any given section of the country.[79] The sociologist Lester Ward, on the other hand, wrote in the 1890s and early 1900s, several decades after Reconstruction had ended, at the height of Jim Crow. In this political climate, when racial segregation was rigidly enforced, Ward argued that interracial contact had played an evolutionarily beneficial role in the development of an advanced civilization.[80]

Shaler studied geology and zoology under Louis Agassiz at the Lawrence Scientific School in Cambridge from 1859 to 1862, and after serving two years in the Union army as a captain of the Fifth Kentucky Battery, he returned to Cambridge to become an assistant to Agassiz for two years. He then spent another two years abroad in study and exploration, returned to Harvard as a lecturer in 1868, and was made professor of paleontology in 1869. He remained at Harvard for the rest of his life—nearly forty more years—also serving as dean of the Lawrence Scientific School from 1891 until his death in 1906. An active and innovative scientist who was in charge of the Atlantic Coast Division of the United States Geological Survey (in this connection, it seems, he traveled almost the whole length of the coast from Maine to Florida on foot), Shaler was also a public intellectual who published his views on a myriad of social issues, including the "Negro problem," in popular journals such as the *Atlantic Monthly, Scribner's,* and the *North American Review.* In an article entitled "An Ex-Southerner in South Carolina," which appeared in 1870, Shaler registered his disapproval of sending northern white women down south to school African Americans in civilization. "The all-important question is, What should we do to secure to this people the highest cultivation of which they are capable? Should we begin by trying to force upon them the last product of our civilization, intellectual culture?"[81] For Shaler, the futility of such an endeavor was only equaled by earlier attempts to teach a Comanche English grammar. "He would be a fool, indeed," Shaler continued,

> who expected that the consequences would be the immediate change in the nature and purposes of the Indian. Now the fact is we have almost as much to do in order to change the average negro into an intelligent citizen in a white society as we should have if we tried to embody the Indian into our government. . . . The school has its place in civilization, and, as a teacher, I should be the last to belittle its importance; but it is the last step in the development of a race, not the first. . . . [W]hen we undertake to civilize a race as foreign to us in every trait as the negroes, by imposing upon them this final product of our national growth, we wrong ourselves and them.[82]

Observation convinced Shaler that Africans did not respond to the environmental conditions (both climate and culture) of the United States as other races did. French people in the northern section of the United States, for example, quickly evolved to have more in common with German people living in the North than they did with French people living in the South. Regional difference, according to Shaler, had clearly and definitively altered the racial histories of civilized peoples, but the same did not seem to be true of Africans: "One looks in vain," Shaler wrote in 1873, "for any marks to separate him from his kindred in other regions. . . . This inflexibility of the African is . . . a very striking feature [and] we may venture the opinion that the negroes of the South give many evidences of being a far less elastic race than our own."[83] Shaler was perplexed by these findings because, by the tenets of his own theory, changing geographic and cultural conditions should have had a profound impact on the bodies, minds, and social practices of blacks, who had sustained the greatest climatic and cultural changes in their forced relocation from Africa to the United States. He thus puzzled over his finding that "the negro has changed less in his movement from one hemisphere to another, from tropical to local conditions, from the indolence of savage life to the toil of slavery than has the European in his migration from one side of the Atlantic to the other."[84]

This apparent evolutionary fixity of the African in the face of geographic mobility and cultural transformation confounded Shaler's expectations, and he sought vainly for some sort of explanation that made sense within his evolutionary framework. In so doing, he provides us with a good illustration of the continuum between racial prejudice and enlightened discourse within scientific racism. For example, Shaler wondered whether the discrepancy might be explained by the "general rule, among animals" that the "higher members of any group" seemed "to be more variable in character than the lower," although he was uncertain as to whether blacks and whites were far enough apart within the human genus for this law of the animal kingdom to apply. It was also possible, Shaler reasoned, that the pronounced variability of Europeans was an "acquired capacity"—an evolutionary product of several thousand years of European migrations. In all Shaler's hypotheses, the ruling assumption was that the greater adaptability and variability of whites must have been a consequence, as well as a sign, of their more "advanced" evolutionary development. Simply put, Shaler believed that Africans were less susceptible to environmental change than whites because they were less civilized. "[T]he resistance to change which his body shows is shared by his mind and . . . his intellectual advance will necessarily be slow, even under the most favorable conditions."[85] For Shaler, the political implications of these evolutionary truths dictated that the best course of action was to keep the races apart, as blacks (due to their essential evolutionary fixity) could not benefit from cultural contact with whites.

For Lester Ward, interracial contact, both in the form of cultural integration and sexual intercourse, had been and would continue to be beneficial to Africans struggling to catch up to the superior whites. Moreover, interracial conflict—what Ward called the struggle of the races—was a fundamental principle inherent in the laws of social evolution. The history of mankind was a history of a (superior) conquering race annihilating or absorbing an (inferior) conquered race. Separation of the races was not only an impossibility, it was also an undesirable arrangement, given how evolution and miscegenation worked together to produce racial progress.

Optimistically, Ward predicted that whites and blacks in the United States would eventually learn that they shared common interests, would join together in commercial and other enterprises, and would intermarry with one another until the society became more or less racially homogeneous. *"Race miscegenation therefore begins immediately, but it does not cease after the subjugation is complete. . . . All attempts to keep the superior race pure fail utterly."*[86] White racial purity was an impossibility; miscegenation a social inevitability.[87] Yet Ward wrote in support of whites' double sexual standard with regard to miscegenation, condoning sexual intercourse between white men and black women as advantageous to blacks, while castigating and forbidding sexual intercourse between black men and white women as detrimental to whites.[88] For the purposes of evolutionary progress, according to Ward, sexual intercourse need only occur between men of the conquering race (white men) and women of the conquered race (black women). The other gender pairing (intercourse between white women and black men), would have no evolutionary advantage for blacks, and could only lead to white racial deterioration.[89] Although Ward offered no explanation for why white women's birthing of black babies and white men's fathering of black babies had such different evolutionary outcomes, he claimed nonetheless to sympathize both with the "biological imperative" that black men felt to "elevate" his race, as well as the indignation of whites who were "impelled to pursue, capture, and 'lynch'" the offender because of a "biological law of race preservation."[90]

As we have seen, antimiscegenation laws reflected white men's fears about white racial degeneration and inability to control white women's sexuality and reproduction. To assuage these fears, Ward developed another theory about white woman's sexual conservatism—or her central, conserving role in the preservation of civilization. Many male theorists in this period argued that (white) woman's biological conservatism made her more resistant to evolution and held her responsible for retarding the evolutionary development of the white race. Ward, on the other hand, argued that white women's special role in passing race traits on to children meant that the white race owed all its progress in social evolution to white women. Thus, while Ward agreed that (white) women were less variable than (white) men, he denied that this meant that "the female sex [was] incapable of progress, or that man [was] destined to develop indefinitely, leaving woman constantly farther and farther in the rear."[91] Instead, Ward saw (white) woman's relative biological inflexibility as "the balance-wheel of society, keeping it in a steady and fixed condition of growth."[92] "Accepting evolution as we must," Ward proclaimed:

> [R]ecognizing heredity as the distinctive attribute of the female sex, it becomes clear that it must be from the steady advance of woman rather than from the uncertain fluctuations of man that the sure and solid progress of the future is to come. The attempt to move the whole race forward by elevating only the sex that represents the principle of instability, has long enough been tried. . . . *the way to civilize the race is to civilize woman.* And now, thanks to science, we see why this is so. Woman is the unchanging trunk of the great genealogic tree; while man, with all his vaunted superiority, is but a branch, a grafted scion, as it were, whose acquired qualities die with the individual, while those of woman are handed on to futurity.[93]

In other words, Ward attributed to white woman a specific racial-cultural function— the preserver of racial traits for society—and he tied that function to woman's evolutionary development of a specific race and sex-linked biology. It is worth noting how white women's and black men's racial fixity were given very different valuations in Ward's work: white women assisted evolutionary processes by preserving desirable racial traits among whites, while black men resisted evolutionary processes by not being able to learn and assimilate into white civilization.

By 1903, in *Pure Sociology,* Ward had elaborated fully an alternative evolutionary theory to Darwin and Spencer—what he called his gynaecocentric theory. In contrast to Darwin, who focused on natural selection—males' competition with other males—Ward focused his theory on sexual selection: women's power, especially in primitive societies, to select mates.[94] Primitive women, Ward argued, had played a crucial evolutionary role in determining the racial traits that would appear in offspring, although civilized women had lost this power of sexual selection.[95] Ward was convinced, however, that civilized women retained the power of racial transmission and through this function wielded dominant control over the future characteristics of the race.

This new thinking about woman's role as transmitter of race traits contained several important reformulations of the theory of the inheritance of acquired traits. In effect, Ward was dismissing the usual Darwinian claim that sexual traits were passed on via the laws of partial inheritance—from father to son and mother to daughter. Instead, he proposed that the mother was the source of all race traits, which were passed indiscriminately to both daughters and sons. Charlotte Perkins Gilman would later characterize this theoretical innovation ("woman as the race-type") as the "most important contribution" yet made to "Neo-Feminism."[96] Man—previously thought of as the primary source of new variations—was no longer granted the dominant role in the process of racial inheritance (and thus social evolution) that he had held previously. Woman— previously granted little efficacy in passing on beneficial traits to offspring—took on the central role in this new theory of evolutionary racial development.

Moreover, Ward's modification of the biological laws of inheritance accommodated a subtle and yet powerful reconceptualization of white woman's role in the nation's political life. The reconceptualization reinforced already prevailing notions that women's primary social role was reproductive. Yet in attributing to civilized women the biological power for determining the racial traits of offspring, and for serving as the exemplars and models for other races, Ward's theory endowed white women with a powerful claim to direct the nation's policies and resources in regard to civilizing primitive others.

Ward seems to have believed that all women served the evolutionary function as the preservers and transmitters of racial traits for their respective races. Anna Julia Cooper, a black woman who most likely heard Ward lecture in Washington, D.C. during the mid-1880s, interpreted his theory in this way and built her own theories of black woman's equality on this foundation.[97]

And Otis T. Mason immediately understood the implications of Ward's thinking for reforming the United States' policy in assimilating Indians. Mason served as a curator of the U.S. Bureau of Ethnology (part of the National Museum, now the Smithsonian Institution) in Washington, D.C., from the early 1870s until his death in 1908.[98] Prior to joining the bureau, Mason had been a professor at Columbian College (now George Washington University), a position he retained from 1861 to 1884. In 1885, Mason assisted the newly formed Women's Anthropological Society (WAS) by providing this group with an outline of study, and in 1893, as president of the men's Anthropological Society of Washington, D.C., he presided over a joint meeting held with the WAS.[99]

Mason's own book, *Woman's Share in Primitive Culture,* the culmination of talks he began giving in 1888, advised the country to assess the stored capital, energy, and experience of its most "advanced" women, as these women contained, in his view, the biological-cultural elements on which the future of the country depended in its mission of bringing civilization to others.[100] Moreover, his book argued that the United States ought to redesign its Indian policies, so as to civilize and assimilate Indian *women* : "The longer one studies the subject," he declared, "the more he will be convinced that savage tribes can now be elevated chiefly through their women."[101] Yet whites first had to correct their misconceptions about the biological nature of primitive women. Indian women were not the immoral, promiscuous, or irrational beings that white Americans thought they were. Rather they shared with white women a capacity for morality, sexual purity, and religious devotion, and, most important, they exercised the same kind of "influence" over their husbands that civilized women were presumed to exercise over their men. In his evocative renderings of the common domestic lives of primitive and civilized women, Mason downplayed ongoing political conflicts between whites and Indians. Thus, Mason's work offered a soothing balm for white Americans' longings for racial harmony, as he insisted on the potential for similarity among the races—at least their common femininity—and for the possibility for the universal acceptance of patriarchal domesticity.

White Women and Civilization-Work

Evolutionist discussions about (white) woman's role as an agent of civilization intensified in the 1880s as whites focused on the primitive others within their midst—whether African Americans, Native Americans, southern Europeans, or Asian immigrants. The growing interest in white women's potential contribution along these lines coincided with the country's obsessions with "Americanizing" the immigrant and "uplifting" the Negro.[102] To put this point in a different way, the combination of social anxiety about the presence of nonwhite groups in U.S. society at this time, along with changing social scientific theories in the 1880s, made possible a more powerful public role for elite, white women as civilization-workers. As I have already mentioned, this was not a new role for white women, as some had served as missionary wives in the early nineteenth century, accompanying husbands to foreign missions to demonstrate the advantages of traditional patriarchal families.[103] In the postbellum period, evolutionists' discourses buttressed white women's desire to work alone, without husbands or male protectors, among primitive groups. Increasingly, as the nineteenth century wore on, civilization-work became secularized, although it remained firmly linked to an evangelical worldview. Extensive women's organizations developed through which white women could derive enhanced status and power by serving as exponents of civilization, in carrying the ideals of Christianity to "primitive" peoples, whether they lived within or outside the borders of the United States.

Even suffragists, who had for decades argued that racial distinctions should be irrelevant to the granting of the franchise, began to think about citizenship in relation to the future of the white race, as global questions of empire and civilization began to shape domestic discussions of women's issues. In 1895, voicing her concern over the inclusion of "ignorant foreigners" in the franchise, Elizabeth Cady Stanton declared that the "remedy" for the domination of one sex by the other was "education of the higher, more tender sentiments in humanity, the mother-thought omnipresent in every department of life. . . . This must be done," Stanton insisted, "before we can take another step in civilization." "Women, the greatest factor in civilization" [must] first [be] enfranchised."[104]

Many groups of women found evolutionist discourse a useful way to analyze race and gender problems, but it was also an ideology that bolstered the public authority and power of white women without seeming to transgress traditionally conservative notions about woman's appropriate sphere and activities. To the minds of white contemporaries, women's civilization-work was distinct from male forms of political activity, which they understood to be morally questionable and inappropriate for white women. White women who carried out this civilization-work at home among Native Americans, the urban poor, and immigrants became a part of the ruling class of the progressive era without having to press their own claims for the elective franchise to obtain political power. Mary Lowe Dickinson, president of the Women's National Indian Association in 1885, explained, "That it [our type of work] exists at all is due to that enlightened spirit of philanthropy, which as a natural outgrowth of Christian principle, permeates as never before the sisterhood of the land. It is this spirit that is making [the white] woman a most potent adjunct in the solving of the social problems that press upon the enlightened conscience in this day of grand endeavors for the uplifting of the race."[105]

White middle-class women generally found missionary work appealing because it permitted them to exercise cultural authority over those they conceived as their evolutionary and racial inferiors. Espousing their superior capacities as reformers and civilizers, white women garnered unprecedented visibility and status from their roles as special government agents (Alice Fletcher), as appointed state commissioners on various boards dealing with urban problems (Josephine Shaw Lowell), as leaders of the settlement house (Jane Addams) and temperance movements (Frances Willard), or as missionaries either at home or abroad (Helen Montgomery). The woman's foreign mission movement eventually became the largest movement of white women in the United States, attracting more than three million women as members by 1915, far exceeding in size even Frances Willard's popular National Woman's Christian Temperance Union (160,000 members).[106] Through their roles as civilization-workers, white women's words, actions, and political demands carried power and influence with government officials, church leaders, and social reformers.

"Woman as a civilizing force" became the common rallying cry of all segments of the woman's movement. Yet this notion was deployed by different groups for different political objectives. Antisuffragists drew on this discourse to argue that the franchise might jeopardize the moral superiority of the civilized woman by making her a partisan rather than an impartial political actor. One antisuffragist argued that "woman is not the subject sex, nor will she ever become the subject sex unless we turn to *savagery* and she 'earns her own living' at hard labor just as man does."[107] While suffragists used this ideology to buttress white women's demands for equal political rights with white men, their opponents used it to point out that civilized women were already in a privileged position and did not need any more rights. The elasticity of this hegemonic discourse meant that no group within the United States could make a play for political power without invoking civilizationist ideologies. Because of the ways in which this discourse constructed the alternatives—identify as a (civilized) Christian or be identified as a (barbaric) heathen—every group first had to demonstrate adherence to the precepts of Christian civilization before it could make any demands to be included in the body politic of the nation.[108]

Although in general, social-Darwinian theory posited that the competitive struggle for survival was a beneficial mechanism, a way of weeding out unfit individuals, there were exceptions in these theories that enabled nineteenth-century elites to ig-nore competition if it occurred in troubling instances, such as between white men and white women (whether within the family or in the workplace) or between Anglos and other races, or between Western and non-Western countries. The renowned paleon-tologist and antisuffragist Edward D. Cope explained, "While the *interests* of the mem-bers of the same sex [i.e., white men] often bring them into collision with each other, those of [the] opposite [sex] cannot normally do so."[109] As I have shown, evolutionary processes were assumed to function in different ways in relation to the sexes (white men and white women), to different races (Europeans, Africans, Indians, and Chi-nese), or to the same sexes of different races. The claim that "social progress" de-pended on competition or social conflict (leading to the "survival of the fittest") was invoked only when it sanctioned the interests of white elites, particularly when it jus-tified the dominance of white men in business, government, the professions, and so on. When the conflictual processes of evolution might lead to competition between white men and white women, or between white and black men, these processes were either not recognized as evolutionary, were considered as some sort of undesirable side effect of "natural laws," or were seen as likely to produce white racial or sexual de-generation.

Evolutionist theories also stigmatized the working classes as lesser, uncivilized be-ings. Class divisions and class conflict were increasing in this period, and some social-Darwinists attributed poverty to an inferior racial inheritance—an insufficiently developed cultural heritage that was manifested in the exploitation of working-class women. William Graham Sumner argued, in *What Social Classes Owe to Each Other,* "Strange and often horrible shadows of all the old primitive barbarism are now to be found in the slums of [our] great cities, and in the lowest groups of men, in the midst of civilized nations. Men impose labor on women in some such groups today."[110] Evo-lutionists' stipulation of social progress as a unilinear and normative movement from savagery to civilization helped white elites redefine economic and political problems as cultural-racial problems, characterized by gender abnormalities and sexual perver-sions. Moreover, class distinctions were rarely recognized within uncivilized groups, even when class differentiation was clearly evident. Evolutionist discourse, for exam-ple, recognized educated or privileged African Americans simply as "Negroes," not as members of a multi-racial middle-class.[111]

To white elites who formulated and applied theories of evolution to their social re-form movements, poor peoples' poverty and political marginality were deemed mat-ters of personal ignorance, sin, or deviance rather than of economic exploitation or political oppression. Most often, those who invoked evolutionist theories denied that wealth or class status had any bearing on the differences between the civilized and un-civilized. For the most part, they did not consider reallocation of economic resources or alteration in property ownership relevant to the civilizing process. The charity or-ganization movement of the 1880s, for example, believed that providing "gifts" of food or money was counterproductive to solving problems of poverty and instead focused on instilling the values of white patriarchal civilization—giving the gift of patriarchy. Most groups of impoverished peoples—blacks living in rural areas, and urban immigrants, for example—were not able to gain support for their demands for economic redress.[112]

Even though evolutionist theories made it possible for some to predict the diminishing of sexual, racial, ethnic, or class differences, most white authorities gave elaborate explanations for why this did not, could not, happen. In the case of African Americans, the rate of evolutionary change was too slow and uncertain (Shaler). Or the Negro could only evolve through sexual intercourse between white men and black women (Ward). Moreover, even if evolutionary theory did sanction "progress," there was no guarantee that white women, people of color, or working-class and non-Western peoples could perform the kinds of tasks that would ultimately produce sexual, racial, or class equality. We might read these convoluted discussions, in which white elites went to great lengths to restrict ideas of what evolution could make possible, as an indication of how anxious they felt about the need to maintain their dominant position within a fragile and destabilized social order.

Sexual differences and racial concerns were also at the heart of the suffragist-antisuffragist debates of this period. Historians have argued that suffragists were advocating rights and responsibilities for women identical to those of men, while antisuffragists stressed women's purported sexual differences as the reason for their continued exclusion from the franchise. In fact, suffragists and antisuffragists generally agreed on their perception of (whites') sexual differences and their significance. What they vehemently argued over, as I shall show next, was how to give political recognition to these differences, given the complex ways in which the racial and class hierarchies of society were shifting.

2

The Making of a White Female Citizenry

Suffragism, Antisuffragism, and Race

> We can not make [white] men see that [white] women feel the hu-
> miliation of their petty distinctions of sex, precisely as the black
> man feels those of color. It is no palliation of our wrongs to say that
> we are not socially ostracised as he [the black man] is, so long as
> we are politically ostracised as he is not.
>
> Elizabeth Cady Stanton, "The Degradation
> of Disfranchisement" (1891)

IN THE 1870s, 1880s, AND 1890s, white suffragists used theories of evolution to support a new rationale for their own enfranchisement, one that depended on redefining what it meant to be a white female citizen. The new definitions made use of older beliefs in white women's moral superiority but also drew on a growing conviction that white women's special racial qualities were needed to counteract the influence of the immigrant and African American men who had just been enfranchised. As government representatives, ministers, and church groups discussed how to make citizens out of so-called primitives, white suffragists conceptualized a special role for themselves in assimilating nonwhite peoples into U.S. civilization and made this point one of their primary rationales for their own inclusion in the franchise.

Older notions of patriarchal citizenship, stemming from classical republicanism and Lockean individualism, emphasized the necessity of citizens bearing arms in defense of the republic. Since "woman" was presumed to lack the intellectual and physical strength required to defend herself or her country, white women could not make headway within this framework in convincing men that they should be granted the franchise. Throughout the nineteenth century, white women's relation to politics was supposed to remain indirect, mediated through the family, via their relation to husbands, fathers, and sons. Moreover, the maintenance of their specific forms of moral virtue—purity, piety, empathy, and spirituality—depended on their staying outside existing political institutions and structures. White women were expected to remain in the domestic sphere and to exert their moral influence from within the home through their roles as wives and mothers.[1]

In the second half of the nineteenth century, however, this constellation of beliefs was challenged on several fronts. First, black men were legally admitted to the franchise after the Civil War, implicitly casting them as protectors of white women—an idea that greatly upset white women, who responded by defining their capacities and responsibilities as citizens in new ways.[2] White women began to assert themselves as the rightful, natural protectors of uncivilized races (the protectors of black men, not the other way around) and used this racialized responsibility to assert their rights as *white ("Saxon") female* citizens. Second, as more and more white women began to live part of their lives outside conventional forms of domesticity, slowly the distinction between a private domain for white middle-class women and a public one for white middle-class men became less salient. White women increasingly developed their own institutions—voluntary and charitable societies, church groups, self-improvement clubs, settlement houses, and organizations focused on "municipal housekeeping"— from which they could influence men's political forums and play a direct part on the formulation of social policy. Even though many white women did not consider their activities or institutions political, they themselves became increasingly visible and active as political agents, using demonstrations, petitions, boycotts, lobbying, and pamphlets to express their political views and consolidate their political power.[3]

As I have shown, theories of evolution linked civilization and sexual difference in such a way that calling for change in woman's sphere seemed to threaten the advancement of whites' civilization. The problem facing postbellum white suffragists, then, was how to argue that the franchise would alter woman's sphere but not diminish whites' sexual differences or endanger their civilization. To address this problem, some white suffragists reaffirmed a pre-evolutionist view of woman's nature, insisting on the principle of the stability of sexual differences against the tenet of change in evolutionist theory, to justify the idea that woman's sphere could be modified without producing corresponding changes in woman's nature. Suffragist Margaret Evans explained, "Experience proves that true womanly qualities are too firmly founded on immutable laws to be shaken by the fall of a ballot."[4] Other suffragists, however, accepted evolutionary predictions that woman's nature would evolve in response to changes in woman's sphere and were careful to defend their proposals on the grounds that it would be evolutionarily advantageous for white women to vote.[5]

While much debate occurred over how malleable woman's nature was likely to be in response to the franchise, the vast majority of white activists in the woman's movement insisted that (white) women were different from (white) men. I am using parentheses again to focus our attention on the unarticulated racial component in suffragist ideology during the postbellum period. When suffragists of the period used racial modifiers, they used the terms "Saxon" and "white" interchangeably, and they used "black" as a modifier when they were speaking about "the Negro."[6] Often, though, they made universal claims about man, woman, and the race that they clearly intended to apply only to whites. Regardless of whether they used racial modifiers, ideas about race difference were always present, even if race functioned as an absent presence, as it so often did. At crucial moments, however, white suffragists invoked race explicitly in their arguments, calling attention both to their own racial similarity with white men and to their racial superiority to nonwhite men. For example, at the Seneca Falls convention in 1848, Elizabeth Cady Stanton called for a platform affirming woman's right to vote with the proclamation: "We need not prove ourselves equal to Daniel Webster to enjoy this privilege [of suffrage], for the ignorant Irishman in the ditch has all the civil rights he has. . . . *All white men* in this country have the same rights, however they may differ in mind, body or estate. The right [to vote] is ours."[7]

Thus, even before white women drew on evolutionist ideas to assert their own significance to civilizing missions, white women invoked their racial similarity with (white) men when they insisted on their inherent capacity to vote and their inherent right to the franchise—racial similarity taking precedence over any sexual difference. At the same time, however, suffragists used sexual differences to criticize the government for taxing them without representation, insisting that full representation could not occur without woman's vote, since (white) men could not understand or represent (white) women's very different needs. William E. Channing, speaking at a woman's rights convention on September 6, 1853, declared, "It has never been asserted that [the white] man and woman are alike; if they were, where would be the necessity for urging the claims of the one?"[8] Even after the Civil War, few among white activists would concede that political equality would endanger sexual differences; few activists proposed changes in woman's sphere with the intent of eliminating sexual differences; and few suffragists desired or expected sexual differences to disappear as a result of women's enfranchisement. To make such claims would have meant risking the accusation (which, ironically, was made anyway) that they were actively working for the devolution of civilization. An anonymous contributor to *Popular Science Monthly* argued in 1878, "Advancement toward perfection is reached by differentiation; [the woman's movement] in so far as it aims at breaking down the natural barriers between the duties of the two sexes, is palpably retrograde . . . *anti-differentiation* . . . must be a return to a lower condition."[9]

By situating the debates over woman suffrage in the context of evolution and racial progress, it becomes clear that the prosuffrage arguments were not simply about the right of woman to vote, but about the repercussions of enfranchisement on white women's sexual differences, and thus about the future progress of Anglo-Saxons as a race. Suffrage discussions intensified as whites assessed whether Reconstruction in the South had been a success, debated what to do about the assimilation of Africans, Indians, and the Chinese, and responded to the social and cultural changes that accompanied several decades of massive immigration. The different outcomes of suffrage battles in different parts of the country may reflect the ways in which different regions confronted and dealt with their own specific racial concerns. The western states of Wyoming, Colorado, Idaho, and Utah, which had very few blacks, a relatively small population of Anglo-Saxon women, and which physically removed resident Native Americans from the body politic by placing them in reservations, were the first to pass woman suffrage laws. As early as 1869, Wyoming had such a provision, which it kept in its constitution when it was admitted to statehood in 1890; Utah had woman suffrage as a territory in 1870 but was deprived of it by Congress in 1887 as punishment for its allowance of polygamous marital practices, but put it back into its constitution by referendum when it was admitted to statehood in 1896; Colorado adopted a state constitutional amendment in 1893, having defeated one previously in 1877; Idaho adopted a state constitutional amendment upon its first submission in 1896.[10] West coast states that struggled with the "problem" of Chinese immigration took longer to pass suffrage laws: A woman suffrage amendment finally passed in Washington in 1910 (after the state defeated amendments in 1889 and 1898); California passed a statute in 1911 (after a defeat in 1896 and after national legislation restricting Chinese immigration was passed in the 1880s); and Oregon passed one in 1912 (after defeats in 1884, 1900, 1906, 1908, and 1910).[11] In the Northeast and Midwest, where immigration posed the greatest threat to the political monopoly of Anglo-Saxon elites, woman suffrage was debated along with immigration restriction and eugenic regulations, and the northern states' ratification of the Woman Suffrage Amendment in 1920 was soon followed by the passage of national legislation restricting immigration in 1923. Southern states, grappling with racial strife between blacks and whites, resisted woman suffrage the longest. Many southern states never ratified the Woman Suffrage Amendment of 1920, partly out of a concern that the woman question would reopen the "Negro question."[12]

In the midst of such extreme racial conflict, a new conception of politics emerged, and with this new conception, the ballot's significance changed dramatically. Prior to the Civil War, politics was defined as public service and was reserved for elite (property-holding) Anglo-Saxon Protestant men. "Disinterested" politicians supposedly transcended personal interest to promote the public good. In this paradigm, the ballot was a symbol of the political equality of Anglo-Saxon men, granted on the presumption, and taken as a sign, of the superior moral character, physical autonomy, and economic independence of these white men. After the Civil War, however, politics was no longer the exclusive preserve of Anglo-Saxon elites. In the North, naturalized immigrants gained power in urban areas. In the South, the electorate briefly encompassed former slaves who elected blacks to local and national offices. It was presumed that the new constituencies of immigrant-citizens and enfranchised freedmen lacked the moral character of Anglo-Saxon whites and, because of their imputed racial inferiority, could not be trusted to resist corrupt political leaders. A new understanding of politics as a competitive and corrupt *business* emerged, reflecting white elites' general fear and distrust of immigrants, blacks, and working classes, as was evident in the new political terminology. Politics was discussed in terms of "bosses" and "machines" who supposedly were not bound by traditional republican precepts in their quest for and use of power. From the perspective of white elites, then, politics had become a morally bankrupt realm of activity, in which men of "lower races" manipulated voters through patronage and bribery. From this vantage point, politics was no longer separable from business, and politicians no longer embodied republican ideals of virtue, independence, and disinterestedness. The ballot, previously considered a privilege granted to white men in recognition of their moral virtue and economic independence, was reconceptualized as a tool used by a morally reprehensible leadership to dominate servile and racially inferior classes of men.[13]

White female suffragists offered a complex and ambivalent response to this emerging understanding of politics in the second half of the nineteenth century. On the one hand, they held out a nostalgic promise that (the white) "woman" by virtue of her special moral qualities could help restore politics to its former glory. To borrow from cultural historian Mary Poovey, the rhetorical separation of (white) men's economic and political realm from (white) women's domestic sphere helped consolidate bourgeois power by linking morality to white middle-class women, who were deemed immune to the self-interest and competition integral to the economic and political sphere in which their husbands, fathers, and brothers operated.[14] White middle-class women did not hesitate to use this conception of their race-, class-, and gender-specific forms of moral superiority to buttress their claims to political and social authority, particularly in calling for reform of business, law, education, medicine, and politics. Elizabeth Cady Stanton, the intellectual powerhouse behind the suffrage movement, held firmly to moral distinctions and discussed them in gendered and racialized terms.[15] In 1869 she referred to the "male element [as] a destructive force, stern, selfish, aggrandizing, loving war, violence, conquest, acquisition, breeding in the material and moral world alike discord, disorder, disease and death" and pointed out that "philosophy and science alike point to [white] woman, as the new power destined to redeem the world."[16] In 1890 she stated, "Our civilization today is strictly masculine, everything is carried by force and violence and war, and will be until the feminine element is fully recognized, and has equal power in the regulation of human affairs. Then we shall substitute co-operation for competition, persuasion for coercion, individual sovereignty for absolute authority."[17]

Although they never fully overcame their disappointment and anger at being left out of the Fourteenth and Fifteenth Amendments, white female suffragists eventually resigned themselves to the fact that the electorate included those whom they considered their evolutionary inferiors and found ways to find some advantage in what otherwise seemed to them a deplorable situation. Many argued that the expansion of the electorate to include nonwhite men meant it was no longer meaningful to require that women conform to eighteenth-century standards of republican ideology. If other groups—notably immigrant and black men—could vote and participate in the formal political process, even though they did not embody republican virtues, then, white suffragists argued, all classes of women should be allowed to vote as well.

By the 1880s, when questions of racial assimilation became most heated, resulting in the Chinese Exclusion Act of 1882 and the Indian Allotment (Dawes) Act of 1887, white women already had a fifty-year history of direct public involvement in national debates over race. Many had been abolitionists in their youth and helped create a political discourse in which comparisons were made between women and slaves. Abolitionist-suffragists like Lydia Maria Child, Angelina and Sarah Grimké, Susan B. Anthony, Elizabeth Cady Stanton, Julia Ward Howe, and others had argued before the Civil War that white women and black men shared an analogous type of bondage. Black men were enslaved through the institution of slavery, white women through the institution of patriarchal marriage. Both "woman" and "slaves" were treated as property rather than individuals; both had been denied personal and political rights; both experienced conditions of subjection, sustained through physical coercion.[18]

With the use of two tropes, that of sisterhood and uplift, white women claimed to share the victimization of slaves rather than to identify with the power and privilege of the white male oppressor. The exclusion of enslaved black women from the categories of both "slaves" and "woman" was a common feature of white abolitionist-suffragist discourse, although white women sometimes invoked claims to a universal sisterhood that contained assumptions about a universal womanly character. At the same time, the tropes of sisterhood and uplift began to foster and reflect a new self-understanding among white women that they, as white women, had a moral responsibility to reform an evil social and political system. As historian Jean Fagan Yellin has pointed out, these tropes were readily apparent in iconography that white female abolitionists used on their stationery and transformed into folk art through their needlework. The imagery depicted a kneeling slave-supplicant asking the question "Am I Not a Woman and a Sister?" a phrase that white suffragist Frances Gage put in the mouth of Sojourner Truth when she retold Truth's 1851 address ("Ar'n't I a Woman?") in the article Gage published in 1863 (see chapter 1).[19] In some of the feminist-abolitionist iconography of this period, the question was addressed to a white female figure also represented in the image, who was sometimes depicted holding a torch (representing truth), standing in a print shop (signifying freedom of the press), or carrying scales (to dispense justice). In other instances the white female figure was absent from the image, and the question floated as a slogan, intended to prick the conscience of a white audience. Such iconography was intended to inspire and empower white women to take action. Significantly, what the iconography did not present was an image of slaves rising and breaking their own chains. As Yellin has argued, abolitionist iconography "negat[ed] the possibility of a servile insurrection that would replace black slavery with black mastery" and thus carefully sidestepped whites' fears about slave revolts.[20]

When abolitionist literature did address slave women specifically, it was usually to emphasize their sexual debasement. For many white women, the greatest horrors of slavery were the ways in which slave mothers were exploited as breeders and then deprived of any relation to their children. These were real horrors, experienced daily by enslaved women, and white people often denied responsibility for them, refusing, for example, to acknowledge that white men routinely raped black women. Instead whites often held slave women accountable for their own victimization by attributing to them wanton and excessive sexual desire for intercourse with white men.[21] Abolitionist literature, on the other hand, pointedly tried to get white women to sympathize with the victimization of black women. Elizabeth Chandler's poem "Kneeling Slave," published in Benjamin Lundy's abolitionist newspaper, begins with the line: "Pity the negro . . . [for] hers is not / Like thine, a blessed and most happy lot!" Chandler urges white women to act on the slave woman's behalf:

> She is thy sister, woman! shall her cry
> Uncared for and unheeded, pass thee by?
> Wilt thou not weep to see her sink so low,
> And seek to raise her from her place of woe?[22]

In trying to motivate a white audience to do something about slavery's sexual abuse of black women, however, Chandler's poem, like so much abolitionist literature, emphasized the moral degradation of the slave woman, depicting her as fallen and deserving of pity, not respect. Paradoxically, the effort to get white women to feel compassion for slave women served to emphasize further the slave woman's debasement. The lower slave women were presumed to have sunk, the greater was the need for white women to act as uplifters. Thus, white abolitionist ideology of liberation and uplift created two interdependent roles delineated along racial lines: for the enslaved black woman, the role of a helpless debased victim; for the free white woman, the role of an empowered, sanctified uplifter.

These tropes of sisterhood and uplift endured into the second half of the nineteenth century, lasting well beyond the institution of slavery itself, and remained a dominant feature of the white suffrage debates of the 1880s and 1890s. In particular, these tropes were used by white women to register their resentment that their own so-called slavery and political exclusion continued while the black man's was supposedly ended by his emancipation and inclusion in the franchise. From white women's perspectives, the amendments that granted black men the right to vote worked against their own future enfranchisement by explicitly characterizing citizenship as male (and because white women believed, mistakenly, that black men would oppose woman suffrage even more vehemently than white men). The Fourteenth Amendment, passed by Congress in 1866 and ratified in 1868, provided sanctions against any state that attempted to exclude any of its "male citizens" from the franchise, while the Fifteenth Amendment, passed by Congress in 1869 and ratified in 1870, asserted that the "right of citizens to vote could not be denied or abridged on account of race, color, or previous condition of servitude" but said nothing about sex.[23] The rights of recently freed male slaves were to be recognized, while the rights of prominent white upper-class women were not. Stanton immediately voiced her objections in a letter she wrote to her cousin, Gerrit Smith: "If that word 'male' be inserted [into the Constitution], it will take us a century at least to get it out."[24]

As a consequence of these proposals mandating different legal statuses for black men and white women, a sharp division occurred among the ranks of white suffragists. At the first anniversary meeting of the Equal Rights Association in New York in May 1867, white women debated what the proposed amendments would mean for their ongoing struggle to enfranchise themselves. In opposition to these amendments, Stanton expressed what would become a common refrain in her subsequent speeches: "The Negro should not enter the kingdom of politics before woman, because he would be an additional weight against her enfranchisement."[25] Abby Kelley, another white abolitionist and suffragist, disagreed with Stanton, pointing out that the differences in black men and white women's social conditions mandated different political solutions: "Were the Negro and the woman in the same civil, social and religious status today, I should respond aye, with all my heart to this sentiment [of Stanton's]." But, Kelley continued, "What are the facts? The Negro is treated as a slave to-day in the South. Without wages, without family rights, whipped and beaten, given up to the most horrible outrages, without that protection which his value as property formerly gave him. Have we any true sense of justice . . . if we wish to postpone his security till [the white] woman shall obtain political rights?"[26] Once again, white women's support for the political equality of blacks was articulated within a framework of black victimization.

White abolitionist-suffragists could not agree on whether it was better to accept what the proposed amendments offered, or hold out for amendments that also recognized the rights of white and black women. In 1869, two separate woman suffrage associations with different positions on this issue emerged: the American Woman Suffrage Association (AWSA), led by Lucy Stone, Henry Blackwell, Thomas Wentworth Higginson, and Julia Ward Howe, and the National Woman Suffrage Association (NWSA), led by Elizabeth Cady Stanton and Susan B. Anthony. The AWSA supported the Republican party's effort to ratify the Fourteenth and Fifteenth Amendments out of a conviction that a partial extension of the franchise was better than no extension at all. The NWSA opposed the Fourteenth and Fifteenth Amendments on the grounds that these amendments provided no constitutional protections for women, white or black. Black suffragists found themselves in the position of having to choose between the two new suffrage groups. Harriet and Robert Purvis and Mary Ann Cary attended meetings of the NWSA, while George T. Downing and Frances Harper were affiliated with the AWSA. Frederick Douglass and Sojourner Truth attended meetings of both groups.[27]

As it turned out, Stanton was mistaken in her belief that black men would be more hostile to woman suffrage than white men. Many black men saw the question of woman suffrage as another component of their own struggle for racial equality. There was no organized resistance to woman suffrage among black men as there was among white men. In contrast to prevalent fears among whites that woman suffrage would increase disharmony between husband and wife and interfere with (white) "woman's" social responsibilities to raise children (hence further endangering the race, a fear that was intrinsic to this position but often not articulated directly), most blacks did not believe that enfranchising black women would add to the black race's familial, racial, or political difficulties. Many blacks believed that woman suffrage represented a way to increase the political power and status of black people overall, since it was presumed, correctly, that black women would vote in alliance with black men rather than form a political interest group with white women. Other blacks, however, were cynically realistic about the futility of the franchise for black liberation. Josephine St. Pierre Ruffin, a founding member of the black women's club movement, remarked in 1915 that "many colored men doubt the wisdom of women suffrage"—because they feared that woman suffrage would "increase the number of our political enemies"; enfranchised white women would vote against the interests of black people, while the country would surely disenfranchise black women along with black men.[28]

Where white suffragists conceived of the enfranchisement of (white) women as an antidote to manpower, black suffragists hoped that (black) women's enfranchisement would serve as an antidote to racism. White advocates of woman suffrage emphasized the role that they—elite white women—could play in restoring politics to its former glory and in reforming society to rid it of immoral elements, symbolized for whites by the political activities they associated with blacks and immigrants. Blacks never held this view of suffrage—they did not see eighteenth-century republicanism as some golden age of politics, since the past for them only contained evidence of political slavery, economic exploitation, racism, and social injustice. Occasionally gender tensions were expressed within black circles, as black women invoked dominant ideologies of womanhood to buttress their demands to the franchise. Nannie Burroughs, a leader of the black women's club movement, believed that the moral strength of black women would enable them to escape the exploitation and disfranchisement, to which, she argued, black men had fallen victim.

> Because the black man does not know the value of the ballot, and has bartered and sold his most valuable possession, it is no evidence that the Negro woman will do the same. The Negro woman, therefore, needs the ballot to get back, by the wise *use* of it, what the Negro man has lost by the *misuse* of it. . . . The world has yet to learn that the Negro woman is quite superior in bearing moral responsibility. A comparison with the men of her race, in moral issues, is odious.[29]

On the other hand, black suffragist Mary Church Terrell, at a meeting of the National American Woman Suffrage Association held in Washington, D.C., in 1904, responded to whites' criticism that black men sold their votes by saying, "Much has been said about the purchasability of the Negro vote. They never sold their votes til they found that it made no difference how they cast them."[30]

After the ratification of the Fourteenth and Fifteenth Amendments, white women feared that their racial interests would be compromised by legislators representing nonwhite constituencies, and they remained highly mistrustful of black and immigrant men's ability to legislate on their behalf. In subsequent decades, some white women attributed continued resistance to woman suffrage to the unenlightened notions of "lower races" rather than to the patriarchal and racist beliefs of white men. The feelings of racial superiority that Anglo-Protestant women nurtured concerning their own ancestry, heredity, and evolutionary history led them to insist that they shared the white man's inherited capacity for self-government. White suffragist Dr. Mary Putnam-Jacobi declared, "To the Anglo-Saxon race seems to have been especially committed the mission of securing and developing political freedom among men. . . . [I]n this it has been invariably foremost and easily supreme. [Anglo-Saxon] women cannot fail to share, at least to some extent, in the *inherited instinct of the race* and in its especial and accumulated capacity for [government]."[31]

Putnam-Jacobi, Stanton, and other white suffragists could not have known in 1869 that state governments would soon find ways to circumvent the intent of the new Constitutional amendments by devising extralegal ways to disenfranchise immigrants, the working classes, and blacks. In the late 1860s, it appeared to Stanton as if the "lower orders" would play an active role in state and national governments, or at least she exploited whites' fears that such would be the case in order to motivate white women to oppose any amendment that did not also enfranchise elite white women. "American women of wealth, education, virtue and refinement, if you do not wish the lower orders of Chinese, Africans, Germans and Irish, with their low ideas of womanhood, to make laws for you and your daughters . . . awake to the danger of your present position and demand that woman, too, shall be represented in the government!"[32]

Although some white women were able to reconcile themselves to an amendment that affirmed black men's right to vote, the enfranchisement of black men ahead of white women clearly rankled many white suffragists, even decades after the event. We have already encountered Stanton's expressions of resentment. Other women expressed similar feelings. Julia Wilbur, who had been a member of the Rochester Ladies' Anti-Slavery Society and had served as an agent for the Freedmen's Aid Bureau after the Civil War, later confessed "to feeling a little jealous—the least bit humiliated."[33] Undoubtedly she was thinking of her students, those she was fervently teaching to read and write, walking to the polls, while she was forced to remain at home. Mary Putnam-Jacobi was still enraged over this issue in 1894: "From many points of view, it certainly seemed most absurd to invite to a share in the Popular Sovereignty a million negroes only just emancipated from two hundred years of bondage, and who, moreover, had not themselves dreamed of demanding more than their personal liberty, their 'forty acres and a mule.'"[34] Susan B. Anthony summarized the emotional responses of white women in her *Autobiography*: "What words can express her [the white woman's] humiliation when, at the close of this long conflict, the government which she had served so faithfully held her unworthy of a voice in its councils, while it recognized as the political superiors of all the noble women of the nation the negro men just emerged from slavery, and not only totally illiterate, but also densely ignorant of every public question."[35] As late as 1912, feminist Mary Roberts Coolidge was still expressing the sense of betrayal that white women felt as a result of the government's decision not to include them, along with black men, in the Fourteenth and Fifteenth Amendments.[36]

The split within the white woman suffrage movement after the Civil War has sometimes been characterized in terms of a "collapse" of a "prewar abolitionist unity of women's rights and black rights," and scholars have argued that this collapse was accompanied by a "new racism in the woman suffrage movement."[37] At one level, this characterization is useful, calling our attention to the way that white women in the postbellum period asserted their shared racial ancestry with white men as a justification for their own enfranchisement. But we should not forget that in the antebellum period, abolitionists had their own forms of racism, reflected in arguments that supported universal rights while still upholding white superiority.[38] At their best, antebellum abolitionists asserted that freedom and civil rights could not be justly withheld from purportedly inferior or unqualified groups, since freedom itself was the necessary precondition for the moral development that slaves and white women were deemed to be lacking. Lydia Maria Child argued in her *Appeal in Favor of that Class of Americans Called Africans*:

> [T]he present degraded condition of that unfortunate race is produced by artificial causes, not by the laws of nature. . . . As a class, I am aware that the negroes, with many honorable exceptions, are ignorant . . . but this ceases to be the case just in proportion as they are free. The fault is in their unnatural situation, not in themselves. . . . And even if the negroes were, beyond all doubt, our inferiors in intellect, this would form no excuse for oppression or contempt.[39]

While pre–Civil War abolitionist-suffragists, like Child, used a Christian theological worldview to assert a God-given common humanity that was shared by all races, suffragists in the 1880s and 1890s modified their former position by drawing on civiliza-tionist precepts to argue for white woman's sexual distinctiveness. White suffragists began to consider political questions in relation to the bearing they would have on the future of civilization. "[Woman's] ideal," Stanton declared, "must be represented in the State . . . before we can take another step in civilization."[40] Stanton continued to express her outrage that "all orders of foreigners rank[ed] politically above the most intelligently, highly educated women—native-born Americans." To Stanton, this was "the most bitter drop in the cup of our grief."[41] Still, Stanton was careful to point out that "it is not the principle of universal suffrage that I oppose, but . . . the admis-sion of another man, either foreign or native, to the polling booth, *until women the greatest factor in civilization*, are first enfranchised."[42]

Perhaps the most popular exponent of this type of reasoning was Frances Willard, who helped found the National Woman's Christian Temperance Union in 1874 and became president of the NWCTU in 1879, leading this, the largest prosuffrage organiza-tion with 160,000 members, until her death in 1898. For many white Americans Willard represented "womanhood's apotheosis." (See fig. 2-1.) In the words of one contempo-rary, Willard was the "personification of consummate feminine excellence in thought, purpose and performance."[43] Historian Ian Tyrrell has argued that Willard envisioned a racial hierarchy that linked the "advance of civilization" to woman's emancipation within Christian societies. At the bottom of this hierarchy were non-Christian nations (such as Islamic Turkey); in the middle were Christian Orthodox countries (such as Greece and Bulgaria); at the top were evangelical Protestant nations (Great Britain and the United States). By 1869, when she toured Europe and the Middle East, Willard had reached the conclusion that "only Christian countries treat women kindly."[44]

Despite her disclaimer that she had not an "atom of race prejudice," Willard's racial assumptions were reflected in her favorite slogan, "A white life for two," and emerged most visibly in a four-year confrontation (from 1890 to 1894) with Ida B. Wells, a black journalist who led a movement to abolish lynching.[45] "A white life for two" was Willard's shorthand for calling for the elimination of the double sexual stan-dard (among whites) by insisting that men conform to standards of social purity that were only being demanded of white women. For sexual equality to become possible, Willard believed, all men must adopt "a white life"—defined as lifelong abstention from alcohol, sexual chastity before marriage, and sexual monogamy within marriage. Describing her vision of a white life in 1892, Willard wrote: "[W]hen woman is recog-nized as a human being as distinct as man, with equal rights, equal privileges and an equal claim to develop her own nature . . . she will either accept man's standard of morality, or she will induce him to accept her own. . . . The acceptance of the male standard would be a degradation unspeakable."[46] In Willard's estimation, woman suf-frage was necessary to help (white) women bring about both temperance and sexual purity. "The fire of woman's ballot will burn out the haunt of infamy [houses of pros-titution] and burn in the single standard of a white life for two."[47]

On the surface, Willard's call for "a white life" might seem an innocuous metaphor. Yet Willard, like most white Protestant elites in this period, conflated moral differences with racial and religious differences—only white Christian men were con-

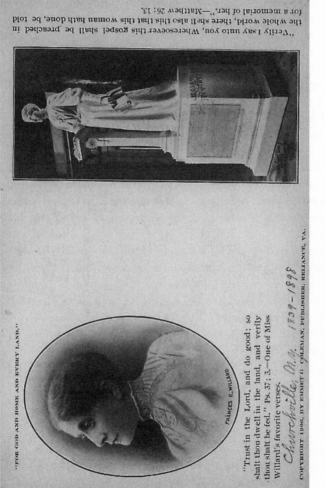

FIGURE 2-1 Apotheosis of womanhood. Frances E. Willard. Postcard, 1906. A portrait of Frances Willard and the statue erected in Washington D.C. in 1906, to honor her after her death in 1898.

sidered moral human beings. Like Stanton, Willard desired an educational qualifica-
tion for the franchise because she feared that the oppression of (white) women would
worsen as "animalistic" males participated in the legislative process. Willard believed
that education was especially crucial, given universal male enfranchisement, as a
means of raising the standard of morality among those she considered "inferior
races."[48]

The confrontation between Frances Willard and Ida B. Wells began with an interview given in October 1890, in which Willard expressed her belief that white Southerners were mostly "kindly intentioned towards the coloured man" and sympathized
with them over their "immeasurable" problem. She went on to portray black men as
illiterate alcoholics who multiplied like the "locusts of Egypt," concurring that in the
South, black men represented a physical threat to white women, who were in constant need of white men's surveillance and protection: "the safety of [the white]
woman, of childhood, of the home," Willard proclaimed, "is menaced in a thousand
localities at this moment, so that the [white] men dare not go beyond the sight of their
own roof-tree."[49]

These pronouncements outraged Wells, and she exposed these depictions as racist
myths in her pamphlet *Southern Horrors*. Wells argued that accusations concerning black
men's lack of sexual control were used to cover up the fact that interracial sexual liaisons between black men and white women were voluntarily engaged in by white
women.

"The miscegenation laws of the South . . . leave the white man free to seduce all
the colored girls he can, but it is death to the colored man who yields to the force and
advances of a similar attraction in white women. White men lynch the offending Afro-
American, not because he is a despoiler of virtue, but because he succumbs to the
smiles of white women."[50]

Willard took great offense at this representation of the moral character of white
women, and attacked Wells for casting doubt on the racial-sexual purity of white
women. "It is my firm belief," Willard wrote, "that in the statements made by Miss
Wells concerning white women having taken the initiative in nameless acts between
the races, she has put an imputation upon [the female] half of the white race . . .
that is unjust." Wells, in turn, objected to this misrepresentation of her position, and
pointed out that she never put such an imputation on white women. All she had said
was that "colored men have been lynched for assault upon [white] women, when the
facts were plain that the relationship between the victim lynched and the alleged victim of his assault was voluntary, clandestine, and illicit."[51]

Willard found it impossible to believe that southern white women would engage
voluntarily in sexual relationships with black men. The most Willard would concede
was that the sexual impulse to rape white women was not inherent in black men's nature but an effect of the loss of control induced in them by the consumption of alcohol. "An average colored man when sober is loyal to the purity of white women,"
Willard acknowledged, "but when under the influence of intoxicating liquors the tendency in all men is toward a loss of self-control."[52] Willard continued to maintain that
black men were lynched in the South for sexual crimes (rape), not, as Wells ultimately

demonstrated, for threatening the economic status of whites. Although Willard eventually supported antilynching resolutions at annual meetings of the NWCTU, she continued to assert that black men's "nameless outrages perpetrated on white women and little girls were a cause of constant anxiety" to white southerners.[53]

The public confrontation between Wells and Willard illustrates how civilizationist ideology jeopardized a potential alliance between a black and white woman. The conflict was never resolved, despite the fact, as historian Gail Bederman has pointed out, that there was much common ground between Wells and Willard: Willard detested lynching, and Wells avidly supported temperance.[54] Willard remained unable to revise her belief that white women would never risk their racial purity through voluntary sexual relations with nonwhite men. Social purity, as Willard's slogan "a white life for two" metaphorically suggested, insisted that white women could only be sexually attracted to whiteness and denied the possiblility that white women might be voluntarily engaging in sexual intercourse with black men.

Preserving White Women's Virtue: Antisuffragists' Defense of a Distinct Political Identity for White Women

In terms of social and class background, marital status, educational accomplishments, and political activism, the white leadership of the antisuffrage organizations did not differ substantially from the white leadership of suffrage organizations; antisuffragism attracted white men and women, primarily of the higher socioeconomic classes.[55] One way in which these two political groups did differ, however, was in their racial composition; suffrage attracted both whites and blacks, and while interracial organizing among suffragists was difficult and black women often formed their own institutions, white and black suffragists were united in their immediate objectives: enfranchisement of *all* women. The antisuffragist movement, in contrast, was an *all-white* movement. Men and women of color, whatever their personal views about the desirability of woman suffrage, did not organize against the enfranchisement of women.[56]

For all concerned in the postbellum period, suffragist and antisuffragist alike, voting meant much more than casting a ballot once a year. Suffrage encompassed sitting on juries, participating in political campaigns, attending political conventions, running for and holding elective office, and enforcing laws. From this perspective, the ballot encouraged types of behavior (disagreeing with men in public, traveling in mixed company, self-promotion, neglect of domestic duties, etc.) that antisuffragist women considered inappropriate or immoral for women.[57] (See fig. 2-2.) Antisuffragist women felt all the "true womanly" virtues—selflessness, subservience, humility, piety, cooperation, obedience, altruism—would either be at odds with, or endangered by, the forms of political activity that had been historically developed by and for (white) men. Mary A. M. M'Intire observed, "The influence of woman standing apart from the ballot is immeasurable. Men look to her . . . (knowing that she has no selfish, political interests to further) as the embodiment of all that is truest and noblest. . . . We be-

FIGURE 2-2 Woman suffrage a threat to domestic life and the family. I
Want to Vote, But MY WIFE WON'T LET ME. Postcard, 1909. Opponents of
woman suffrage feared that the franchise would pervert civilized gender relations, lead (white) women to abandon their homes and families, and result in the domestication and demasculinization of (white) men.

lieve that it is of vital importance that our sex should have no political ends to
serve!"[58] Caroline Corbin wrote that many leading workers in charity and philanthropy "make a special plea for immunity from political responsibilities, on the
grounds that at present women . . . can carry their claims for legal help to both political parties and be sure of a respectful hearing, while if they were voters they would

by their votes be allied with one or the other party and their requests would be subject to party action and the rise and fall of party fortunes. Experience has taught them to prefer decidedly their present independent position."[59]

White women began to organize state antisuffrage societies in the 1890s and for two decades successfully blocked suffragists from winning state referendums. The antisuffragist movement had its greatest number of victories in a single year in 1915, when suffrage referenda were defeated in New York, New Jersey, Pennsylvania, and Massachusetts. Between 1912 and 1916, twenty-one state referenda on woman suffrage came to a vote, and only six passed. At its height in 1916, the antisuffrage movement, coordinated by the National Association Opposed to Woman Suffrage, encompassed twenty-five state organizations with a total membership of roughly 350,000.[60]

White women's opposition to suffrage, however, must not be construed as part of a blanket opposition to the woman's rights movement overall. Boston reformer and antisuffragist woman's rights advocate Kate Gannet Wells could not have been more explicit on this point: woman antisuffragists, she affirmed, believed in "woman's capacity for advancement in every direction; in her right to receive the highest education, to demand equal wages with men, to work as physician, lawyer, minister, lecturer . . . [to] serve on school committees, on State boards of charities, and on all kindred institutions, so that we wish to effect *no curtailment of a woman's sphere except in the direction of suffrage.*"[61] Ruth Lyman, an antisuffragist member of the Woman's Municipal League in Boston, insisted, "It is not a "woman's rights' question; it is a *which* woman's rights question."[62] In other words, with the sole exception of suffrage, suffragists and antisuffragists often agreed on the other social changes they desired; in Lyman's words, "both desire the same end—namely, a better world to live in—[but] they differ fundamentally as to the method of attaining it."[63] While on the surface it might seem that white suffragist and antisuffragist women disagreed over sexual differences, what they were really debating was how to make best political use of the racialized sexual differences that they agreed set elite white women apart from other groups of women. Suffragists like Frances Willard argued vehemently that (white) women should extend their activities explicitly to encompass politics, believing that women's special womanly virtues would be well suited to solving urban problems of poverty, crime, the assimilation of foreigners, urban mismanagement, and so forth ("municipal housekeeping").

Nonetheless, campaigning against suffrage raised practical problems for female antisuffragists, who struggled to find ways to oppose suffragists without contradicting their own ideals of what constituted acceptable political activity for women. According to historian Louise Stevenson, members of the all-female Massachusetts Association Opposed to the Further Extension of Suffrage to Women developed special tactics (e.g., displaying placards that they hoped would be "silent speeches" rather than addressing people directly) that allowed them to participate in a "political campaign without violating their self-imposed domestic standards." Insisting that their organization was a women's and not a political organization, they coordinated their activities with their male counterparts in such a manner as to permit them to relinquish "the 'political' aspects of the campaign while managing its 'educational' aspects."[64]

Not only did antisuffragist women largely share suffragists' views about (white) women's racial-sexual differences, they also often disagreed vehemently with male antisuffragists' blanket statements concerning the inferiority of "woman's nature." Alice George emphasized: "No question of superiority or equality is involved in the opposition to votes for women"; educator Annie Nathan Meyer declared forthrightly that "there is no longer [any] question of the capacity of woman's brain to be trained to wield the suffrage"; and journalist Jeanette L. Gilder agreed, stating that she was "a great believer in the mental equality of the sexes."[65] While male antisuffragists summoned biological and evolutionist theories to "prove" (white) women's inferiority, female antisuffragists emphasized the need for women to develop themselves along separate and different lines and to adopt a division of social labor that did not overlap with men's.[66] Mrs. Herbert Lyman (an antisuffragist) argued as follows at the turn of the century:

> The strikingly progressive message the new century presents us is this: Give equal opportunity to men and women for expression along their *different* lines. Government, law making, law enforcement, with all the allied problems of tariff, taxation, politics, railroads, interstate and international relations, etc., must still be the business of men. The business of women must be to work out a national ideal of domestic life and juvenile training.[67]

Many antisuffragist women supported other planks of the woman's movement, including women's right to higher education, equal pay for equal work, access to male professions, and so forth, and continued to work alongside white suffragists from the 1870s through the 1890s, serving together in organizations such as the Association for the Advancement of Women, and the National Council of Women, the International Council of Women, and in temperance and missionary societies. Leaders of organized antisuffragism included women who considered themselves integral to the woman's movement, among them Catharine Beecher (1800–1878), founder of the Hartford Female Seminary and promoter of women's education; Caroline Fairfield Corbin (1835–c.1900?), who helped establish the Association for the Advancement of Women; Annie Nathan Meyer (1867–1919), one of the original founders and trustees of Barnard College, who promoted college education for women; Minnie Bronson, an agent of the U.S. Labor Department, who lobbied for protective labor legislation for women; Kate Barnard (1875–1930), a labor and prison reformer, who worked for the abolition of child labor, state support of widows, and humane prison conditions for women; Alice N. George, a labor organizer who belonged to the National Civic Federation of the Woman's Trade Union League; Helen Kendrick Johnson (1844–1917), a member of the National League for the Civic Education of Women; Clara Leonard (1828–1904), who was a leader of the prison reform movement in Massachusetts in the 1870s; Catherine Robinson, who was active in a variety of social service organizations in Massachusetts; and Kate Gannett Wells (1838–1911) who worked for the Massachusetts Moral Education Association to combat prostitution and alcoholism, led the Woman's Education Association of Boston in the 1870s, and was an active member and secretary of the Association for the Advancement of Women in the 1880s.

White women's opposition to suffrage, therefore, should not be misconstrued as opposition to woman's rights or to the woman's movement overall. Antisuffragist women believed that their opposition to the franchise was perfectly compatible with, indeed requisite for, their continuing efforts to "advance" (white) women, improve (whites') civilization, and foster (white) racial progress. Critical of the existing male system, female antisuffragists wanted to remain outside of electoral politics so that they could use their position as outsiders as a form of moral leverage, to exercise their "influence" with male elites to achieve the reforms they supported. They did not deny the need to bring about social change or to alter the status and position of (white) women. "That there are still unfair and degrading laws is granted," wrote Kate Gannett Wells, but "will a brutal, an intemperate husband be any less brutal or intemperate because his wife has the power to vote?"[68]

In keeping with the antidemocratic sentiments of their class, antisuffrage women wanted to preserve their own power relative to that of immigrants, blacks, and working-class people, whom they felt were not competent to take on political responsibilities. In explaining her opposition, Annie Nathan Meyer, a proponent of women's higher education and a founder of Barnard College, pointed out: "It must be remembered that the suffrage—at least in America—is almost certain to be refused to *all* women, or given to *all* women; that a vote to one woman will be a vote to *all* women, vicious and virtuous, ignorant and educated, lowest and highest."[69] Grace Goodwin reiterated the same point in her own arguments: "In this day of frenzied democracy, limited suffrage is not popular. . . . Suffragists desire full female citizenship [for all women] with all the rights of men. It is against these wholesale claims that the antisuffragists level their objections."[70] Catharine Beecher also advocated a partial suffrage, and the famous writer Margaret Deland explicitly stated that she would support a limited extension of suffrage to educated women only, but as so long as suffragists insisted on a universal extension, she would not approve of the reform.[71] Goodwin, for example, argued that the United States should not follow the lead of other nations who were considering enfranchising women, stressing that the United States was unique in that it had "a negro and alien problem. . . . Our American negroes . . . have not yet ceased to be a political menace. In the Southern states, where white control is held only by the rankest bribery, it is proposed to add, for further exploitation and bribery all the negro women, who are more helpless and ignorant than the men."[72]

Like their suffragist counterparts, many ideas of the antisuffrage movement's older leaders, including Catharine Beecher and the prominent political journalist Mary Abigail Dodge (1833–1896), were shaped by the debates over slavery, and their views about white women's role in politics were racialized at the very core. Beecher's views were formed at the height of debates over abolition during her residence in Cincinnati during the 1830s, in the midst of violent confrontations between whites and blacks. Dodge, who came into public view under the pseudonym Gail Hamilton in the late 1850s and emerged full-blown on the national journalistic scene in the 1860s, formulated her views during the years of struggle preceding the Civil War and then in the fiery debates over Reconstruction.

Despite the difference in their ages, Dodge and Beecher were similar in background, self-identity and aspiration. Raised in evangelical Protestant families in small northeastern towns (Beecher in Litchfield, Connecticut, Dodge in Hamilton, Massachusetts), both women received the best private education available to young girls in their day. Both began their careers as schoolteachers, but eventually shifted their energies from schoolteaching to writing, as they consciously sought to enlarge their own public "influence."[73] Dodge even taught at the Hartford Female Seminary for a brief period of time in 1854, although Beecher had long since left the school by then. Both women remained single throughout their lives and so found themselves outside the conventional boundaries of middle-class white women's domestic sphere.

Together, these two women did as much as any suffragists to imbue white women with a new political identity. Beecher transformed the subordinate role of the white woman vis-à-vis the white man into a sign of "woman's" superior moral sensibility and made it the foundation from which white women might act in the political arena. Historian Kathryn Sklar has argued that Beecher "defined the home not as the place isolating [white] women from political affairs, but as the base from which their influence on the rest of the culture was launched."[74] But if Beecher was proposing a new role for (white middle-class) women as mediators, working behind the scenes to mitigate social conflict, it must not be forgotten that such drastic action was required because the nation was facing a racial crisis: white women's skills were needed to soothe and diffuse immanent racial violence.[75]

More than thirty years younger than Beecher, and having more models to emulate (including Beecher), Dodge eventually achieved a reputation only slightly less prominent than Beecher's famous sister, Harriet Beecher Stowe. Where as Beecher had had to defend her decision to publish treatises on race questions, Dodge accepted her political authorship as a natural extension of a white woman's moral authority. Whereas Beecher had had to go to great lengths to show why white women, as the best-trained mothers of society, had much to contribute to political debate (a position that suffragists would take up and exploit to full benefit in the 1880s), for Dodge, motherhood was beside the point. Even in the 1880s, Beecher still held on to the hope that "woman's influence" could reinvigorate Jacksonian forms of republicanism, eliminate racial and class conflict, buttress white racial supremacy, and peacefully resolve social conflicts. In contrast, Dodge accepted social and racial conflict as an inevitable component of public life, in accordance with laissez-faire and evolutionist notions that competitive conflict led to progress, and so did not argue that it was white women's responsibility to purge politics of contentiousness and conflict. Indeed, rather than celebrate domesticity, Dodge criticized it, exposing the cultural myths that depicted marriage, motherhood, and domesticity as fulfilling occupations for white women.

The lives of these two antisuffragists reveal the meaninglessness of trying to define antisuffragism as a conservative or conventional defense of domesticity in contrast to suffragists' purported attack on the home, for Beecher helped to make domesticity and motherhood the basis for white middle-class women's political activity in ways that suffragists would later emulate and adopt, while Dodge's criticism of white women's subordination within middle-class homes was so trenchant that she was often mistaken for a radical suffragist. What these two antisuffragists shared, both between themselves and with their white suffragist opponents, however, was a determination to create political roles for white women that would maintain white civilization and advance "the race."

The Gender Politics of Catharine Beecher

> But while [the white] woman holds a subordinate relation in society to the other sex, it is not because it was designed that her duties or her influence should be any less important, or all-pervading. But it was designed that the *mode of gaining influence and of exercising power* should be altogether different and peculiar.
>
> Catharine Beecher, *An Essay on Slavery and Abolitionism* (1837)

Catharine Beecher's public visibility as a political commentator was consolidated, ironically enough, in the series of "Letters" she exchanged with Angelina Grimké on the slavery question in the late 1830s. At issue in this exchange was not only the question of the future legal status of African Americans but also the redefining of white women's role in the political struggle over slavery and abolitionism. Beecher took the position that white women should not assume a direct role in the antislavery movement, and she argued for their remaining "impartial" actors so that they could consolidate their power as "moral" arbiters of social problems.

In Beecher's day, public opinion was traditionally shaped in three main ways: through the press, through the pulpit, and through the party. All these vehicles were the domain of elite Anglo-Saxon men, but by the mid 1830s, white middle-class women were beginning to develop their own forms of political activity: circulating petitions for signatures, offering talks and lecture courses in the homes of prominent women, and publishing monographs, letters, poems, and columns expressing their political views.[76] Beecher herself used these kinds of tactics in a campaign to assist the Cherokees in 1828, as they were being expelled from Georgia, when she wrote a circular addressed "To Benevolent Women of the United States." Seeking "the aid and council of some of the most judicious and influential ladies of Hartford," Beecher convened a meeting, read the circular, sought signatures on a petition, and offered prayers calling for "the intervention of the National Government to protect the Indians." She then sent the circular as an anonymous chain letter to "lady friends" in other northern, midwestern and western cities, asking recipients to keep their identity secret but to mail the circular to "the most influential and benevolent ladies of [their] acquaintance."[77] In keeping with this approach, eight years later Beecher would argue against the propriety of white women taking active roles in abolitionist societies, although she fully approved of these other activities. If Beecher did not directly challenge the terms of the dominant discourse, in which politics was considered a "male" activity, she nonetheless helped fashion a culturally sanctioned role for white women in political affairs.

In 1832, Catharine, at age thirty-two, moved to Cincinnati with her father and her two younger sisters, Harriet and Isabella, so that her father, Lyman Beecher, could assume the presidency of Lane Seminary, a liberal institution whose students were sympathetic to the antislavery cause. Catherine worked to establish a new school for young ladies, the Western Female Institute, and devoted her time to raising money for her project and attracting prospective students.

When the Beechers arrived in the early 1830s, Cincinnati was embroiled in a decade-long period of racial conflict. Because of its location on the north bank of the Ohio River across from slaveholding Kentucky, Cincinnati served as a stopping-off point for many slaves trying to escape the South, and had a significant black presence. Moreover, Ohio, as a free state, was attractive to white liberals from both New England and nearby southern slaveholding states, but a large majority of prominent white families in town had commercial ties to the South and were antiblack and proslavery.[78] In 1826, The Cincinnati Colonization Society was formed to restrict the size of the black population, which had grown since 1810 to roughly 10 percent of all residents.[79] In 1829, racial tensions culminated in white riots against blacks, and the town instituted "black laws" requiring black residents to present certificates of freedom to city officials. The new laws and the white antipathy prompted roughly 50 percent of the local black population to flee the city in the early 1830s.[80] In the midst of this racial turmoil, Beecher was hard pressed to stay neutral: she needed to remain on good terms with prominent white families (whose patronage she required to keep her institute functioning), and yet members of her own family would soon declare themselves in support of abolition.

Catharine was present in 1834 when white students at Lane Seminary discussed the relative merits of colonization (freeing individual blacks and repatriating them in Africa) versus immediate abolition (ending slavery and allowing freed blacks to remain in the United States) in a series of debates that was organized by a student, Thomas Weld. The immediate result was the conversion of the majority of Lane's students from colonization to abolition. The trustees outlawed the students' antislavery society, and Lyman Beecher, when he returned to town, sided with the trustees, perhaps at his daughter's recommendation. Student leaders, including Weld, were threatened with expulsion, whereupon most resigned and left for the newly established Oberlin College, which openly welcomed blacks.[81]

In August 1836, tensions escalated further in Cincinnati. A group of prominent white men destroyed the press of James Birney, a well-known abolitionist and follower of Weld, who had been publishing an abolitionist journal, the *Philanthropist.* The white society in which the Beechers traveled was divided. Some prominent citizens, such as Nathaniel Wright and Jacob Burnet, were sympathetic to those who had destroyed Birney's newspaper. Others, like Samuel P. Chase, an abolitionist, and Charles Hammond, a local newspaper editor, defended Birney's right to free speech.[82] Catharine apparently attended a meeting between Jacob Burnet and James Birney, in which Burnet had urged Birney to stop publication—in an unsuccessful attempt to forestall the planned action to sack the press if publication continued.[83] Shortly after these riots, Catharine's sister Harriet wrote to her husband, Calvin Stowe, that "a large body, perhaps the majority of citizens, disapprove [of the violence] but I fear there will not be public disavowal. . . . Mr. Hammond (editor of the 'Gazette') . . . has condemned the whole thing, and Henry [Catharine's brother, who edited the Cincinnati *Journal*] has opposed, but otherwise the papers have either been silent or in favor of mobs."[84]

Unlike her sister and brother, Catharine did not immediately defend Birney's right to free speech, nor did she join the local female anti-slavery society when one of its members came to her home with abolitionist literature just after Birney's press was destroyed.[85] While she lived in Cincinnati, Beecher remained opposed to the formation of abolitionist societies and held local abolitionists personally accountable for stirring up civic unrest. In a letter written to members of her family in January 1838, Catharine gave her reasons for keeping her distance from the Cincinnati abolitionists: "I have yet to . . . see that Abolitionism and all that help it along are not doing more harm than good—retarding the prospect of a *speedy* ending of it [slavery]—and making more and more probable the result of a *dangerous and bloody* issue to what might have been accomplished by safer and gentler means. . . . As to *freedom of speech* and all that matter I never saw less of it than since the Abolitionists have begun to take care of it."[86]

Meanwhile, Angelina Grimké (1805–1873), whom Beecher had met briefly years before when Grimké visited Catharine's school in Hartford, had joined the Philadelphia Female Anti-Slavery Society and had become well known as an abolitionist who had formerly been a slaveholder herself.[87] Grimké's pamphlet, *An Appeal to the Christian Women of the South* published in 1836, attracted a great deal of attention, and by the fall of 1836, the American Anti-Slavery Society had engaged her to hold meetings in private homes in New York City to recruit white women to the cause.[88] Beecher received a copy of Grimké's *Appeal* and was asked to circulate it. Instead she decided to respond to Grimké publicly, a decision she justified to her readers by explaining that she needed to show "ladies of the non-slave-holding States" why it would be "unwise" and "inexpedient" for them "to unite themselves in Abolition Societies."[89] Beecher's published response, *An Essay on Slavery and Abolitionism with Reference to the Duty of American Females,* was answered in turn by Grimké's *Letters to Catharine Beecher,* first published in Garrison's *Liberator* and then collected in book form in 1838.

Although Beecher opposed both male and female participation in abolitionist societies, she felt that abolitionism was particularly unsuitable for (white) women, as abolitionist tactics were "calculated to stimulate pride, anger, ill-will, [and] contention." "A man may act on society by the collision of intellect, in public debate;" Beecher wrote; "he may urge his measures by a sense of shame, by fear, and by personal interest; . . . he may drive by physical force, and he does not outstep the boundaries of his sphere." But (white) women, Beecher believed, ought to act in accordance with a higher moral standard: "But all the power, and all the conquests that are lawful to woman, are those only which appeal to the kindly, generous, peaceful and benevolent principles."[90]

Beecher's understanding of what was necessary for a political system to function without disorder or conflict was built upon a republican ideology that emphasized self-restraint, disinterestedness, and rationality as necessary qualities for political leaders and republican citizens, qualities that up until this point were thought to be available only in white men. Beecher invoked this ideology both to counter blacks' challenges to whites' racial domination (she believed whites were superior in these respects to blacks) as well as to buttress white women's race-specific claims to a political role. Although Beecher was working out of a political philosophy in which political leaders (presumed to be white Protestant men) were expected to control and suppress strong feelings as they legislated for the "public good," she became increasingly concerned that white men could no longer restrain themselves—and that the special skills of white women had to be employed. For example, in critiquing Garrisonian opposition to the Colonization Society, Beecher wrote:

> The peaceful and christian method of meeting the difficulty would have been, to collect all the evidence of this supposed hurtful tendency, and *privately*, and in a respectful and *conciliating* way, to have presented it to the attention of the wise and benevolent men, who were most interested in sustaining their institution. If this measure did not avail to convince them, then it would have been safe and justifiable to present to the public a temperate statement of facts, and of the deductions based on them, drawn up in a respectful and candid manner, with every charitable allowance which truth could warrant.[91]

In effect, Beecher began to advocate for white women the model of political action that she could no longer find in male leaders.[92]

Although Beecher lessened her opposition to abolitionism when she left the Midwest, she never lost her conviction that white men's control over politics and the social order were deteriorating as the country was entering a period of heightened racial conflict. In the 1850s, Beecher's sense of a growing national crisis grew more acute, and she singled out conflict between immigrants and the native-born; sectarian strife; partisan politics; and a corrupt political press as the worst ills.

> Meanwhile, as men are losing the restraints of self-government, family discipline, and law, the causes of dangerous excitement are multiplying. The *clashing interests* of foreigners and native-born citizens, the deep-rooted prejudices of Catholics and Protestants, the *threatening* aspects of slavery, the *demoralizing influences* of party politics and the political press, the all-pervading malaria of corrupt literature, the low tone of piety in the Christian church, the consequent increase of sectarian bitterness, and finally, the wide prevalence of rationalism, infidelity, and skepticism—all these present portentous omens of danger.[93]

The solution for ills of this nature, Beecher believed, no longer lay with men or their organizations: "It is WOMAN," Beecher wrote," who is to come in at this emergency, and meet the demand . . . if this country is ever [to be] saved, it must be by woman more than by man."[94]

Beecher's efforts to politicize the home and bring white women into the public arena as peacemakers and moral mediators went hand in hand with her attempts to make teaching a respected profession for women and to professionalize motherhood.[95] (White) woman's role as savior of her country had to be acted out through her contact with and influence over children—both as mother and teacher. For this she needed specialized training. Homemaking needed to be practiced seriously as a professional occupation, bringing to bear all the new developments in "domestic science" on daily chores.

Beecher's call for a profession of homemaking that was "as honorable and as lucrative for her [the white woman] as the legal, medical and theological professions are for [white] men," was not just a means of increasing the status of white women.[96] It also instantly forged new class divisions among white women on the basis of education and training. Not all women could become "professionals" in mothering, teaching, and homemaking—the status of the professional depended on many women falling below the "professional" standard, since the very concept of "professionalizing" meant creating occupational categories into which access was carefully regulated.[97] Prior to the demand for domestic training, all mothers, regardless of class or ethnic background, potentially had been equals in their mothering because mothering had been understood as a "natural" quality inherent in womanhood, not a skill to be taught and learned. In demanding training for motherhood (and training for teachers to train mothers), Beecher introduced a new class hierarchy among women—creating new categories of better and worse mothers. Moreover, Beecher's demands for domestic reform and the professionalization of motherhood introduced new racialized divisions among white, immigrant, and black women, since many groups—including enslaved, immigrant, and Native American women—were automatically excluded from Beecher's conception because they did not have the kind of homes Beecher conceived as the foundation for "woman's" political authority.

In sum, by redefining (white) woman's role in the family, school, and government, Beecher solidified the class and racial components of a social hierarchy that were not always explicitly recognized but existed nonetheless. As teaching, mothering, and homemaking were invested with moral qualities and requirements that were not matched in any other domain; as the home became the locus of ethical learning; and as the schoolhouse (beginning to be dominated by white middle-class women) became the reinforcer of moral rules, white women could lay claim to a kind of authority to which they had previously been unable to appeal, and from which nonwhite women were excluded.

The Racial Politics of Mary Abigail Dodge

> [White] women in not voting are not unrepresented in the sense or to the
> extent to which non-voting negroes are unrepresented. The African is a
> separate race from the Caucasian, with its own ambitions and traditions.
> Either, without the other, is an entire and a distinct race; but the men and
> women of an American community are one race.
>
> Gail Hamilton [Mary Abigail Dodge],
> *Woman's Wrongs* (1868)

In 1858, at age twenty-three, Mary Abigail Dodge left New England for Washington, D.C., to take a position as governess in the family of Gamaliel Bailey, the abolitionist editor of the *National Era,* in which he had two years earlier published some of Dodge's poetry and essays. Bailey lived the life of a prominent, influential political journalist, in a large house staffed with black servants—a life very different from the one Dodge had known in the reserved New England Congregational household in which she had grown up. Despite Bailey's recent illness and increasing financial problems, his residence remained a social center for politicians, journalists, and foreign expatriates. During the day, Dodge made the acquaintance of the social elite of Washington; in the evenings, she engaged in literary and political conversations with guests, including many prominent Republican politicians.[98] During this period she sent political commentaries to the *Congregationalist* under the assumed name Cuntare, becoming one of the first female political correspondents in Washington, D.C.[99]

In 1860, after Bailey's death, Dodge moved back home to Hamilton, where she remained for the duration of the Civil War, and where she wrote the columns published in the *Atlantic Monthly* that instantly brought "Gail Hamilton" fame and public appreciation, causing one of her admirers later to remark that "in sarcasm and invective [Gail Hamilton] has hardly a peer among American authors. She is incisive, even combative, by nature, and thoroughly enjoys a good, hot old-fashioned controversy."[100] After the death of her father in 1864, Dodge stayed on to nurse her mother through a final illness, which ended in her death in 1868. In 1871, at age thirty-eight, her journalistic reputation secure, Dodge moved back to Washington, D.C., spending her winters in the household of James G. Blaine, who was married to her first cousin, and her summers up north, in her home in Hamilton.

Dodge quickly became an integral and beloved member of the Blaine family, assisting her cousin with the hosting of dinner parties, serving as a sounding board for Blaine's political ideas, and enjoying the political influence that she wielded through her close association to powerful politicians.[101] Outwardly, at least, the Blaine household was similar to Bailey's: large, well staffed with servants, a social center for liberal Republican political circles. Blaine was a prominent national politician, holding the positions of Speaker of the House (1869–1876), senator from Maine (1877–1881), and secretary of state (1880–1881, 1888–1892).[102] The Blaine household was an ideal place from which to wield the kind of political influence that antisuffragists desired to preserve. Harriet Prescott Spofford, a political journalist in her own right and close friend of Dodge's, wrote several years after Dodge's death: "[G]reat men and charming women clustered about her, senators, cabinet officers, diplomats, and titled Englishmen of the High commission, the President himself, all attended on her court, at first entertained and delighted with her brilliancy and pleasantness, and then discovering her as a woman of affairs, having her part in statecraft, and of great value with her advice and her work."[103]

As Spofford's reminiscence suggests, when Dodge returned to Washington, D.C., in the 1870s, she attracted a great deal of attention. Women who wrote about meeting her often noted how she immediately drew men to her. Men who wrote about their first encounters with Dodge said they found her "brilliant." Dodge herself was proud of the impression that she made, as a woman, upon men. The care and expense that Dodge assumed to outfit herself were known throughout the city. Her decision to remain single was not the result of a lack of suitors. On the contrary, Dodge had many male friends and admirers, including a George Wood, who was interested in her from the first day he met her in Washington in 1858, an interest that did not abate throughout their long correspondence in the 1860s.[104] Rather, Dodge had no romantic illusions about the bliss of wedded life, and in a private letter she ruminated, "I assure you with entire seriousness that nothing which my own life has missed given me a tithe of the disturbance, I might almost say despair, which I have found in the terrible bewilderments of the married lives I have seen."[105]

In keeping with this sentiment, much of Dodge's writing in the late 1860s and early 1870s exposed the cultural myths that celebrated middle-class marriage, motherhood, and domesticity.[106] She often remonstrated with (white) married women for not paying adequate attention to their appearance and personal development, arguing that they ought to resist and change their domestic condition rather than merely submit to it with quiet forbearance. Refusing to idealize domesticity or to make it the basis for women's politicization, she called housework necessary drudgery and saw it as something that prevented white women from engaging in other more interesting and rewarding activities, anticipating the arguments that Charlotte Perkins Gilman and Mary Roberts Smith Coolidge would set forth decades later. For Dodge, the solution lay in finding ways to escape domestic work. Thus, Dodge recommended that mothers hire servants to care for their infants so that they could continue to read, ride, play music, and cultivate themselves.[107]

The assumption of a pseudonym enabled Dodge to develop two personas: as Mary Abigail she was a charming, witty hostess—the epitome of "true womanhood" (except for her lack of a husband, but her position in Blaine's household was an excellent substitute). As Gail Hamilton, however, Dodge was biting, argumentative, confrontational, and aggressive—qualities that made some of her readers certain that she had to be a man. The use of the pseudonym allowed her to express a wide range of political ideas without having to bear the consequences of her political outspokenness in her private life. Her family humorously nicknamed her "Mary the Dodger" and John Greenleaf Whittier, an intimate friend, reportedly told her that it would be better if she wrote under her real name, as that "might keep her within the bounds of good behavior."[108] The assumption of the pseudonym did not serve so much to mask Dodge's growing power as to further enlarge her public sphere of influence without endangering her private life.

Because of the lucidity with which Dodge critiqued the misogynist views of male antisuffragists, she was sometimes mistaken for a supporter of woman suffrage. Her first antisuffrage treatise, entitled *Woman's Wrongs: A Counter-Irritant,* was devoted (in Dodge's words) to "tearing in pieces some of the flimsiest of these anti-female-suffrage arguments; . . . set[ting] in their strongest light the arguments for female suffrage." But in the end, Dodge concluded "that these [prosuffrage] arguments also availed nothing, and that female suffrage would not mend matters."[109] Even so, Dodge's political analysis was so incisive that Susan B. Anthony wrote to her, asking if she would be willing to write for the *Revolution,* the newly founded journal of the National Woman Suffrage Association.[110] Two decades later, in the mid 1880s, the *Woman's Journal* quoted Hamilton out of context, giving the impression that she was a suffragist.[111] In 1912, the feminist Mary Roberts Smith Coolidge included Dodge among her pantheon of early advocates of women's rights in a history of the woman's movement.[112]

This longstanding confusion over Dodge's antisuffrage stance is fully understandable, given her scathing criticism of white men's political misogynism and her lifelong commitment to critiquing the ideology of woman's sphere.[113] Arguing against those who opposed woman suffrage because it contravened woman's nature and natural sphere, Dodge wrote, "If the right of suffrage shall result in bringing woman from the domestic hearth to the public hall, it will only show that we have all been wrong together in restricting her to the former." To those who claimed that (white) men could be trusted to represent the interests of their families, Dodge replied scornfully, "Certainly they cannot [be trusted]. Men are in the constant daily habit of doing injustice to wife, mother, daughter, sister."[114] Dodge also dismissed the argument that (white) women's involvement in politics would be unseemly or that these women should not have (or did not need) a political voice, and she insisted that her opposition to woman suffrage was not to be taken as a slight upon the general intelligence or political readiness of "American" women:

> Are American women, as a class, more unfit to vote than Irishmen? Are they less capable of understanding issues involved, and of passing judgment upon measures proposed, than negroes who have been slaves for generations? . . . It will not be denied that the Mrs. Stowes, the Miss Mitchells, the Mary Lyons, the Mrs. Mills, the Madame de Staels, [the Gail Hamiltons!] are as able to form an intelligent opinion, even upon questions of finance and internal improvements, as the laborers who are digging in the canals, and the shoemakers pegging on their benches.[115]

She lamented the naturalization and enfranchisement of "illiterate foreigners," considering it "utterly irrational" for them to "make laws for the nation, while an educated and intelligent woman is not allowed to cast a vote to keep him at home."[116] Yet Dodge remained unconvinced that the "indiscriminate" enfranchisement of women would bring any definite benefit to women as a group or to the nation. Had Dodge had the alternative of a partial or limited franchise—one that restricted suffrage on the basis of education to the racial groups she thought suited for it—she probably would have lent her support to the measure.[117]

Although Dodge did not support the universal enfranchisement of women, believing that the contributions of women like herself would not make up for the involvement of lower-class women, she adopted a different approach to the enfranchisement of black men. In 1868 Dodge argued that racial differences, unlike sexual differences, mandated immediate political recognition:

> Women in not voting are not unrepresented in the sense or to the extent to which nonvoting negroes are unrepresented. The African is a separate race from the Caucasian, with its own ambitions and traditions. Either, without the other, is an entire and a distinct race; but the men and women of an American community are one race. . . . The life of our [i.e., white] men and women is constantly and inextricably intertwined;

in the house, in the church, in the assembly, in work and worship and recreation, they are inseparable companions, every moment giving and receiving influence.[118]

Dodge's terms reveal how magnified for her racial difference appeared: Negroes were of a different continent—they were "African," not "American." It was the profundity of this racial difference that justified the enfranchisement of African American men but not "American" women.

Yet Dodge's support of black enfranchisement went hand in hand with a belief in black inferiority and a deep antipathy for blacks as a race, which, if it was not already evident in the late 1860s, was clearly present in an article she wrote on "Race Prejudice" in 1885 for the *North American Review*. In this piece, Dodge was outspokenly critical of the Congregational church, the Home Missionary Society, and the American Missionary Association for allowing racially mixed congregations. Dodge defended whites' right to attend all-white churches, calling whites' maintenance of a color line an "ethnological fact, utterly without moral quality." Her claims were formulated using social-Darwinian language, as is evident in her attribution of "much of his [the Negro's] inferiority . . . to his longer apprenticeship at barbarism, his longer servitude to degradation." Moreover, Dodge went on to explain that "race prejudice" did not exist "all on one side. . . . The colored people have as strong an objection to mingling with their Caucasian brethren as the Caucasians have to mingling with the Africans." These statements elicited a vehement response from Charlotte Forten, a prominent black poet and writer in Philadelphia, who pointed out that one reason blacks seemed to Dodge to prefer to remain in their own churches was that they were mistreated by whites when they visited white churches.[119]

It is not clear whether Dodge always harbored these racist views or grew more strident after Reconstruction. Although her writings from the 1860s do not contain such explicit claims about blacks' racial inferiority, nothing I have seen in the primary sources suggests that these remarks were a departure for Dodge. Abolitionism and a belief in black inferiority were never mutually exclusive ideologies, and Dodge's commitment to political liberty for enslaved blacks was not meant to challenge white supremacy. As Dodge wrote in the mid-1880s: "The old question, put in abolition days, 'Do you want your daughter to marry a nigger?' was impertinent, irrelevant, ignorant. A 'nigger's' marriage had nothing whatever to do with a 'nigger's' freedom. The question was of political and personal liberty, not of social status."[120] In the 1880s, however, debates about sexual difference, race, empire, and miscegenation raised the question of black men's social relations to white women directly, and Dodge was not embarrassed to express the distaste she felt for intermarriage. "But when we come to this question of mixed churches, we come plumply [sic] and squarely upon the question of 'marrying a nigger.'"[121]

Dodge's life and writings are full of interesting contradictions that serve as a caution against overstating the conservative dimensions of antisuffragism, despite the pervasive racism contained therein. Dodge opposed woman suffrage, yet she encouraged intelligent (white) women to take an active interest in politics. She advocated a

"Hands-off government" policy in the industrial realm, departing from most other antisuffragists in this regard, because she believed that working-class women, like everyone else, should be treated as independent, responsible agents. Like her suffragist opponent, Caroline Dall, she believed that women had a right to "equal pay for equal work."[122] Finally, while she disavowed the wisdom of the government intervening in the economy, this was not meant to be a full rejection of patriarchal protection. Rather, she insisted that women deserved the protection of husbands, even though she was also critical of women's financial subordination in the home and personally could not bear the emotional dynamics produced by financial dependency.

Dodge's life also exemplifies the way that antisuffragists of her generation exploited dominant cultural beliefs about the need for (white) women to be protected, even as they themselves gradually moved to take on the agency of the protector of others. For this reason, many antisuffragists opposed what they called "equal suffrage"—a term they used with disapprobation—because they feared it would jeopardize the roles of moral arbiters that they had developed since Beecher's activism of the 1830s. In their view, "equal suffrage" threatened (white) women's traditional means of serving the state, for such women demonstrated their sense of civic responsibility by having children and by exercising their "influence" over husbands and legislators, as well as through social work and holding appointive office. For antisuffragists, it was clear: "protection" signified "privilege," and they offered lists of the sex-specific "privileges" that (white) women would have to forgo if they agreed to be enfranchised. They were allowed to acquire a settlement without paying a tax; they were exempt from supporting indigent husbands (even though men always had to support their wives); they could divorce husbands who failed to provide for them and were frequently entitled to alimony even if they remarried (husbands had no equivalent rights); they were not liable for their husbands' debts, even though husbands were liable for wives' debts; they could not be arrested in a civil action until a judgment was obtained against them, while men could be so arrested; they received more favorable terms in life insurance policies than men; they were treated more leniently by juries than men and, if unmarried or widowed, they were exempt from taxation.[123] All these "special privileges" were accorded "in recognition of the fact that as a woman she has a special service to perform for the state . . . in order that the *motherhood of the race may be protected* and that future citizens shall have the birth right and the inheritance of a strong and vigorous childhood."[124] All these privileges, antisuffragists believed, would have to be forgone if women were recognized as the legal equals of men. Most significant, female antisuffragists opposed woman suffrage because they anticipated that the principle of equality embedded in suffrage demands would endanger special protective labor laws that had been introduced in the 1880s. Mrs. Arthur M. Dodge succinctly summed up the conflict: "*Equal* suffrage would demand that woman should enter into competition with man in a fair field with favor to none, but woman's welfare demands protection under the laws."[125]

The awareness of the conflict between "equality" and "protection" that was expressed in antisuffragist writings in the 1890s did not elicit much response from suffragists prior to the ratification of the Nineteenth Amendment in 1920. It was not until the mid-1920s that advocates of the Equal Rights Amendment directly clashed with proponents of protective labor legislation over the meaning of "political equality" and the significance of "equal rights." In 1923, many women who had previously advocated woman suffrage, including Carrie Chapman Catt, Florence Kelley and Jane Addams, opposed the introduction of the Equal Rights Amendment because they believed the latter would jeopardize sex-specific, special protective labor legislation. They too were now confronting a tension between "difference" and "equality" that antisuffragists had identified a generation previously. The origins of that struggle can be traced to the debates over coeducation and industrial education that took place in the 1870s, as I will show in the next chapter.

3

The Politics of Patriarchal Protection

Debates over Coeducation and Special
Labor Legislation for Women

> For both sexes, there is no exception to the law, that their greatest
> power and largest attainment lie in the perfect development of their
> organization. . . . The physiological motto is, Educate a man for
> manhood, a woman for womanhood, both for humanity. In this lies
> the hope of the race.
>
> Edward Clarke,
> *Sex in Education* (1873)

D URING THE POSTBELLUM PERIOD, the woman's movement fashioned a politics out of protection that eventually made it possible for white middle-class women to become political actors and agents of the state, despite dominant cultural assumptions about sexual differences that characterized women as unsuited for these roles. Yet protection—which encompassed white men offering white women financial support, supervision, polite courtesies, and a general solicitousness that was not extended to other groups of women—was conceived as a "privilege" to be granted only so far as (white) women lived in conformity with patriarchal norms of middle-class domesticity. White women sensed that these kinds of protections would be withdrawn if they did not conform to their primary roles as homemakers and childrearers. Freeing themselves from the category of the protected and becoming protectors themselves was a difficult maneuver, yet it became, as I shall show, one of the most effective ways that white, middle-class women began to assume political power without transgressing culturally prescribed notions of womanhood and civilized gender relations.

In the 1870s, physicians accused middle-class women who aspired to college educations of willfully flouting motherhood and domesticity, and they castigated these women for any illnesses that later beset them. It was generally assumed that college women *voluntarily* brought reproductive harm upon themselves by removing themselves from the domestic realm of patriarchal protection so carefully constructed for their benefit. The same physicians were much more sympathetic toward women industrial workers, whom they cast as victims of the "disarrangement of economic forces in society," believing that these women worked only because the structures of patriarchal protection had malfunctioned. Dominant cultural prescriptions held that women employed in industry were not working out of "choice"—that they would have preferred to remain at home and that they would happily leave the paid labor force as soon as it was economically feasible for them to do so. Thus, in contrast to the dangerous expressions of autonomy that many conservatives saw in middle-class women's attempts to secure higher education, most labor reformers construed women's industrial work and other forms of wage labor as the consequence of a broken-down patriarchal system (men's inability to protect women) that was itself proof that the country was regressing faster and faster in the direction of barbarism and savagery. Most white people viewed industrial work for women either as a temporary occupation for young women still seeking husbands; as a necessary stopgap measure for women whose fathers and husbands could not earn adequate livings; or as the last resort for widows and other single women who lacked male protectors.[1]

This chapter examines the contradictory responses of the woman's movement to these two issues during the 1870s: its opposition to one physician's (Edward Clarke's) invocation of sexual difference to protect women from the purportedly harmful effects of higher education, and its support of another physician's (Azel Ames's) use of sexual difference to protect women who labored in industry. Examining these debates side by side, we can see a fundamental paradox operating at the heart of "the politics of protection," in which class and racial dimensions were central but rarely articulated explicitly. In the context of higher education, advocates of woman's rights exposed as a myth the claim that (middle-class white) women needed men's "protection." But in the context of labor reform, these advocates embraced the position that (working-class) women's sexual differences mandated special treatment in the form of protective labor legislation. In so doing, women's rights advocates helped fashion a new role for themselves as protectors of the laboring classes, a role that superseded their own status as protected middle-class homemakers.

IN 1872, AT THE INVITATION OF SUFFRAGIST Julia Ward Howe, Dr. Edward H. Clarke, a retired faculty member of Harvard Medical School, gave a controversial address on "Sex in Education" to the New England Woman's Club of Boston.[2] Women's rights advocates had considered Clarke an ally of their cause because three years earlier he had denounced male medical students in Philadelphia for harassing female classmates. In his address to the Woman's Club, however, he warned that men's colleges and universities were potentially harmful to women's health because women's unique physiology mandated a different educational system from that designed for men.[3] Clarke insisted that he was not arguing for a full restriction in (white middle-class) women's education or woman's sphere, only for a change in the *way* that these women were educated: "Women who choose to do so," Clarke acknowledged, "can master the humanities and the mathematics, encounter the labor of the law and the pulpit, endure the hardness of physics and the conflicts of politics." But, he added, "they must do it all in woman's way, not in man's way. In all their work they must respect their own organization, and remain women, not strive to be men, or they will ignominiously fail."[4]

Clarke's talk sparked a vehement discussion among woman's rights activists—and physicians, professionals, and scientists more generally—about the ways in which (white) women differed from (white) men.[5] Yet in some respects, the vehemence of women's responses is surprising, for in his arguments about the need for a "special" educational program for women, Clarke was merely following a position well outlined by female educators of the previous forty years—educators such as Caroline Kirkland, Emma Willard, and Catharine Beecher, all of whom had been demanding separate educational institutions for (white) women on the grounds that (white) women's sexual differences and unique sexual roles necessitated a different training.

Indeed, many of Clarke's critics, including Caroline Dall, an organizer of the New England Woman's Rights Convention of 1859 and author of *Woman's Right to Labor* (1860) and *The College, the Market, and the Court* (1867), insisted that they shared Clarke's views on sexual difference. Dall wrote, "I start from the same premises with Dr. Clarke; for I believe the spiritual and intellectual functions of men and women to tend differently to their one end; and their development to this end . . . to be best achieved by different methods."[6] Why, then, if they agreed with the basic premise—that women fundamentally differed from men and thus needed different educational methods—did women like Dall find Clarke's book so objectionable? Most advocates of woman's rights saw Clarke as a significant adversary in a battle in which much was at stake. Eliza Duffey, another woman's rights activist in Boston, wrote that she considered Clarke's "line of attack masterly" and feared that "if he convinces the world that woman is a 'sexual' creature . . . the battle is won for those who oppose the advancement of women."[7]

Clarke's remarks, and the vehement debates that ensued, were part of an extensive, broad-based response to the influx of young white women into higher education that took place in the first decade after the Civil War. In 1870, five years after the war's end, roughly eleven thousand women attended institutions of higher education, 4.6 percent of these in coeducational colleges. By 1880, however, there was a fourfold increase in the numbers of women attending college to approximately forty thousand, almost a quarter of them enrolled in coeducational institutions.[8] Higher education—gaining access to it, and using it to obtain occupational and financial reward—had become a crucial issue for middle-class women aspiring to economic independence in the early 1870s, as they increasingly realized how significant education had become for their fathers, husbands, and brothers in differentiating themselves from men of nonprofessional or lower-class status. In effect, Clarke was denying these women access to the same avenue of class differentiation, financial improvement, and status elevation that middle-class men had already used most effectively.[9]

Conservatives who had read Clarke's book were alarmed by the developments in higher education, which they interpreted in light of reports about falling birth rates among college-educated (white) women. Although the fertility of white women had been steadily dropping since 1800 (as documented in 1843 by George Tucker, a professor of moral philosophy and political economy at the University of Virginia)[10] national debates in the 1870s, 1880s, and 1890s conveniently forgot about the antebellum period and instead placed the beginning of this trend in the 1860s. Census observers believed that the drop in (white) women's fertility rates worsened significantly in the 1870s and 1880s, at the height of (white) women's demand for higher education. The

Census Bureau published birth rate statistics every decade, and U.S. commentators grew increasingly alarmed with every subsequent study, especially as it appeared that the birth rates of purportedly inferior "darker races"—southeastern Europeans and African Americans—were increasing.[11] (See figs. 3-1 and 3-2.) Francis A. Walker, director of the U.S. Census in 1870 and 1880, struck an alarm bell among whites in the early 1890s when he compared the birth rates of native-born whites with foreign-born immigrants, blaming the declining fertility of whites on immigrants themselves.[12] By the 1890s, it was well publicized that more than half the women who had graduated from college in the 1880s still had not married. At the turn of the century, the trend seemed stable and indisputable: in 1900, still less than half of women who attended college during the postbellum period had married; and of those who had, approximately 20 percent remained childless. As early as 1867, an anonymous critic, identified only as an "anti-reconstructionist," attributed the declining birth rates of (white) women to the "doctrine of the woman's rights movement" that originated in New England and had spread elsewhere. "The anti-offspring practice has been carried [by women] in New England and wherever New England ideas prevail. . . . It is not that the New England women are unable to bear as many children as formerly, but that they will not."[13] In 1875, Oliver Wendell Holmes, professor of anatomy and physiology at Harvard, in a review of Clarke's book, restated what was clearly already at the crux of the debate for many white middle-class Americans: "We have heard a great deal . . . of the rights of woman. . . . It may be very desirable that she should vote, but it is not essential. . . . It *is* essential that she should be the mother of healthy children well developed in body and mind."[14]

Clarke associated the woman's movement with the evolutionarily regressive position of "sexual sameness" and blamed the movement for reducing the birth rate of white elites and impeding the advancement of civilization. His genius was to make it difficult for advocates of woman's rights to use the ideology of sexual difference for their own purposes. He labeled them in ways they disliked, attributing to them ideas about sexual identity that they insisted they did not advocate. Speaking of woman's physiological differences from man, Clarke declared:

> All this is so well known that it would be useless to refer to it, were it not that much of the discussion of the irrepressible woman-question, and many of the efforts for bettering her education and widening her sphere, *seem to ignore any difference of the sexes; seem to treat her as if she were identical with man,* and to be trained in precisely the same way; as if her organization, and consequently her function were masculine, not feminine. Woman seems to be looking up to man and his development, as the goal and ideal of womanhood. The new gospel of female development glorifies what she possesses in common with him, and tramples under her feet as a source of weakness and badge of inferiority the mechanism and functions peculiar to herself.[15]

By reformulating the "irrepressible woman-question" in this manner, Clarke constructed an ideological conflict over sexual difference that had never in fact existed between the woman's movement and its opponents, obscuring a much more critical struggle occurring between middle-class white men and women over political authority and educational resources that had been in progress for more than fifty years.

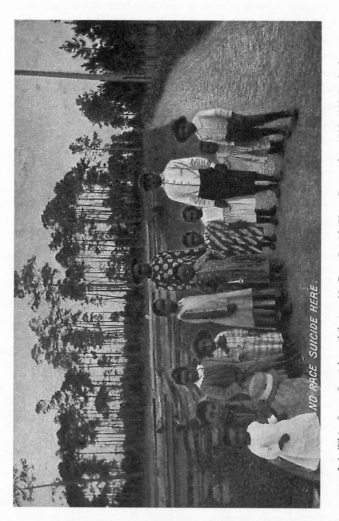

NO RACE SUICIDE HERE.

FIGURE 3-1 White fears of racial annihilation. No Race Suicide Here. Postcard, c. 1905–1907. In the late nineteenth and early twentieth centuries, whites worried incessantly about their falling birth rates in comparison to the much higher birth rates of nonwhite peoples. The presence of the elegant young black woman (second from left) and the well-attired children suggests that the photograph was posed under quite other pretexts than the one for which it was ultimately used.

Many who responded to Clarke, including Thomas Wentworth Higginson, Julia Ward Howe, Caroline Dall, Mercy B. Jackson, Elizabeth Garrett Anderson, and Eliza Duffey, vehemently objected to the way in which Clarke appropriated the concept of sexual difference in order to characterize the position of the woman's rights movement as insisting on sexual similarity. Higginson, for example, denied that sexual identity was the "gospel" of the woman's movement and reiterated that "the strongest arguments in favor of Woman Suffrage are based not on the identity, but on the difference of the sexes."[16] The woman's movement had carefully negotiated the question of sexual difference in its quest for higher education and its demands for the suffrage (see chapter 2), often basing arguments for female seminaries on the grounds that (white middle-class) women required special institutions to train themselves for sex-specific social roles. That Clarke understood that there was such a struggle for power taking place was apparent in the way he sought to reassure his female opponents that in making his specific claims about the ramifications of women's sexual differences he was not calling for the perpetuation of sexual inequality.[17] As white women moved into the cultural spaces that were defined as "male" and were seen as potential competitors for economic and political power, conservatives like Clarke made claims that woman's sexual differences made it racially dangerous for (white) women to "compete" politically with (white) men.

The *Woman's Journal,* a prosuffrage publication, of which Howe was an editor, re-

Copyright, 1905, by U. Co., N. Y.   "COMPARING NOTES."

FIGURE 3-2 Keeping up the birth rate. Comparing Notes. Postcard, 1905. In both overt and subtle ways, white women were commanded to fulfill their social responsibility to have children for the race.

ported Clarke's speech on December 21, 1872, and covered the ensuing debate in the months that followed.[18] So much public interest was generated by his lecture that Clarke extended his original remarks and published them several months later under the title *Sex in Education: Or, a Fair Chance for the Girls* (1873). Among academics and intellectuals the book was an immediate bestseller. In Ann Arbor, where women had been attending the University of Michigan for only three years, a bookseller reported selling two hundred copies in a single day.[19] About a dozen editions were issued within the first few months of the book's appearance, yet *Sex in Education* still did not exhaust its readership. From 1875 to 1887, it was reprinted at least seventeen more times, and reviews appeared in magazines and newspapers around the country.[20] In 1875, the editor of *Scribner's Monthly* reported that the controversy had grown so large and so heated that it had become a "matter for criticism, [simply] on its merits as a controversy."[21] M. Carey Thomas, founder of Wellesley College, would later remark, "We did not know when we began [admitting women to universities] whether women's health could stand the strain of education. We were haunted in those days by the clanging chains of that gloomy specter, Dr. Edward Clarke's *Sex in Education.*"[22] As late as 1904, the psychologist G. Stanley Hall, who served as president of Clark University from its founding in 1888 until 1920, a solid opponent of coeducation himself, affirmed that "even though he may have 'played his sex symphony' too harshly, E. H. Clarke was right."[23]

Clarke succeeded in removing the debate from the realm of politics or ethics—a realm that woman's rights advocates had been learning to address with some assurance by invoking their superior moral status as civilized women—by insisting that woman's access to higher education was not a moral issue (it could "not be solved by applying to it abstract principles of right and wrong").[24] The solution "to the problem of woman's sphere," Clarke declared, "must be obtained from physiology. . . . The *quoestio vexata* of woman's sphere will be decided by her [physical] organization."[25] In the process, Clarke elaborated a biological theory of the development of (white) womanhood that divided human physiological maturation into three periods: childhood, which extended from birth to the onset of adolescence, characterized by similarity between the sexes; adolescence and mature adulthood, when "the sexes diverge[d]" as part of a natural process of maturation; and, for women, a third stage, menopause, which continued into the "unknown" and involved a return to sexual similarity with men. Adolescence or young adulthood, as Clarke constructed it, was a stage of sexual divergence, a turbulent and fragile period during which young women experienced a "rapid expenditure of force" that resulted in the creation of a "delicate and extensive mechanism"—a stage that had no counterpart in men, whose growth was presumed to occur steadily from birth through maturity.[26] In Clarke's book, adolescence became identified with (white civilized) women's physiological departure from a male norm. "Overworking" women's brains during this crucial phase of maturation meant risking the normal development of the female reproductive system and endangering the future evolution of civilized society.[27]

Within the woman's movement, Clarke's remarks generated an immediate and angry response. In a year, four volumes had appeared: Howe's edited collection *Sex and*

Education, which included essays by prominent reformers, educators, and writers, including such luminaries as Thomas Wentworth Higginson, Mrs. Horace Mann, Caroline Dall, and Elizabeth Stuart Phelps, among others; Eliza Bisbee Duffey's treatise *No Sex in Education*; a monograph, coauthored by Professor George Fish Comfort and his wife, the physician Anna Manning Comfort, *Woman's Education and Woman's Health*; and *The Education of American Girls*, edited by Anna Callender Brackett, which included contributions from well-known physicians, educators, ministers, and suffragists, among them Antoinette Brown Blackwell and Mary Putnam-Jacobi.[28]

Many of these respondents rushed to do combat with Clarke by marshalling "scientific" studies to show that college education (even if they were designed originally for men) did not, in fact, impair female students' reproductive health. In 1874, when the Harvard Medical School announced that the next topic for its Boylston Prize would be the effects of menstruation on women's health, a group of women in Boston went looking for a female physician to counter Clarke's claims. In the fall of 1874, C. Alice Baker wrote to Mary Putnam-Jacobi, a physician trained at the Ecole de Médecine (in Paris, 1869), urging her to submit an essay. Jacobi interviewed several hundred women about the effects of work on their experience of menstrual pain. Her study, "The Question of Rest for Women during Menstruation," found that most women were able to do intense intellectual work during their periods without debilitating pain or a need for rest. "Nothing in the nature of menstruation," Jacobi found, "impl[ied] the necessity, or even the desirability, of rest for women whose nutrition is really normal."[29] A decade later, women were still conducting scientific studies to rebut Clarke's pronouncements. In 1885, a special committee of the Association of Collegiate Alumnae surveyed 1,290 female college graduates and found that 19 percent of them reported experiencing a deterioration of their health while in college, in comparison to 21 percent who reported experiencing an improvement.[30] Mary Roberts Smith Coolidge, associate professor of sociology at Stanford, published a study in 1900 to show that the marriage and fertility rates of college-educated women were roughly the equivalent of noncollege women of the same race, class, and social background.[31]

Despite these attempts to demonstrate that college-educated women were not impaired physiologically by their educations, most female advocates of coeducation did not give up the argument that (white) "woman" differed from "man." Nor did they argue for the "identical" treatment of women as a means of obtaining educational equality for women, in part because they firmly believed in the existence of sexual differences. Mercy Jackson, for example, explicitly rejected Clarke's depiction of the woman's movement and pointed out that what was at stake in this debate was who would be able to claim sexual difference for their own purposes: "We regret to find," Jackson wrote,

> that one who should be informed of the views of the prominent advocates of co-education should permit himself to talk of their wishing to make women as nearly as possible like men, and of women as wishing to become like men, and despising those differences in themselves which distinguish the sexes, *when in fact these are the opprobriums of their opponents instead of arguments to defeat the cause.* . . . What women now struggle for is not to be like

men, not to get their education by the same mental processes as men, but to have the same opportunities to use in a woman's way. . . . Why the Doctor supposes it necessary to co-education that women should study like men . . . I cannot imagine.[32]

Maintaining the ability to appeal to sexual difference was crucial to many of Clarke's opponents, in part because they did not have the credentials or training to argue as scientists or physicians (having been excluded from most colleges and medical schools). Needing to find other ways to assert authority for their position, female respondents emphasized their differences from men of their race and class to establish the validity of their own forms of knowledge. This special "woman's knowledge," they argued, had developed as a result of their experiences as wives and mothers. These experiences, they insisted, gave them as (white middle-class) women a perspective that no white male scientist could match or counter. Hence, Eliza Duffey defended her "qualifications" to write on the subject of "woman's" health and physiology in the following way:

> The writer of this book—a book designed for women exclusively—is a woman, a wife and a mother. These facts alone, with the *experiences* they involve, seem to give her qualifications for the work she has undertaken superior, in many respects, to those possessed by any man, professional or otherwise. . . . Men have had their say. It is but fitting now that a woman should have hers, especially as the woman who assumes to speak does so with an authority man cannot venture to claim.[33]

Thus, one tactic was to insist upon the superior knowledge that sexual difference afforded them as (civilized) wives and mothers—without mentioning, of course, their specific racial or class position in the prevailing social hierarchies of the 1870s. But another tactic involved focusing attention on their racial similarity with white men, shifting the terms of the debate away from their sexual differences, and onto their evolutionary racial sameness with white men. For example, in her effort to defend (white middle-class) women's right to higher education, Julia Ward Howe drew on prevailing ideology that held that Europeans exhibited greater responsiveness to climatic influences than other racial groups, initiating what was to become a recurrent strategy among the white woman's rights movement.[34]

Howe began by questioning Clarke's assumption that there was a direct connection between higher education and arrested physical development among (white) women. First, she claimed that "savage" women in other parts of the world also had reproductive problems, and these, Howe believed, were clearly not the result of overeducation. In citing this example, Howe did not mean to suggest any point of sexual likeness between civilized and savage women—she was merely pointing out that reproductive troubles (anywhere) were generally attributable to climatic factors, not education. Howe's alternative explanation for the failed health and imperfect physique of educated New England women focused on the role that cold winters played in producing these results. Climaticly induced physiological changes in (white) women, Howe believed, also had their counterpart in (white) men residing in New England, who were widely recognized to be less robust than men of other regions and less strong than men of other racial groups. Here Howe was drawing on a long tradition, dating back to the eighteenth century and George Louis Leclerc Buffon's claims in his *Natural History* (1761), but more recently argued by British scientists and reported in the *Atlantic Monthly* in 1872.[35] To buttress these arguments, Howe drew on the recent experience of Western colonizers.

> English families resident in India soon lose the freshness of their coloring and the full-ness of their outline. . . . The writer has seen an American official long resident in Turkey whose physiognomy had become entirely that of his adopted country. The po-tent American climate works quickly in assimilating the foreign material offered to it. Two generations suffice to efface the salient marks of Celtic, Saxon, French, or Italian descent. The Negro alone is able to offer a respectable resistance.[36]

Thus, Howe insisted that it was not college but climate that produced the physical weakness and reproductive ills within the white race residing in New England, includ-ing the Anglo-Saxon women attending universities in this region.

Because the debates over Clarke's book focused on sexual differences that were un-derstood as sufficient grounds to lump all women together as a group, the class and racial dimensions embedded in these claims to difference (and in the politics of protec-tion more generally) remained hidden in the debates over coeducation. Yet, in this same decade, other discussions erupted that exposed the underlying tensions among race, class, and gender, when Azel Ames, a Boston physician who became interested in labor reform, read Clarke's book and instantly saw the value of extending it to "woman's employment in industry." Although the two discussions occurred simulta-neously, Ames' remarks elicited no outpouring of scorn from the woman's move-ment. Rather, woman's rights activists agreed with Ames that working-class women deserved "protection." A special rationale for "protective labor legislation" was devel-oped during the 1880s and 1890s that defined "woman" as a special class of worker who, because of her vulnerable position in the labor force and her unique reproduc-tive system, deserved different legal status and economic treatment from that ac-corded to working-class men.

"Sex in Industry": Historical Origins of Protective Labor | Legislation for Women

Inspired by the visibility and success of Clarke's book, Azel Ames, a special commissioner of investigation for the Massachussetts State Bureau of Statistics of Labor, produced his own study, *Sex in Industry: A Plea for the Working-Girl,* in 1875, in which he documented the suffering of thousands of young women employed in factories in Massachusetts—women who worked exceedingly long hours for pitifully low wages, under brutal condi-tions. Rooms were poorly ventilated, and the heat and noise were overwhelming. Ade-quate restroom facilities were rarely available, and these women were not permitted to take breaks during the day. *Sex in Industry* set forth guidelines for fundamental changes in the economic structures and labor policies affecting such women.[37]

Broader analyses of the "labor problem" in this period, Ames's included, often stressed that working-class men were not paid enough to support their families. Labor reformers generally favored solutions that they believed would help guarantee working-class men a "family wage," solutions that would raise the standard of living among working-class families while at the same time encouraging working-class women to stay at home to take care of their families in accordance with middle-class ideals of domesticity.[38] In Ames's state of Massachusetts, for example, the State Bureau of Statistics of Labor reported in 1873 that the average income earned by an adult male worker was less than $550 per year, although a family of five required approximately $650 per year to eke out a minimal subsistence. According to the Bureau's report, without the "assisting labor" of wives and children, the average laborer could not make ends meet. Many labor reformers maintained that the best solution was *not* to raise women's wages to make up this difference or to make it easier for women to obtain jobs but rather to bar women from the most dangerous jobs and create other incentives to induce women to leave the paid labor force.

So-called special protective labor legislation for women appealed to both "progressive" reformers as well as "conservatives" on the woman question for different reasons: progressives, like Caroline Dall and Florence Kelley, believed they were acting in accordance with social evolution by calling for the elevation of working-class women into a patriarchal world of domestic protection. Conservatives believed they were buttressing patriarchal domesticity, protecting a vulnerable group of women from economic abuse and preserving the domestic morals of civilization. Both sides could agree on maximum-hour legislation for women, seeing this legislation as a means of "protecting" women's health and making it possible for women to devote more time to domestic responsibilities. Both could also support minimum-wage laws for women since these were expected to help women earn the same salaries as previously, but with fewer hours, and therefore enable them to spend more time in the home caring for their families. Because the labor market was segregated in ways such that men and women (and blacks and whites) rarely competed for the same jobs, the proposal to guarantee women a minimum wage was not construed as a competitive threat to male labor. If anything, minimum wage laws, by raising women's wages (making them more expensive as laborers than they had been previously) would reduce the large disparity in the cost of female versus male workers and might even help dissuade employers from hiring female workers as a way to reduce their labor costs. Moreover, in the late nineteenth century, the demand for "equal pay for equal work" did not embody the view that (white) women should or would become permanent employees. Rather, it was a measure that was seen as supportive, not subversive, of domestic ideologies, as it was intended as a method of raising (white) women's wages so that they could earn more money by working fewer hours and consequently be able to spend more time at home, caring for their families. In other words, proposals for protective labor legislation—whether they took the form of maximum-hour or minimum-wage laws, "equal pay" slogans, or night-prohibition statutes—reinforced and perpetuated dominant ideologies of patriarchal domesticity, buttressing white middle-class ideals about manhood that attributed to (white) men the role of financial provider and physical protector of women.[39]

Many participants in the woman's movement, as well as male labor reformers and male unionists, agreed that the work environment itself also endangered the morals of young women. Middle-class society claimed it needed to protect itself from the moral degradation that threatened to engulf it, particularly in urban areas. Ames argued that state regulation of women's employment was justified because it was the public, not the employer, who had to assume the costs of rehabilitating working-class women, whose health and morals, he asserted, were damaged by industrial labor. However, women in the woman's movement often wanted to correct the work environment (put older elite women in charge as managers, for example), while male reformers wanted to remove the victim, arguing that labor itself was degrading to women and that industrial employment accelerated girls' physical development and made them sexually precocious—an ironic criticism since they were also concerned that the hard work would impair these young women's reproductive systems, making it impossible for them to reproduce "the race."

This ironic contradiction was at the heart of Ames's work. In one breath, Ames worried about infertility in working women, and in the next breath, he warned that "the stimulus of a heated atmosphere, the contact of opposite sexes, the example of lasciviousness upon the animal passions—all have conspired to produce a very early development of sexual appetencies [sic]."[40] Ames's greatest fear was that moral deterioration and increased sexual activity among working women would mean that even if reproduction took place, it would not ensure the perpetuation of "civilization" but instead might lead to evolutionary regression. Ames was preoccupied with the deciviliz-ing effects of industrial work, which he believed would produce "primitive" sexual appetites among (working-class) whites, and he articulated his fears by saying that "the female population engaged in manufactures approximates very closely to that found in tropic[al] climates."[41]

Some women reformers tried to counter these views by arguing that moral and racial deterioration was not intrinsic to an industrial economy that employed women but stemmed from the behavior of immoral men who took sexual advantage of young girls in these settings. The fault was with the men who abrogated the civilized, manly role of protector. For example, Caroline Dall, who, as I have already shown, objected to Clarke's arguments concerning the dangers of coeducation, insisted that the labor problem had nothing to do with girls' unique physiological and reproductive systems, or with the effects upon women's morals that were attributed to wage labor. Instead, Dall ascribed the degradation of working-class women to the lack of respect that men generally demonstrated toward all women, and to the special (class) stigma that was attached to paying women for their labor.[42]

For Dall, the labor problem encompassed intertwining economic and moral issues: male employers did not pay women as good wages as they paid men, in part because they knew that women, out of desperation and lack of organization, would work for less money. Because women worked for less money, Dall argued, male employers had less respect for woman's work. The volunteer work of middle-class women, Dall noted, only made the problem worse. So long as "ladies" refused to accept money for their labor, feeling that payment would somehow lower them, they perpetuated the notion that wages degraded female laborers. At bottom, Dall believed the economic problem would disappear when the ethical one was solved: "When men respect women as human beings, consequently as laborers," Dall wrote, "they will pay them as good wages as men." Dall also urged "women of rank" to help counter the stigma that attached to working women by demanding payment for their own work. "Plenty of employments are open to [women]," Dall argued, "but all are underpaid. They will never be better paid til women of rank begin to work for money, and so create a respect for woman's labor."[43]

Dall's efforts to break down the moral distinctions held to differentiate middle-class "ladies" (who did volunteer or charity work) from working-class women (who received wages for their labor) predated later arguments that would reject the social-Darwinian assumption that economic hardship was synonymous with moral failure. In the 1880s, labor reformers and charity workers, including women like Josephine Shaw Lowell, began to introduce new moral distinctions among the working classes, differentiating between the worthy and unworthy poor. Ames himself was a forerunner of this new group of reformers who attributed poverty to systemic and institutional factors—a malfunctioning economy—rather than to character flaws of the poor person. This type of analysis was crucial to gaining acceptance for protective labor legislation: if the poor woman herself was not to blame for her condition, she deserved protection.

Ames put forward his call for state protection of women at a time when governmental intervention in economic processes concerning male workers could not be sustained. For male workers, equality and protection could not be reconciled: to ask for state protection for men was interpreted as involving an admission of personal inadequacy, some fundamental lack of manhood. This perspective was clearly encapsulated in the economist William Graham Sumner's defense of laissez-faire notions of liberty in 1883:

> Certainly liberty, and universal suffrage, and democracy are not pledges of *care and protection*, but they carry with them the exaction of individual responsibility. The State gives *equal rights and equal chances* just because it does not mean to give anything else. It sets *each man* on his feet and gives him leave to run, just because it does not mean to carry him. Having obtained his chances, he must take upon himself the responsibility for his own success or failure.[44]

Ideologies about individual responsibility, that linked equality with manhood, liberty, suffrage, and democracy (in opposition to "protection"), were employed by court decisions in the 1880s and 1890s: to be a free *man* meant to be free to enter into contracts with employers without any state regulation or interference. Thus, protective labor laws that were written in universal or gender-neutral language and were tested in the 1880s were generally invalidated.[45] In the 1880s and 1890s, the United States Supreme Court ruled repeatedly that general (sex-neutral) labor legislation was unconstitutional because it interfered with the [male] individual's and the corporate entity's right to enter freely into a labor contract, a right that the court found was guaranteed under the due process clause of the Fourteenth Amendment.[46]

Hence, labor reformers began to argue that the state could legitimately treat "woman" as a "special class" of citizen by virtue of her sexual differences so as to obtain special protective labor legislation for women workers only. As legal historian Nancy Erickson has argued, the courts slowly developed sexually differentiated notions of liberty—one for male workers and one for female workers—beginning in the mid-1870s through the mid 1890s.[47] Yet, while sexually distinct notions of liberty for women had their origins in this period, it is also true that such notions of liberty were strongly resisted.[48] In 1876, as the case of *Commonwealth v. Hamilton Mfg. Company* reveals, it was still possible to uphold maximum-hour legislation for women without drawing on the kinds of arguments that Ames was developing, and without perpetuating the constructions of sexual and class differences that made the legislation necessary in the first place.[49] The Massachusetts court simply argued that no infringement of an individual's right to contract had occurred, without reference to the sex of the employee or arguments about her sexual differences.[50] Twenty years later in 1895, however, the State Supreme Court of Illinois, in *Richie v. People*, reviewed the Massachusetts finding and found its reasoning inadequate. The Illinois court accused the Massachusetts court of "begging the question," skirting what was the heart of the issue: the fact that maximum-hour legislation *did* place restrictions on the *female* individual's right to contract freely.[51] Unlike the Massachusetts court, the Illinois court felt it had to take up the question of whether sexual differences could be deemed relevant in justifying different treatment for women. It reached the conclusion that sexual differences were not relevant and decided to strike down its own maximum-hour law because it could find no other appropriate legal justification.[52]

By the end of the 1890s, however, a legal consensus had developed that agreed that the state could legitimately regulate women's employment—even though in so doing, the state restricted the freedom of individual women to enter into labor contracts—so as to ensure that (white) women would be able to bear adequate numbers of children in the future. The rationale for this legislation drew on several types of argument: first, that such legislation was needed to alleviate women's oppression in light of their sexual differences; second, that the state's interest in ensuring a future (white) population justified regulation of woman's employment to ensure (civilized) motherhood; and third, that the state had a responsibility to protect the public's moral welfare and ensure the future evolution of civilization.[53]

The Supreme Court sanctioned such reasoning in a 1908 case that is now well known among scholars of women's and labor history, *Muller v. Oregon.* Using arguments prepared by Josephine Goldmark of the National Consumers' League, Louis Brandeis, the lawyer who argued the case in front of the Supreme Court, cited women's "special physical organization," "child-bearing and maternal functions," and the need to prevent "laxity of moral fibre which follows physical debility" as adequate justifications for the state's different treatment of men and women employed in industrial wage labor.[54] The Court upheld maximum-hour legislation on the grounds that women's sexual differences and unique role in reproduction mandated and justified state intervention, even when no such intervention could be mandated or justified in the case of men.[55]

The politics of protection, so strongly resisted by white middle-class women in the

1870s when it was applied to their educational options, had now been fully endorsed by most segments of ruling white elites. "Home protection"—the slogan used by the NWCTU to call for woman suffrage and temperance legislation—had achieved its legal counterpart. (See fig. 3-3.) This approach to politics would become so dominant in the early decades of the twentieth century that the National Woman's Party could not muster much support from within the woman's movement for the Equal Rights

FIGURE 3-3 Mobilizing women under a politics of protection. The Home vs. the Saloon. Postcard, 1910. Members of Frances Willard's National Woman's Christian Temperance Union supported woman suffrage because they believed that women needed to vote to protect their home and children.

Amendment when it was first introduced into Congress in 1923; most white activists, including the National Consumers' League, the General Federation of Women's Clubs, and the National Women's Trade Union League opposed the amendment because they feared that it would jeopardize the special protective labor legislation that they had worked so hard to secure.[56]

Protection was a problematic strategy in woman's movement politics, implying dependency, victimhood, and vulnerability on the one hand but also privilege, high status, economic well-being, and personal security on the other hand. In the context of late-nineteenth-century U.S. political culture, to accept the status of the protected implied a certain lack of autonomy, a curtailment of freedom and economic opportunity, even as protection supposedly insulated white women from the sullying aspects of competition and worldly activity. In the late 1890s, as the nation specifically justified its imperialist ambitions with the explanation that it had a moral obligation to "protect" vulnerable (i.e., incompetent) peoples from other, more brutal, colonizers, "protection" became even more problematic for white women, as it was associated with "protectorates." Woman's rights advocate Lizzie Holmes explained in 1898, "A free woman will not choose to be 'protected' in the old sense. Protection has ever been an implication of weakness and a willingness to occupy a subordinate position. Nations which call upon other nations for protection must needs give up for that protection some portion of their independence."[57] Moreover, in the context of laissez-faire versions of social Darwinism, protection of primitives was deemed a dubious strategy, as social evolution was supposedly most efficient at weeding out the racially unfit when permitted to operate without interference. Finally, the move to protect so-called primitive races had different consequences for primitive men and women: protection diminished the primitive male as lacking in manliness, unable to protect his own women himself, while it raised the status of the primitive woman closer to that of the protected homemaker, deemed to be the first step in cultural assimilation. The next two chapters examine the complexities in such a politics, as white women began to throw off the mantle of protection for themselves and to act on a newly claimed right to serve as protectors for others.

4

A Feminist Explores Africa

May French-Sheldon's Subversion
of Patriarchal Protection

[I]f anyone would start schools among them [African primitives]
. . . [and] teach them a better way of living . . . lifting them
up by degrees, they would in time become Christians.
> Fannie C. Williams, "A 'White Queen' in Africa" (1893)

The whole future of this world rests upon the status of women, and
those who have influence should see that [others] who have not had
their advantages should be brought up to their standard.
> *Evening Sun*, quoting
> May French-Sheldon (1915)

O N THE EVE OF HER DEPARTURE for Africa in 1891, May French-Sheldon was, by all
accounts, a strikingly beautiful forty-four-year-old American woman, happily
married to a prosperous London banker, who enjoyed entertaining prominent businessmen in her own drawing room. Nothing in the public record gives any indication
that she was dissatisfied with this role. No personal illness, singular ennui, family crisis, or other necessity prompted her to leave her comfortable home to venture on a
three-month safari into a remote region of East Africa. Unlike other Victorian British
women who embarked on their own travels through what was known as the dark
continent, the flamboyant French-Sheldon never tried to make her voyage palatable
to Europeans or Americans by cloaking her actions in socially acceptable forms. She
was leaving a husband behind for no compelling reason other than that she desired to
prove to the world (and perhaps to herself as well) her ability to pull off such a dangerous trip without any white men to "protect" her. Resourceful, energetic, strong-
willed, and outspoken, with definite tastes and opinions, May French-Sheldon was asserting her independence from and picking up the gauntlet laid down by the
suffocating protectionism of Western patriarchy.[1]

As remarkable as the action itself, however, was the way in which French-Sheldon
was received as an "American heroine" by the U. S. press on her return. The *Chau-*
tauquan praised her for her "perseverance and . . . pluck" and for demonstrating that
a woman could perform such a masculine endeavor without any diminishing of her

womanliness.[2] The *New York Times* called it simply "the most remarkable performance in recent travel and exploration."[3] Reporters and the public alike marveled at the accommodations French-Sheldon fashioned for herself (which she exhibited at the World's Columbian Exposition in Chicago in 1893 for all to see). French-Sheldon had slept in an elaborate, portable bed (her palanquin) "made of wicker and furnished with luxurious and downy pillows in plenty, and with silk curtains." She had dined formally with linen tablecloths and silver cutlery, and she had served proper English tea to visitors she met along the way. There were even rugs on the floor of her tents.[4] "Tall and slender . . . [with] graceful figure, dark sparkling eyes and . . . fine complexion," May French-Sheldon embodied the "culture of a true woman"—a model homemaker, even in the bush.[5]

French-Sheldon's singular accomplishment was that she had survived an excursion that had defeated many a white man before her, all without sacrificing her womanliness or needing white men's protection or supervision. Alice Fletcher, the nationally famous Indian reformer of the 1880s who had had her own share of experiences among the "primitives" on Indian reservations, was duly impressed. She awarded French-Sheldon a prize for "best exhibit" at the Chicago Columbian Exposition, noting that she "was the first of her race and sex to enter [an unfrequented region]" and commending her for a "heroic and successful expedition."[6] (See fig. 4-1.)

Popular celebration of French-Sheldon's safari in East Africa lasted for nearly forty years, from 1892 through the 1920s. Her lecture tours were well received by both the public and the media throughout the first two decades of the twentieth century. Her celebratory reception as an "American" explorer of Africa (she was received much more enthusiastically in the United States than in Great Britain, where she was sometimes castigated as a "vulgar American")[7] spoke to the pride that Americans took in the fact that they now had an explorer of their own—one that even knew and had corresponded with the famous Henry Morton Stanley. Had French-Sheldon so boldly circumvented patriarchal domesticity in the United States, she would have been ignored or even denigrated. But from the perspective of white elites, her gender transgressions, having taken place in Africa, served a good cause: French-Sheldon was understood as demonstrating the superiority of white civilization to primitive peoples. The story of her life makes manifest how the United States's desire to assert itself as an imperialist nation, on a par with other European nations, helped make emerging feminist challenges to patriarchal protection more palatable.[8]

In the 1890s, the U.S. media saw French-Sheldon as the embodiment of a "true woman" who had proven herself the equal of white male explorers—and an emblem of the civilizing mission, even though she herself expressed little interest in Christianizing heathens. Journalist Fannie C. Williams acknowledged that French-Sheldon "did not go as a missionary . . . simply as an explorer," yet she credited French-Sheldon with introducing African natives to the superior virtues of white civilization. "Mrs. Sheldon has left behind her in Africa an influence which cannot fail to be felt . . . her example, worshipped as she was by them, was emulated in every possible way by these poor ignorant savages." For Williams, the primary symbolic act, signifying the great transformation that French-Sheldon wrought by her mere presence among

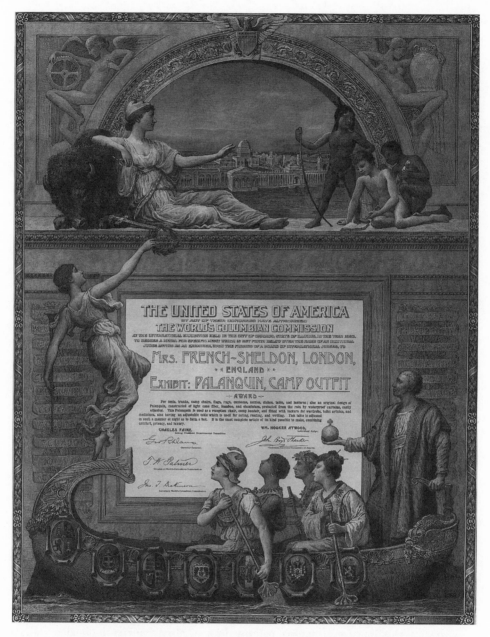

FIGURE 4-1 Celebrating civilization. Award for "best exhibit" at the World's Columbian Exposition, Chicago 1893. Reproduced with permission of the Library of Congress. Alice Fletcher was among the judges who awarded May French-Sheldon this prize for her exhibit of African artifacts acquired during her safari to East Africa in 1891. The iconography of a white woman in classical garb, symbolizing the United States, supervising the education of young savages, was a common way to represent the supposed benefits of imperialism and assimilation.

primitives, was the natives' improved table manners. "These tribes were in the habit of mincing their food all together . . . and crowding it down their throats with force, in a horribly gluttonous fashion. Sometimes a thousand at a time would come down from the mountains to see the white woman eat; and now where she has passed through, they eat with knives and forks."9

In contrast, in the 1910s and 1920s, the U.S. media promoted her, without censure or ridicule, as a "feminist" who had not needed a woman's movement to secure her liberation. The kind of feminism May French-Sheldon came to represent was that of the universalized liberal subject whose liberation from patriarchy was manifest in a personal autonomy that was purported to result from individual character—will, courage, and determination—disproving the need for structural change or "special rights." Moreover, an unprecedented outpouring of excitement over women travelers in this period (including the excitement generated by Margaret Mead's work *Coming of Age in Samoa* in 1928) marked the full transformation of French-Sheldon from an anomalous female explorer into a prototypical feminist ethnographer—signaling an extraordinary shift in popular conceptualization concerning the advancement of women that occurred between the 1890s and the 1920s. Despite the media's representation of French-Sheldon as a feminist, however, she never lost her cultural cachet as a true woman. Rather, she reinvigorated the image of the white woman as sexually pure, chaste, and refined (at a time when flappers were putting this into question), even while she exploited, for her public's titillation, the sexual tension between a white woman and male primitives. As late as 1924, when French-Sheldon was seventy-seven years old, she was still considered an exemplar of liberated womanhood—a woman who had "blazed the way for [other] women in the fields of geology, geography, exploration and science."10 Her success in this regard was due directly to her deployment of whiteness within a master narrative of colonial domination, which authorized her to embody, for at least three generations of American women, what was best in white civilization.

French-Sheldon's safari also symbolized for her white female audiences the possibility that colonization did not have to be based on male force or coercion: even the most "brutish" of African savages, French-Sheldon's experiences indicated, instinctively had recognized and responded to her authority. As she wrote in the foreword of *Sultan to Sultan,* her account of her safari, one of her purposes had been "to demonstrate that if a woman could journey a thousand and more miles . . . among some hostile tribes . . . without bloodshed, [then] the extreme measures employed by some would-be [male] colonizers is unnecessary, atrocious, and without the pale of humanity."11 On her death in 1936, writers of her obituaries exaggerated this aspect of French-Sheldon's self-presentation, propounding a distorted view of her as an opponent of colonization (when in fact this had not been the case).12

From the start, May French-Sheldon was aware of her safari's potential historic significance, both in demonstrating to skeptical European and white American men the full capabilities of a true woman and in altering contemporary European colonial practices. She purposefully chose what others considered a dangerous route, and she repeatedly turned down requests from "professional and scientific men entreating [her] to allow them to accompany [her]."[13] Later she boasted that over two thousand men and women had asked to join her expedition, but she had refused them all, telling the *Evening Sun* that she wanted "to show how easy it was for a woman to . . . travel about on friendly terms with the natives where a man would probably have to make his way by force."[14] French-Sheldon went on to explain that a female travel companion "might fall ill, and out of common humanity I should have to stop and care for her and perhaps be obliged to change my plans entirely." As for a white man: "I was afraid he would want to take care of me, shoulder all the responsibilities &c., and it would turn into *his* expedition instead of mine."[15]

Part of the reason that French-Sheldon could venture abroad without white male protectors was that she was acutely aware of the symbolic power that her whiteness would have among African natives, and she emphasized this to full effect by dressing up as a "White Queen" (her term, and one that U.S. reporters repeated with evident delight) to receive African princes, in a kind of oneupmanship that signified that she knew that she had European colonial power backing her. Garbed in a spun-silver sequined gown, bedecked with jewels and a blond wig, French-Sheldon appeared as the literal embodiment of Miss Britannia. Transforming herself into a White Queen allowed French-Sheldon to create a new identity, one that highlighted her race, along with her gender, in asserting her superiority in relation not just to the African leaders she encountered along the way but, more important, to white men. Her other favorite title for herself, one that she used throughout her life, long after her return from East Africa, was *Bébé Bwana,* a term supposedly given to her by her African porters. *Bébé,* a polite form of address, meant "Madam," *Bwana* "leader," but French-Sheldon often translated this expression for her readers as "woman-master" or "woman-man," to emphasize the anomaly and uniqueness of her role.[16] Stressing the special attributes that she believed were part of her whiteness (ingenuity, courage, self-discipline, intelligence, leadership), French-Sheldon fashioned an identity that countered both African and American understandings of "woman" as incompetent and vulnerable, in need of men's protection, and incapable of governing others.

Assuming the role and demeanor of a European monarch, perhaps also ridiculing it even as she invoked it, French-Sheldon was able to mitigate the public condemnation she otherwise would have received in the United States for her utter disregard of gender conventions. In evidently sincere appreciation of the outrageousness (and splendor) of French-Sheldon's self-presentation, the *New York Times* wrote, "Who but an American woman would have conceived the idea of making a Worth gown help her win her way into the interior of Africa?" The *Times* also lamented the fact that French-Sheldon's husband, Eli Sheldon, who financed the fifty-thousand-dollar excursion, died soon after his wife's return, so he could not be present to enjoy the publicity (or to signal French-Sheldon's return to the patriarchal fold). But the *Times* was consoled by the thought that Eli had gone to his grave a happy man, for his wife had been supremely successful—"an American woman had won distinction as an African explorer."[17]

French-Sheldon luxuriated in this public praise and attention, clipping newspaper accounts and preserving them carefully in a scrapbook.[18] On her return to England, she set to work on *Sultan to Sultan* and prepared to exhibit her artifacts in the Chicago Exposition. Her book and exhibits were reviewed in glowing terms by the *New York Times*, The *Critic*, the *Chautauquan*, and the *Nation*; furthermore, during the 1890s and early 1900s she was a popular speaker on the U.S. lecture circuit, and gave many talks in Great Britain and Canada as well.[19] During this time she assiduously promoted herself as a scientist and ethnographer. *Sultan to Sultan* mixed the conventions of nineteenth-century travelogues, evangelical ethnology, and the newly emerging scientific genre of anthropological ethnography. In addition, she wrote formal academic pieces on East African women and England's commercial future in Central Africa, which were published in the *Journal of the Anthropological Institute* and the *Journal of the Tyneside Geographical Society*, respectively.[20] For her research, monographs, and collecting, she was honored by the Royal Geographic Society in London in 1892, which admitted her into its ranks, along with a number of other women. French-Sheldon was fiercely proud of this achievement, and always referred to herself (somewhat misleadingly) as the society's first woman member, frequently signing her public correspondence with the initials F. R. G. S. (Fellow of the Royal Geographic Society) to remind readers of the honor.[21]

MAY FRENCH (1847–1936) WAS BORN IN BEAVER, PENNSYLVANIA, to a wealthy and prominent family. Her mother was a respected physician, among the first generation of women to practice medicine in this country. Her father derived his fortune from sugar, cotton, and tobacco plantations. In the 1860s, May and her sister, Belle French-Patterson, were educated by private tutors and then taken on an extended trip to Europe to round out their education. May French's early adult life has been lost from view. It is not clear what happened to the family's fortunes after the Civil War; and extant records in the United States reveal few details about her life in the 1870s. It may be that she had an early, unsatisfying first marriage while she was in her twenties.[22] By the mid-1880s, however, May was living in London with a new husband, Eli Lemon Sheldon, who managed successful banking and publishing businesses.

French-Sheldon seems to have enjoyed a happy and prosperous life in London. She was wealthy and well connected among British businessmen and scientists. She spent a lot of time in artistic pursuits (painting and fiction writing), outdoor activities, and physical exercise. In 1886, she published a translation of Gustave Flaubert's *Salammbo*, which brought her immediate recognition as a serious student of French literature. Then, in January 1891, for reasons that remain unclear, French-Sheldon, at age forty-three, made plans for an expedition to East Africa, writing in earnest to the famous explorer Henry Morton Stanley for assistance. French-Sheldon evidently had already mapped out an itinerary that would take her on a thousand-mile trek, through parts of what are now Kenya and Tanzania and into the territory around Mt. Kilimanjaro claimed by Germany. These areas were known to be sites of violent resistance to colonial power; the Masai were challenging German authority, and other African peoples in the surrounding regions of British-held Kenya were reluctant to venture inland.

Knowledgeable Europeans considered French-Sheldon's plan foolhardy. Stanley advised her "not to go further than the Free Methodist Mission nine miles beyond Mombasa" and cautioned her that "a long stay will bring out any lurking malady that you may have, and you will certainly lose your good looks."[23] Still, he agreed to provide her with several letters of introduction to British officials in the region. Even with Stanley's letters, however, French-Sheldon met with resistance from George MacKenzie, the representative of British colonial authority in Mombasa, whom, it seems, doubted that French-Sheldon could successfully manage the type of expedition she envisioned. "The fact was," French-Sheldon related afterward, "it was feared that the consequences of a woman's leading a caravan might throw the natives into a frenzy, [and] bring difficulties about which would involve the Imperial British East African Company in trouble and expense to come to my rescue."[24]

Knowing in advance that the European men she would encounter in Africa were unlikely to assist her, May French-Sheldon was still determined to proceed. She left London in January 1891, parted from her husband in Naples, and caught a boat that took her to Mombasa (on the coast of what is now Kenya). Finding the British officials unhelpful if not hostile, and assured that it would be impossible to hire any porters in Mombasa (due to an excess number of recent expeditions), French-Sheldon went on to Zanzibar, a small island just off the coast of present-day Tanzania, to outfit her expedition. In Zanzibar, European residents greeted her with the same antagonistic skepticism she had encountered in Mombasa, but she was able to engage a Mr. Boustead, an employee of a caravan-outfitting concern, who agreed to help her hire fifty porters. Moreover, the American consul general, a Mr. Ropes, arranged an audience for her with Abdal Aziz bin Mohammed, the sultan of Zanzibar, who endorsed her proposed safari, writing a letter that made it possible for Mr. Boustead to engage the men she needed. Returning triumphantly to Mombasa to make final preparations for her expedition, French-Sheldon found that George MacKenzie had overcome his initial opposition sufficiently to write her an affidavit of support, which read as follows (French-Sheldon translated it from Arabic for her U.S. readers):

> To all Arabs and Swahilis traveling in the interior: This is to inform you that this lady, to whom I have given this letter, is my friend, and I wish every one who meets her caravan to be kind to herself and her porters, and to do everything to help her *safari*. Any one who does this, and brings a letter from her to say she is pleased with what has been done for her, will receive thanks on arrival at Mombasa. Should any one interfere with her caravan, annoy her in any way, and do any act of disrespect to her, [that person] will be considered to have offended the company, and will be treated and punished accordingly.[25]

Thus prepared, and disregarding Stanley's advice to stay close to Mombasa, French-Sheldon set off for the interior on an expedition that ended up lasting three months, from March to May 1891. In the end, at least 153 people accompanied her: 138 porters and a number of palanquin-bearers, soldiers, and headmen, as well as several interpreters.[26]

Captain William E. Stairs, a British officer renowned for his own expeditions, advised French-Sheldon to have "as many women as possible . . . as it shows peaceful intentions," and so, probably as a result of his advice, French-Sheldon hired several female attendants.[27] (One, named Suzani, was a "black woman" who had a "natural gift of massage," and French-Sheldon employed her in this capacity during afternoon breaks.)[28] Yet French-Sheldon rarely mentioned these African women in her written accounts (newspaper interviews never mentioned these women either). French-Sheldon may have preferred to keep silent on this point to emphasize her own singular capacities. Only once in *Sultan to Sultan* did French-Sheldon express admiration for the strength and perseverance of her female attendants. Mostly, she claimed that she "found the few [women she] had a perpetual nuisance. They were always inciting disputes among the porters, and resorted to all sorts of measures to win from them portions of food and other things which they coveted."[29]

In part to highlight her managerial abilities, French-Sheldon stressed the extraordinary magnitude and complexity of her caravan. "A caravan going into the interior," she explained to her English and American readers, "is like a migratory community and must be provisioned and armed for the entire expedition."[30] She needed sufficient goods to prevent hunger, purchase rights of way through native-controlled territories, provide presents for negotiations, afford protection against the elements, and offer defense against wild beasts. Thus, French-Sheldon's provisions included beads (for trade), carried in boxes or canvas sacking; cloth (for her porters' wages and trade with other natives) in long bales covered in coconut matting; rice in sacks; pots, pans, and kettles; tents and poles; chairs and folding tables; large waterproof canvases to protect her goods; ground cloths to protect her tents; boxes of candles, soap, cartridges, matches, flints, and steel; cotton to clean guns; coconut oil and kerosene in large square tin cans that, when emptied, were used for water or bartered to natives; coffee in sacks; lanterns; water bottles; photographic apparatus and observation instruments; tools (rope, canvas, nails, sail needles, great hanks of linen thread, aluminum, wire, solder, irons); medicine cases; large tin buckets for water; a bathtub (French-Sheldon insisted on bathing every evening); hammocks for the sick; and "all manner of trifling accessories."[31]

Furthermore, French-Sheldon traveled well provisioned with gifts for the natives she expected to encounter along the way:

> the most valued among which will be the British soldier coats, flaunting red, with gaudy gold-lace and plenty of brass buttons, European hats, and red umbrellas, tooting horns, music boxes, clocks, matches, razors, knives, bells, rings, bracelets, metal belts and jeweled weapons, needles, sewing thread, pins, fishhooks, tops, kites, dolls, picture books, clay pipes, tobacco snuff, tea, sugar, silverware, china cups, knives, spoons and forks, paint boxes, mirrors, sewing machines, tools.[32]

All of these items were weighed, numbered, and allotted to individual porters, and then rearranged and reallotted on a daily basis, as articles were traded, used, consumed, or redistributed.

Because of the reported Masai disturbances, French-Sheldon's caravan was heavily armed, rendering her the commander of a small army (and indirectly disproving antisuffragist claims that women were unable to defend themselves or others). Most of her porters (at least seventy men) carried guns; the rest carried knives. French-

Sheldon emphasized, for her American readers, how threatening the group appeared: "I looked with amazement over all these strange black and every shade of brown faces, with much brutality imprinted thereupon, and marveled if I should always be able to control them and make them subservient to my commands."[33] Her doubts, French-Sheldon quickly added, were instantly dispelled, as she had faith that the "savages" would intuitively respond to the superiority of her whiteness. To wield power over these men, she knew discipline was crucial. She first tried to govern in a "womanly" way, but her initial attempts to direct "by kindness and moral suasion," she reported, were ineffectual, and she unabashedly adopted more masculine means. "I found that discipline could only be maintained by chastising serious offenders in the accepted way [i.e., flogging]. . . . Coaxing arguments and persuasive talks were disregarded and sneeringly laughed at, probably the more so because I, their leader, was a woman."[34] Taking charge and inverting the politics of protection with gleeful pleasure, French-Sheldon constructed herself as the leader and protector of her porters, rather than the other way round, even though on several occasions, French-Sheldon conceded, her porters saved her from injury and death.[35]

Knowing, too, that her white audiences would be titillated by her intimate encounters with primitive men, yet concerned that her sexual purity never be in question, French-Sheldon stressed the many ingenious stratagems she came up with to elude the sexual advances of the sultans who "courted" her. The titles of her most popular lectures from the 1920s, "Thrilling Experiences in Savage Africa," "Camp Life with Natives in the Jungle," and "Thrilling Adventures of a Lone White Woman in Savage Africa," invoked these same sexual themes.[36]

Most crucial, French-Sheldon's narrative of 1892 recounts how her porters, despite their respect, loyalty, and devotion, could never quite "reconcile my office with that of a woman." "I would open my tent-flap and say, 'Boy!' Back would come the answer, 'Sabe!' (sir); and they never got over it. If I addressed a porter he would respond, 'Dio, Bwana' (yes, master)."[37] French-Sheldon took credit for winning African respect by means of her strength of character, courage, and indomitable will—her successful projection of herself as a White Queen fully in command.

> It is therefore with a sense of personal pride [that] . . . surrounded constantly by these black porters, the majority of them culled from the roughest specimens of natives, deficient in intellect, devoid of any certain knowledge as to the proper attitude that men should assume to a white woman, and many of them full of brutish instincts, that they universally treated me with deference and obedience. . . . All this I firmly hold was due to [a] certain regime I adopted, based upon the combined experience of many white explorers and an innate conviction that individual prestige, consisting in personal dignity and self-respect on the part of a leader, must be maintained wherever you may be, if you expect to inspire those whom you aim to guide and command with your personal importance.[38]

French-Sheldon's tone, a mixture of fondness and condescension, suggested that she found Africans' acceptance of her as their leader natural and in keeping with her status as a white woman. She clearly believed in a personal superiority that entitled her to lead and govern men she felt were "deficient in intellect" and "brutish." Yet her reportage of these observations, on the surface meant to point to the inability of Africans to fully comprehend white women's leadership abilities, also signaled her ironic awareness that Africans could overlook her gender because of her race and call her "sir" with respect, when white men never could.

French-Sheldon's challenge of white male patriarchy is manifest in her continual defense of herself as a competent explorer and superior administrator. Sometimes she made such assertions directly, but more often she compared her own actions—taken as a woman—with those of other white male explorers in ways that affirmed her judgment of herself as a superior leader. Occasionally, French-Sheldon offered admonishments to previous explorers, who, in her view, falsely misrepresented Africans as unclean or sexually licentious; always the underlying subtext was a pointed affirmation that Africans had been misrepresented as savages by white men and that they were indeed capable of assimilating Western civilization. This subtext can be seen operating in French-Sheldon's narration of a conversation with a young sultan who asked her for an English saw and hammer so that he could "live like a white man."

> I asked, "What do you want these for?"
>
> He answered, "Ah, Bébé Bwana, I want to build an English house and live like a white man." I promised to send him the saw.
>
> He said doubtfully, "Ah, yes, white men all promise, but they all forget; the *mzungu* always lies."
>
> I interrupted him sharply, "Stop, Miriami, you must not speak to Bébé Bwana in that way. I will send you the saw."
>
> And upon my return, while the delirium was raging during my illness, this thing haunted me with other promises I had made those poor trusting natives, and I never rested, day or night, until every one had met a fulfillment. . . . Miriami has his saw.[39]

French-Sheldon's frequent references to herself as a *white* woman, her repeated declarations of how profoundly she had won the allegiance of black subjects ("Stay, Bébé Bwana, Stay; you shall be more powerful even than all the sultans"),[40] her proud display of her skills as a hunter and disciplinarian—all of these were part of a strategy to demand respect from white men on the grounds that she was a competent ruler of African savages known to resist and disobey white male rulers.

IN 1903 FRENCH-SHELDON RETURNED TO AFRICA, this time to the Belgian Congo, where she went to investigate accusations of Belgian abuses among rubber plantation workers. Belgium had been one of the ruling European authorities in this region since the division of the Congo in 1885. Under the guise of international humanitarianism, King Leopold II had created a protectorate called the Congo Free State, and he eventually assumed full control in 1908, administering the colony through a partnership of government, church missions, and interlocking companies. Initially Belgium exploited the Congolese ivory trade, becoming one of the main European traders in ivory. By the late 1890s, however, elephants were "shot out," and with ivory supplies dwindling, Belgium turned to wild rubber, which was used to manufacture hoses and later motor tires and other industrial products. Rubber was much more lucrative than ivory, accounting for sixteen million francs in 1896 and forty-three million francs in 1904, or about 83 percent of the Congo's foreign trade.[41] Thus, much was at stake when William Stead, editor of the *Review of Reviews* in London, offered to pay French-Sheldon five hundred pounds for a series of letters to begin January 1, 1904, about the Belgian Congo's use of African labor on rubber plantations. Stead wrote her that she was "absolutely free to describe things exactly as they are" and warned her that "the man who goes out to the Congo with the intention of investigating the evil deeds of the Congo State, and going out unattached [to] the missionary societies, State or Co's. takes his life in his hands."[42] Although she departed for the Belgian Congo ready to expose imperialist exploits, French-Sheldon found herself becoming sympathetic to the Belgian rubber operators, and she ended up a lifelong apologist for King Leopold II.

Indeed, her observations of the plantation system in the Belgian Congo inspired French-Sheldon to try to develop a similar scheme for exploiting the timberlands of Liberia, using the labor of African Americans, whom she intended to "repatriate" to Africa for this purpose. She negotiated with both the Liberian government and the U.S. Secretary of State, Elihu Root, for two years, hoping to create a business enterprise that would establish her as a colonial entrepreneur. Ultimately, the Roosevelt administration refused to assist her, and the Liberian government never granted its approval.[43]

During World War I, French-Sheldon left London, her primary residence since the 1880s, and returned to the United States for the duration of the war. Accompanied by her longtime companion, Nellie Butler, the two went on a lecture tour of the United States and Canada to raise funds for the Belgian relief services.[44] It was during this period that U.S. reporters explicitly linked French-Sheldon's earlier safari with the recently emerging feminist movement. "Before the feminist had been made one of the issues of the day," the *New York Press* reported in 1915, "a woman explorer had found her way into the heart of Africa."[45]

After World War I, French-Sheldon resumed her residence in London, but she continued to return to the United States annually in the early 1920s to do lecture tours. In her mid-seventies now, but still a beautiful and stylish woman of much younger appearance, French-Sheldon continued to fascinate young white women and to draw the attention of the local press as she traveled around the country with Nellie Butler and gave presentations before women's clubs, schools, universities, art galleries, bookstores, and amateur societies, such as the Women's Athletic Club, the Woman's Press Club, the American Pen Women, and the Daughters of the American Revolution. Most of her talks took place in the South, in New York state, and in California. Between 1922 and 1925, when she was most in demand as a speaker, French-Sheldon gave multiple presentations in about a dozen cities each year.[46] In September 1923, a journalist in Covina, California, gave notice of a talk that French-Sheldon was to give at the Woman's University Club, identifying her as "one of the outstanding figures among the great women of modern times."[47]

French-Sheldon offered young white people an alternative to more contentious forms of feminism. She firmly believed in higher education and individual ability and thought white women should be treated the same as white men. She did not support special protective labor legislation. Although she had been a suffragist, she was not what might be called a movement woman. She simply offered herself as evidence that the "old prescriptions of former days which were so galling, so unfair and unjust" were gone.[48] Young white college women in the 1920s were inspired by her example, which they took to mean that anything was possible for them, as long as they had adequate strength of will and purpose.[49]

Yet French-Sheldon was not fully recuperable by the U.S. media as a nonthreatening feminist, and in some ways she challenged her society to rethink its conventional assumptions about the civilized West and the African primitive. Whereas whites thought of primitive women as the most debased of all creatures, French-Sheldon offered a modified view, responding that "the African woman seems to have achieved that economic independence for which our women are [still] clamoring."[50] Yet she also contributed her own orientalist stories about the depraved institution of the harem, relating how the sultan of Zanzibar discouraged her from greeting the women in his harem with the words, "Do not trouble yourself for them. They are too many, all alike, and not worth it."[51]

On the other hand, French-Sheldon wrote sympathetically of polygamy, challenging the dominant view that polygamy signified African women's sexual debasement. Rather, French-Sheldon emphasized the economic efficiency of the institution, seeing it as a system that could alleviate household drudgery and increase female pleasure, autonomy and power:

A man accumulates more land or more cattle than his first wife can attend; he purchases another wife, and so on. The wives are far from being jealous of each other; in truth are delighted to welcome a new wife, and make great preparations for her. Each wife has her own hut. . . . She has control of her own plantations, and has the supreme right to her children. Her moral standard is exactly the same as her husband's.[52]

Implicit in this statement was a criticism of gender relations in the United States, where married women had difficulty retaining title to their own property, had no legal right to their children, and needed to maintain their own sexual fidelity regardless of the sexual liaisons their husbands might form.

Nonetheless, French-Sheldon's white audiences thought of African men as sexual beasts and sat on the edge of their seats waiting to hear how she had managed to preserve her chastity in the face of so much licentiousness. And while French-Sheldon exploited these assumptions in the ways she framed her stories about sultans "courting" her, she always insisted in the end that she had never been treated more chivalrously by men anywhere in the world than she had been by the so-called savages of Africa. In depicting African men as chivalrous, French-Sheldon put white men on notice: to prove their superiority to the African, they would have to treat the white woman with the same respect and deference that she claimed to have received while on safari.

On French-Sheldon's death in 1936, an obituary in a London newspaper interpreted the significance of her 1891 safari, forty-five years earlier, as follows:

For months she lived alone except for head-hunters and cannibals. She had at least 60 proposals of marriage from native sultans, kings and chiefs. "Not that they loved me for myself," she used to say. "They simply thought that the acquisition of Bébé Bwana would add to their prestige. It requires some tact and nerve to refuse a native potentate when he has you at his mercy." She added, nevertheless, that in all her experience of savage races she had never known a savage [to] insult her. "It is only when one gets back to civilisation that one is reminded of one's sex."[53]

This account contains many of the classic themes that surfaced in popular discussions of white women among primitives during the late nineteenth and early twentieth centuries: the emphasis on the physical danger that the primitive represented ("headhunters and cannibals"); the hint of miscegenation ("60 proposals of marriage"); the dismissal of any possible sexual desire on the part of white women, along with a subtextual rendering of the primitive as rapist ("It requires tact and nerve to refuse a native potentate when he has you at his mercy"). Indeed, the sultans are depicted as incapable of Western-type love ("Not that they loved me for myself"). Yet the final line of the obituary contained the unexpected paradox: "It is only when one gets back to civilisation that one is reminded of one's sex." Despite everything, encounters with the primitive were coming to symbolize a realm of freedom and power, personal independence and control over others that was not available to white women at home in England or the United States. Taking on the role of the protector of primitives, French-Sheldon traveled widely and independently at her own discretion. Her trips to Africa quite literally enabled her to escape the suffocating protection of white men at home.

Obituaries published in U.S. newspapers went even further in representing French-Sheldon as an emancipated woman who also had worked for the emancipation of African natives. The *New York Times* reported:

> Mrs. French-Sheldon was not only a pioneer among women explorers in Africa but one of the few of either sex who in her generation returned with kind words for the natives. In a day when they were described as treacherous and bloodthirsty she insisted their white exploiters were more guilty. For many years she argued the cause of the blacks, and [the] decrease in the cruelty with which natives were handled was in some part attributed to her championship.[54]

What wasn't noted in this obituary was French-Sheldon's long and vigorous defense of Belgium's rule of the Congo and her justifications of the brutal system of indentured servitude that King Leopold II and his successors enforced among African laborers on Belgium-owned rubber plantations. Nor did the writer mention French-Sheldon's advocacy of immigration restriction legislation for the United States during 1915 or her unsuccessful lobbying attempts on behalf of the Americo-Liberia Company.

The elevation of May French-Sheldon to the status of a national heroine came about through her specific negotiations with the discourses of the 1880s and 1890s, that positioned white women as potentially ideal civilizers of primitive peoples. For French-Sheldon, however, the supposed savagery of African natives was not innate in primitive nature but a logical response to the aggression of white men; substitute the refined white woman in the place of the aggressive white man, and imperialism need not generate opposition. Thus for French-Sheldon, African men's acceptance of her as their superior indicated a new way to go about colonizing primitives, even as it provided evidence that African men were not hopelessly mired in savagery. As a role model for young women and the embodiment of a feminist esprit for the nation, French-Sheldon helped shape a feminist alternative to male imperialism, while upholding the white woman as the prime measure of the superiority of U.S. civilization.

French-Sheldon's life was clearly extraordinary in her access to great wealth, her connections to powerful men in Great Britain, her self-confidence, and her racial pride as a white woman. Yet she had much in common with other woman's rights activists of this period whose lives and commitments were shaped by prevailing discourses of civilization and empire that enabled them to make their own race-specific claims to equality with white men. By her example, French-Sheldon proclaimed white women's capability as explorers and scientists and embedded this construction within an emerging discourse of Western imperialism. In the next chapter, I will examine how Alice Fletcher's involvement in the Indian reform movement of the 1880s and 1890s drew on and consolidated the special attributes that white women purportedly had in bringing civilization to the primitive.

5

Assimilating Primitives

The "Indian Problem" as a "Woman Question"

Never, before I came out among the Indians, did I realize the power
of woman's work, and how she is indeed the mother of the race.
Alice Fletcher, "Among the Omahas" (1882)

Let *us* women give to the destitute tribes Christian homes and missions, for without these no race can rise.
Amelia S. Quinton, Annual Address in Indian's Friend (1899)

Does anybody suppose that if Amelia S. Quinton, Alice Fletcher
and Elaine Goodale [White leaders of the Indian Reform move-
ment] had been given power over our bewildered Indians of the
plains,—that pitiful remnant of a race cut down as ruthlessly as
the forests of the Adirondacks,—[that] this winter's tragedy would
"have crimsoned" our military records?
Frances Willard, address in Transactions of the
National Council in the United States (1891)

IN 1891, THE SAME YEAR THAT May French-Sheldon sailed to Africa, Frances Willard
addressed the National Council of Women, a gathering that included the heads of
most of the major women's organizations from around the country.[1] Willard tried to
clarify what she thought was at the heart of the woman question. "Women as a class
have been the world's chief toilers; it is a world-old proverb that 'their work is never
done.'"[2] Although she could have been thinking about women working in factories,
or as teachers, nurses, and domestic servants, or even all women's unpaid domestic
labor in their own homes, Willard did not make reference to any of these instances. Instead, she drew upon the observations of one of her temperance workers on an Indian
reservation in Florida. As Willard reported, this temperance worker

> saw oxen grazing and a horse roaming the pasture, while two women were grinding at
> the mill, pushing its wheels laboriously by hand. Turning to the old Indian chief who
> sat by, the temperance woman said, with pent-up indignation, "Why don't you yoke
> the oxen or harness the horses and let them turn the mill?" The "calm view" set forth
> in his answer contains a whole body of evidence touching the woman question. Hear
> him: "Horse cost money; ox cost money; *squaw cost nothing.*"[3]

This statement, meant to inspire white women to take a larger view of the woman question and the important civilizing work still before them, contained a number of core truths for white reformers in this period. First, the label "squaw" conjured up an image of an overworked, prematurely aged Indian woman, exploited by a husband who had long since lost any sexual interest in her.[4] Second, this scenario drew on social Darwinian beliefs that Indians remained in a state of barbarism because they refused to allocate labor along acceptable gender lines, protect their women in monogamous family structures, and adopt individualist, capitalist understandings of property ownership. Willard and other white women were convinced that Indians remained inferior to whites as a race *because* they oppressed their women. For white women, successful assimilation of Indians could not come about without the "emancipation" of Indian women from the barbaric practices within their own culture.

After the passage of the Dawes Act in 1887 (which made the granting of U.S. citizenship conditional on Indian conformity to the gender, economic, and religious structures of patriarchal, capitalistic Christian civilization), white women increasingly encouraged each other to expand their understanding of "womanhood" to include the "squaw" and took it upon themselves to mediate between what they defined as a brutal primitive male and his exploited female subject. "There is a sense," Amelia Quinton, president of the Women's National Indian Association (WNIA), wrote in 1888, "in which the Indian Question must become more and more a woman question. When all legal rights are assured, and all fair educational facilities provided, the women and children of the tribes will still be a sacred responsibility laid upon the white women of the land. The true civilization that begins with the child and the home must come through women's work."[5] A feeling of sympathy ensued (reminiscent of abolitionist appeals to a common sisterhood with enslaved black women), since all women everywhere were considered "mothers of the race," responsible for their own races' advancement into civilization. Still, white women believed they had "progressed" further than Indian women because they had had Christian men as protectors. Eventually Indian men would have to become Christians and assume the correct patriarchal role vis-à-vis Indian women. In the meantime, however, white women like Alice Fletcher and the members of the WNIA would assume this role themselves.

At the base of such views was an ambivalence about Indian women's capacity for civilization. On the one hand, white women posited that all women, civilized and primitive, could serve as the agents and promoters of civilization—hence the focus on sending Indian women to schools like Hampton in Virginia and Carlisle in Pennsylvania to train them to become homemakers, teachers, and missionaries. On the other hand, white women considered Indian women, especially ones who "return to the blanket," the main impediment, not just to the racial progress of the tribe, but also to the future of the United States.[6] The primitive woman was therefore heralded as embodying the solution to the Indian problem and at the same time castigated for holding back "the nation." The discourse worked simultaneously as an evangelical declaration of solidarity between white and Indian women, even as it reinforced the superiority of white Christian civilization over heathen Indian cultures. "Let the women then give to the destitute tribes Christian homes and missions, for without these, no nation can rise, for as the women are so will the nation be," stated Quinton, echoing an ambiguous refrain that was becoming axiomatic in white women's political ideology, without specifying exactly which women (or nation) she meant.[7]

In white female reformers' rhetoric, evolutionist theory linked the future of white women, the United States, and destitute Indian tribes by suggesting the need to save, protect, and elevate Indian women. To accomplish this purpose, it was essential to "educate" Indian women about white middle-class norms of domesticity and home-making, and the WNIA made this their prime concern. In 1884, Alice Fletcher, a prominent white reformer and an advocate of dismantling the existing reservation system by allotting individual homesteads to nuclear families, recommended at a Lake Mohonk conference that a fund be started to build homes for the young people returning from the boarding schools at Carlisle and Hampton Institutes. The idea was picked up by Sara Kinney, president of the WNIA's Connecticut chapter, and implemented by the WNIA, which helped build roughly forty new homes on reservations over the next four years.[8] Kinney explained in 1890:

> If we could excite . . . in [Indian women and children] a desire for home-life which should have in it the elements of decency and comfort and progress, we need have no fear for the men. Indian men are curiously like their white neighbors, they can be influenced through their affections, and may be led towards better ways of living by the women and children whom they love. Save [Indian women], and we may be reasonably certain of the salvation of [Indian] men.[9]

For Fletcher and other activists in the WNIA, the most needed reforms were individual (male) ownership of land; monogamous family structures; male support of women and children through farming; traditional log cabins instead of Native American dwellings; Indian women's assumption of white women's domestic duties; learning of English; conversion to Christianity; education of children in missionary, common, or industrial training schools; and adoption of white styles of dress and appearance. Even something so simple as a short haircut for boys became crucially significant, symbolizing the acceptance of "civilized" practices and values. (One missionary reported that as she cut away the locks, she felt barbarism retreating.) Hampton and Carlisle trained Indian boys in agriculture, cattle raising, and mechanical skills and taught Indian girls to tend house, do laundry, cook, and sew. "It is not enough to teach these girls *how* to sweep and scrub and wash and iron, " another missionary teacher explained. "[W]e must strive so to get them in the *habit* of being neat in person and surroundings [so] that they cannot be comfortable otherwise."[10]

Work in anthropology appearing in the 1890s lent support to this approach. For example, Otis Mason argued in *Woman's Share in Primitive Culture* that previous attempts to civilize Indians had failed because earlier policies had been misdirected toward male rather than female Indians. Past attempts to turn Indian men into farmers had been futile because they required a profound transgression of primitive gender relations. To ask the "savage man . . . to lay down a bow and arrow and take up the hoe, a woman's implement" imposed too great a humiliation. "See how this racks his whole being," Mason wrote, "bodily, mentally, and spiritually." Mason believed that less cultural trauma would result from transforming Indian *women's* gender roles, and ultimately the same purpose would be achieved: that is, a gendered division of labor in accordance with the ideology of separate spheres. Having primitive women become the domestic keepers of western-style homes, according to Mason, "need modify their [the Indians'] conceptions and their opinions very little."[11] In keeping with this perspective, reformers measured their success by the degree to which Indian women modeled themselves after middle-class white women and rejected their former practices. "They have fallen out with their old ways of doing things. The hair must now be arranged becomingly, the colors that adorn their persons must correspond, and there is a certain dignity exhibited in their carriage."[12]

Most white reformers in the 1880s and 1890s, including Fletcher, Quinton, and Willard, initially had no doubt that civilization would improve Indian women's lives; rather than have to do backbreaking labor while their menfolk loafed, they would experience the joys of domesticity; they would be protected from sexual exploitation within monogamous, nuclear family structures; and they would become citizens of a home-loving republic and receive the blessings of democracy, even without the vote. In short, Indian women were to be given the gift of patriarchy, with all the protection it afforded.

As I shall show, the discourses of civilization, evolutionary progress, and patriarchal protection brought certain perspectives into view and obscured others, making it difficult for white women to comprehend the ways in which their work to "save" the Indian was the culmination of a cycle of cultural annihilation that had been taking place for more than two centuries. Yet the influence was not entirely in one direction. Civilization-work brought white women like Fletcher, Quinton, and Elaine Goodale into extended contact with Indian cultures, and these women were deeply affected by the experience, both in their personal lives and political outlooks. Goodale married Dr. Charles Eastman, a Santee Sioux, with whom she lived for thirty years, bearing him six children. Fletcher developed a lifelong attachment to an Omaha Indian, Francis La Flesche, a man seventeen years her junior, with whom she lived for forty years. Both women spent years living on western reservations and made Indian rights their lifelong cause, and both became nationally known for their political activism and their philanthropic work among Indians—Fletcher as well for her prolific contribution to the newly developing field of anthropology. Perhaps more than any other person of her day, Fletcher was responsible for developing the severalty policy, which conferred citizenship on "allotted" Indians (Fletcher's term).[13] Due to the efforts of white reformers, the country came to adopt the view that in relation to Indians, separate could not be equal. In the end, however, the main beneficiaries of this civilizing work were white women themselves, as in an odd and unexpected way, their work among Indians brought white women great public visibility and political power, smoothing over any nascent tensions between white women's assumption of a new public role and performance of their traditional responsibilities as mothers and homemakers.[14]

THE FOUNDING OF THE WNIA IN 1879 occurred during one of the most violent periods in the history of white–Native American relations. The decade of the 1870s was one of unceasing raids and counterraids, including the Modoc War of 1872–1873, the Red River War of 1874–1875, and ongoing battles with the Sioux, Nez Perces, Utes, and Apaches, among others. By 1881, as the surrender of Sitting Bull marked the close of the Plains Indian wars, all tribes in the West, except the Apaches, had been compelled to relocate to reservations designated for them in Indian Territory, in what is now Oklahoma.[15]

The white women who became active in the WNIA recognized that whites had a shameful past to overcome in their relation to the Indian.[16] Helen Hunt Jackson's exposé, *A Century of Dishonor* (1881), had laid out this history in detail, and her premature death in 1885 only strengthened other white reformers' resolve to continue in her stead.[17] They knew that the U.S. government routinely made treaties that it did not honor and used the military to squelch resistance. They were highly sensitive to the fact that white administrators of Indian reservations personally profited from the distribution of government rations and were unable to restrain white settlers and railroad developers bent on appropriating reservation land for themselves. Even though the government was helping to finance industrial education programs at Hampton and Carlisle Institutes to buttress ongoing efforts to "civilize" Indians, these programs were widely acknowledged to be insufficient to meet the need. Moreover, despite taking certain initiatives, the government had been unsuccessful in its attempt to purge the reservation system of gross abuses or to end armed conflict between Indians and whites.[18]

At this critical historical juncture, then, Mary Lucinda Bonney, principal of the Chestnut Female Academy, and Amelia Stone Quinton, a former teacher of the school, both members of the First Baptist Church in Philadelphia, founded the Indian Treaty-Keeping and Protective Association in late 1879 (renamed the Women's National Indian Association in 1883).[19] Quinton, born in Jamesville, New York, near Syracuse, had been involved in the woman's movement for several years, most recently as a temperance worker in Brooklyn, but she had also worked among inmates of charitable and correctional institutions in New York City and taught in women's seminaries in Syracuse, New York, and Madison, Georgia.[20] Bonney, born in Hamilton, New York, had had a career as a teacher at girls' seminaries in New Jersey, South Carolina, and Rhode Island. She also served as an officer of the Philadelphia branch of the Woman's Union Missionary Society of America for Heathen Lands and had contributed money to support the sending of female missionaries to eastern countries. Their decision to take up Indian reform and "home missionary" work was sparked by Ponca Chief Standing Bear's lectures about the Ponca relocation of 1877 and newspaper accounts that Bonney had read concerning proposals in Congress to allow whites to acquire land in Indian Territory.[21]

In 1877, the Ponca tribe had been compelled to move from one reservation located in Dakota Territory to a new one in Indian Territory because the government had inadvertently assigned the former reservation to the Sioux. Subjected to great pressure, the Poncas agreed to relocate, but they experienced so much hardship in Indian Territory that, in the spring of 1879, Standing Bear decided to move his people back home. When Standing Bear stopped at the Omaha Agency, he was arrested. With the help of

Thomas H. Tibbles, a white reporter from Omaha City who publicized the cause, the case reached a federal court, which ordered Standing Bear and his party released from jail, and ruled that an Indian, as a person in the eyes of the law, could not be deprived of life, liberty, or property without due process of law, as mandated by the Fourteenth Amendment. The Poncas were allowed to remain in Nebraska, but the question of where they were to live remained unresolved. To keep national attention focused on their plight, Standing Bear embarked on a speaking tour in the east, accompanied by a young Omaha interpreter, Suzette La Flesche, her half-brother Francis La Flesche, and her future husband, Thomas Tibbles.[22]

Standing Bear's eloquent lectures prompted Bonney and Quinton to take action in ways that, by this time, were conventionally understood as appropriately feminine. Among white women active in church work in the Philadelphia area they circulated petitions calling for the honoring of government treaties and presented them to President Rutherford Hayes and the Congress: the first, in February 1880, had thirteen thousand signatures; another one later that same year had over fifty thousand signatures and also demanded the granting of citizenship to Indians; a third, circulated in late 1881, which bore one-hundred thousand signatures, called for the allotment of separate plots out of the collectively held reservation land to individual Indian householders. This third petition, with its "lands in severalty" policy, was introduced in the Senate by Henry L. Dawes of Massachusetts in 1882.[23]

Standing Bear's speeches also profoundly affected Alice Cunningham Fletcher, (1838–1923), who was to become the most famous woman in the Indian Reform movement and a key formulator of the final version of the severalty policy that was contained in the Dawes Act of 1887.[24] Decades later, Fletcher tried to recapture for a younger audience the effect that Standing Bear and Suzette La Flesche ("clad in the garb of a white woman") had had on white audiences in Cooper Union in New York City and Faneuil Hall in Boston: "The old stereotyped picture of the savage faded. . . . The need to push the question as to whether or no the Indian was 'a person' vanished. . . . [T]he skill with which the eloquence of the Chief was rendered into ringing English by the young Indian woman, showed that the door of language could be unlocked and intelligent relations made possible between the two races."[25]

Fletcher immediately took up the cause and within a few years had become a very powerful advocate of Indian rights—a power that she garnered through a number of channels: the organized woman's movement, women's clubs and philanthropies, church groups, missionary societies, Hampton and Carlisle Institutes, Peabody Museum of Harvard University, the Bureau of Ethnology in Washington, D.C., the Bureau of Indian Affairs, the Department of the Interior, and Congress, as well as the organizations of the Indian reform movement—the WNIA, Herbert Welsh's Indian Rights Association, and Albert Smiley's Lake Mohonk Conferences of Friends of the Indian. The outlines of her career show how an individual white woman could develop extraordinary political power even before women could vote or hold elective office. In 1883, Fletcher was appointed as a special agent of the Department of the Interior, employed to implement the new allotment policy among the Omaha in Nebraska. In 1885, in response to a request from the Senate, Fletcher drew up a lengthy

(693-page) compendium of U.S. policies, entitled *Indian Education and Civilization,* a document that solidly established her as a foremost expert on Indian affairs. After the passage of the Dawes legislation in 1887, Fletcher was again hired as a special agent, this time to administer allotments among the Winnebago Indians of Nebraska (1887–1889) and the Nez Perces in Idaho (1889–1893). During the 1880s and 1890s, in addition to her government work, Fletcher also became a highly acclaimed and widely published ethnographer, respected for her scientific expertise on the Omaha and Nez Perces. In 1890, she was awarded a lifelong fellowship through the Peabody Museum, which removed all pressure of having to earn her living, and which transformed her into the foremost woman scientist in the nation (the astronomer Maria Mitchell having died in 1889).

Fletcher grew up in New York City and was raised by a widowed mother and a stepfather with whom she did not get along. Educated in private schools, she eventually became a governess in the family of a school friend (the father, Conis Conant, was a wealthy Brooklyn merchant) and was supported with a large salary for many years (from age eighteen to thirty-two). When she left the Conants in the early 1870s, financially independent, she moved to Manhattan, joined Sorosis, and helped plan the first Woman's Congress, at which the Association for the Advancement of Women (AAW) was founded in October 1873. As secretary and later cochair of one of the AAW's key committees, Fletcher planned its annual congresses from 1873 through 1881, becoming acquainted with some of the most influential and important women in the woman's movement of this period, including AAW presidents Mary Livermore, Maria Mitchell, and Julia Ward Howe.[26]

Then, unexpectedly, the financial depression of the mid-1870s wiped out Fletcher's investments, and she was forced to turn to public speaking to earn her living. In 1879, when Fletcher first met Standing Bear and Suzette and Francis La Flesche in Boston, she was forty-one years old and had been lecturing on topics dealing with Indians for several years. She had become a serious student of ethnology, informally studying under Frederick Ward Putnam, the director of the Peabody Museum at Harvard University. When Suzette La Flesche and Thomas Tibbles returned to Boston in early 1881, Fletcher approached them about the possibility of visiting them on their reservation along the Missouri River in Nebraska, about one-hundred miles north of Omaha City. They arranged for her to spend several weeks during the summer camping in Dakota Territory among the Sioux—a tribe that for whites was (in)famous for its longstanding conflict with the government, its defeat of General George Custer at Little Big Horn on June 24, 1876, and the recent surrender and imprisonment of Sitting Bull and his followers at Fort Randall. Thus, when Fletcher set off for Omaha City in the summer of 1881 (just five years after Custer's defeat), she did not know what to expect, but she left with a plan: she was going to focus her study on the life of Indian women in the hope, as she wrote Lucian Carr, an associate at the Peabody Museum, that there would be "something to be learned in the line of woman's life in the social state represented by the Indians that . . . will be of value not only ethnologically but help toward the historical solution of 'the woman question' in our midst."[27]

As historian Joan Mark so perceptively points out, what Fletcher saw on this first trip was deeply colored by her study of ethnology and the preconceptions she had about Indian women's degradation.[28] At this juncture, she believed that Indians were mired in barbarism because they did not know how to cooperate with one another. Later she would add that their backwardness also resulted from tribal restrictions on individual initiative and the absence of individual ownership of land.[29] Yet she was deeply impressed by how much work Indian women did, admitting, "[N]ever before . . . did I realize the power of woman's work, and how she is indeed the mother of the race. I knew theoretically that from her lap sprang the industries; here I see them starting from her knees."[30] Moreover, while it was clear to her that Indian women controlled their own property, and that the economic well-being of the family was dependent on their labor, Fletcher believed that they would have to give up much of their traditional work in order for their race to progress from barbarism to civilization. She was also profoundly moved by what she interpreted as Sitting Bull's request that she help Indian women adjust to what they both knew would be a painful transition. "'You are a woman,'" Fletcher recorded Sitting Bull's words in her diary, publishing them in the *Woman's Journal* in 1882. "'You have come to me as a friend. Pity my women. We men owe what we have to them. They have worked for us . . . but in the new life their work is taken away. For my men I see a future; for my women I see nothing. Pity them; help them, if you can.' It was a touching natural speech," Fletcher added. "The women had been the tillers of the soil and now the men must take their work in the change of life. What shall the faithful women find to do?"[31] For Fletcher, this was to be the beginning of a lifelong rumination on the Indian Problem as a woman question.

In May 1883, Fletcher went to the Omaha reservation, with Francis La Flesche as her interpreter, to implement an experimental policy in individual allotments, out of a belief that if Indians were to "progress" they would have to adopt the monogamous family structures and gendered economic division of labor encompassed in whites' ideology of separate spheres. The policy was controversial among the Omahas, and a group of twelve families who banded together as "the Council Fire" opposed individual allotments of the reservation land. However, Chief Joseph La Flesche, Francis's father, was among the first to take possession of his assigned land, and others followed. Then, Fletcher got soaked in a sudden downpour on July 3, caught a chill, and lay in bed for eight months, recovering slowly from what was eventually diagnosed as inflammatory rheumatism, an illness that aged her prematurely and left her lame. During these months, her authority among the Omahas declined precipitously, as many who had been opposed to allotments interpreted her illness as divine retribution.[32]

Fletcher had La Flesche set up his desk by her bed so that she could continue with her work. After seven months, with still one-third of the allotments to make, Fletcher decided to implement her policy with force. According to Mark, Fletcher had the reservation police round up the resistors, force them to appear before her, and compel them "to make their mark in the presence of witnesses indicating that they accepted a designated piece of land."[33] Mark estimates that roughly one-fourth of the Omahas actively supported the allotment program, one-third actively opposed it, and the rest were persuaded to go along.[34] In all, Fletcher allotted 75,931 acres in 954 separate allotments to 1,194 persons. About 50,000 acres were sold to white settlers, and the remaining 55,450 acres were reserved for the children who would be born during the next twenty-five years. In line with whites' patriarchal customs, wives were not given their own allotments. Heads of families received 160 acres; single persons over eighteen (of both sexes) received 80 acres each, and children under eighteen received 40.[35]

In June 1884, her work allocating land among the Omaha completed, Fletcher took the train back east to Washington, D.C. For the next several years, she worked both as an employee and lobbyist of the national government, continuing all the while to write ethnographic papers for publication in the newly emerging professional journals of anthropology. She prepared the U.S. government's Indian Bureau exhibit for the New Orleans Exposition of 1884, and in the fall she attended her first Lake Mohonk conference, where she was "made quite a heroine of," as she confided to her friend Caroline Dall. As Mark informs us, the Lake Mohonk reformers were generally suspicious of ethnologists like Fletcher, whom they believed wanted to keep Indians mired in barbarism in order to study their traditional cultures. But according to Indian reformer Philip Garrett, Fletcher was deemed "'the single brilliant exception'; her 'philanthropy swallowed up her anthropology.'"[36]

It is during this period, the mid-1880s, that Alice Fletcher came to a comprehensive view of the task facing the nation and decided on a final strategy. She understood there to be a total of 262,000 Indians living in the United States. Approximately sixty-four thousand were part of the so-called Five Civilized Tribes residing in Indian Territory (Oklahoma) and the Six Nations of New York—groups that were eventually exempted from the Dawes legislation. This left 197,973 Indians, as Fletcher computed it, whose relations to whites had to be reconfigured and whose rights to citizenship needed to be recognized. These 198,000 Indians controlled 123 million acres of land on 124 reservations (excluding Indian Territory) and were under the authority of fifty-six agencies that were scattered across eleven states and nine territories. To some reformers—Lyman Abbott, for example—the problem seemed easily manageable; less than two hundred thousand was a small number, especially in comparison to eight million blacks. But Fletcher fully appreciated the difficulties: only a small percentage of the reservation land (roughly eight million acres, or less than five acres per Indian) was believed to be tillable, and this land was unevenly distributed across the 124 reservations. Complicating the problem still further was a reluctance on the part of Indian men to enter into the occupation of farming, which in Indian societies, Fletcher understood, was conventionally assigned to the opposite sex.[37]

Fletcher also understood that Indians had very different understandings of land tenure from Europeans, and this was the first thing Fletcher believed would have to be altered if Indians were going to adopt "proper" gender relations. Fletcher declared, "Tribal control, therefore, which ignores the individual and the family (as established in civilized society) must be overturned, and this can only be effected surely, by giving individual ownership of the land, and thus setting up the legal homestead. Until these changes are made, all labor in behalf of the elevation, education, and civilization of the Indian will be but partially effective."[38]

Ultimately, Fletcher came to the conclusion that Indians' traditional beliefs and practices about self-government, land, property, family, and gender could not be accommodated. Evolutionary progress demanded that Indians adopt the same economic and household arrangements as whites; private property, patriarchal marriage, a gendered division of labor that conformed to whites' ideology of separate spheres—all these, she believed, were crucial to bringing about Indian equality with whites. Based on her experience among the Omaha, Fletcher knew how difficult it would be to get two-thirds of the tribes to vote in favor of allotment policies. The solution, therefore, was to make allotments mandatory. "The work must be done for them [Indians]," Fletcher insisted, "whether they approve or not."[39]

The final version of the Dawes Act of 1887, therefore, made no provision for tribal consent and had several main features intended to do away with collective land ownership, matriarchal forms of gender practices, and tribal authority. First, it provided for allotments of land to individual Native Americans as a first step toward granting U.S. citizenship. Second, it specified different amounts of land to be granted to different categories of people, thereby encouraging Native Americans to give up their traditional forms of kinship relations and to adopt white forms. The same numbers were used as in the Omaha allotments: male heads of households would receive 160 acres (wives none), unmarried men and women 80 acres each, and children 40 acres. But discretion about how to categorize individuals—whether to recognize specific individuals as married or not—was left up to government agents. Third, and most important, the Dawes Act deprived tribal authorities of unallotted land, specifying that all "surplus" lands would be sold to the government and opened to white settlement. Since the targeted Indian population was under two hundred thousand and reservations included 123,000,000 acres—or more than six hundred acres per person—this provision had tremendous significance. In the end, the Dawes legislation provided for a forced transference of a large portion of Indian land from tribal control to the United States government. (Since the policy was mandatory, tribal authorities could not vote to accept or decline these provisions.)[40] There were whites at the time who were critical of this legislation, predicting that "under the profession of enabling the Indians to become citizens" the United States would destroy Indians' sense of themselves as independent peoples and nations. As one unidentified editorialist remarked, severalty bills were a "sham disguise. . . . They ought to be entitled bills for annihilating the Indian nations, in order to steal their lands."[41]

Fletcher, in contrast, believed that these vast landholdings were not "fully utilized" by Indian tribes and actually impeded the "advance of the Indian by isolating him from the industries that teem throughout the length and breadth of our land." Isolation on remote reservations, Fletcher argued further, increased the Indian's "dependence upon the government," kept him ignorant "of his own short-comings," did nothing to foster ambition, and left him impoverished.[42] She thus praised Severalty legislation for opening the way "for the legal release of the Indian from his hitherto anomalous position in our midst. . . . The Indian may now become a free man; free from the thralldom of the tribe; free from the domination of the reservation system; free to enter into the body of our citizens. This bill may therefore be considered as the Magna Charta of the Indians of our country."[43]

In defense of the decision to deny tribes the right to vote to decline allotments, Fletcher offered the following rationale.

> Under the combined influence of the chiefs and the agency system, the Indians are kept in the irresponsibility of perpetual childhood. The only door of release opens through the breaking-up of the Reservation and giving individual ownership to tracts of land greater or less in extent, according to the nature of the soil, thereby extinguishing tribal ownership, and in a great measure, tribal authority. By such a division of the land, the *individual would be set free and become the inheritor of his own labor,* and *the important point in social advance would be gained by having the legal family established.* . . . It seems clear that in any legislation upon land for the Indians, the allotment of the land in severalty should be made the rule, and the matter not left permanently optional with the Indians. . . . To leave severalty optional and dependent upon a two-thirds vote of any tribe, is to rivet the chains which bind the Indian to a hopeless position. . . . [I]t is surely imposing too grave a task upon the Indian to bid him decide his own future condition; particularly as he is now standing facing the forward rush of civilization with its difficult ideas, laws and customs, already closing him in with irresistible force.[44]

By likening Indians to children who lacked the maturity and experience to know what was good for them, Fletcher justified depriving them of power over their own lives, arguing it would be pointless to consult with or defer to them on questions concerning their future. This metaphor was widespread in national discourse during the period (see fig. 1-1 and the discussion thereof in chapter 1), but this fact should not absolve Fletcher of responsibility for her role in perpetuating the view of Indians as dependents. The metaphor of the Indian as a child clearly worked to bolster the authority that Fletcher, as a white woman, wanted to assume. The custom of referring to Indian men as children or wards made it possible for the gender inversion that was necessary for white *women* to become rulers and protectors of Indian *men.* Casting Indians as children and wards also made it easier to placate white men who resented white women's increasing political visibility, and to argue for the naturalness of white women assuming positions of authority and power. Who better than a white woman would make a suitable protector for a vulnerable child? "We have inherited the guardianship of the Indians," Fletcher insisted, and "we must therefore act for the benefit of our wards in a way that shall fit them to enter upon their majority." "We owe it to our own honor . . . to act as faithful guardians."[45]

Fletcher used prevailing ideologies about evolutionary progress, the supremacy of white civilization, and white women's natural role as mothers to take the sting out of a policy that would have been roundly rejected as antidemocratic had it been formulated for whites. Interestingly, ideas about motherhood and guardianship also figured in the way Fletcher conceived of her lifelong relationship with Francis La Flesche, the young Omaha man who had served as her interpreter during her first stint as an allotment officer on the Omaha reservation in 1883. Despite the difference in their ages, a deep attachment formed between them, with Alice claiming to feel toward Francis what a mother would feel toward a son. At one point, she even began adoption procedures, giving this up when it became obvious that Francis would have to relinquish his surname. Regardless, the two lived together in Washington, D.C., from 1884 until

Fletcher's death in 1923. From 1890 to 1906, Fletcher also shared her life and home with Jane Gay, with whom she had a loving, if not erotic, relationship. Fletcher never married; La Flesche did. His marriage, to Rosa Bourassa, which took place March 15, 1906, a date carefully chosen to coincide with Fletcher's sixty-eighth birthday (La Flesche was fifty), lasted less than a year and reconfigured the household in an unpredictable way. Within weeks of the wedding, Francis, Jane, and Alice all became ill. In May, a "scene" occurred at Fletcher's bedside, and two weeks later Jane Gay packed up and left the household permanently. Two weeks after that, Fletcher went to Mexico, where she stayed for six months, leaving La Flesche alone in the house with his wife. By the end of December, after a night-long conversation with Fletcher, La Flesche had decided to end his marriage. Rather than becoming a family of four, La Flesche's marriage reaffirmed Francis and Alice's commitment to each other. Francis left Rosa, Alice gave up Jane.[46]

The unconventional way in which Fletcher lived her own personal life makes it even more ironic that she took it upon herself to enforce monogamous domestic arrangements among Indians. She did this, she insisted, for Indian women's own protection. In one instance, Fletcher told of her decision to prevent a sixteen-year-old girl from being forced to marry a man she did not love. The girl, Fletcher related, was sold by her brother to become the second wife of her older sister's husband and repeatedly tried to run away from her appointed husband. Each time her family forced her to return to the man she was supposed to share with her older sister (in part to protect the family's property from being taken by their brother-in-law). Finally, the girl managed to run off with another young man, against the wishes of her mother and brother. At this moment, Fletcher "allott[ed] the girl as the wife of the young man" and refused to "yield to the pleading of mother or any other one to give her land separately." Fletcher explained that she was acting merely "to protect the young people," but she feared that her attempts would prove futile: "the Indian custom[s] hold good, and there is no [white] law to guard the girl, or the property of the brother, who certainly did wrong in selling his sister. . . . Were there law, these customs would cease to be practiced; as it is, they will continue in spite of agents' attempts to have a better state of affairs."[47]

IN THE 1880s, FLETCHER COMBINED HER dual identities as an ethnographer and government agent into the single role of advocate of political equality for Indians. Where her contemporaries saw a tension between the two identities, Fletcher did not experience any contradiction. In fact, she was delighted when she received her first appointment on the Omaha reservation because she thought that this position would enable her to continue her ethnographic work almost full-time. As a scientific expert, she would be able to assemble the knowledge that she believed would help the government determine the best methods to elevate, purify, and assimilate evolutionary inferiors into a higher civilization. Like most ethnologists in this period, Fletcher did not study other cultures in order to criticize or find alternatives to Anglo-Saxon practices. (Margaret Mead would introduce this practice in the 1920s.) Because of her evolutionist perspective on the world, she never doubted the superiority of her own culture or saw any reason to look for alternative models elsewhere.

In 1899, however, a fundamental change occurred in her thinking about assimilation. Joan Mark attributes the change to a second trip that Fletcher took to the Omaha reservation in the summer of 1897, which revealed to her that Indians' lives on the reservation had deteriorated from what they had been four years earlier when she had made her allotments.[48] It is also possible that the Spanish-American-Filipino War helped to alter her perspective, allowing her to see more clearly the cultural annihilation that was the flip side of racial assimilation. Now Fletcher began to advocate the importance of every racial group "having a [rightful] claim to [its] past history, a right to build one's life into its present." Fletcher even began to sense that Indian cultures might be able to bring a new perspective to *white* women's rights: "We must endeavor to reach the Indian's standpoint if we would learn what was the true relation of man and woman to each other," Fletcher claimed for the first time.[49] Fletcher also felt it imperative to correct misreadings from the past (some of which she had helped to promote) so that "they [Indians] who are the natural inheritors, and we [whites] who share their heritage, may more truthfully estimate the past history of this continent."[50]

To further this end, Fletcher urged young Indians, especially those who were "thoughtful and educated," to embark on the recording of cultural practices that were quickly disappearing from everyday life. She wanted to "rescue" these rituals before they all "pass[ed] away with the life of the old people." But here we must be careful not to make too much of this change in Fletcher's thinking. Although she insisted on the importance of recording native culture so that it "could foster a noble pride in the Indian" and serve as a "contribution to the enlightenment of the future," Fletcher's identification as a full-time ethnographer made this new position one that was solidly in her interest. No longer needing to balance the dual careers of government agent and ethnologist, Fletcher's main ambition was to record and publish as much as she could. Fletcher never relinquished her role as the preeminent scientific authority on Indian culture and reserved for herself the status of final arbiter, noting she would be careful not to "encourage false estimates of ideas born under conditions of limited knowledge."[51]

Fletcher continued to reflect on the early conversation about the status of Indian women that she had had with Sitting Bull during her first visit to the Sioux in 1881. In 1899, she published another version of it:

> Sitting Bull . . . turned to me, saying: "You are a woman; take pity on my women, for they have no future. The young men can be like the white men, till the soil, supply the food and clothing, they will take the work out of the hands of the women, and the women, to whom we have owed everything in the past, will be stripped of all which gave them power and position among the people. Give a future to my women!" He drew a ring from his finger, and said; "Take this to remind you of my request. Help my women."[52]

Now, in 1899, at the height of public debate about the United States' role in the Philippines, Fletcher saw a new lesson in these words—a warning about the deterioration in the status of *all* women, not just Indian women, that came about as societies moved from savagery through barbarism into civilization. Intending her remarks to encompass white women in the United States as well as Indian women, Fletcher issued a solemn warning: "Woman's work has been taken from her by man, and with each appropriation she has been bereft of importance in the community."[53] But Fletcher still could not move beyond this insight to a more forceful critique of patriarchal gender relations within the supposedly advanced civilization of whites. The best she could do was to entreat white people to be more sympathetic with the Indian woman's "longings for her previous life," in which her labor had been valued and her status in relation to Indian men greater than it had become under "civilized" conditions.

Fletcher's willingness to revise old ethnographic approaches to grant Indians more agency in recording their past marked her as a radical in her day. This radicalism is even more salient if we compare her to other women reformers, like Mary Collins and Alice Crane, who also wrote on the Indian Question—for the *Arena* and the *Southern Workman* respectively—in the early 1900s. By this time, Collins and Crane had lost patience with what they understood to be missionaries' misguided attempts at kindness and sympathy toward "backward" peoples. They did not consider rations a just system of economic redress, but rather a foolish and ineffective form of almsgiving. They blamed the government for its pampering of the Indian—calling government support "degrading to [Indian] manhood," and they held the Indian responsible for a willful, illogical resistance to the white man's civilization.[54] In contrast to Kinney, who had argued twenty years earlier that Indian men would follow their women eagerly into civilization, Collins stated flatly, "The needs of wife and children do not appeal to him." Collins understood this as "the natural result of [the Indian's] heredity" yet insisted that "these traits [be] altered" through a system that would give Indian men more incentive to work. "They will only learn to work for the sake of results. . . . If the government would hire more Indians, pay better wages, and give less, it would help to forward this cause."[55] Crane was even more adamant about ending all economic supports: "let him loose and make him work or starve."[56] In contrast, Fletcher never relinquished her belief that Indians were the equals of whites in their capacity for civilization, a conviction that coexisted without any tension with her cultural ethnocentrism. If Indians had not yet fully been assimilated, the fault lay not with them but with the failure of whites to properly execute their civilizing missions.

EVOLUTIONIST DISCOURSES OF CIVILIZATION provided the lens through which white women focused their efforts to address "the Indian problem" as a "woman question," but their work among Indians also prompted them to turn the lens back upon themselves, reaffirming their conviction that motherhood and homemaking were woman's highest callings. Paradoxically, their work among Indians gave them renewed appreciation for the racial significance of their own domesticity. As early as 1882, Alice Fletcher had remarked that only after living among the Omaha did she realize the "power of woman's work." Twenty years later, she was still trying to comprehend what she had seen. Evoking the same image that Frances Willard had offered to the assembly of white women at the National Council of Women, Fletcher wrote for the *Woman's Journal*:

There is a picture frequently presented to illustrate the degraded position of the Indian woman and the lazy selfishness of the Indian man. She is seen trudging with burdens on her back, driving the laden pony or dog, and looking after the children concerned with nothing but her duties; while he, with quiver slung over his shoulder, bow in hand, or his gun resting across his saddle, rides on horseback in picturesque costume, apparently free from labor or care. When the journey ends, the woman sets up the tent, gathers the wood, makes the fire, cooks the food and serves the family; while the man, after watering his horse, and turning it out to graze, returns to the tent, drops on the ground, and smokes, or falls asleep until called to partake of the meal.[57]

As Fletcher knew, this image was sure to raise white women's ire: for here was the by now classic inversion of civilized gender relations: the Indian man nonchalantly enjoying his leisure while the Indian woman labored from morn to night. From the perspective of middle-class white women, it was supposed to be the reverse: man laboring in business, supporting a wife who no longer had to perform domestic chores. The leaders of Christian missionary societies, as women with means, employed others to help them with domestic tasks. They knew, as Mary Abigail Dodge had put it, that domestication was the death of women. But where Willard and most other white women were affronted by this "abuse" of the squaw, Fletcher was trying to get her audience to have renewed appreciation for the value that Indian culture placed on Indian women's work. "Under the old tribal regime woman's industries were essential to the very life of the people," Fletcher explained, "and their value was publicly recognized. . . . [H]er work was exalted ceremonially. . . . Her influence in the growth and development of tribal government, tribal ceremonies, and tribal power, shows that her position had always been one of honor rather than one of slavery and degradation."[58] Fletcher knew that her outlook would seem to her white audience "to run counter to ordinary observation," but she knew herself to be the better judge, and she cautioned her colleagues in the woman's movement against making "superficial observation[s] from a foreign standpoint." She felt the irony poignantly: Indian women, who had been honored for their work, were now to give it up to become ordinary housewives.

It was an irony that women of Fletcher's generation could never fully examine; nor could they cover it up entirely. These women shunned housework themselves; they occupied themselves in activities outside the home, for which they adamantly refused payment so that they could perpetuate the myth that as women of leisure, they did not work. Fletcher's own feelings must have been deeply conflicted. Fletcher herself had never known domestic drudgery or financial dependence on a husband, and these were not experiences she lamented missing. She knew firsthand what it meant to fall from the leisure class to laboring status (she had been independently wealthy in the early 1870s); and she knew how she felt when she was once again relieved of the need to work for her living (as a result of having received a lifetime fellowship).

Primitive women's labor, and the respect it was accorded in their own cultures, presented a potential opening for feminists who were critical of their own dependency and confinement within the domestic sphere. But evolution's construction of racial progress prevented them from proceeding down this road. Fletcher tentatively headed in this direction (and Margaret Mead would take up this lead in the late 1920s, soon after Fletcher's death), but in the intervening decades from 1900 to 1920, feminists like Charlotte Perkins Gilman and Mary Roberts Smith Coolidge would choose a different path. Rather than celebrate primitive society for offering civilized women a better alternative, Gilman held primitives responsible for white women's relegation to the home. On the face of it, the argument seems patently absurd—how could primitives who did not have a gendered division of labor that relegated woman to the home bequeath this legacy to civilized societies? Yet Gilman's contribution to feminism was to explain how this indeed had taken place. For her, there was no doubt about it: patriarchy was an invention of the primitive, and sexual differences were a constraining legacy that would have to be overthrown if the white race were ever to advance beyond its primitive heritage. Gilman's generation—the "new woman" of the 1890s—disavowed the domestic sphere as a site of woman's protection and emancipation, insisting that escape from the home, rather than protection within it, was the only means by which white women could attain their freedom and equality.

IN THE NEXT CHAPTER, I turn to the evolutionist feminism of Charlotte Perkins Gilman and Mary Roberts Smith Coolidge, two important theorists who offered searing critiques of white women's oppression under civilization. Yet, remarkably, their critiques served only to fix more firmly the evolutionary boundary between the primitive and the civilized even as they severed the link between civilization and sexual difference. Their feminism both drew on and reinforced dominant discourses that constructed the white middle-class woman as the symbolic and physical embodiment of civilization.

6

Eliminating Sex Distinctions from Civilization

The Feminist Theories of Charlotte Perkins Gilman and Mary Roberts Smith Coolidge

[A]ll that makes for civilisation, for progress, for the growth of humanity up and on toward the *race* ideal—takes place outside the home. This is what has been denied to the lady of the house— merely all human life! . . . *Race characteristics belong in equal measure to either sex,* [my emphasis] and the misfortune of the house-bound woman is that she is denied time, place, and opportunity to develop those characteristics.

Charlotte Perkins Gilman, The Home (1903)

It is scarcely half a century since China was an unknown country, and the Chinese—to our complacent view—a weird, incredible, uncivilized people; yet in that time China has risen to be one of the greater powers. . . . Surely, if in so short a time the "Heathen Chinee" can rise to be a progressive human being in our estimation, *it is not impossible that [white] women may become social entities,* [my emphasis] whose acquired "femininity" may be modifying faster than the carefully digested ideas of scientific observers.

Mary Roberts Smith Coolidge,
Why Women Are So (1912)

It is necessary, then, to understand Feminism as an evolutionary development.

Beatrice Forbes-Roberston Hale,
What Women Want (1914)

WHITE WOMEN WHO SUPPORTED THE abolition of the Indian reservation system were intent on eliminating racial differences in order to transform primitive women into civilized women. They believed this endeavor was crucial both to saving the entire race of Indians from evolutionary extinction and to freeing Indian women from the sexist oppression of their own cultures. To do this, Anglo-Protestant women insisted on the incorporation of patriarchal gender relations into Native American cultures as part of an assimilationist strategy to eliminate the racial traits that they deemed primitive. Even when Anglo-Protestant women were able or willing to acknowledge (and usually they were not) that Native American women would have to give up power, economic advantages, and status to assimilate into white civilization, they still insisted on assimilation as the first step toward making Christian citizens out of Indian primitives.

Charlotte Perkins Gilman (1860-1935) and Mary Roberts Smith Coolidge (1860-1945), two important feminist theorists of the early twentieth century, sympathized with this assimilationist endeavor and, like Alice Fletcher and other members of the WNIA, looked to the government to play a major role in this process. Gilman, who was five years old when the Civil War ended, thought that Reconstruction and its aftermath had demonstrated the possibilities for an enlarged assimilationist program and that "the African race" had progressed rapidly since emancipation. She was optimistic that this progress would continue.[1] But Gilman also believed that a large segment of American Negroes were rejecting white cultural norms; refusing to work and support families; and creating havoc and social disorder—in short, interfering with the ongoing evolutionary progress of whites. Gilman wrote:

> Transfusion of blood is a simple matter compared with the transfusion of civilization; yet that is precisely what is going on between us and the negro race. . . . We have to consider the unavoidable presence of a large body of aliens, *of a race widely dissimilar and in many respects inferior, whose present status is to us a social injury.* . . . What can we do to promote the development of the backward race so that it may become an advantageous element in the community?[2]

Gilman argued that all African Americans, men and women, who had not yet attained "a certain grade of citizenship" should be forced to join "industrial armies" and compelled to perform menial labor. Universal education should be provided for the children. "Decent, self-supporting, progressive negroes" would not need to enlist in these armies, "but the whole body of negroes who do not progress, who are not self-supporting, and who are degenerating into an increasing percentage of social burdens or actual criminals should be taken hold of by the state."[3] In other words, Negro men who, by breeding or education, could demonstrate their civilized status by working hard, supporting families, living temperately, and worshipping Christianity were to be accorded the rights of citizens; those who acted as primitives (were lazy, drunk, lascivious, or unable to support themselves and their dependents) were to be imprisoned and compelled to work so that white Americans could continue, unencumbered, in their efforts to evolve a more perfect civilization. Gilman admitted that "a certain percentage of degenerates and criminals would have to be segregated and cared for," but if they were placed in institutions that would prevent them from reproducing, she argued, the state would benefit greatly from "cutting off the supply of these degenerates." . . .[4] Even in her day, Gilman's solution seemed harsh, and an anonymous critic in the New York *Literary Digest* called her proposal "a system of enforced labor, like those which have disgraced countries like Egypt."[5]

Gilman's proposals for blacks' assimilation were grounded in her enduring conviction of the superiority of white civilization. Gilman believed that whites were a superior race because they had created an advanced civilization, and she was convinced that the racial advancement of nonwhite peoples was conditional on their having contact with white civilization. This ethnocentrism, sometimes dismissed by white scholars as a puzzling inconsistency within Gilman's gender egalitarianism, has recently been understood as the foundational basis of Gilman's feminism. As Gail Bederman has shown, Gilman's "feminism was inextricably rooted in the white supremacism of 'civilization' [discourse]."[6]

Gilman saw no contradiction between these views: for her, white supremacy was entirely consistent with a belief in equality between the sexes. Nor would she have considered herself a racist because she believed that individuals, while inheriting the acquired characteristics of their race, could ultimately transcend their racial heritage through education and upbringing. In this way, Gilman, like other white progressives in the early twentieth century, downplayed blackness as a permanent category of social inferiority: Negroes were not to be branded uncivilizable as a race but judged individually on the basis of their adherence to middle-class, gendered social norms. Civilization was a crucially important category in Gilman's thought—the key to how she envisioned (white) women's sexual equality with (white) men. In Gilman's view, civilized women were both racially superior to noncivilized peoples generally, and racially similar to civilized men—the racial similarity more than compensated for any sexual inferiority. Shared racial inheritance meant that men and women of the same race had more in common with one another than they did with the same sex of different races. In Gilman's words, "there is more difference in social evolution between a civilized man and an Ainu man than there is between their relative degrees of masculinity; and similarly there is more difference in social evolution between a civilized woman and an Ainu woman than there is in their relative femininity."[7]

Like Fletcher, Gilman believed that the key to uncivilized peoples' racial advancement lay in their adopting the gender practices (the cult of domesticity, the separation of spheres, and the ideals of Victorian womanhood) that she, as a feminist, found oppressive in her own life and was determined to abolish from white civilization. Yet the contradiction, so apparent to us, was not visible to Gilman for the same reason that it was not visible to Fletcher: these women understood social evolution as an unilinear stage process. As each race proceeded from savagery through barbarism to civilization, the matriarchal structures of savage or primitive societies would be replaced with the patriarchal structures of civilization. Only after industrial civilization had been attained could a race become fully egalitarian in its treatment of women.

What is imperative to grasp, however, is not simply the cultural ethnocentrism or racial prejudice of these early feminist thinkers, but the historical relationship between the simultaneous emergence of feminist ideology and assimilationism as two components of a culturally comprehensive racial politics. Both Gilman and Mary Roberts Smith Coolidge drew important lessons from the assimilation of foreigners and primitives as they articulated a new ideology that they and others explicitly, self-consciously identified as "feminist." If racial traits could be eliminated from foreigners and primitive peoples by their conformity to the gender roles of civilized society (enabling them to move up the hierarchy of evolution), then certainly the historically developed sexual traits of white women—now redefined as "primitive survivals" within Christian civilization—could be abolished as well. As Coolidge put it, "if in so short a time the 'Heathen Chinee' can rise to be a progressive human being in our estimation, *it is not impossible that women may become social entities, whose acquired 'femininity' may be modifying faster than the carefully digested ideas of scientific observers.*"[8] In this way, Gilman and Coolidge applied assimilationist ideologies toward a new goal, calling for the eradication of so-called primitive sexual traits within (white) women so as to accelerate the evolution of civilized society.

In other words, white feminist thinkers of the early twentieth century, unlike their nineteenth-century predecessors, reviewed their country's recent treatment of primitives and came to an optimistic conclusion: assimilation of these nonwhites had worked. "The African race," Gilman declared, "with the advantage of contact without more advanced stage of evolution, has made more progress in a few generations than any other race has ever done in the same time, except the Japanese."[9] Traits previously considered to be biologically fixed in a racial primitive had proven amenable to change. If primitives could be so improved within such a short time, then so could (civilized) women. The supposed biological fixity of the white woman's sexual difference—her greater emotionality, inability to reason well, physical weakness—all this could be altered within a relatively short period. This is what Coolidge meant when she said that "in some aspects, the woman-questions are analogous to race questions."[10] Gilman agreed. "Our own general history," Gilman wrote, "with its swift, resistless Americanization of all kinds of foreigners, shows the same thing. . . . From the foreigner of every sort the American is made."[11]

The key, however, was convincing others that sexual difference *should* be eliminated—for it was not just misogynists or social conservatives who were insisting on the naturalness and social benefit of sexual difference. As I have noted repeatedly, sexual difference had been accepted by the woman's movement of the late nineteenth century as the defining feature of white women's contribution to white civilization. Gilman's key contribution to feminist theory was to recast sexual difference not as the touchstone of Christian civilization but as a "primitive survival" within Christian civilization—a detrimental vestige of less evolved societies that blocked the ongoing evolution of white society. Gilman effectively dismantled her society's hegemonic association of (the civilized white) "woman" with the supposedly natural and ineradicable sexual differences produced by woman's relegation to the home.

Moreover, while most participants in the woman's movement of this period—suffragists, temperance workers, protective-labor advocates, missionaries, and so forth—continued to base their particular demands for political and social change on woman's centrality to the home, Gilman and Coolidge rejected and departed from this strategy. Rather than argue that the world was the home writ large, Gilman and Coolidge conceived of the home as a primitive institution, one that had not kept up with the evolving industrialism of the late nineteenth century. Gilman declared that "all that makes for civilisation, for progress, for the growth of humanity up and on toward the race ideal—takes place outside the home."[12] Her proposals for communal living arrangements, with public dining halls, maid service, and childcare facilities on the premises, were fashioned out of a desire to free (white) women from the daily chores of housekeeping and domestic life so that they could partake in the supposedly more advanced forms of economic production and social interaction.

However, Gilman's dismantling of nineteenth-century constructions of (white) domesticity and womanhood did not alter the prevailing racial beliefs and hierarchies that were embedded within those constructions. In fact, her new theories of (white) womanhood—her feminism—while dismissing sexual difference as crucial to evolutionary progress, nonetheless continued to encode assumptions of white racial superiority. Gilman's discursive tactics, formulated in response to the racial anxieties (and in light of the assimilationist policies) of whites during the progressive era, were based on an ongoing denigration of the "primitive" as the antithesis of "civilization." She never intended to challenge the civilizationist hierarchy of evolutionary theories. She only wanted to remove the sexual difference of (white) woman as its defining feature. To do this, she and Coolidge emphasized the racial similarities, or the potential for such similarities, between white women and white men, and thus the racial distance between white women and nonwhite women. In this way, Gilman's own theories of social evolution reinscribed many of the same racial assumptions about white women's superiority that were contained in earlier social Darwinian constructions of (civilized white) womanhood.

In sum, then, the specific feminist visions of Gilman and Coolidge were historically and discursively intertwined with the assimilationist politics of the late nineteenth and early twentieth centuries. Anglo-Protestant feminism developed as an integral member of the family of discourses that emerged as a response to laissez-faire versions of social Darwinism, discourses that included socialist strategies to deal with labor conflict; eugenics and birth control strategies to deal with fears of racial degeneration; and state regulation to deal with immigration, poverty, alcoholism, prostitution, and other social ills. To put this point another way, feminism and assimilationism were historical siblings, the offspring of a marriage between democratic liberal ideals that held forth the promise of equal citizenship for all who conformed to the gendered ideals of Anglo-Protestant civilization and contemporary evolutionist premises about the superiority of the civilized in relation to the primitive.

Unlike many white women of this period who remained ambivalent about changing woman's nature, Gilman and Coolidge embraced this aspect of social-Darwinian theory. How profound the potential changes in white women might be, Gilman and Coolidge proclaimed, no one could yet foresee. As Coolidge explained, just as it was impossible to know what "degree of civilization" nonwhite peoples might attain under "the stimulus of new environments," it was also not possible to predict what (Anglo-Saxon middle-class) women might become in a world in which sex segregation was not rigidly enforced.[13] Just as racial differences of blacks or the Chinese could be made to disappear, given appropriate measures to assimilate them into civilized society, so might primitive sexual differences of (white) women disappear with analogous types of changes.

Gilman and Coolidge worked to dislodge sexual difference from the realm of normative white civilization by arguing that sexual differences would disappear as civilized women became less like the primitive. Whereas white women in the WNIA understood sexual differences as a positive feature of Anglo-Saxon civilization, evidence of white Christians' superiority and membership in the "higher races," Gilman and Coolidge identified sexual differences *for whites* as a negative vestige of their primitive past. Thus, a fundamental contradiction existed at the intersection of early feminist and assimilationist strategies: sexual difference was to be inserted into primitive cultures as a way to lessen the racial difference between primitives and the civilized; but sexual difference was to be removed from civilization as a way to promote equality between white men and white women. Gilman and Coolidge's assimilationist policies called for the diminishing of racial differences between whites and nonwhites, while their feminist demands were based on a reassertion of racial differences between the civilized and primitive.

For civilized (white) peoples, sexual difference needed to be expunged because it interfered with the further development of industrial efficiency and individual and social morality in modern civilization. For primitive peoples, however, sexual difference needed to be injected into the society to help accelerate "racial inferiors" along the path of social evolution. Hence for Gilman, the development of patriarchal economic and familial structures was an evolutionary consequence *of the gender relations of specific racial groups.* "The Teutons and Scandinavian stocks seem never to have had that period of enslaved womanhood, that polygamous harem culture; their women never went through that debasement; and their men have succeeded in preserving the spirit of freedom which is inevitably lost by a race which has servile women."[14] In other words, Gilman held primitives responsible for originating and perpetuating "androcentric" doctrines that held woman in subjection to man. Literary critic Susan Lanser has stated it most succinctly: "for Gilman, patriarchy [was] a racial phenomenon."[15]

Moreover, by transferring responsibility for the origin of patriarchal oppression from "civilized" Anglo-Saxon men to "savage" or "primitive" African and Asian men, Gilman made it possible for Anglo-Saxons to continue to assert their racial superiority over other "races" without having to invoke permanent sexual differences as the determining causal factor of their racial superiority. It was clear to Gilman that the danger of allowing "androcentrism" (or patriarchy) to continue was that so long as (white) women were subjected to androcentric practices, the racial development of whites would be slowed. In 1911, Gilman expounded in *Man-Made World*:

> Nature did not intend him [man] to select [a woman as his sexual partner in marriage]; he is not good at it. . . . When women became the property of men; sold and bartered; "given away" by their paternal owner to their marital owner; they lost this prerogative of the female, this primal duty of selection. The males were no longer improved by their natural competition for the female; and the females were not improved; *because the male did not select for points of racial superiority, but for such qualities as pleased him.*[16]

So long as (white) women remained economically dependent upon (white) men, (white) men would maintain control over sexual selection. And because white men chose to reproduce with women whom they found attractive for superficial reasons—

because "the male did not select for points of racial superiority"—the future development of the white race would remain in jeopardy. This was Gilman's answer to those who blamed (white) racial degeneration on the declining birth rates of (white) women. Gilman held that the solution to the problem of "race suicide" was to make (white) women economically independent of men so that (white) women could once again resume control over sexual selection.

In Coolidge and Gilman's discussions of sexual difference, the traditional qualities associated with (white middle-class) womanhood—virtue or chastity, emotional sensitivity, and physical delicacy—were no longer deemed positive or permanent traits, although both theorists continued to posit these qualities as biologically transmittable traits. Because of their adherence to evolutionary explanations for the appearance of "feminine" qualities, neither woman was ever able to fully differentiate between biological notions of sex and social constructions of gender, although Coolidge understood hyperfeminine qualities to be a "pretense" that (Anglo-Protestant middle-class) women assumed in order to secure economic support. In Coolidge's words, woman had "pretend[ed] to be extremely delicate, elusive, and emotional in order to enhance her charms [to secure a husband]."17

Gilman also denigrated the so-called womanly virtues, characterizing "obedience, patience, endurance, contentment, humility, resignation, temperance, prudence, industry, kindness, cheerfulness, modesty, gratitude, thrift, and unselfishness" as "convenient virtues of a subject class."18 She continued to believe that (white) woman's sexual differences from (white) man had become a part of her biological and racial inheritance through her relegation to a "primitive" sphere of life. The assimilationist strategy of feminizing primitives to address their inferiority was reversed in Gilman's mind; now the (white) woman was primitivized as a part of a critique of Western gender relations. Yet the biological inheritance of white women could be reformed by altering the prescribed social activities and duties of (white) women—first by removing the cultural restrictions that kept these women confined to their primitive (domestic) sphere. The "woman problem," as Gilman redefined it, was that Anglo-Protestant women had been "denied time, place and opportunity" to develop those "race" characteristics that were part of every white woman's shared racial heritage with white men but were now mistakenly referred to as "male," when in fact they were "human" traits, potentially available to both white men and women.

Gilman and Coolidge demanded that woman's "human"—as opposed to "female"—traits be given due recognition by society, but what they really meant was that the humanity of *white* women be recognized as essentially the same as and equal to *white* men. Most of the time, the racial component of their argument was obscured by universal or racially neutral language about "the race," which as historian Linda Gordon has pointed out in relation to eugenic discourse of this period, was revealingly ambiguous: "race" could mean either the human race or the white race.19 Occasionally, though, Coolidge and Gilman voiced their racial views so explicitly that it became evident that they were self-consciously fashioning their theories about sexual equality on a foundation of racial superiority. Quoting from Thomas Wentworth Higginson's work of the 1880s, for example, Coolidge espoused what were by now longstanding truisms about the lack of sexual differentiation among primitives and the evolutionary gulf between white women and women of the lower races.

> This is not denying the distinctions of sex , but only asserting that they are not so inclusive and all-absorbing as is supposed. It is easy to name other grounds of difference which entirely ignore those of sex, striking directly across them, and rendering a different classification necessary. *It is thus with distinctions of race or color, for instance. An Indian man and woman are at many points more like one another than is either to a white person of the same sex.*[20]

Coolidge also believed that sexual differences were less relevant to theories of social equality than were racial differences, and she too was convinced that racial differences could be overcome by Americanizing immigrants, educating blacks, reforming Indians, and assimilating the Chinese. Similarly, Gilman's statement that "race characteristics belong in equal measure to either sex" should not be read as an egalitarian assertion about all women's potential equality or common humanity with all men. "Race characteristics belong in equal measure to either sex" meant that men and women of any particular race shared equally in their own race's specific racial heritage.

IN AN EFFORT TO EXPLAIN THE personal roots of Gilman's feminism, historians have called attention to the tensions within Gilman's difficult childhood and young adulthood.[21] By the time she was nine years old, Charlotte knew firsthand how the ideology of separate spheres, which promised women protection and care within the domestic realm, often left women impoverished and vulnerable. Her mother, Mary Perkins, had had three children in quick succession before being advised by her physician that further childbearing would endanger her life. Embittered by this news, Charlotte's father, Frederick Perkins, distanced himself from his family and either refused or was unable to support his wife and children. "Forced to take up the itinerant lifestyle of genteel 'poor relations,'" as historian Gail Bederman notes, the family was constantly on the move to escape creditors. They ranged across three states—Rhode Island, Connecticut, and Massachusetts—often living with resentful relatives.[22] Gilman later described her mother's life as "one of the most painfully thwarted I have ever known. . . . The most passionately domestic of home-worshipping housewives, she was forced to move nineteen times in eighteen years, fourteen of them from one city to another."[23]

The alienation, poverty, and dislocations must have been even more galling, however, because Charlotte Perkins was related to the prominent (and wealthy) Beecher family. Her father was the grandson of the evangelical preacher Lyman Beecher. Catharine Beecher, the proponent of women's education, and Harriet Beecher Stowe, author of *Uncle Tom's Cabin,* were Gilman's great-aunts. Through her sporadic contact with these various relatives, Gilman was introduced to the reigning radical ideas (abolitionism, suffragism, evangelicalism, evolutionism) of the 1860s and 1870s. However, while this kinship brought her into proximity with a northeastern intellectual elite, it would also serve to remind her that she was denied full access to this elite world—an exclusion she felt as a denial of a rightful inheritance.

In Charlotte's family, then, as historian Gail Bederman points out, the Victorian doctrine of separate spheres was clearly ever-present as a religious dogma and social ideal, yet entirely nonfunctional. Even as a child, Charlotte sensed that predicating civilization's advance on separate spheres was costing women financial security and happiness. Reacting against a society that valued frailty and dependency in elite women, Charlotte took great pride in her robust health and strong body. She reformed her dress, eschewed corsets and uncomfortable shoes, and began a serious program of strenuous exercise, getting plenty of fresh air, and taking cold baths to increase her physical endurance and self-discipline.

Determined not to share her mother's fate, Charlotte began to prepare herself for a life of intellectual activity outside the home. Because her family could not find the money to send her to school, Charlotte took charge of her own education. In 1877, at age seventeen, Gilman wrote her father (he was assistant director of the Boston Public Library) to ask him to suggest books for her to read. (Throughout her life she would repeat this pattern by corresponding with other academic men, developing a close intellectual relationship with the sociologists Edward Ross and Lester Ward.) She later described this moment as "the beginning of [my] real education."[24] Charlotte avidly read the books her father suggested, including Edward B. Tylor's *Researches into the Early History of Mankind and the Development of Civilization* (1865) and *Primitive Culture* (1871); John Lubbock's *Pre-historic Times* (1869) and *The Origin of Civilization and the Primitive Condition of Man* (1870); and a large number of issues of *Popular Science Monthly,* a magazine that had recently been established to disseminate the views of Herbert Spencer and other evolutionists' to an American public.[25] Out of these works, Charlotte set about "building my own religion," and social evolution soon became the basis of her political views and social commitments. Looking back on her life when she was writing her autobiography in the 1920s, Gilman reflected, "[T]his religion of mine underlies all my Living, is the most essential part of my life, and began in [those] years."[26]

Eventually, Gilman conceptualized an alternative to living her life as a woman doomed to the confinement of the domestic sphere. Instead, she would live as an Anglo-Saxon, and accept the mission to "carry out the evolution of the human race." Like so many other white women of this period, Gilman would come to see Anglo-Protestant women as central to the civilizing mission. But for Gilman, this choice came at great cost, because she experienced the two components of her identity—her race and her sex—as fundamentally at odds. Initially, at least, she could not reconcile her life as a woman with her aspirations as an Anglo-Saxon civilizer. As Bederman summarizes the conflict, "either she could follow the claims of sex—marriage, motherhood, domesticity and dependency—or the claims of race."[27]

By the time Charlotte was twenty-one years old, she had begun to experience profound psychological turmoil over which avenue to take. She had just received a marriage proposal from a handsome young artist, Charles Walter Stetson, to whom she was very much attracted. At first she refused him, but then she wavered: "on the one hand, I knew it was normal and right" for a woman to marry; "On the other, I felt strongly that for me it was not right, that the nature of the life before me forbade it."[28] She eventually accepted Stetson, was married on May 2, 1884, and then promptly fell into paralysis and despair, an illness from which she suffered acutely throughout her brief marriage and which recurred in periods throughout her life. The initial depression was diagnosed as neurasthenia, and she sought treatment for this illness from S. Weir Mitchell, an experience that nearly cost her her sanity and which she fictionalized in her short story *The Yellow Paper* (1891).[29] Finding that her symptoms abated when she was away from her husband, Gilman eventually left Stetson permanently in 1888, to embark on a new life in California as a writer and reformer.[30] Years later, in 1900, at age forty, she entered into a happy second marriage with a younger cousin, Houghton Gilman.

Although Gilman's case is the most famous, many other white women activists of the 1880s and 1890s experienced similar tensions with traditional forms of patriarchal domesticity. Some of the women I have discussed in this book took similarly unconventional approaches to their personal life. After the death of her second husband, which occurred when she was forty-three, May French-Sheldon developed an intimate relationship with Nellie Butler, which apparently lasted for the rest of her life. Alice Fletcher never married but shared her life with Francis La Flesche, a man who was seventeen years younger than herself. Susan B. Anthony never married, drawing her sustenance from her close friendship with Elizabeth Cady Stanton. Mary Roberts Smith Coolidge married for the first time at age thirty, later divorced, and eventually settled into a happy second marriage with Dane Coolidge, a man fifteen years her junior.

Within ten years of divorcing Stetson, Charlotte Perkins Gilman had become the most influential and prominent feminist theorist in the United States, a reputation she maintained until the mid-1910s. *Women and Economics,* her first monographic treatment of these problems published in 1898, brought her instant fame and worldwide acclaim. It remained her most successful book, going through nine U.S. printings by 1920, and was published in translation in Japan, Hungary, Holland, Denmark, Italy, Germany, and Russia.[31] Reviewers called it "the book of the age" and recognized it as the most valuable contribution on the woman question since John Stuart Mill's essays on *The Subjection of Women* (1869).[32] Thirty-five years after its publication, the *New York City Review of Literature* was still asserting that *Women and Economics* was "considered by feminists of the whole world as the outstanding book on Feminism."[33]

In *Women and Economics,* Gilman argued that (white) women's relegation to the home and economic dependence on (white) men meant that they had not had the opportunity to evolve socially. While (white) men had learned how to organize their efforts collectively and to form industries with specialization of labor and economies of scale, (white) women were still replicating each other's labor in the home in ways that had not changed much since the beginning of time. "The economic progress of the race," Gilman wrote, "involve[s] the collective activities of all the trades, crafts, arts, manufactures, inventions, discoveries and all the civil and military institutions that go to maintain them."[34] As these were the exclusive domain of (white) men within the civilization of the United States, (white) women's present degree of economic development was still very primitive, not because of "any inherent disability of sex" but because of the "present condition of woman," which "forbid[s] . . . the development of this degree of economic ability." Were it not for the transmission of acquired traits to both sexes, (white) women would be even further behind (white) men in social evolution. But because they too inherited transmissable traits from their fathers, they shared in (white) men's evolutionary development.[35] These were themes that Gilman would return to repeatedly in future books: *Concerning Children* (1900), *The Home,* (1903), *Human Work* (1904), *The Man-Made World* (1911), and *His Religion and Hers* (1923).

Women and Economics drew heavily on social-Darwinian precepts. The main problem was that (white) women were excluded from much social activity and thus had not been able to evolve as much as (white) men. Gilman believed that sexual distinctions between white men and women had increased so much that "we have in all the higher races two markedly different sexes, strongly drawn together by the attraction of sex, and fulfilling their use in the reproduction of species."[36] Unfortunately, the higher races had evolved a "morbid excess" in sexual attraction (i.e., white men wanted to have sex with white women much more frequently than was necessary for the purposes of reproduction, and more frequently than white women wanted), and this problem was compounded by the fact that white men did not choose their wives for their usefulness to the race's survival but merely for their sexual attractiveness. "Man, as the feeder of woman, becomes the strongest modifying force in her economic condition. . . . For, in [woman's] position of economic dependence in the sex-relation, sex distinction is with her not only a means of attracting a mate, as with all creatures, but [also] a means of getting her livelihood."[37] Herein lay the central problem: when woman stopped working for her livelihood, she was selected by men for her sexual attractiveness alone, and her sexual function became the raison d'être of her existence. As the middle-class white woman stopped producing goods (while working-class and nonwhite women continued to do so because their husbands did not earn enough for them to withdraw from productive labor), she became more highly sexed, more emotional, less rational, and less useful in the world.

The negative impact of civilization's sexual differences was not born by (white) women alone. Sexual difference was also having a negative effect on (white) men, who were in danger of regressing from strong, rational agents back into primitive aggressors—men who would mistreat and abuse women. To illustrate this contention, however, Gilman did not cite signs of regression among white men. Rather, she took her evidence from "oriental nations" that overbred women for sexual attraction. Not only were these women much smaller and weaker than women elsewhere, but also they had not produced vigorous male offspring. "The female in curtained harems," Gilman wrote, "is confined most exclusively to sex-functions and denied most fully the exercise of race-functions. . . . In such peoples the weakness, the tendency to small bones and adipose tissue of the over-sexed female, is transmitted to the male, with a retarding effect on the development of the [entire] race."[38] Conversely, Gilman maintained, Europeans had had a different evolutionary history: "in early Germanic tribes the comparatively free and humanly developed women—tall, strong, and brave—transmitted to their sons a greater proportion of human power and much less of morbid sex-tendency."[39] White Europeans then had developed advanced civilizations not just because the men were the most advanced men in the world but because the women had had a past history in which they had been active and strong. From

Gilman's perspective, the Victorian moment was merely a recent phase in a much longer history, and needed to be recognized as a potential threat to the future progress of the (white) race.

Gilman's contribution to evolutionary theory, then, was to hypothesize that increasing sexual difference to such extremes that women were only valued for their sexual attractiveness would lead to racial regression. In other words, women everywhere were the key to racial progress: strong intelligent women bred strong intelligent men; weak, oversexed women bred weak ineffectual men. Civilization, although initially brought about by sexual difference, was now in danger of producing too much sexual difference: excessive sex was threatening the future progress of the white race.

These ideas, while distinctive to Gilman, were not created by her in a vacuum. Others were heading in similar directions. In fact, a community of intellectuals, whom Gilman knew personally and whose work she read carefully, assisted her in coming to these formulations. This community of scholars included (but was not limited to) the sociologists Lester Ward (1841–1913) and Edward A. Ross (1866–1951), as well as the economist Thorstein Veblen (1857–1929).[40]

Gilman first met Ward in Washington, D.C., in early 1896, where she was attending the annual suffrage convention of the National American Woman Suffrage Association and was scheduled to address the Judiciary Committee of the House of Representatives. The Wards hosted a reception for Gilman, having known of her since the publication of her poem "Similar Cases" in the *Nationalist* in 1890. Gilman was also familiar with and impressed by Ward's work. She had read his article "Our Better Halves," which had appeared in the *Forum* in 1888 (see chapter 1).[41] In her own work, Gilman drew heavily from Lester Ward's theories. Ward had posited that there had been a time very early in human history when women had controlled the process of sexual selection, choosing their mates and thus determining the racial traits that would appear in offspring. Women in these matriarchal societies could exercise this power of sexual selection because they were self-sufficient laborers—the primary economic producers in their societies—and economically independent of men.[42] Gilman agreed with Ward about this early prehistory and believed, too, that primitive men had usurped all forms of women's productive labor, made women their slaves and took possession of them as property, enforced women's economic dependence upon male providers, and assumed control over sexual selection. With the advent of modern Christianity, however, the condition of women had improved dramatically. Civilized Christian men no longer treated (white) women as slaves or property and were slowly permitting them access to economic opportunities.

Moreover, as Ward also argued, (civilized) women now played a crucial role in the perpetuation of the "race" because children inherited their core racial traits from their mother, not their father.[43] This was the point that Gilman recognized as critical in revaluing (civilized) women's role in evolution, appreciating the radical potential in Ward's reformulation of social-Darwinian ideas about (white) women's role in the transmission of racial traits. Gilman dedicated *The Man-Made World* to Lester Ward, in acknowledgment of the influence that his "gynaecocentric theory" had had upon her work, stating "nothing so important to humanity [as gynaecocentrism] has been advanced since the Theory of Evolution, and nothing so important to women has ever been given to the world."[44]

Ward's insistence that (white) women were the cornerstone of future racial progress for "the race" meant that society could no longer afford to ignore the intellectual and psychological stagnation of (white) women. Gilman's abbreviated formulation of this point was that the "female was the race type, the male, originally a sex type only."[45] Or "the [white] child is born to a progressive fatherhood and a stationary motherhood. . . . We rob our children of half their social heredity by keeping the mother in an inferior position."[46]

Yet, Gilman's use of evolutionary theories differed from Ward's in significant ways. Where Ward had posited an evolutionary advantage to sexual differences among whites, Gilman argued that existing differences between (white middle-class) women and (white middle-class) men were not *sexual* differences at all but primitive survivals that continued to manifest themselves in (white middle-class) women only because of their relegation to a primitive sphere, an idea that she adapted from the work of Tylor and Veblen. It was not that (white) women had a "feminine brain" and (white) men a "masculine brain" but that (white civilized) women had a "home-bred brain" and (white civilized) men a "world-bred brain."[47] Whereas Ward assumed that men's control over sexual selection was beneficial to *all* "racial" progress, Gilman posited that the control primitive men had wrested over sexual selection had led to (white) women's mental, physical, and psychological stagnation.

Through the Wards, Gilman became close friends with Edward Ross, who was six years younger than Gilman and at the time of their earliest acquaintance was just beginning to establish himself as a scholar.[48] (Ross had married Ward's niece in 1892 while Ross was employed in the sociology department at Stanford.)[49] Like Gilman, Ross eventually became a key figure among a generation of progressive academics and reformers who opposed laissez-faire versions of social Darwinism and devoted their lives to creating the intellectual foundations to justify state intervention in economic and social practices. In the mid-1890s, just before Gilman's reputation as the author of *Women and Economics* was established, Ross was becoming known as a vocal advocate of free silver—he wrote speeches for William Jennings Bryan's presidential campaign in 1896. In the early 1900s, when Gilman's national reputation was secured, Ross also became famous for his views on "race suicide" and for his support of immigration restriction legislation as a way to protect native-born American laborers from declining wages.[50] President Theodore Roosevelt read Ross's early monographs and found his ideas extremely valuable in justifying the nation's foreign imperialist and domestic assimilationist programs.

Throughout Gilman's life, Ross was warmly supportive of her work, and she depended on him to keep her up to date on an ever-growing sociological literature. Despite his frank opinions of her work—and they were not always favorable—Gilman was able to confide in him her feelings about her "scandalous lack of education and most unscientific method of work."[51] She looked to him to supply her with the references that she felt her arguments needed to be acceptable to academic audiences. She wrote Ross in November 1900, "Can you not—without taking much time to it, jot me down a little list of Standard Authors on Scientific Subjects who would have been authorities if I'd read 'em? . . . [G]ive me a few of the big progressive sociologists, whose work bears out mine or mine theirs."[52] He lent her copies of books he thought would interest her—including William Graham Sumner's *Folkways* (1906) and Sumner and Albert Galloway Keller's *Science of Society* (1927)—sent her copies of his own books, and wrote her criticism of her works.[53]

Ross also introduced Gilman to Thorstein Veblen by lending her a copy of *A Theory of the Leisure Class* which she claimed to find "most interesting and suggestive."[54] As colleagues in the social sciences, Ward, Ross, and Veblen regularly reviewed each other's works in academic journals and shared their ideas through their personal correspondence. Ross also sent Ward a copy of *A Theory of the Leisure Class*, which the latter reviewed for the *American Sociological Review.* In turn, Veblen expressed warm appreciation of Ward's *Pure Sociology* (1903). Although Gilman never went to college or held an academic appointment, she followed these intellectual developments closely and took it upon herself to become a popularizer of these men's theories.[55]

By the early 1900s, Ward, Ross, and Veblen were all influential in academic as well as progressive reform circles, although none of them had obtained Gilman's international stature. Only Ward, in addition to Gilman, received an entry in the 1899 edition of the *Dictionary of American Biography.* Within several more years, however, Ross's national reputation would become well established, despite or perhaps because of, his controversial dismissal from Stanford in 1900.[56] In 1901 he published two important works: an article, "The Causes of Race Superiority," and a monograph, *Social Control.* In the former, Ross coined the phrase "race suicide" to describe the declining birth rates of Anglo-Saxons, a phenomenon that was deeply troubling to whites of Ross's generation.[57] Ross was explicitly pro-imperialist in his views, and *Social Control* brought him widespread recognition not only within academic sociology but also among politicians and reformers. Roosevelt wrote Ross a letter of appreciation, as did the jurist Oliver Wendell Holmes, Jr.[58]

Veblen, on the other hand, had been opposed to the United States assuming a protectorship over the Philippines in 1901. Yet, even though Veblen's work was intended as a thoroughgoing attack on so-called civilized practices, his formulations were useful to and were recuperated by those people who wanted to give imperialist policies a central role in the civilizing mission. Ross and Gilman found Veblen's work immensely helpful in explaining how Anglo-Saxons had remained fit for the task of colonizing purportedly inferior peoples despite the strains of civilization. At the turn of the century, as I have already shown, extensive debates occurred about whether the United States was overstepping ethical boundaries and evolutionary possibilities when it made the decision to bring civilization to primitives residing outside its geographic borders. Veblen's and Ross's works, taken together, provided new and much needed evidence that Anglo-Saxon Americans were racially suited to the role of foreign imperialist and that primitives residing in remote lands could indeed be transformed into well-assimilated subjects.

Veblen's *Theory of the Leisure Class* rejected the Spencerian-Sumnerian assumption that social evolution, if left to its own devices, would lead to ever more advanced and better societies. The book also rejected the assumption, widespread among white elites, that primitives were unrelentingly, inherently hostile, brutal, and aggressive. According to Veblen, civilized men manifested more aggression than primitive men, as a result of an evolutionary process he called "the direct transmission of archaic traits." Aggression had survived in civilized societies, while the "peaceable" qualities of primitive societies had not.[59] Veblen reconstituted the so-called civilized Anglo-Saxon male as capable of much more physical aggression and racial stability than had previously been acknowledged, and he characterized primitives as more peace-loving, cooperative, and racially flexible than previously believed.

Indeed, it was this type of reasoning that Gilman might well have had in mind when she called *A Theory of the Leisure Class* an "amazing" book.[60] Veblen had taken up a trait—aggression, which was previously thought to be primitive—and explained how it had originated in primitives but now survived only in civilized peoples. Appropriating this theoretical move, Gilman accomplished the same kind of intellectual transmutation for sexual difference: sexual difference originated in primitives, but had come to manifest itself as an archaic survival in civilized peoples.

From Veblen's perspective, the fact that the best traits of the most primitive societies (peacefulness and solidarity) had not endured, while the worse traits of less primitive societies (aggression) had survived in civilized societies, was simply proof that the Spencerian predictions about the survival of the fittest were mistaken: if Anglo-Saxons were the "fittest," clearly they were not the most fit in moral terms. Thus, Veblen ironically maintained that the "energetic aggressiveness and pertinacity" of "predatory [primitive] man is a heritage [enjoyed by present-day white men] of no mean value," and concluded that the "bellicose temperament [was] in some appreciable degree a *race* characteristic . . . appear[ing] to enter more largely into the make-up of the *dominant, upper-class ethnic type—the dolicho-blond of the European countries.*"[61] In other words, white, upper-class Anglo-Saxon men (like Roosevelt) were inherently, biologically, racially aggressive—this was a part of their ethnic or racial makeup.

Veblen found this conclusion deeply ironic and hoped that it would prompt readers to question the benevolence of imperialist claims that the civilized had a responsibility to assimilate primitives. For some readers, it may have had this effect, but for others, like Ross, Veblen had provided plenty of evidence to make pro-imperialists feel optimistic that the white race could and would physically conquer nonwhite races. With Veblen's work fresh in mind, Ross wrote in his own book, *Social Control*, that "certain shocking practices of primitive folk which were formerly held to indicate great ferocity . . . are now differently interpreted." The savage was not, after all, "savage at all, [save in his mode of warfare, but] on the contrary [was] amiable and peaceful."[62]

Veblen and Ross' arguments that primitives were really peace-loving and not combative enabled many whites to reclaim violence and aggression as an inherent, inevitable part of the racial inheritance of civilized white men and to rejoice in this reappropriation. Many imperialists saw this ideal of tough masculinity as an antidote to the problems of "over-civilization" and a way to reassure skeptics that the United States would prevail in its attempts to civilize primitives on foreign terrain. To shrink from this civilizing mission would be to acknowledge that white men had degenerated racially from earlier standards of white manliness. In 1899 Theodore Roosevelt argued in "The Strenuous Life":

> We cannot avoid the responsibilities that confront us in Hawaii, Cuba, Porto Rico, and the Philippines. . . . If we drove out a medieval tyranny [Spain] only to make room for savage anarchy, we had better not have begun the task at all. It is worse than idle to say that we . . . can leave to their fates the islands we have conquered. . . . Some stronger, manlier power would have to step in and do the work, and we would have shown ourselves weaklings.[63]

Moreover, to preserve yet temper the "adaptability" and "violence" of Anglo-Saxon men, white racial ideology reconceptualized the reproductive role of Anglo-Saxon women as a desirable sexual characteristic because it lent "racial stability" to the white race.[64] With this new balance of white male aggression and white female racial stability, imperialists could feel confident that they would be able to withstand what they assumed would be the debasing effects of primitive cultures as they set off to colonize foreign peoples living in tropical climates.

Ross thought of imperialism as part of an ongoing evolutionary process, necessary for the continuing racial development of Anglo-Saxons. Yet, while he had no doubts that Anglo-Saxons had evolved to become superior to all other races, he had serious misgivings about how the "race" would fare now that the United States was entering a more "static" period in its development. Along with historian Frederick Jackson Turner, who wrote about the closing of the frontier in 1893, Ross gave credence to the notion that the country had used up its "wilderness," in which Anglo-Saxons had developed the traits of "self-reliance" and "independence" that had given them their evolutionary advantage. A new frontier was needed so that whites could continue evolving. Thus, Ross advised (white) Americans to look to territories outside the continental United States to continue their racial development, for in Ross' words, a "dynamic epoch" was required to ensure that Anglo-Saxons would remain superior to other races.[65]

For Gilman, these reconfigurations of violence and aggression as natural and beneficial racial traits in white manhood constituted a significant challenge and can help us understand some of the contradictions in her theoretical work—for example, why she often asserted that (white) women were "naturally" more peaceful than men even as she was attempting to subvert the traditional sexual dichotomies of evolutionary theory. Her assertion that (white) men were inherently more violent and (white) women inherently more peaceful derived from her desire to oppose the overt violence of imperialist policies yet still call for other tactics to assimilate racial inferiors into the superior civilization of the United States. Faced with the claim that aggression in white men was an advantageous racial trait in a world where conflict with uncivilized peoples was presumed to be necessary for white racial advancement, Gilman responded that (white) women offered a viable alternative in whites' racial struggles to preserve the cultural dominance of Anglo-Saxon civilization.

Most important, Gilman rebutted the notion that modern warfare was of evolutionary benefit to whites—by denying that modern warfare served the same evolutionary function for civilization that ancient warfare had served for primitive societies. In "primitive warfare," where women were "promptly enslaved, or, at the best, polygamously married," Gilman maintained, war and conquest might be in the interest of social evolution. But as "civilization advances and monogamy obtains," Gilman argued, "whatever eugenic benefits may have sprung from warfare are completely lost, and all its injuries remain."[66] In primitive societies, in which women had been economically independent of men and thus able to care for themselves and their young without men's assistance, combat had served the interests of human progress by weeding out weak men and leaving only the strongest males as sexual mates for women. In modern societies, however, where women were selected for their sexual attractiveness and were dependent on men for their economic survival, warfare had disastrous effects: the strongest men, who served as soldiers, were likely to die in combat, leaving their wives and children destitute, while those men who were "too old or too young, [or were] the sick, crippled [or] defective [would be] left behind to marry and be fathers."[67]

Thus war no longer constituted a "eugenic" solution to whites' racial difficulties but would lead only to a further diminishing of the white population, exacerbating the problem of "race suicide" and producing what she called "surplus" women who lacked husbands and so by necessity remained single and childless. Instead, Gilman proposed widespread adoption of what she called the "female process": "The female process is to select the fit [as mates with whom to reproduce]." This (white) women could not do if the "best" men were enlisting in imperialist wars.[68] Refusing to accede to explanations that attributed the declining birth rates among the white middle classes to white women's selfishness or ambition, Gilman railed, "All this talk, for and against and about babies, is by men. One would think the men bore the babies, nursed the babies, reared the babies. . . . The women bear and rear the children. The men kill them. Then they say: 'We are running short of children—make some more.'"[69] (See figs. 6-1 and 6-2.) Gilman's explanation placed responsibility squarely on white men and their proclivity for warfare: "The birth rate is lowered," Gilman wrote, "in quantity, by the lack of husbands, and in quality both by the destruction of superior stock and by the wide dissemination of those diseases which invariably accompany the wifelessness of the segregated males who are [hauled] off to perform our military functions."[70]

Because of the ways in which white femininity and white masculinity were being reconstituted in an imperialist era (white women have babies for the race; white men fight wars for the race), Gilman faced a difficult theoretical task: to dislodge the supposedly natural sexual dichotomies constructed by evolutionist theories, while opposing the overt violence of political imperialism. Yet she took great care not to weaken the foundation of Anglo-Saxon racial supremacy (which previously had been based on assertions of biological sexual differences). These conflicting and competing theoreti-

FIGURE 6-1 An antidote to race suicide. What would Col. Roastwell Say to this? Six in one year! Postcard, 1903–1907. Roosevelt is credited with having popularized the term "race suicide" in his call to the white middle classes to raise their birth rates, which had been falling steadily since the early nineteenth century. Feminists like Charlotte Perkins Gilman and Mary Smith Coolidge resented President Theodore Roosevelt's (Col. Roastwell) commandment to "propagate the race."

FIGURE 6-2 Refiguring relations between white men and white women. The White Man's Burden. Postcard, c. early 1900s. The slogan "white man's burden" was generally used in this period by pro-imperialists to defend the United States' imperial and assimilationist policies. Using it to characterize white men's relation to white women was meant to be funny, but an edge to the humor can be detected in this image of an oversized woman who has practically pinned her partner to his seat, an unfriendly representation of the woman's movement's political demands.

cal and political objectives account for many of the peculiar tensions in Gilman's feminist ideology, in which sexual differences (for whites) were simultaneously asserted and discredited.

For Gilman, the key to the improvement of each race as a race-species and the key to the improvement of the United States as a civilized nation inhered in the *system* of labor adopted by each racial group and by the country as a whole. Gilman reminded her readers, "By labor the individual man [has] grown from a naked cannibal to a civilized human being."[71] It was also through the system of labor that what were now taken to be permanent racial and sexual differences would be shown up to be false and would eventually disappear.[72] The woman problem, as Gilman reformulated it, was that (civilized) "woman," denied the opportunity to engage in advanced forms of labor, had not had the same chance for equivalent growth permitted to "the individual man." Thus she had not been able to develop the types of "cooperative" labor for the domestic sphere that (civilized) man had developed in the industrial sphere. Since cooperative labor was also what led to altruism, Gilman disputed the notion that (white middle-class) women were more altruistic than men. The solution to the woman problem, as Gilman saw it, was for (white middle-class) women to embrace cooperative forms of labor for its ability to free them of their dependence on (white middle-class) men.

Gilman's peculiar and particular exemption of Anglo-Saxon men from responsibility for the origins of patriarchal oppression and her granting to them the credit for originating industrial civilization permitted her to support the United States' efforts to assert cultural and political supremacy over the "uncivilized" world. Yet her dismissal of sexual difference as the foundation of Anglo-Saxon civilization threatened the entire racial hierarchy to which she adhered, so she substituted the organization of labor as an alternative criterion on which to base assertions about the superiority of Anglo-Saxon civilization. Gilman clearly did not intend her theories to prompt others to reconsider the civilizationist hierarchy constructed by evolutionary theories. The evolution from matriarchy to patriarchy—*despite the decline in woman's status and economic freedom that it produced*—was, for Gilman, an example of evolutionary progress: she could not recognize nonwhite or non-Christian women as laboring agents, as this would have necessitated acknowledging their superior status in relation to nonlaboring white women, which in turn would have required a fundamental rejection of the civilization hierarchy that she was determined to support. Thus, although Gilman posited that "human labour comes by nature from the woman [and] was hers entirely for countless ages" and that "during all those ages of savagery the woman was the leader," still she believed that it was a good thing that savage men usurped savage women's labor. "Well it was for the human race," Gilman declared, "that the male savage finally took hold of the female's industry . . . [for] in the hands of the male, industry developed."[73] As was the case for Fletcher, Willard, Stanton, Jacobi, and so many others in the woman's movement, Gilman's advocacy of Christian, Anglo-Saxon civilization prevented her from altering her presumptions regarding the higher status of (white) women in "civilized," as opposed to "primitive," societies.

Mary Roberts Coolidge on "Chinese Immigration" and "Why [White] Women Are So"

Mary Roberts Smith Coolidge, an exact contemporary of Gilman, was also part of the intellectual network described above. Mary Roberts received her bachelor's and master's degrees from Cornell University in 1880 and 1882. She then assisted Marion Talbot with her survey of the health of women college graduates, designed to disprove Edward Clarke's contentions that higher education wrecked the health of women. From 1886 to 1890 she was an instructor of economics at Wellesley. In 1890, at the age of thirty, she married Albert Smith, a professor of mechanical engineering, and left her position at Wellesley to accompany her husband to Cornell and then to the University of Wisconsin, where he served on the faculty and she continued to research the sexual practices of college women, with one of her former students, Clelia Duel Mosher. By 1893, the Smiths had left Wisconsin for Stanford, where Mary Roberts Smith studied for her doctorate under Edward Ross, as well as the historian George E. Howard and the economist Amos Warner. In 1896 she received her doctorate from Stanford and became an assistant professor of sociology, teaching in the same department as Ross. Years later, Ross played a crucial role in getting Coolidge's book *Why Women Are So* quickly accepted for publication.[74]

I have not been able to determine whether Gilman and Coolidge ever met one another, although they moved within the same intellectual and reform circles. From 1893 to 1895, when Coolidge was studying at Stanford, Gilman was living in San Francisco and involved in women's reform and nationalist clubs. By this time, Gilman had secured a prominent local reputation, publishing hundreds of articles in a variety of publications: the San Francisco *Call*, the Los Angeles *Porcupine*, the *Pacific Monthly*, the *California Nationalist*, the *Pacific Rural Press*, *Kate Field's Washington*, and the *Oakland Times*. Coolidge also might have come across Gilman's work in any of a number of nationally circulating magazines: *Woman's Journal*, *Woman's Tribune*, *Cosmopolitan*, *Century*, *Harper's Bazaar*, *Scribner's*, and the *Christian Advocate*, among others. Moreover, Gilman's divorce from her first husband, Walter Stetson, in 1894 and her subsequent decision to send her daughter east to live with her ex-husband and his second wife, Grace Ellery Channing, Gilman's best friend, were widely covered by the local press. In addition, Coolidge had studied under Richard T. Ely at the University of Wisconsin in the early 1890s, close to the time that Helen Campbell, a good friend of Gilman's, was also enrolled at Wisconsin as a graduate student of Ely. Through Campbell, Coolidge may have had an opportunity to meet Gilman. At any rate, by the late 1890s, if not before, Coolidge probably had heard of Gilman, since *Women and Economics* (1898) brought its author national attention. Gilman, in turn, may have read some of Coolidge's writings, in particular *Why Women Are So* (1912), which was published with the assistance of Ross, their mutual friend and mentor.

Coolidge's *Chinese Immigration*, published in 1909, was, simply, a remarkable book for its time.[75] In it, Coolidge positioned herself against those academics and reformers, among them her mentor Ross, whose antipathy for the Chinese as an unassimilable immigrant group was especially fierce. Coolidge's goal was to rescue the Chinese from the category of the "primitive"—to depict them as the "inheritors" of an ancient civilization, one just as democratic and morally sound as that of Anglo-Saxons, despite the adherence of the Chinese to non-Christian religions.

To prove her claim that the Chinese were a civilized people, Coolidge cited at length the many ways in which the Chinese living in the United States conformed to dominant constructions of civilized gender relations. Chinese men were kind to their wives. Chinese women were excellent housekeepers. Chinese parents cared lovingly for their children, sent them to public school, and protected them from "premature labor." In Coolidge's words, "The Chinaman is above all a lover of home and children, and if married men were allowed to bring in their wives freely the conditions of life of the Chinese entitled to live in this country would become much more normal."[76] Furthermore, the Chinese, according to Coolidge, learned English; they dressed in Western-style clothing; they fed their children American food; the men cut off their queues to fit in with white middle-class notions of masculine appearance; and many families adopted Christianity.

With these assertions, Coolidge was responding, one by one, to whites' prejudices concerning the Chinese. To the charge that Chinese labor lowered the wages of "American" (i.e., white) labor, Coolidge presented a statistical survey showing that the labor force was racially segregated so that the Chinese rarely held jobs that whites desired. To the charge that the Chinese remained "heathens" and refused to convert to Christianity, Coolidge pointed out that missionaries generally converted non-Christians through the women of a race, and the Chinese who failed to convert were generally single men without wives. Hence, the fault was not with the Chinese men, Coolidge maintained, but with laws that made it illegal for them to bring their wives and families to the United States. Coolidge advised simply that the laws be changed and appealed to whites to put into practice their espousals of religious tolerance.[77]

In short, Coolidge wanted to prove that the Chinese occupied a higher place on the evolutionary hierarchy than most whites believed, and she offered example after example to demonstrate that the Chinese assimilated as quickly as any other immigrant group. Coolidge insisted that emigration to the United States resulted in immediate emancipation for Chinese women, which for her was symbolized in the unbinding of their feet. ("In no one respect have the Chinese in America altered more than in their ideas about women. Wives have a far greater amount of freedom in America than in China. . . . The women like to live here, they say, because they have so much more freedom.")[78]

Even though Coolidge ostensibly took the side of the Chinese against those whites who demanded harsher treatment and more restrictive immigration laws, nonetheless her arguments served to reinscribe the racial and gender hierarchies that placed Anglo-Saxons at the pinnacle of civilization because of their supposedly superior ways of treating women. To some extent, Coolidge's assimilationism also prevented her from formulating a more thoroughgoing critique of Western gender relations. For example, in stressing that Chinese men married Chinese women who were "perfectly chaste" and that they drew the same rigid "line between respectable and lewd women

. . . as . . . Americans," Coolidge wanted only to show that Chinese adhered to American standards of domestic relations. She could not, at the same time, question the constructions of respectability and chastity that were inherent in U.S. patriarchal gender relations.[79]

Coolidge's study of the Chinese and her use of the assimilationist paradigm also shaped her analysis of the woman question. Her subsequent book, *Why Women Are So,* surveyed the nineteenth-century woman's movement. Preceding Mary Beard's *Woman as a Force in History* (1946) by thirty-two years, it is one of the earliest examples of the genre now referred to as women's history.[80] The title immediately served notice that Coolidge, like Gilman, embraced evolutionary notions of change and attributed (white women's) sexual differences to (their) specific social functions. To use Coolidge's words, "the characteristic behavior which is called feminine" was not "inalienable" but rather "an attitude of mind produced by the coercive social habits of past times."[81]

Why Women Are So had a dual purpose. Coolidge's first objective was to explore the historical origins of the modern "feminist" movement, a term Coolidge used to describe both herself and a movement of women who were demanding careers outside of middle-class domesticity. Yet Coolidge asserted continuity with the past, locating the origins of her own contemporary feminism in the missionary, temperance, suffragist, and literary movements of the nineteenth century. Although Coolidge believed that the missionary women had had a different ideology from suffragists, still, she insisted, they had been the unwitting allies of these more explicit proponents of woman's rights. As Coolidge argued, missionary and temperance women both demonstrated an "unconscious expression of precisely the same expanding spirit as that displayed . . . [by] the suffragists . . . and the literary amateurs." Of Willard's NWCTU, Coolidge stated simply: its "contribution to the feminist movement was also considerable." "Thousands of housemothers learned to work in small groups for the public welfare outside the church and home; these women of a purely domestic type emancipated themselves into a world of larger ideas."[82] In short, Coolidge's criterion for inclusion in the ongoing woman's movement was the freeing of (middle-class white) women from domestic ideology, enabling them to assume a public role outside the church and home.

Yet Coolidge was also critical of what she saw as the limitations of the institutions that she credited with the emancipation of (white middle-class) women from their narrow domestic world. Her second objective was to expose the falsity of the ideologies of domesticity and sexual difference that were actively promulgated through women's missionary and temperance organizations. Like Gilman, Coolidge had personal reasons to be wary of these ideologies. In her first marriage to Albert Smith she experienced conflicting emotions and much sexual dissatisfaction. According to historian Rosalind Rosenberg, she had previously been financially independent but found herself upon this marriage "a dependent creature, keenly sympathetic with wives who 'wept in secret humiliation' to have to ask for what they considered their due."[83] Because she remained childless, she could not put her energies into the one avenue that might have brought her social recognition, if not personal happiness. Her husband's

career took priority over her own, and she constantly moved from one academic institution to another so that he could accept faculty promotions. After a decade of increasing unhappiness, she surrendered to a nervous breakdown in 1903. She was dismissed from Stanford, institutionalized briefly, and then divorced. In 1906 she married
again, this time to Dane Coolidge, a writer who was fifteen years her junior—a marriage that Coolidge described as "exceptionally happy."[84]

Why Women Are So focused on what Coolidge recognized to be disjunctures between
the nineteenth- and twentieth-century women's movements. In particular, Coolidge
emphasized that the twentieth-century movement provided an essential corrective to
the earlier movement's overemphasis on (white) women's sexual difference. "Aside
from the monotony of such a society," Coolidge wrote, "its worst aspect lay in the in-
breeding of sex characteristics." She continued, "In village communities, in church
gatherings, and temperance and missionary societies, men herded with men and
women flocked with women, losing the stimulus of the social and intellectual com-
radeship enjoyed by the sexes in modern life." For Coolidge this type of sex segregation accounted for the ongoing existence, biological transmission, and cultural rein-
forcement of (white) women's sexual differences, which she now viewed primarily in
negative terms. Drawing on Lamarckian principles of sexual inheritance, Coolidge
wrote, "Men, associating constantly with men, perpetuated the standards and habits
inherited from their fathers; women, corraled by themselves, gossiped of their narrower
experiences, perpetuating their own pettiness."[85]

The "new" or "modern" (white) woman, by contrast, had become an entirely reconstituted physiological entity from her nineteenth-century predecessor because her
life had been spent in heterosocial, as opposed to homosocial, institutions. "[T]here
has been developed in a single generation a large number of American women who
are less excitable than a Frenchman, less sentimental than a German, and less emotional than an Italian—in short, almost as reasonable and self-poised as the men of
their own class and race."[86] By denying that sentimentality and emotionality inhered
in all women's nature, Coolidge drew on a discursive strategy that proponents of
woman's rights had articulated for over forty years. Julia Ward Howe, it may be re-
called, made this point in her debates with Edward Clarke in the early 1870s when she
argued that (the white) woman's sensitivity to the cold climates of New England was a
trait she shared with men of her race and class, and that it was her racial sensitivity,
not her sexual difference, that accounted for whatever weakness of constitution educated women manifested. Thomas Wentworth Higginson, Elizabeth Cady Stanton,
Francis Willard, Mary Putnam Jacobi, and other suffragists invoked the same strategy
in their arguments for suffrage in the 1880s, urging opponents to remember that
white women had much more in common with white men than they did with other
races of women (and should be enfranchised on the basis of that racial similarity, in
addition to that of their sexual differences). Indeed, the argument that (white)
women's sexual differences were either not sexual in nature, or that they were over-
shadowed by some other racial trait held in common with men of their race and class,
appealed to many white elite women in the woman's movements of the late nineteenth and early twentieth centuries.

Like Gilman, Coolidge was concerned about the social outcry over increasing divorce and falling birth rates. Like Gilman, she defended educated Anglo-Saxon women against the charge that they were failing to reproduce the "race."[87] But where Gilman insisted that (white) men take responsibility for the wars that led to declining fertility among whites, Coolidge argued that these lower birth rates were a logical consequence of the false teachings of domestic ideologies of the nineteenth century. Coolidge found it no surprise that (white) women divorced their husbands more frequently and took measures to limit the size of their families. "[T]he transition from unalterable wedlock to more and more divorce, the resistance of many women to involuntary motherhood, the entrance of protected women into wage-earning occupations; these and many other symptoms," declared Coolidge, *are phases of evolution engendered in part by the hiatus between the high rank which women believed motherhood should hold, and the realities of [white] married women's lives in the past generation.*"[88]

Coolidge also pointed out that in the past, large families were often "produced at the cost of the first wife's life" and that when women managed to survive a large number of pregnancies, they were unable to "enjoy a vigorous, intelligent old-womanhood, but [lived] in a state of premature decrepitude, similar to that of women among primitive races."[89] Coolidge's invocation of the primitive, like Gilman's, served frequently as a gauge of the social evolution or racial progress of whites in the United States. If the trait under scrutiny was present in both "modern" and "primitive" women, Coolidge argued that the social practice under examination was a survival of primitive times and needed to be eradicated. If the "modern" (Anglo-Saxon middle-class) woman could be shown to differ from the primitive, then, Coolidge argued, social (racial) progress had occurred. Coolidge frequently used the term "modern" as a substitute for the term "civilized," but its meaning was established by the same evolutionary discourses that prevailed into the early twentieth century.

In sum, white women's racial difference from the primitive served as Coolidge's replacement for sexual difference (among whites) as the touchstone of evolutionary progress. For Coolidge, sexual differences were stigmatized as a quintessential feature of primitive societies, even though they might be absent in present-day primitive societies.[90] Evolutionary distance from the primitive enabled these white feminists in the early twentieth century to demonstrate their equality—or potential for equality—with (white) men.

As Gilman may have intuited when she titled her journal the *Forerunner*, she and Coolidge were transitional figures in the emergence of early feminist discourses. They were scornful of nineteenth-century ideologies of domesticity that revered (white) women for their sexual differences, and they were leery of social practices that segregated (white) women from (white) men. Yet they were equally uncomfortable with the emerging theories of a younger generation of feminists that rose to cultural authority after World War I destroyed both the physical and intellectual manifestations of European civilization. This new generation, which eventually included women like Elsie Clews Parsons (1875–1941), Ruth Benedict, (1887–1948), and Margaret Mead

(1901–1978), rejected the evolutionism of Charles Darwin, Lester Ward, and Havelock Ellis and looked to cultural anthropology and Freudian psychology for new intellectual frameworks to help them in their reconceptualizations of the relations among feminism, race, and civilization. My final chapter examines these developments through the work and life of Margaret Mead.

7

Coming of Age, but Not in Samoa

Reflections on Margaret Mead's Legacy
to Western Liberal Feminism

> In the case of anti-colonial critique, it is the *similarity* of past and present that defamiliarizes the here and now and subverts the sense of historical progress.
>
> Nicholas Thomas,
> *Colonialism's Culture* (1994)

Coming of Age in Samoa, one of the most famous and popular works ever published by an American anthropologist, first appeared in 1928, when its author Margaret Mead was twenty-seven years old.[1] By the mid-1930s, Mead had gained a national reputation as an expert on "primitive cultures" and was recognized by the public, if not by her colleagues, as one of the leading anthropologists of her day. Prolific, outspoken, charismatic, unconventional, provocative, controversial, and brilliant, Mead achieved a widespread public renown that was remarkable for a woman who constructed herself as a scientist and intellectual. She recognized instantly that her audience extended far beyond the elite worlds of the university and museum, and she cultivated her public by publishing hundreds of articles in such venues as *American Anthropologist, Natural History, Redbook, Vogue, Good Housekeeping, Seventeen,* and the *New York Times Magazine,* to name just a few. Mead also gave numerous interviews on domestic issues and international politics. From the appearance of *Coming of Age in Samoa* until her death fifty years later, Mead was sought after for her opinions on marriage, homemaking, childrearing, feminism, civil rights, and race relations.[2]

Among the general public old enough to remember her, Mead is probably best known for the role she played in the 1930s in prompting Westerners to question their sense of cultural superiority, using so-called primitive societies to critique patriarchal gender relations in the United States. Mead was not alone in this endeavor, as she wrote at a moment when artists, professionals, and other elites were drawing from such cultures to reinvigorate Western arts—literature, music, dance, visual arts, photography, and film.[3] Among historians of anthropology, Mead is remembered as one of the many students of Franz Boas who helped bring about a paradigm shift from evolutionism to cultural relativism by challenging biological explanations of cultural differences and refuting the explicit racism in eugenics and mainstream anthropology.

In addition to seeing Mead as someone who helped foster cultural relativism within anthropology of the 1930s, this chapter places Mead within a tradition of white feminist thought on racial questions that I have been tracking throughout this book. Mead's work became (and remains) popular because it touched on the collective unconscious of a society long accustomed to ruminating on what it took to be the unrestrained and unrestrainable sexuality of the primitive, which it then used (and still uses) to form an identity of itself as a civilized nation. Mead's brilliance was to redeploy these constructions of primitive sexuality to prompt white Americans to reconceptualize their understanding of sexual differences and gender relations.

Yet Mead's credibility as a "scientific" authority on primitive societies would not have been possible had not a renegotiation of the social relations between white women and the primitive taken place during the late nineteenth century. For the profession of the woman anthropologist even to exist, it first had to be demonstrated that single white women could live safely among primitives without the protection of husbands or other white authorities (something French-Sheldon had demonstrated during her safari to East Africa and Alice Fletcher during her residences on Indian reservations) and that she could have something of value to contribute to Western knowledge about the primitive. Through exploration and ethnography, Anglo-Saxon women transformed themselves from perceived victims of the sexual and physical aggression of savages into the civilizers and protectors of peoples presumed to be facing physical and cultural annihilation.

Situating Mead in this context requires that we view Mead as an integral part of a nineteenth-century tradition that combined notions of white or "civilized" women's sexual restraint and black or "primitive" men's bestiality in order to reinforce the dominant cultural taboo against miscegenation. Whereas Mead is usually understood as challenging the racism of such constructions, these dualisms nonetheless informed her work. In other words, this chapter highlights the continuities between the Victorian ethnography exemplified by women like Alice Fletcher and May French-Sheldon, on the one hand, and Mead's modern anthropology, on the other hand, in order to reconsider the nature of Mead's antiracism. To grasp my central point—that Mead's work was implicated in and shaped by Victorian race politics—we must be willing to embrace the idea that opposition movements retain residues of that which they oppose.

Mead's early monographs, *Coming of Age in Samoa* (1928) and *Sex and Temperament in Three Primitive Societies* (1935), broke with an earlier tradition of evolutionary or Victorian anthropology that supported Anglo-Americans' definitions of themselves as a superior race because of their supposedly unique, race-specific, biological forms of sexual difference.[4] Yet, while Mead challenged Anglo-Saxons' beliefs in their inherent biological superiority to primitive peoples, she did not challenge their belief in the cultural superiority of Western civilization. Mead invoked primitive societies to critique U.S. gender relations, but at the same time she dismissed those primitive societies for lacking freedom and circumscribing individual choice. For Mead, primitive societies provided Americans with conceptual alternatives to reflect on, but she never advocated that the United States remake itself in the image of the primitive.

The nineteenth-century discourses linking race, sexual difference, and civilization that I have traced in this book were central to Mead's work, enabling her to transform, without transcending, the racist formulations of evolutionary anthropology. Although we are not used to contextualizing Mead's work in this way, her corpus can be understood as a logical *culmination* of three nineteenth-century traditions: that of the woman missionary, the woman explorer, and the woman ethnographer. These traditions, as I showed in chapters 4 and 5, helped solidify a role for the Anglo-Saxon woman as a legitimate practitioner of anthropological science, a role that emanated from her previous role as Christian civilizer and governor of the primitive. Relating Mead to these traditions will enable us to comprehend how she became so popular at a time when many still questioned the suitability and capability of women as scientists and will help us expose the vestiges of nineteenth-century racism that form part of Mead's legacy to U.S. feminist discourse today.

Margaret Mead's Departure from Evolutionary Anthropology: Invoking the Primitive to Reassess Civilized Gender Relations

In the context of academic anthropology of the early twentieth century, both *Coming of Age in Samoa* and *Sex and Temperament in Three Primitive Societies* were extraordinary books, helping to contribute to the dissolution of evolutionary anthropology.[5] In these works, Mead represented the "primitive" as having something valuable to teach "civilized" society about reforming its present institutions, rather than serving merely as an embarrassing reminder of a shared and discredited past. As Mead mentions in her autobiography, *Blackberry Winter,* "We had, of course, had lectures on evolution. . . . But we went to the field not to look for earlier forms of [our past] human life, but for forms that were different from those known to us. . . . We did not make the mistake of thinking, as Freud [did] . . . that the primitive peoples . . . were equivalent to our ancestors."[6]

In this statement, Mead registers her rejection of Victorian evolutionary anthropology—in particular, her disagreement with the presumption that all societies followed the same path of development. Positing a unilinear, universal path of development, most social Darwinists located primitive societies at an earlier stage of development than civilized societies and often measured a society's relative position in the hierarchy of primitive-to-civilized nations by woman's "status" or "condition." One justification for Western colonialism was formulated in terms of protecting primitive women from various forms of social, economic, and sexual mistreatment.[7] For over a century, Westerners had presumed that primitive women were overworked, sexually abused, or otherwise badly treated by men of their cultures.

Within evolutionist paradigms, another indicator of a society's evolutionary ranking was the existence of pronounced physical-moral-sexual differences: tall strong dispassionate men, small delicate emotional women. Evolutionist accounts held that the "progress of a race" depended on the adoption of specific sex roles that were in turn supposed to bring about specific manifestations of sexual differences. Mead challenged the evolutionist beliefs that held primitive races as characterizable by either a lack of sexual differentiation or by an uncontrollable, rampant sexuality. She argued in *Sex and Temperament* that primitive societies differed substantially from one another in how they understood sexual differences and in the ways they structured gender relations. Mead concluded that sexual differences varied so substantially from one society to another that they must be understood as culturally, not biologically, determined. Or, as she put it, "the personalities of the two sexes are socially produced."[8]

Following her teachers and mentors, Franz Boas and Ruth Benedict, Mead helped consolidate a new paradigm in anthropology, which scholars often refer to as cultural relativism. Anthropologists working in this new paradigm understood cultures as developing along different, noncommensurable lines and no longer held up Western practices as the only morally legitimate forms of cultural arrangements. Nonetheless, Mead was not a moral relativist, nor was she attempting to write value-free ethnographies. Her understanding of cultural relativism did not prevent her from making moral distinctions among various cultural practices. Thus, I prefer the term "cultural comparativism," for it enables us to retain the idea that Mead did not validate indiscriminately all other cultural practices but studied primitive cultures to determine whether other societies had created alternative ways of living from which the United States could learn.[9] Such a perspective meant that Mead and others who worked within this paradigm resisted normative judgments of the sort that automatically called for "primitives" to adopt "civilized" gender roles—but these anthropologists did not suspend all judgments. Mead wanted to expand Americans' repertoire of conceivable alternatives, so that Americans might envision new ways of reforming their social institutions.

Positing a distinction between "social constructs" (Mead's term for culturally specific beliefs about sexual differences) and "biological facts" (universal aspects of sex difference manifest in all known cultures), Mead assisted modern anthropology in creating new distinctions between culture and biology. Evolutionary anthropology had preferred the term "civilization" to culture and understood the former as comprising social practices that were passed from one generation to another, partly through learning and partly through heredity. As the term "culture" eventually replaced the term "civilization," culture became fully distinguishable from biology. The older term "civilization" (which was still used) was eventually fully divorced from the idea of heredity: that is, cultures (civilizations) were presumed to pass from one generation to the next only by social processes, not through heredity.

Furthermore, in Mead's anthropology, culture was generally used to account for the differences among peoples and biology was used to account for the similarities. The fact that all women lactated and could bear children was an attribute of biology (or sex); the fact that only some women in some societies were passive or gentle was an attribute of culture (or civilization). Mead's particular contribution to this paradigm shift was to show how varied were different societies' views of sexual differences (regardless of race), thus shifting both sexual and racial differences from the category of biology to the category of culture. According to Mead, Western nations were not the only ones to consider (white) men and women fundamentally different from one another; other cultures considered their men and women fundamentally different as well. Indeed, constructions and manifestations of sexual differences varied so much from one society to another that it was no longer possible to account for these by appealing to biological notions of innate maleness or femaleness. In other words, "racial superiority" (of Anglo-Saxon whiteness) and "sexual difference" (of genteel Anglo-Saxon womanhood), which had been fundamentally linked concepts in Victorian evolutionary schema, were, in Mead's work, separated and emptied of their usual content.

In short, where nineteenth-century social evolutionists had believed that civilization was a *racial* trait, *inherited* by advanced white races, Mead assisted in redefining what was culturally transmitted through teaching and learning (civilization, culture, many sex-race differences) and what was genetically or biologically transmitted. Along with other social scientists of the 1910s and 1920s, Mead argued that "sex" and "race" were not significant variables of biological transmission. Mead wrote: "one by one, aspects of behavior which we had been accustomed to consider invariable complements of our humanity were found to be merely a result of civilization, present in the inhabitant of one country, absent in another country, and *this without a change of race.*"[10]

These theoretical innovations had profound implications for the development of subsequent feminist analyses, for they permitted new critiques of Western patriarchy. As I have just shown, evolutionist feminists, like Charlotte Perkins Gilman and Mary Roberts Coolidge, had invoked the primitive to argue for the elimination of the traces of primitivism that remained in the patriarchal civilization of the United States. For them, evolutionary or social progress meant increasing the distance (measured in terms of cultural differences) of civilized peoples from existing primitive groups.[11] Mead's revaluation of primitive cultural arrangements made possible a new strategy for Anglo-American feminists. The primitive could now be invoked as an alternative to be emulated rather than a vestige to be eliminated—an idea that was incipient in Fletcher's thinking of 1900, but which she never fully articulated.

Studying the Primitive to Reform Western Civilization: *Coming of Age* and *Sex and Temperament*

Mead's intent in *Coming of Age* was to question the inevitability and intransigence of the emotional "stress and strain" that others believed were inherent in the biological stage of maturation known as adolescence. Mead explicitly situated her study in opposition to works like G. Stanley Hall's *Adolescence* (1904), a book that, building on Edward Clarke's earlier works, ascribed young people's restlessness and rebellion to inescapable maturation processes.[12] Mead desired to show that behaviors and feelings that Hall and others identified as intrinsic to adolescence were dependent on social processes (culture) and not on physical development (biology and sex). Mead succinctly summed up her doubts about this biological-developmental explanation of young people's behavior: "Were these difficulties due to being adolescent or to being adolescent in America?"[13]

In particular, Mead attributed the pain of adolescence for young American women (thinking only of white, middle-class, heterosexual women) to the changing social mores of the 1920s. These women, Mead argued, were no longer compelled to adhere to traditional forms of heterosexual marriage, but could now choose from among a broad range of marital arrangements: "half a dozen standards of morality," to use her phrase. Mead noted these alternatives as including premarital sex; open marriage (marriages that included extramarital sexual relations); trial marriage (marriages that could end voluntarily after a trial period without divorce proceedings); companionate marriage; marriage without children; and marriage combined with a career.[14]

Another problem for Mead was that this "American girl" had little experience or knowledge of sex. Once married, she was less likely than her Samoan counterpart to experience a satisfying sexual life, in part, Mead believed, because U.S. society had such a limited notion of what constituted acceptable sexual behaviors. Samoan society, in contrast, was supposed to have a wider range of practices, which served to prevent sexual problems of both an individual and social nature: guilt, frigidity, marital unhappiness, and prostitution.[15] Yet Samoan society, while it enabled its girls to enjoy sex without shame or guilt, appeared to demand more "conformity" and allow less "individuality" among its women. This apparent contradiction troubled Mead greatly. The Samoan girl appeared more content, but she also seemed to Mead to have less freedom than her American counterpart. In one sense, Samoa could serve as a model to the United States demonstrating that young women there were able to enjoy sex, but in another sense, Samoa offered Americans a warning: sexual enjoyment for Samoan women entailed restrictions on their individuality and freedom. In Mead's view, then, the explanation for why adolescence was characteristically a pleasurable period of sexual expression for Samoan girls and a painful period of sexual repression for American girls could be boiled down "to the difference between a simple, homogenous primitive civilisation [where there was "but one recognised pattern of behavior" in which all Samoan girls had no choice but to engage] . . . and a motley, diverse, heterogeneous modern civilisation" in which various types of sexual behavior for girls were possible.[16] In other words, Samoan culture served as a means of pointing out what was wrong in U.S. gender relations but at the same time was devalued for exhibiting a more extreme gender oppression than that which existed in the United States.

Although Mead rejected certain assumptions of evolutionary anthropology, she retained its tendency to use gender to encode and assess cultural "progress." This practice of measuring the status of a society by the degradation of its women had a long history in Western imperial and anthropological thought, in particular in the way Westerners understood Pacific societies, including Samoa.[17] Although Mead rejected the crude judgments of nineteenth-century anthropologists that primitive women were debased, nonetheless the belief was implicit in her work that Samoa was a flawed society because it restricted the freedom of its women. In making this claim, Mead helped foster a liberal feminist critique of U.S. society that attacked patriarchy for

placing restrictions on women's expression of sexuality and conceptualized a "free" society as one that permitted women "choice" in how they lived their sexual lives.

Mead never advocated that the U.S. model itself after Samoa. For one thing, she
would have understood this as a practical impossibility. The United States could not
make its culture simpler or less diverse, and Mead would have seen an attempt to do
so as necessarily authoritarian and repressive, involving an elimination of social options and resulting in less freedom for women. Mead also believed that young women
in the United States had more freedom than young women in Samoa, and she would
not have been willing to trade freedom for happiness.

However, for Mead, individual freedom and personal happiness did not need to be
at odds, particularly if one defined these ideals in terms of being "free" to "choose"
what best suited one's innate temperament. The American girl's pain and suffering,
Mead argued, resulted not from having too many choices but from being unable to
live out, without social stigma or economic repercussions, the option(s) she was best
suited for by nature or temperament. Mead was a subtle enough observer of her own
society to realize that the array of alternatives that appeared to be available were often
not livable possibilities, and she realized too that class, race, ethnicity, and religion,
among other factors, prescribed the "choices" of particular groups and individuals.[18]
What the United States must do, Mead believed, was to make the sexual alternatives
that were conceptually available real options for all women.

In 1935, with the publication of *Sex and Temperament in Three Primitive Societies,* Mead
moved from a perspective that emphasized sexual conformity within a given primitive
society—all men adhering to the same ideal of maleness; all women adhering to the
same ideal of femaleness—to a perspective that emphasized the differences *among*
primitive societies.[19] Her analysis of the Arapesh, Mundugumor, and Tchambuli
stressed that each had a different understanding of what constituted natural sexual
differences. The Arapesh and Mundugumor, Mead argued, both believed that men
and women shared a similar temperament, but the Arapesh assumed both sexes were
gentle and unassertive, while the Mundugumor understood men and women to be
violent, competitive, aggressively sexed, jealous, and quick to avenge insult. On the
other hand, the Tchambuli, like Americans, believed in innate or natural sexual differences between men and women but had "a genuine reversal of the sex-attitudes of
our own culture, with the woman the dominant, impersonal, managing partner,
[and] the man the less responsible and the emotionally dependent person."[20]

Mead drew an explicit lesson from her study of these three primitive societies, arguing that they showed that many so-called sexual traits of American men and
women were arbitrary and not an inevitable emanation of biological difference. In
other words, it was possible to change how men and women behaved and to eliminate
many forms of apparent sexual difference.

> [U.S.] society can take the course that has become especially associated with the plans of
> most radical groups: admit that men and women are capable of being moulded to a sin-
> gle pattern as easily as to a diverse one. . . . Girls can be trained exactly as boys are
> trained, taught the same code, the same forms of expression, the same occupations.
> . . . If this is accepted, is it not reasonable to abandon the kind of artificial standardiza-

tions of sex-differences that have been so long characteristic of European society and admit that they are social fictions for which we have no longer any use?[21]

Mead tried to convince her society that there were other ways to structure gender relations than the ways that most middle-class white Americans felt were natural, inevitable, and good. She also challenged Americans' belief that men and women had sex-linked differences in temperament that were impossible to change. "We are forced to conclude," Mead wrote, "that human nature is almost unbelievably malleable, responding accurately and contrastingly to contrasting cultural conditions. . . . Standardized personality differences between the sexes are of this order, cultural creations, to which each generation, male and female is trained to conform."[22]

This finding that primitives differed in their attitudes about sexual difference and sexuality represented a significant break from the evolutionary belief that all primitives were blatantly sexual beings, unable to exercise any restraint over sexual impulses, an idea that was still vestigially present in *Coming of Age*.[23] *Sex and Temperament* was thus a far more radical work (Mead commented later that it was her "most misunderstood book") and unsettled readers in a way that *Coming of Age* had not.[24] Some readers had difficulty grasping the distinctions that Mead was trying to make between sex and temperament. Mead used sex to mean sex-associated differences, some of which were innate (biologically transmitted through heredity), some of which were not. She used temperament to designate innate individual endowments, which were not sex-linked but were nonetheless biologically transmitted through heredity.

Some readers also mistakenly thought that Mead was denying the existence of *any* biological sex differences, when all she hoped to show was that most so-called sexual differences thought to be innate were not. Other readers found this point obvious, even trite. The sociologist Hortense Powdermaker pointed out that the notion of cultural or social conditioning of human character had been introduced over fifty years earlier. As Powdermaker wrote in a review of *Sex and Temperament*, the idea "that men and women follow roles culturally assigned to them is not . . . new . . . even to the intelligent layman."[25] Powdermaker was disappointed that Mead had focused her work on such an obvious point and called for additional work assessing the significance of those sex differences that were innate and universal. Mead eventually answered Powdermaker's call with *Male and Female*, only to find that readers used this book to discredit her earlier one. In a new preface to the 1950 edition of *Sex and Temperament*, Mead responded to her critics: "In our present day and culture . . . there is a tendency to say: 'She can't have it both ways, if she shows that different cultures can mold men and women in ways which are opposite to our ideas of innate sex differences, then she can't also claim that there *are* sex differences.' Fortunately for mankind, we not only can have it both ways, but many more than both ways."[26]

Although *Sex and Temperament* represented a major break from *Coming of Age* by introducing variability into primitive sexuality, it operated on the same premise that had so fundamentally shaped the earlier book. For Mead, the point of intercultural comparisons (despite her often stated belief in the incommensurability of different cultures) was to prove that alternatives to U.S. gender relations were possible. She used knowledge of these alternatives to argue that Americans could and should reform their culture and themselves—establishing a fundamental principle that still operates within Western feminist anthropology today.

In short, Mead never relinquished the belief that intercultural comparisons could be put to the use of social reform. Nor did she doubt or challenge Americans' belief in the cultural superiority of Western civilization. What she did instead was propose a new set of criteria on which to base that judgment. Mead believed that the United States was superior to the primitive societies she studied, not because of sexual differences, but because only it had the potential—due to a presumably greater complexity and sophistication—to maintain a larger range of gendered behaviors from among which individuals could pick and choose.[27] Challenging the United States to eliminate its rigid and "artificial" sex-typing, Mead ended *Coming of Age* with this injunction: "Samoa knows but one way of life and teaches it to her children. Will we, who have the knowledge of many ways, leave our children free to choose among them?"[28]

Cultural Resonances between Mead's Work and the Late-Nineteenth-Century Traditions of the Woman Missionary, Woman Explorer, and Woman Ethnographer

As I showed in chapter 1, Anglo-Saxon women came to be seen as central to the "civilizing" process—in part because of their special attributes as moral guardians and teachers; in part because they were held up as a model of gender relations imposed on primitives for emulation; and in part because they were imbued with new biological functions in the transmission of civilization-race traits.[29] Anglo-Saxon women assumed responsibility for transmitting civilization not just to their own children but also to primitives, whom they presumed resembled children in their supposed simplicity and naiveté.

Middle-class Anglo-Protestant women found missionary work especially appealing because they could act as representatives for the primitive without violating their notions of "woman's sphere" or abrogating their conventional duties as wives and mothers. But missionary work also terrified white women who were frightened of peoples whose dark skin color and nakedness they interpreted in light of their preconceived notions about primitives' unrestrained and wanton sexuality. This fear was exacerbated in the post-Reconstruction era by the highly publicized lynchings of black men that were often justified on the grounds that the black male victims had attacked or molested white women. In this climate of racial tension, Anglo-Protestant women often saw themselves as potential rape victims, even when no sexual interest was shown them, and projected this sexual dynamic onto territories beyond the United States. Missionary reports sent back to the United States contained stories of white women having to fend off unwanted sexual advances of nonwhite men (similar types of stories were also contained in Indian captivity narratives). Because of the cultural taboo against miscegenation and the imperative to remain sexually chaste, any feelings of sexual attraction that white women might have felt towards these men had to be denied through the projection of an exaggerated and aggressive sexuality onto the primitive.

A vivid illustration of how such repression and denial operated may be ascertained from Mrs. M. F. Armstrong's "Sketches of Mission Life," written in 1881 during her stay in Hawaii and sent back to the U.S. for publication in the *Southern Workman,* the school newspaper of Hampton Institute. Armstrong was the wife of Samuel Armstrong, the founder of Hampton Institute, a vocational training school in Virginia established to "civilize" blacks and, later, to help achieve the assimilation of Native Americans during the postbellum era. In several of these sketches, Armstrong's sexual fascination with the primitive centers on Papatutai, a man she describes as "most savage in his appearance, some six feet tall, erect, and with a fine athletic form." Emphasizing his imposing height—his "erectness"—Armstrong's selection of details revealed how great an interest she takes in Papatutai's physical person, an interest she could never register so directly were she describing a white man. This type of description is possible only because Armstrong and her audience consider Papatutai not a man but a savage.

Despite the fact that Armstrong expresses a strong dislike and feelings of repulsion toward Papatutai, she nonetheless decides to sketch his portrait so that she can send a picture of him home "for friends to see what sort of neighbors [she] had." (Unfortunately, the picture itself was not published but only described in the school newspaper.) For this purpose, she has "Papatutai stand, spear in his hand" as if he "were about to thrust it into a victim." At her request or insistence (we do not know whether she formulated it as a question or command), Papatutai dons a war costume; "his appearance as he thus stood . . . was revolting beyond expression."[30]

Savagery is here quite literally Armstrong's creation. She positions Papatutai in what she thinks of as a suitable and typical pose—with little clothing, a fierce expression, and a weapon about to be launched. Clearly, the spear that Armstrong invokes is the warrior's long shaft, but another spear, one more phallic, is suggested by her description. Armstrong is simultaneously so attracted to Papatutai that she wants him near her yet so afraid of him that she will only sketch him when her husband is close by. Mr. Armstrong seems oblivious to his wife's feelings and decides to hire Papatutai to look after his wife and child when he goes on a brief expedition. Armstrong does not protest or remonstrate with her husband about this decision. Describing her feelings during her first evening alone with Papatutai, she writes:

Papatutai pompously accepted the proposal, and on the first evening came into the house and was quite talkative and friendly. My heart throbbed with fear, but I had to conceal it as best I could, and at length I mustered courage to say that my baby must be put to sleep, and that little Hape [sic] would wake up if there was so much talking in the house. Upon this he went, and I locked the door behind him, feeling that it was a frail protection against savage passions. . . . My condition while under this wild guardianship was no enviable one, but it was well to have trusted this man, for he was capable of much evil, and the promise of the reward no doubt exercised a strong restraining influence over him.[31]

Armstrong projects her own feelings outward onto Papatutai. Although it is her heart that is "throbbing," she attributes the sexual tension in the air to his "savage passions." Although Papatutai seems unthreatening ("quite talkative" and "friendly"), Armstrong struggles to conceal her fear. Heart pounding, Armstrong turns the key in the lock—the locked door serving as the symbol of a "civilized" patriarchal order, for the moment still intact. In her view, to accept Papatutai as a temporary substitute for her husband's protection perverts a civilized Christian order—represents a "wild" guardianship from which she cannot escape but which she does not support. Armstrong represents this experience in terms of having narrowly escaped a fate worse then death, crediting her own ingenuity with having staved off an imminent sexual attack. Although the anticipated rape never occurs, indeed is not even fully stated as a possibility, it nonetheless serves as the backdrop to this account, adding drama and tension to what otherwise would be an uninteresting and uneventful narrative.

Armstrong makes no reference to savage women in her account. Whether Papatutai has a wife or family is never raised as an issue—a textual absence that reinforces his place outside the "civilized" order of gender relations. Furthermore, Armstrong's sexual attraction to Papatutai surfaces through a subtext that strains against the bounds of Victorian sexual propriety. By imagining that it is Papatutai who desires her and not the other way around, Armstrong secures her identity as a sexually chaste Christian woman, obscuring the source of what for her society was an illicit interracial sexual attraction. Not having white male protectors (her husband is presented as entirely oblivious to her profound sense of sexual danger), Armstrong believes that her proper ladylike comportment, her Christian faith, and her civilized womanhood provide a shield around her through which Papatutai cannot penetrate.

For Armstrong, the possibility of having an intimate relationship with Papatutai is automatically foreclosed, yet it constantly resurfaces as a dangerous threat. By reading between the lines of Armstrong's narrative, it may be surmised that Papatutai has no personal interest in her but is merely fulfilling a promise to her husband to look after her when he is away on one of his frequent trips. Mr. Armstrong, himself, is represented as entirely at ease in making this request of Papatutai (bonding with him as a patriarch in their shared role of protecting the weaker sex), and Armstrong seems to resent her husband for entrusting her to Papatutai. Thus the repressed attraction that Armstrong feels for Papatutai but cannot express, given the bounds of Victorian propriety, is born of a mixture of loneliness, frustration, anger at her husband, and dissatisfaction with her domestic life.

In these accounts, Armstrong experiences herself as powerless and a potential victim—two feelings she clearly was not accustomed to feeling in relation to her Hampton students back home—and the act of writing itself serves as a way to restore her sense of control and autonomy. For other white women, like the Indian reformer and ethnologist Alice Fletcher, and the explorer May French-Sheldon, contact with primitive cultures represented opportunities to experience themselves as powerful political and intellectual leaders, helping them to forget and overcome their frustrations with the patriarchal aspects of white culture.

In the late nineteenth century, Anglo elites like Armstrong perceived primitives as dangerous and wild, not in control of their sexual feelings, lusting after white women. Margaret Mead tapped into this long-standing cultural fascination with primitive sexuality and was accepted as an expert on the primitive because she skillfully maneuvered within a discourse that had come to recognize Anglo-Protestant women as the ideal protectors (rather than the sexual victims) of the primitive. (See figs. 7-1–7-4.)

FIGURE 7-1 Parodying primitivism. Truly, Here is a Man After My Own Heart. Postcard, c. early 1900s. In its lighthearted mockery of the primitive rapist, this Valentine Day's postcard indicates how deeply embedded white fears of black men's sexuality were in the United States' popular and political unconcious.

I do not know the Indian tongue
And don't know how to sing it,
But slap your tom-tom, Heap Big Chief,
And swing it, brother, swing it.

C-193

© C. T. & Co.

FIGURE 7-2 Post-assimilationist primitivism. I do not know the Indian tongue. Postcard, c. early 1940s. With the United States government long past the point of trying to civilize Indians, popular culture began to look to exotics to provide whites with vibrant but safe pleasures. Notice how the possible sexual tension between a white woman and a primitive man is textually foreclosed by the infantilized primitive boy as her dance partner and the voyeuristic white cowboy as her chaperone.

FIGURE 7-3 Whitening primitives and sexualizing violence. Ooh! You're so Primitive. Postcard, c. 1960. Here's another way that mockery of the primitive rapist has figured in U.S. popular culture.

"Yes, we find the primitive existance to be quite exhilarating."

Y-18

FIGURE 7-4 Gone primitive. Yes, We Find the Primitive Existance [*sic*] to be Quite Exhilarating. Postcard, 1982. An effete upper-class man paired with a masculinized woman explorer, juxtaposed with a camping vehicle sporting a church, chandelier, and television antenna—a hybrid mix of many of the symbolic motifs of colonial adventuring—and the dangers thereof. Has decadence descended or is this an ironic vision of postimperialism?

By the time that Mead embarked for Samoa in 1925, the belief that white women could serve both as protectors and liberators of savages had received full play in the U.S. print media. Although her upbringing was steeped in Protestant evangelicalism, Mead was not a missionary and did not want to convert others to Christianity. Nor did Mead conceive of her own scientific expeditions to primitive societies as a way to demonstrate white women's independence and courage to a skeptical world, although the mainstream and feminist press reported on Mead's achievements under headlines (recalling French-Sheldon's) like "'Going Native' for Science" and with lead phrases like "Here's the only white woman to live alone among cannibals."[32]

Furthermore, Mead went to extreme lengths to differentiate her own "scientific" practices from those of evolutionary anthropologists, including Alice Fletcher. Speaking of the relationship between the modern fieldworker and her subject, Mead proclaimed, "[The 'pure' anthropologist] does not want to improve them, convert them, govern them, trade with them, recruit them or heal them."[33] Opposed to what she called "culture-wrecking," Mead characterized this earlier anthropology as poor science, distorted by assimilationist goals. She understood the role evolutionary anthropology had played in accelerating the deculturation of Native American societies. Mead differentiated her methodology from those of her predecessors, constructing herself as an objective scientist, whose practice, in distinction to Alice Fletcher's, was politically detached, morally neutral, theoretically valid, and empirically sound.

Despite her disavowals, however, Mead depended on nineteenth-century traditions to construct her own authoritative relationship to primitive societies (as their protector) and to maintain her authority as a scientific expert in the eyes of her Western audience. Anthropology attracted Mead initially and continued to compel her allegiance because it empowered her to act as a cultural mediator (or barrier when necessary) between the civilized and primitive. Like Fletcher in the 1890s, Mead believed that anthropologists were under severe time pressure to provide knowledge about primitive cultures before they were entirely subsumed within or destroyed by Western societies. Although in Mead's view, Fletcher had assisted in the annihilation of Native American cultures, and Mead saw her role as somehow preserving what was left of primitive cultures (or if not the cultures themselves, then Westerners' knowledge of them), the two positions were not that different. Mead's anthropology was riddled with the same tensions that existed in Fletcher's (although the way they defined the source of danger was very different.) Fletcher's intervention into Indian societies was justified, in her mind, by the necessity of protecting Indian women from brutish savage men and protecting Indian men from white people's rapaciousness (the gendered metaphor that feminized the Indian as a violated object is hers, not mine); Mead was willing to intervene in primitive cultures to "protect" them from "contamination" by the West. Despite her avowals about the necessity of the "pure" scientist remaining uninvolved, as a citizen sensitive to the injustices of Western imperialism, Mead sometimes found a neutral stance impossible.

Nor was Mead above taking advantage of imperialist power relations when it served her purposes to do so. In 1932, for example, she explained how Reo Fortune, her husband at the time, coerced unwilling men to help them carry their belongings by "unearth[ing] their darkest secrets which they wished kept from the government, and then order[ing] them to come and carry."[34] Mead's biographer, Jane Howard, also relates how Mead was shouted down when she gave speeches in Manus and in Port Moresby, Papua New Guinea, in 1953 (her first return since the 1930s) because she refused to acknowledge that she had made her "fortune . . . telling their stories around the world."[35] Howard tries to defend Mead, offering the observation that Mead would have been the first to encourage New Guineans to write down their own stories. Indeed, during the 1940s, Mead had urged Western anthropologists "to *study with* members of other cultures," cautioning them that it was "imperative to phrase every statement about a culture so that those statements are acceptable to the members of the culture itself."[36] Whether Mead called for this kind of collaboration because she believed it would promote more accurate accounts or whether she simply believed that Westerners had a moral obligation not to offend their informants remains unclear. Whichever the case, Mead seemed not to fully appreciate how imperialist dynamics gave her power and authority over her informants, a power they clearly resented.

Like Armstrong and French-Sheldon before her, Mead played to Western fears that a single white woman among primitives was always at some physical risk. This aspect of Mead's self-presentation can be most clearly discerned in her radio conversations with James Baldwin (transcribed and published in 1971 under the title *A Rap on Race*). In these exchanges Mead recollected one incident from her field work in New Guinea in the 1930s, in which she thought she had to retrieve a book of matches that strange men from another village had stolen from her. Recalling that she was all "alone in a village where there wasn't a single white person within two days' walk," Mead recounted:

> I had to get that box of matches back. If I didn't, I would have been as good as dead. White people who let a thief go used to be killed; they had shown themselves as weak. So I stormed up to the end of the village. This was a fine exercise of sheer white supremacy, nothing else. . . . I walked up to the end of the village and they were all sitting around in a circle and I said, "Give me those matches back." And one man put his hand his bag and said, "I didn't steal them; I just took them," and handed them back. Then we were all safe. Now if I had made one misstep I'd have been dead, and then the administration would have sent in a punitive expedition and they would have been dead.[37]

What interests me most in this account is the responsibility Mead invested in herself for ensuring everyone's safety—her ease with the Anglo-Saxon female role of protector. While she clearly feared for her life, she claimed greater fear for their lives and argued that their fate lay in her hands—not her fate in theirs. This sense of having greater power, knowledge, and skill than the primitive at maneuvering within the primitive's own world links Mead to both French-Sheldon and Fletcher and attributes to the white woman an agency and authority that simultaneously denies the "primitive" corresponding agency, knowledge, and power. It does not occur to Mead that these men might have understood the risks of retribution that the colonial government represented for them and that it might have been simply this recognition, and not any skillful maneuvering on her part, that lay behind their compliance with her orders.

Yet Mead also felt burdened by what she understood to be her complicity in maintaining the racist boundaries required by the strictures of white supremacy, for, as she immediately added in her conversation with Baldwin, she imagined that this was what it must have been like for white women in the antebellum U.S. South. "This is the burden, in a sense, that in this country the black man and the white woman carried in plantation days. If a white woman made a mistake, or didn't remember who she was every single second, everyone would suffer."[38]

Finally, there is one other tendency in Mead's work that owes its cultural resonance to the embeddedness of nineteenth-century constructions and that continues to be of great relevance to feminists in the late twentieth century. This has to do with the responsibility that Mead vested in women as mothers to abolish racial discrimination and oppression. Although Mead did not believe in the theory of the maternal transmission of racial traits, in the 1950s she set forth a cultural theory of mothering that held that better mothering could eliminate racial prejudice. Downplaying economic and social structures that perpetuated racial oppression, and conflating all forms of racism with individual prejudice, Mead argued that prejudice developed and served primarily as an "educational device" which the "average mother [uses] to bring up her children." Believing that all forms of racial oppression could be overcome through an alteration in childrearing practices, Mead recommended that mothers be taught not to make negative references to other groups as they raised their children.[39]

To illustrate the importance of unprejudiced childrearing methods, and in response to the query "Do the children of mixed marriages usually grow into more tolerant adults?" Mead cited an anecdote she claimed to be "render[ing] from memory of a story recorded on p. 168 in John Dollard's *Caste and Clan in a Southern Town* (1937)."

> There is quite a good anecdote that is told of a group of Negro children in the South who were picking on one sibling who was much lighter than the others. . . . [T]he mother comes out and says: "you chillun stop apickin' on dat pore white chile. He'd be jes' as black as you are if I hadn't got behind in mah insurance."[40]

Mead called this "a counter-racial joke," "a Negro-American joke which denies the fact that white people are the least interesting or attractive [to black people] except for economic reasons." Mead employed the joke in an attempt to allay fears among her white audience that black people constantly desire and seek sexual intercourse with white people. The context in which Mead repeated it suggested that it was a joke that black people told about themselves, and she used it to allude to the information it supposedly contained concerning actual childrearing practices among black people— practices, Mead seemed to be saying, that white people might consider as a model in raising their own children to be free of the racial prejudice that disparaged blackness.

However, when we compare Mead's analysis to the one that Dollard provided (since Mead gave the precise page number from Dollard, we can presume she knew of his interpretation), we find that Mead dramatically revised the significance of the joke by neglecting to mention that Dollard heard it from white women of the middle and upper classes. Dollard's interpretation, in fact, is quite different from Mead's. He found the joke interesting because it seemed to him "to convey an amusement [on the part of white women] at the freedom with which Negro women do sexual things," "to express a rather simple sort of envy of the superior freedom of Negro women, who . . . have access to men of both castes, as the white women do not." In short, for Dollard, the joke represented "the fleeting forms in which forbidden [sexual] interests can be socially expressed although they could not be seriously declared."[41]

This clearly, then, was not a joke that black people told about themselves, as Mead's reading implied, but a joke that elite southern white women told about black women in the 1930s. The joke does not contain information concerning actual child-rearing practices, as Mead's citing of it suggested, but expresses white hostility toward black women (masking the repression of white women's interracial sexual desires). Mead read "choice" into black women's imputed behavior, seeing freedom from, not entrapment within, racist economic structures, as the lesson the joke contained. Or to put this point in even stronger terms, Mead's analysis of "choice" transformed what might have been interpreted as the disparagement and sexual victimization of the black woman into a justification for her just punishment due to her own lack of industry and thrift (she should not have gotten behind in her insurance).

Had Margaret Mead been born several generations earlier, in 1850 rather than 1901, she very likely could have been a missionary in the vein of Mrs. M. F. Armstrong, or an ethnologist and advocate of Indian reform, like Alice Fletcher, or, with a little more money, an explorer of Africa, such as May French-Sheldon. As it was, Mead came of age at a moment when academic anthropology was consolidating its authority as a modern "science" of "primitive" nature and society. Mead's use of anthropology drew on her culture's longtime prurient fascination with the primitive as a racial other, on whom white women projected or worked through their own sexual and racial anxieties as they continued to reflect on what they should do about their own perceived sexual oppression.

Mead's insistence that the "pure" anthropologist was merely a neutral observer was disingenuous—or rather, it was a point of considerable instability upon which she seesawed throughout her career. The objectivity she insisted on when she claimed to be merely observing and recording cultural practices of primitive societies (as a pure anthropologist) was something she easily dispensed with in her critiques of both Western and non-Western patriarchal relations (as a feminist). Mead's relation to "primitives" was equally complex. Part of Mead wanted to "protect" primitive societies from what she saw as the contaminating influences of Western colonialism and modernization, and part of her wanted to spur primitive societies, as well the United States, into altering their gender practices.[42] To get primitives to change immoral practices without imposing Western values on them was not necessarily, for Mead, a contradiction, as she believed that certain values were universal and that human beings were often in agreement on moral questions. "Practices that are repugnant to our ethical system, often [are] also to the natives who practice them. . . . It is very interesting to see the way these practices which are most repugnant to humans disappear quickly when primitive people are given a chance at something else."[43]

As others have argued, by the standards of her day, Mead's science was not just competent, it was at the cutting edge of progressive anthropological practice. Yet, while Mead conceived of her work as an antihegemonic challenge to social Darwinism, eugenics, and evolutionary anthropology, this does not mean that her work was devoid of racism. Mead offered a radical critique of evolutionary anthropology and its political corollary, assimilationism, but her dependence on liberal constructs of "choice" and "freedom" impeded her ability to critique domestic racism. Her work was implicated in the history of Western imperialism in ways that she herself refused to acknowledge.

Envisioning a Future for Feminist Ethnography

> Feminist-inspired anthropological research and writing on gender rela-
> tions, after two decades of practice, has come of age. . . . We now see
> both the adjective of location—we are *Western* feminists . . . and the
> noun's contingent, historically determined existence. . . . It is necessary
> to break out of the closed system of ethnographic liberalism, to recognize
> that no ethnography is ever entirely nonevaluative, that *ethnography itself is a*
> *genre made possible by ongoing Western imperialism.*
>
> Micaela di Leonardo,
> *Gender at the Crossroads of Knowledge* (1991)

Despite her profound impact on our society, Mead does not figure prominently in most recent cultural histories, and she only occasionally appears among the pantheon of elite women whose works now constitute the canon of early feminist writings for the modern women's movement in the United States. Although Mead wrote columns about the women's movement for *Redbook Magazine* in the 1970s, the history of anthropology and feminism remain two separate and distinct fields of inquiry.[44] The dismissal of Mead as properly belonging to an early feminist tradition may also have been encouraged by Betty Friedan's interpretation of Mead (post-1949) as a biological essentialist: Friedan comments in *The Feminine Mystique* that Mead's writings, infused with Freudian ideas, "glorif[ied] the mysterious miracle of femininity, which a woman realizes simply by being female." Still, Friedan herself recognized that Mead had a "profound effect on the women in [her] generation, the one before it, and the generation now growing up."[45]

Unfortunately, much recent debate surrounding Mead's work still centers on the question of whether she wrote accurate or true ethnographies—in part because she herself was so emphatic about defending anthropology as a positivistic science that produced "objective" accounts of other cultures, and in part because so many social scientists today remain committed to positivism as an ideal to strive for, even if, as they understand, it can never be obtained. In the early 1980s, Derek Freeman's *Margaret Mead and Samoa: The Making and Unmaking of an Anthropological Myth* sparked a controversy over the scientific worth (accuracy) of Mead's ethnography.[46] As a result, Mead emerged once more as a subject of intense public scrutiny and debate. Freeman argued that Mead did not properly differentiate truth-telling and jesting among her adolescent informants and so had produced an ethnography that inaccurately represented Samoan sexual practices.

In response, academics published a flurry of articles reassessing the empirical methods and scientific validity of Mead's early work. The debate has tended to fixate on whether Mead's depictions of Samoan society correspond to other anthropologists' knowledge about the "reality" or "truth" about Samoan society and cultural practices in the early 1920s.[47] The few feminist scholars who have defended Mead against charges of shoddy science have done so from the perspective that no scientific practice is ever fully "objective" and have argued that the ethnocentrism in Mead's work was unavoidable and insignificant in light of the dominant practices of her day.[48]

I would argue otherwise. Mead's legacy for Western liberal feminism demonstrates that what counts as "good" ethnography is neither self-evident nor measurable in any objective sense, and most certainly does not derive from attempts to be "fair," "rational," or "scientific." Science cannot resolve the problems posed by the fact that the anthropological author-reader is always already *historically* as well as culturally positioned in relation to the object of study, as Micaela di Leonardo perceptively notes that "ethnography itself is a genre made possible by ongoing Western imperialism."[49] But this statement, so subtly put, raises other significant questions. How precisely should we characterize the relationship between ethnography and imperialism? If ethnographies are inescapably "evaluative," are they inescapably ethnocentric? To try to understand how previous forms of ethnography facilitated certain types of ethnocentric visions of the world, which in turn helped define the West and consolidate its power and authority over what was constituted as the non-West, does not explain how ethnography will function in the future, although it does focus our attention where it needs to be: on the contemporary effects of ethnographies, assessed in relation to a range of political contexts. The problem we must engage, then, is whether some kind of new ethnography can be created that might help undermine Western imperialism.[50]

Both the debates over Mead's competency as a scientist as well as feminist historians' relative neglect of her deflect us from examining how racism and ethnocentrism continue to inform an American liberal feminist tradition, not just in the most esoteric realms of feminist theory but also in popular expressions of feminist politics. The posing of the question, Was Mead's science "objective" (free from cultural ethnocentrism)? as well as the answer frequently offered by feminists today—No science is ever "objective"—excuse us from having to examine the *effects* of Mead's comparative cultural criticism on Western feminist thought today.

To identify these effects, it may be worth reflecting on an article that recently appeared in the *New York Times.* This article, written by Susan Chira and entitled "Nursing Becomes a Feminist Battlefield," describes the emotional difficulty that some middle-class U.S. women experience as they decide whether or not to breast-feed their infants.[51] The author attributes the dilemma to the psychological and cultural pressures resulting from the medical community's campaign to promote breast-feeding. Aware that the medical profession did not always advocate breast-feeding as the best form of infant care, Chira cautions American women against capitulating to the newest dogmas of scientific authority. Chira fears that the medical community's injunction to breast-feed will result in further restriction of U.S. women's economic opportunities, and she wants women to be able to resist, without guilt, the cultural pressure to nurse their babies. Thus, she demands of U.S. society that mothers be given the greatest "freedom of choice" in making such a decision.

So far, there is nothing particularly striking in the linkage of women's freedom with individual choice, which has become an intellectual mainstay of liberal feminism. What is remarkable (or rather unremarkable, if we understand the historical antecedents) is the way Chira attempts to defend "choice" as the basis of *Western* women's freedom. She does so by invoking an implicit assumption that freedom of choice differentiates the United States from the developing world. In a discussion that is, up until this point, clearly focused on a conflict between U.S. mothers and U.S. physicians, Chira introduces ethnographic evidence about breast-feeding practices of women in unspecified "developing countries." Desiring to show that breast milk is not always the best milk, that breast-feeding does not necessarily or automatically promote the health of child and mother, Chira marshals her evidence from interviews with Penny Van Esterik, an anthropologist from York University in Ontario, and Dr. Nafis Sadik, the executive director of the United Nations Population Fund.

Both Esterik and Sadik go on record as advocates of breast-feeding, but they provide Chira with conflicting data about the significance of nursing practices in developing countries. Sadik offers Chira examples of nursing mothers who suffer anemia and iron deficiencies, which for Chira serves as evidence that breast-feeding does not necessarily promote women's health. Esterik points out that bottle-feeding among women in developing countries does not change their status as full-time childrearers. For Chira, this fact serves as evidence that bottle-feeding does not liberate women from restrictive gender roles.

The evidence, then, is both contradictory and meaningless. Chira has no interest in determining whether breast-feeding or bottle-feeding is a better method of nursing infants for a specific group of women, in a specific sociohistorical context. The cultural logic and power of such an argument—why it is that Esterick's and Sadik's contradictory testimony about women in developing countries is seen as relevant for assessing U.S. cultural practices—only becomes evident when we reflect on Margaret Mead's legacy. For it was Mead who consolidated the idea for Western feminists that the "primitive" could be used to critique western patriarchy, even as primitive societies themselves were criticised for an even more extreme gender oppression. For Chira, the same logic is operable: such evidence can point us in the right direction (be wary of breast-feeding because women in developing countries who breast-feed suffer from nutritional deficiencies), even as such societies are devalued for their extreme misogynism (even when such women bottle-feed, they remain oppressed by restrictive gender roles). For these comparisons to have any meaning at all, we must understand ourselves as somehow connected to these women of developing countries (don't breast-feed, or you too may suffer health problems) yet consider our culture incommensurably superior in its gender relations (bottle-feeding would promote freedom for women in the United States, even though it doesn't promote freedom for women in developing countries). The developing world is invoked as capable of providing the United States with a critique of its own patriarchal gender relations, while at the same time, such a critique discredits the developing country as a model because of its own purported extreme and intransigent gender oppression.

Chira's assumption that situations in "developing countries" (generically and abstractly conceived) are relevant to Americans' assessment of their own patriarchal, misogynistic gender practices is logically possible only because Western liberal feminism has succeeded, since the late nineteenth and early twentieth centuries, in forging analytical comparisons between "civilized" and "primitive" women.[52] This tradition is a deeply problematic one, as I have shown, not the least because Western feminist theory has enabled the carving-out of a cultural space that empowers the "civilized" woman as morally superior to those "primitives" with whom she seeks to compare herself. In so doing, Western liberal feminism has perpetuated a cultural ethnocentrism that the Western speaker rarely intends and often cannot acknowledge. It's not simply that crosscultural forms of sisterhood are difficult to enact because of misunderstandings that stem from cultural differences. Rather, the history of Western liberal feminism has produced theoretical claims that position Western societies as superior to non-Western ones in terms of women's freedom from oppression, defined in terms of "individuality" and "choice."

I do not share di Leonardo's optimistic assessment that in the last two decades feminist anthropology has come of age. Too often, positivist feminist ethnography continues to assert that empiricism will somehow solve these conundrums, positing unproblematically that "systematic approaches" are better than "armchair reasoning."[53] Conversely, poststructuralist feminist ethnography too often assumes that exposing contradictions within imperialistic discourses will somehow automatically take the gale out of imperialist winds. Both traditions believe that writing "good" feminist ethnography (now acknowledged to be inescapably "evaluative" rather than value-free) is *only* a question of coming up with a better methodology or a more nuanced theory. Most practicing feminist anthropologists, I would suspect, would agree with di Leonardo that our recognition that "we are *western* feminists" somehow moves us beyond the ethnocentrism of Margaret Mead.

If Mead cannot be emulated as a capable scientist, neither can we reject her work on the grounds that our own practices and theoretical insights have nothing in common with hers (as she did in regard to her relation to evolutionists like Fletcher). Her ethnocentrism notwithstanding, Margaret Mead was grappling with important questions, that we still need to consider. If cultures are fundamentally untranslatable or incommensurable, what then is the point of and how shall we conduct comparative analyses? How does the attempt to understand other cultures help us grapple with our own? Given that we are always already historically and culturally positioned in relation to our objects of study, how do we write ethnographies that do not merely impose our views and morals on an "other" (or rather, to adopt Ann duCille's term, on the "othered")?[54] We must not be too quick to deny our historical embeddedness within the liberal feminist and anthropological traditions that Mead so centrally represents and embodies. Mead helped give authority to and popularize a framework that invoked the primitive for the articulation of Western feminist ideals—a framework that, if Susan Chira's article is any indication, we are still a long way from abandoning.

Conclusion

Coming to Terms

Compared to their sisters in the rest of the world, American women have it pretty easy. Just listen to the stories coming out of the Fourth UN Conference on Women. Parents killing their babies for being born female. Genital mutilation of pre-teenage girls. Bride-burning. Forced abortions. Mass rape.

> Louise Kiernan,
> *Chicago Tribune* (1995)

It would be a mistake to ask which comes first in the process of conceptual transformation—the "excess" of daily life, or the introduction of a different discursive repertoire . . . [because] the line of causality mov[es] in both directions.

> Ruth Frankenberg,
> *White Women, Race Matters* (1993)

THIS BOOK HAS OFFERED A HISTORY of the woman's movement that rejects the premise that feminism, in any of its late nineteenth- or early twentieth-century incarnations, was an egalitarian movement. Instead I have argued that the discourse we call woman's rights was shaped by the turbulent debates over race during the 1870s through 1890s and must be understood in relation to the nation's civilizing missions and imperial projects, both at home and abroad. The creation of early feminism was intricately connected to specific terrains of social struggle and transformation: enslavement, emancipation, evangelicalism, expansionism, immigration, and empire. Feminism developed in conjunction with—and constituted a response to—the United States' extension of its authority over so-called "primitive" peoples, and feminism was part and parcel of the nation's attempt to assimilate those peoples whom white elites designated as their racial inferiors.

I have also argued that white women used evolutionist discourses—unintentionally at times, at other times very purposefully—to expand the range of their political and social authority. White women's ability to become more powerful and visible as political agents was facilitated by their success in combining Victorian ideologies of patriarchal domesticity with ideologies of social evolution as they addressed the increasingly momentous questions of citizenship and empire. Excluded from positions of leadership in church and government, yet intent to offer a feminine alternative, white middle-class Protestant women formed their own organizations dedicated to applying the principles of woman's separate sphere and Christian civilization to the lives of Native Americans, formerly enslaved blacks, immigrant groups, and colonized peoples in Africa, the Caribbean, and Asia. Increased political power and freedom for white women was, in a material as well as ideological sense, dependent on asserting the racial inferiority and perpetuating the political subordination of nonwhite others. Paradoxically, elite white Anglo-Protestant women like Alice Fletcher and May French-Sheldon personally subverted the ideological juncture of domesticity and protection to escape the confinement of patriarchal homes themselves, only to export civilizationist patriarchy to those whom they racialized as primitives. In arguing for women's higher education, protective labor legislation, temperance, suffrage, and missionary activity, white women drew on an entrenched patriarchal tradition that made moral claims valuing the domestic sphere as the locus of white women's racial superiority. By century's end, white middle-class women's separate sphere, conceptualized initially as the antithesis of politics and a transcendent moral realm, had become synonymous with a political activism that was of critical importance to the nation in its efforts to colonize others.

Women's social-biological role as mothers and homemakers, white woman's rights activists often claimed, made women's unique experiences indispensable to their communities, to society, to politics, to civilization, and, finally, to outposts of primitivism in newly acquired colonies. The argument was often phrased just this way, without reference to race, but the racial dimension of the claim was apparent to all: white women, by virtue of their social evolutionary development, asserted themselves as the best qualified to reform the nation so that colonizing need not be so brutal. Assimilation and civilizing missions were conceived as humane alternatives to the violence and coercion that male politicians had condoned in whites' dealing with the so-called primitive groups of Indians, Chinese, Africans, and Filipinos. (See fig. 1-2.)

The Indian Reform movement was a crucial arena in which white women tested out the discourses of social evolution and civilizing missions—an arena in which social evolution reached its territorial limits before being exported to Hawaii, Cuba, and the Philippines. Indeed, by asserting their authority to act as *peaceful* agents of civilization, white women contributed a discursive innovation that was useful to those calling for the United States to embark on a more ambitious imperialist project—to eliminate "savagery" not just within the borders of the United States but throughout the world. In 1899, Harriet B. Bradbury justified the United States–Philippine war as "a necessity of evolution," a war fought in "defense of the weak."[1] A male apologist for annexation declared, "I believe in imperialism because I believe in foreign missions," explaining that subjugation of the Philippines was "not for domination but for civilization."[2]

For feminist theorists in the early twentieth century—women like Charlotte Perkins Gilman and Mary Roberts Smith Coolidge—assimilation appeared to have been remarkably effective in closing the gap between "the civilized" and "the primitive." Both Gilman and Coolidge interpreted this fact as evidence that society and the state might take the same attitude toward white women, that is, acknowledge that their nature was mutable, and that white racial advancement could be engineered by educating, enfranchising, and employing white women outside the home in cooperative industries. Gilman reassured her audience that the abolition of sexual differences would not bring about white racial degeneration, since sexual differences were an archaic vestige of primitivism, not the product of civilization. Gilman's insistence that (white) racial progress was not dependent on the maintenance of woman's separate sphere freed white women to take part in those activities defined as "masculine" without having to fear that they were jeopardizing "the race." This was indeed a radical critique of patriarchy, but one that placed responsibility for patriarchal oppression squarely on the primitive. Rather than subvert existing racial hierarchies that privileged white elites, Gilman strengthened them: she made the racial distinctiveness of civilized whiteness the foundation of her claim that *white* women were the equals of *white* men.

After 1920, Margaret Mead rejected evolutionary theories' racial hierarchies. But despite this rejection, Mead and other modern feminists retained certain nineteenth-century ideas about the cultural superiority of the United States as a Western, civilized society: notably, the idea that its advocacy of political democracy, free speech, freedom of choice, individual rights, and (ironically enough) woman's rights granted this superiority. The idea that white woman could serve as protector, or mediator, for vulnerable peoples was retained by feminist social scientists in the 1930s and 1940s: (white) woman's experience of sexism purportedly enabled her to sympathize with nonwhite peoples' experiences of racism and colonialism; her experience of freedom, liberalism, and democracy supposedly transformed her into a model of emancipation for women all over the world to look up to and follow.

In other words, racism was not just an unfortunate sideshow in the performances of feminist theory. Rather it was center stage: an integral, constitutive element in feminism's overall understanding of citizenship, democracy, political self-possession, and equality. Feminism offered race-specific ideas about gender, citizenship, social development, and racial progress that enabled white women to fashion moral arguments for altering (white) "woman's nature" and for bringing about radical change in gender relations, not just among whites but also between whites and those they deemed primitives. Feminism was a discourse about the evolutionary advantages that accrued to white women because of their race, and a demand that power should be reconfigured in U.S. society to take account of this fact. Beatrice Forbes-Robertson Hale, a self-proclaimed feminist of Charlotte Perkins Gilman's generation, put it most succinctly when she wrote, "It is necessary, then, to understand Feminism as an evolutionary development."[3] Or, as Elsie Clews Parsons explained in 1916, "the main objective of feminism is . . . the defeminisation, the declassification of [white] women as women."[4]

So how are we to come to terms with a history as disheartening as this one? Could feminists have specified a different relation to those they posited as racial others, in which "Africans," "Indians," and "primitives" would have been allowed their own distinct cultural projectories, their own forms (or absence) of patriarchy? Was it a problem of limited vision? Of good intentions but inadequate analysis? Of false exclusions or false inclusions?

Recently, similar questions have emerged in the debates within the National Organization for Women (NOW) over Tammy Bruce's comments in reference to the racism exhibited in the O. J. Simpson trial, about which she purportedly said, "We don't have to teach our children about race; what we have to teach them about is violence against women."[5] When Denny Blackwell, a black community leader in Los Angeles, protested that Bruce's remarks "somehow give domestic violence a priority over racism," Bruce was adamant that the two issues required ideological and political separation: "I'm an advocate for women," Bruce, at that time the head of the Los Angeles chapter of NOW, retorted. "What I work on is to try to improve the quality of women's lives."[6] As feminists noted at the time, Bruce's remarks left women of color out of the picture altogether, figuring neither as victims of domestic violence (in Bruce's usage, "women" meant white women) nor as victims of racism. How different in their effects, we may wonder, are Bruce's statements from the one that Susan B. Anthony gave to the press in 1884 when asked to comment on Frederick Douglass's marriage to Helen Pitts? "I have but one question, that of equality between the sexes—that of the races has no place on our platform."[7] Perhaps we can take some heart in the fact that NOW's board of directors, one-third of whom are women of color, issued a resolution censoring Bruce, while Patricia Ireland, the president of NOW, gave interviews in which she discussed the reasons for the reprimand. "[Bruce] violated very directly NOW's position that says we do not create a hierarchy and say that one type of oppression is more important. We consider that it's every bit as important to rid the world of Mark Fuhrmans as it is those nameless, faceless police officers who did not respond appropriately . . . after Nicole Simpson called 911."[8] NOW tried to get Bruce to recant, but Bruce refused to do so. She saw herself as representing a constituency of white women who were concerned that the issue of "violence against women" (read white women) was being set aside and subsumed into the issue of police misconduct against black men. We may remember that we have been down this road before: Abby Kelley rebuked Elizabeth Cady Stanton for her decision to fight against the Fourteenth Amendment, and Stanton's response, like Bruce's, was to create a new organization—one that would focus solely on "woman" and not on "race."

The problem facing NOW, however, is much larger than refusing to "create hierarchies" of oppression. Rather it is one of effective management of the irresolvable tensions that emerge because women experience oppression along multiple, intersecting, and competing axes. There is no singular "woman," no abstract "person" representing us all—only embodied subjects whose lives are governed by ever-shifting axes of power that are aligned and fragmented along lines of race, class, gender, sexuality, ethnicity, nationality, religion, and so forth. Universal principles of human rights, equality, and freedom are espoused as if these axes do not exist. But they do, and thus implementation of universal principles will always bring to the surface the conflicts and contradictions that the principles themselves are designed to cover over.

Clearly, this is not a problem for feminists alone but for all groups committed to social justice. Managing these kinds of tensions is required in every cultural and political arena: in "objective" reporting of the news; in the composing of nonethnocentric ethnographies; in the filming of documentaries; in representing "accurately" another's history; in forging political alliances between First World and Third World, Western and non-Western peoples; in protesting forms of patriarchal abuse that take place outside the borders of the United States. What the future holds depends on our learning to undo feminism's historical complicity with racism and imperialism; in subverting the unproblematic construction of the West as morally superior to the nonWest because it treats its women better (i.e, "the West is best" reflex). In the previous chapter, we saw how such constructions of the "West is best" informed one journalist's representation of breast-feeding debates in the United States. Similar constructions also permeate the media's reporting of the UN women's conference at Beijing ("Compared to their sisters in the rest of the world, American women have it pretty easy") and shape public discussion of the patriarchal abuses in Third World countries (e.g., the wearing of the bourqa in Afghanistan; the ban against women driving cars in Saudi Arabia; the practice of female genital mutilation in Egypt, etc.).[9] In short, feminists must find ways to challenge patriarchy without reinscribing discourses of Western domination or white superiority.

Unfortunately, there is a great deal of confusion (and purposeful obfuscation) of the inevitable conflicts among feminist, anticolonial, anticapitalist, and antiracist discourses. But we must not make the mistake of assuming that multiculturalism, postcolonialism, antiracism, and Western feminism are hopelessly at odds. Multiculturalists want to protect the cultural heterogeneity of U.S. society and so battle against the assimilationist impulses of conservatives, liberals, and others. Postcolonialists work to identify and address the long-lasting and insidious effects of imperial domination, even while understanding that colonialisms have so insinuated themselves into their "host" cultures that to purify the latter of the former is a herculean task. Antiracists challenge structures of racial domination, and feminists struggle to expose and subvert the patriarchal hierarchies that oppress women, whatever their cultural manifestation and geographic location. In their broadest formulations, feminism, antiracism, multiculturalism, postcolonialism, and anticapitalism (the list could be expanded infinitely) share a vision of a world free of domination, and thus the potential for interalliances is real and compelling. But we must first come to terms with the past in order to develop new strategies for the future, so that such a vision of social emancipation can be realized.

Notes

Introduction

1. *Report of the International Council of Women, Assembled by the National Woman Suffrage Association, Washington, D.C., U.S. of America, March 25 to April 1, 1888* (Washington, D.C.: Rufus H. Darby, 1888), p. 48.

2. Cited without attribution in Kathleen Barry, *Susan B. Anthony: A Biography of a Singular Feminist* (New York: New York University Press, 1988), pp. 318–319.

3. Susan B. Anthony to Elizabeth Cady Stanton, January 27, 1884, University of Rochester Library Archives, cited in Barry, *Susan B. Anthony,* p. 319.

4. For an account of racial conflict within the suffrage movement, see Ellen Carol DuBois, *Feminism and Suffrage: The Emergence of an Independent Women's Movement in America, 1848–1869* (Ithaca: Cornell University Press, 1978), pp. 162–202.

5. Anthony to Stanton, January 27, 1884, University of Rochester Archives, cited in Barry, *Susan B. Anthony,* p. 319.

6. "Address to the National Woman Suffrage Convention," Washington, D.C., January 19, 1869, reprinted in *The Concise History of Woman Suffrage: Selections from the Classic Work of Stanton, Anthony, Gage and Harper,* ed. Mari Jo Buhle and Paul Buhle (Urbana: University of Illinois Press, 1978), p. 254.

7. Stanton, "Address to the National Woman Suffrage Convention," p. 254.

8. For a discussion of these associations, see Barry, *Susan B. Anthony,* pp. 322–323, 346–347.

9. Robert H. Terrell, "Our Debt to Suffragists," *Crisis* 10 (August 1915): 181.

10. Terrell, "Our Debt to Suffragists," p. 181.

11. Terrell, "Our Debt to Suffragists," p. 181.

12. See Nancy F. Cott, *The Grounding of Modern Feminism* (New Haven: Yale University Press, 1987); Hazel Carby, *Reconstructing Womanhood: The Emergence of the Afro-American Woman Novelist* (New York: Oxford University Press, 1987); and Paula Giddings, *When and Where I Enter: The Impact of Black Women on Race and Sex in America* (New York: Bantam Books, 1984).

13. Cott, *Grounding of Modern Feminism*, pp. 69–70.

14. Barry, *Susan B. Anthony*, p. 319.

15. "True womanhood" has become shorthand for the way the dominant white gender system defined feminine virtue in the United States during the nineteenth century. See Barbara Welter, "The Cult of True Womanhood: 1820–1860," *American Quarterly* 18 (Summer 1966): 151–174.

16. Giddings, *When and Where I Enter*, p. 93.

17. Carby, *Reconstructing Womanhood*, p. 5. The six women were Frances Harper, Fannie Barrier Williams, Anna Julia Cooper, Fannie Jackson Coppin, Sarah J. Early, and Hallie Quinn Brown.

18. Cited only as Nancy Boyd Willey interview in Jean Howard, *Margaret Mead: A Life* (New York: Simon and Schuster, 1984), p. 53.

19. Joan Jacobs Brumberg, "Zenanas and Girlless Villages: The Ethnology of American Evangelical Women, 1870–1910," *Journal of American History* 69 (September 1982): 349. Brumberg explains in n. 6 that a seraglio is the portion of a Muslim house where women are secluded, similar to a Hindu zenana. A bagnio is a brothel or bathing-house. Suttee is the self-immolation of the Hindu widow on her husband's funeral pyre. Bastinado, a form of corporeal punishment, means being beaten with a stick on the buttocks.

20. Woman's Occidental Board of Foreign Missions, *Annual Report*, 1904, p. 53; cited in Peggy Pascoe, *Relations of Rescue: The Search for Female Authority in the American West, 1874–1939* (New York: Oxford University Press, 1990), p. 121.

21. "Address of Josephine St. P. Ruffin," *Woman's Era* 2 (August 1895): 15, 13.

22. Anna Julia Cooper manipulated evolutionary paradigms to combat the racism implicit in dominant ideologies, arguing that black women had the same evolutionary functions in relation to black racial progress as white women claimed for themselves in relation to white racial advancement. See Anna Julia Cooper, *A Voice From the South* (Xenia, Ohio: Aldine, 1982; reprint, New York: Oxford University Press, 1988), pp. 9, 11, 18–21, 51–55, 91, 116–123, and Kevin Gaines, *Uplifting the Race: Black Leadership, Politics, and Culture in the Twentieth Century* (Chapel Hill: University of North Carolina Press, 1996), pp. 128–151.

23. Louis Harlan, ed., *The Booker T. Washington Papers*, vol. 2 (Urbana: University of Illinois Press, 1972), p. 305; cited in Giddings, *When and Where I Enter*, p. 99.

24. Gaines, *Uplifting the Race*, p. 2.

25. Gaines, *Uplifting the Race*, p. 4.

26. Azel Ames, Jr., *Sex in Industry: A Plea for the Working Girl* (Boston: James R. Osgood, 1875), p. 9.

27. The term "Anglo-Saxon" was also sometimes used to mark the absorption of specific European races, including the French, Dutch, Norwegian, and Italian races; see Sir Walter Besant, "The Future of the Anglo-Saxon Race," *North American Review* 163 (August 1896): 136. According to Besant, Anglo-Saxon countries included England, the United States, Canada, Australia, South Africa, and New Zealand (p. 139). For other uses of "white," "Anglo-Saxon," and "Caucasian," see Gail Hamilton, "Race Prejudice," *North American Review* 141 (October 1885): 475–479, and "What is an American?" *Atlantic Monthly* 35 (May 1875): 561–567.

28. See, for example, Goldwin Smith, "Anglo-Saxon Union: A Response to Mr. Carnegie," *North American Review* 157 (1898): 170–185, and Philip Schaff, "Protestantism and Romanism," *Independent* 26 (February 26, 1874): 1.

29. Matthew Jacobson argues brilliantly that "the civic story of assimilation (the process by which Irishmen, Russian Jews, Poles, or Greeks became Americans) is inseparable from the cultural story of re-racialization (the process by which Celts, Hebrews, Slavs, or Mediterraneans became Caucasians)." See Matthew Frye Jacobson, *Becoming Caucasian* (Cambridge: Harvard University Press, forthcoming).

30. Anne McClintock, *Imperial Leather: Race, Gender and Sexuality in the Colonial Contest* (New York: Routledge, 1995), pp. 54–55; emphasis in original.

31. Gustave Le Bon, *La Psychologie des Foules* (1879), pp. 60–61; cited in McClintock, *Imperial Leather*, p. 54; also cited in Stephen Jay Gould, *The Mismeasure of Man* (New York: Norton, 1981), pp. 104–105.

32. Pascoe, *Relations of Rescue*, p. 13.

33. Pascoe, *Relations of Rescue*, pp. 17, 24.

34. My analysis here is drawn from Anne McClintock's discussion of Victorian Britain in *Imperial Leather*, p. 34.

35. For an especially insistent espousal of this view, see David Starr Jordan, *The Question of the Philippines: An Address Delivered before the Graduate Club of Leland Stanford Junior University on February 14, 1899* (Palo Alto: John J. Valentine, 1899). Also see Felix Adler, "The Philippine War: Two Ethical Questions," *Forum* (June 1902): 387–399; Francis A. Brooks, *The Unlawful and Unjustifiable Conquest of the Filipinos* (Boston: George H. Ellis, 1901); James L. Blair, *Imperialism: Our New National Policy. An Address Delivered before the Monday Evening Club, January 9, 1899* (St. Louis: Gottschalk, 1899).

36. David Starr Jordan, *"Lest We Forget": An Address Delivered before the Graduating Class of 1898, Leland Stanford Jr., University on May 25, 1898* (Palo Alto: John J. Valentine, 1898), especially pp. 31–32. For excellent secondary treatments of this issue, see Walter L. Williams, "United States Indian Policy and the Debate over Philippine Annexation: Implications for the Origins of American Imperialism," *Journal of American History* 66 (March 1979): 821–822, and Robert Beisner, *Twelve against Empire: The Anti-Imperialists, 1898–1900* (New York: McGraw-Hill, 1968).

37. Mrs. Jefferson Davis, "The White Man's Problem," *Arena* 23 (January 1900): 2; emphasis in original.

38. Carl Schurz, *American Imperialism: The Convocation Address Delivered on the Occasion of the Twenty-Seventh Convocation of the University of Chicago, January 4, 1899* (Boston: Dana Estes, 1899), p. 4. Also see Carl Schurz, "Imperialism," *Independent* (July 14, 1898): 83–86. This debate lasted well into the twentieth century. See, for example, Albert Ernest Jenks, "Assimilation in the Philippines, as Interpreted in Terms of Assimilation in America," *American Journal of Sociology* 19 (May 1914): 773–791.

39. Aileen S. Kraditor, *The Ideas of the Woman Suffrage Movement, 1890–1920* (New York: Norton, 1981 [1st ed., New York: Columbia University Press, 1965]), pp. 44–45, 86, 137. DuBois, *Feminism and Suffrage*, pp. 187–189.

40. Suzanne Lebsock, "Woman Suffrage and White Supremacy: A Virginia Case Study," in *Visible Women: New Essays on American Activism*, ed. Nancy A. Hewitt and Suzanne Lebsock (Urbana: University of Illinois Press, 1993), p. 63.

41. Lebsock, "Woman Suffrage and White Supremacy," p. 62. These scholars include Rosalyn Terborg-Penn, "Discrimination against Afro-American Women in the Woman's Movement, 1830–1920," in *The Afro-American Woman: Struggles and Images*, ed. Sharon Harley and Rosalyn Terborg-Penn (Port Washington, N.Y.: Kennikat Press, 1978), pp. 17–27; Angela Y. Davis, *Women, Race and Class* (New York: Random House, 1981), pp. 70–86; Giddings, *When and Where I Enter*, pp. 159–170; and Barbara Hilkert Andolsen, *"Daughters of Jefferson, Daughters of Bootblacks": Racism and American Feminism* (Macon, Ga.: Mercer University Press, 1986).

42. Cott, *Grounding of Modern Feminism*, p. 7.

43. Cott, *Grounding of Modern Feminism*, p. 19.

44. Jean Fagan Yellin, *Women & Sisters: The Antislavery Feminists in American Culture* (New Haven: Yale University Press, 1989).

45. In addition to the works cited in n. 41, see Hazel Carby, *Reconstructing Womanhood*; Evelyn Brooks Higginbothan, "African-American Women's History and the Metalanguage of Race,"

Signs 17 (Winter 1992): 251–274; and Higginbothan, *Righteous Discontent: The Women's Movement in the Black Baptist Church, 1880–1920* (Cambridge: Harvard University Press, 1993).

46. Carby, *Reconstructing Womanhood,* p. 18.

47. Gail Bederman, *Manliness & Civilization: A Cultural History of Gender and Race in the United States, 1880–1917* (Chicago: University of Chicago Press, 1995); T. J. Boisseau, "They Called Me *Bebe Bwana':* A Cultural Study of an Imperial Feminist," *Signs* 21 (Autumn 1995): 116–146; Ruth Frankenberg, *White Women, Race Matters: The Social Construction of Whiteness* (Minneapolis: University of Minnesota Press, 1993); Jane Hunter, *The Gospel of Gentility: American Women Missionaries in Turn-of-the-Century China* (New Haven: Yale University Press, 1984); Carolyn L. Karcher, *The First Woman in the Republic: A Cultural Biography of Lydia Maria Child* (Durham: Duke University Press, 1994); Peggy Pascoe, *Relations of Rescue;* Laura Wexler, "Tender Violence: Literary Eavesdropping, Domestic Fiction, and Educational Reform," *Yale Journal of Criticism* 5 (Fall 1991): 151–188; and Jean Fagan Yellin, *Women & Sisters.*

48. David Roediger, *The Wages of Whiteness: Race and the Making of the American Working Class* (New York: Verso, 1991), and *Towards the Abolition of Whiteness: Essays on Race, Politics and Working-Class History* (London: Verso, 1994); Noel Ignatiev, *How the Irish Became White* (New York: Routledge, 1995); and Matthew Jacobson, *Special Sorrows: The Diasporic Imagination of Irish, Polish and Jewish Immigrants in the United States* (Cambridge: Harvard University Press, 1995).

49. Antoinette Burden, *Burdens of History: British Feminists, Indian Women, and Imperial Culture, 1865–1915* (Chapel Hill: University of North Carolina Press, 1994); Nupur Chaudhuri and Margaret Strobel, eds., *Western Women and Imperialism: Complicity and Resistance* (Bloomington: Indiana University Press, 1992); Kimberle Crenshaw, "Demarginalizing the Intersection of Race and Sex: A Black Feminist Critique of Antidiscrimination Doctrine, Feminist Theory, and Antiracist Politics," *University of Chicago Law Forum* 139 (1989): 139–167; Laura E. Donaldson, *Decolonizing Feminisms: Race, Gender and Empire Building* (Chapel Hill: University of North Carolina Press, 1992); Donna Haraway, *Primate Visions: Gender, Race and Nature in the World of Modern Science* (New York: Routledge, 1989); Anne McClintock, *Imperial Leather;* Chandra Mohanty, "'Under Western Eyes': Feminist Scholarship and Colonial Discourse," *Feminist Review* 30 (Autumn 1988): 61–88; Susan Thorne "'The Conversion of Englishmen and the Conversion of the World Inseparable': Missionary Imperialism and the Language of Class in Early Industrial Britain," in *Tensions of Empire: Colonial Cultures in a Bourgeois World,* ed. Frederick Cooper and Ann Laura Stoler (Berkeley: University of California Press, 1997), pp. 238–262; Gayatri Spivak, *In Other Worlds: Essays in Cultural Politics* (New York: Routledge, 1988); George Stocking, *Victorian Anthropology* (New York: Free Press, 1987); Ann Laura Stoler, "Making Empire Respectable: The Politics of Race and Sexual Morality in Twentieth-Century Colonial Cultures," *American Ethnologist* 16 (1989): 634–660; Margaret Strobel, *European Women and the Second British Empire* (Bloomington: Indiana University Press, 1991); and Vron Ware, *Beyond the Pale: White Women, Racism and History* (London: Verso, 1992).

1. Evolution, Woman's Rights, and Civilizing Missions

1. Richard T. Ely, Introduction to *Women Wage-Earners: Their Past, Their Present and Their Future,* by Helen Campbell, (Boston: Roberts, 1893), p. v.

2. Jos Rodes Buchanan, "The Cosmic Sphere of Woman," *Arena* 1 (May 1890): 669, 679.

3. See, for example, Margaret W. Noble, "What Next in Women's Societies?" *Chautauquan* 14 (February 1892): 600–602; Buchanan, "The Cosmic Sphere of Woman," pp. 666–681.

4. Buchanan, "The Cosmic Sphere of Woman," pp. 666–681.

5. Katharine Coman, "The College Settlement," *Southern Workman* 29 (November 1900): 650, 652.

6. Anne McClintock, *Imperial Leather: Race, Gender and Sexuality in the Colonial Contest* (New York: Routledge, 1995), p. 33; emphasis in original.

7. For discussions of the 1893 Columbian Exposition in Chicago, see Gail Bederman, *Manliness & Civilization: A Cultural History of Gender and Race in the United States, 1880–1917* (Chicago: University of Chicago Press, 1995), pp. 31–41, and Robert W. Rydell, *All the World's a Fair: Visions of Empire at American International Expositions, 1876–1916* (Chicago: University of Chicago Press, 1984). For discussion of the exhibits at the Museum of Natural History in New York, see Donna Haraway, "Teddy Bear Patriarchy: Taxidermy in the Garden of Eden, New York City, 1908–36," in *Primate Visions: Gender, Race and Nature in the World of Modern Science* (New York: Routledge, 1989), pp. 26–58.

8. Such a box cover still exists and trades on the rare book/ephemera market. I thank Barbara Walzer, a rare book dealer in Providence, Rhode Island, for providing me with a photograph of it.

9. Cynthia Russett, *Sexual Science: The Victorian Construction of Womanhood* (Cambridge: Harvard University Press, 1989), p. 3.

10. Catherine Clinton, *The Other Civil War: American Women in the Nineteenth Century* (New York: Hill and Wang, 1984), p. 75.

11. Noble, "What Next in Women's Societies?" p. 601.

12. Clinton, *The Other Civil War*, p. 81.

13. Clinton, *The Other Civil War*, p. 90.

14. Nathaniel Shaler, "An Ex-Southerner in South Carolina," *Atlantic Monthly* 26 (July 1870): 59.

15. Alice C. Fletcher, "The New Orleans Exposition," *Southern Workman* 14 (July 1885): 79.

16. Clinton, *The Other Civil War*, p. 125.

17. Historian James McPherson explains that of the total 620,000 soldiers killed, 360,000 were Union and 260,000 Confederate. He does not break these statistics down by race but notes only that a total of 179,000 black soldiers fought in the war. James McPherson, *Ordeal by Fire: The Civil War and Reconstruction* (New York: Knopf, 1982), pp. vii, 355, 488.

18. Alice Kessler-Harris, *Out to Work: A History of Wage-Earning Women in the United States* (New York: Oxford University Press, 1982), pp. 76–80.

19. Clinton, *The Other Civil War*, p. 127.

20. Clinton, *The Other Civil War*, pp. 91–92, 124.

21. David Starr Jordan, "Evolution: What It Is and What It Is Not," *Arena* 18 (August 1897): 146.

22. Tayler Lewis, "The Highest Thing in Humanity," *Independent* 26 (January 8, 1874): 1.

23. Editor's Literary Record, *Harper's New Monthly Magazine* 49 (September 1874): 591. For an excellent overview of the development of evolutionary theory in Great Britain from the 1850s through the 1910s, see George W. Stocking, Jr., *Victorian Anthropology* (New York: Free Press, 1987).

24. Nancy Leys Stepan and Sander L. Gilman, "Appropriating the Idioms of Science: The Rejection of Scientific Racism," in *The Bounds of Race: Perspectives on Hegemony and Resistance,* ed. Dominick La Capra (Ithaca: Cornell University Press, 1991), p. 80.

25. Editor's Literary Record, p. 591.

26. Herbert Spencer, *The Principles of Biology* (New York: D. Appleton, 1864), p. 444. Although Spencer was the first to use the terms "struggle for existence" and "survival of the fittest," Darwin later adopted these phrases in subsequent editions of his own works. For a detailed explanation of both Darwin's and Spencer's use of the phrase, see the later edition of Spencer, *Principles of Biology* (New York: Appleton, 1898), p. 530.

27. The teleological cast to Spencer's theory was evident as early as 1852 in his "Theory of Population," *Westminster Review* 57 (April 1852): 499–500, and received its classic expression in *Principles of Biology* (1864), p. 444.

28. Herbert Spencer, "Psychology of the Sexes," *Popular Science Monthly* 4 (November 1873): 30–38; reprinted in *Men's Ideas/Women's Realities: Popular Science, 1870–1920,* ed. Louise Michele Newman, (New York: Pergamon Press, 1985), pp. 17–24. Richard Hofstadter, *Social Darwinism in American Thought* (Boston: Beacon Press, 1955), p. 195.

29. Louis Agassiz, "Evolution and Permanence of Type," *North American Review* 33 (January 1874): 98–99.

30. For a good example of the racial significance that evolutionary theory had for early proponents, see "The Progress from Brute to Man," *North American Review* 117 (October 1873): 255, 259, 261.

31. Chauncey Wright, "The Genesis of Species," *North American Review* (July 1871): 64, 63.

32. See Antoinette Brown Blackwell, *The Sexes throughout Nature* (New York: Putnam, 1875), p. 21, and Margaret N. Wishard, "Sex Nature or Human Nature?" *Chautauquan* 15 (September 1892): 748–750; "The Weaker Sex," *Revolution* 5 (February 10, 1870): 91. Also see Frances Emily White, "Woman's Place in Nature," *Popular Science Monthly* 6 (January 1875): 292–301, Miss M. A. Hardaker, "Science and the Woman Question" *Popular Science Monthly* 20 (March 1882): 577–584, and Mary T. Bissell, "Emotions versus Health in Women," *Popular Science Monthly* 32 (February 1888): 504–510, reprinted in Newman, *Men's Ideas/Women's Realities,* pp. 25–53. For secondary sources, see Marie Tedesco, "A Feminist Challenge to Darwinism: Antoinette L. B. Blackwell on the Relations of the Sexes in Nature and Society," in *Feminist Visions: Toward a Transformation of the Liberal Arts Curriculum,* ed. Diane L. Fowlkes and Charlotte S. McClure (University, Al.: University of Alabama Press, 1984), pp. 53–65.

33. Charles Darwin, *The Descent of Man, and Selection in Relation to Sex* (London: John Murray, 1871), p. 64; cited in Sue V. Rosser and A. Charlotte Hogsett, "Darwin and Sexism: Victorian Causes, Contemporary Effects," in *Feminist Visions,* p. 44.

34. Spencer, "Psychology of the Sexes," in Newman, *Men's Ideas/Women's Realities,* pp. 17–18.

35. Charles Darwin, *The Descent of Man and Selection in Relation to Sex* (New York: Appleton, 1906 [1st ed. 1871]), pp. 568–569, 576–578. Spencer also adhered to this theory of "partial limitation of heredity by sex"; see "Psychology of the Sexes," in Newman, *Men's Ideas/Women's Realities,* p. 21. The theory was complicated, however, as not all sexual traits were acquired through sexual selection or governed by the law of partial inheritance. Some sexual traits were passed from each parent to offspring of both sexes, while other traits were sex-linked, that is, passed from father to son or mother to daughter. Still other characteristics could be transmitted through both sexes but would develop only in the offspring of the same sex. For example, via the "equal transmission of characters," a woman could pass along her father's musculature to her sons, even though she herself had not developed her father's musculature. Her daughters, in turn, would share either their mother's or their paternal grandmother's feminine musculature, yet still have the capability of transmitting their father's or their maternal grandfather's musculature to their own sons. These specifics attracted notice from women commenting on social Darwinian theory in the 1870s. See Blackwell, *Sexes throughout Nature,* p. 21, and Frances Emily White, "Woman's Place in Nature," in Newman, *Men's Ideas/Women's Realities,* p. 25.

36. The most virulent expressions of woman's intellectual inferiority are contained in Darwin, *Descent of Man,* p. 576. For women's responses, see Blackwell, *Sexes throughout Nature,* and the discussion in chapter 2.

37. Spencer, "Psychology of the Sexes," in Newman, *Men's Ideas/Women's Realities,* p. 18. Also repeated in Herbert Spencer, *Study of Sociology* (New York, 1893), p. 373, cited in Jill Conway, "Stereotypes of Femininity in a Theory of Sexual Evolution," in *Suffer and Be Still: Women in the Victorian Age,* ed. Martha Vicinus (Bloomington: Indiana University Press, 1973), p. 141. For Antoinette Brown Blackwell's repudiation, see *Sexes throughout Nature,* pp. 13–15.

38. Edward H. Clarke, *Sex in Education; Or, A Fair Chance for the Girls* (Boston: Osgood, 1873), and G. Stanley Hall, *Adolescence: Its Psychology and Its Relations to Physiology, Anthropology, Sociology, Sex, Crime, Religion and Education,* 2 vols. (New York: Appleton, 1904). See chapter 3 for a fuller discussion of this debate.

39. Patrick Geddes and J. Arthur Thomson, *The Evolution of Sex* (London: Scott, 1889), p. 271; see Stephanie Shields, "The Variability Hypothesis: The History of a Biological Model of Sex Differences in Intelligence," *Signs* 7 (Summer 1982): 769–797.

40. See Rosalind Rosenberg, "The Dissent from Darwin, 1890–1930: A New View of Woman among American Social Scientists," (Ph.D. diss., Stanford University, 1974), p. 13.

41. For a discussion of ancient Greek thought on "Nature" and "woman's nature," see Susan Moller Okin, *Women in Western Political Thought* (Princeton: Princeton University Press, 1979).

42. Barbara Welter, "The Cult of True Womanhood: 1820–1860," *American Quarterly* 18 (Summer 1966): 151–174.

43. Lucretia Mott, *Discourse on Woman* (Philadelphia: T. B. Peterson, 1850), p. 7.

44. Samuel Longfellow, "Speech to the Tenth National Woman's Rights Convention," May 10–11, 1860, in *History of Woman Suffrage,* ed. Elizabeth Cady Stanton, Susan B. Anthony, and Matilda Joslyn Gage, vol. 1 (Rochester, N.Y.: Susan B. Anthony, 1889), p. 712.

45. Abba Goold Woolson, *Woman in American Society* (Boston: Roberts, 1873), p. 50.

46. Elizabeth Cady Stanton, "Letter to George G. Cooper, Editor of the *National Reformer,* Rochester New York, September 14, 1848," in *Elizabeth Cady Stanton as Revealed in Her Letters, Diary and Reminiscences,* ed. Theodore Stanton and Harriot Stanton Blatch, vol. 2 (New York: Harper, 1922; reprint, New York: Arno Press, 1969), p. 19.

47. See Gail Bederman, "'Civilization,' the Decline of Middle-Class Manliness, and Ida B. Wells's Antilynching Campaign (1892–94)," *Radical History Review* 52 (Winter 1992): 5–30, and Bederman, *Manliness & Civilization.*

48. W. I. Thomas, "On a Difference in the Metabolism of the Sexes," *American Journal of Sociology* 3 (July 1897): 41.

49. See Spencer, "Psychology of the Sexes," in Newman, *Men's Ideas/Women's Realities,* pp. 19–20.

50. Barbara Welter, "She Hath Done What She Could," *American Quarterly* 30 (Winter 1978): 627 n. 12. Also see Patricia Hill, *The World Their Household: The American Woman's Foreign Mission Movement and Cultural Transformation, 1870–1920* (Ann Arbor: University of Michigan Press, 1985), pp. 213–222.

51. Joan Jacobs Brumberg, "Zenanas and Girlless Villages: The Ethnology of American Evangelical Women, 1870–1910," *Journal of American History* 69 (September 1982): 350.

52. Brumberg, "Zenanas and Girlless Villages," p. 350. In 1868 Congregational women organized the Woman's Board of Missions; in 1869, the Methodist Episcopal women created the Woman's Foreign Mission Society; in 1870, Presbyterian women founded the Ladies Board of Foreign Missionary Societies; and in 1873, Baptist women formed the Woman's Baptist Foreign Missionary Society. These were the most active of the postbellum organizations. The Woman's Foreign Missionary Society of the Methodist Episcopal Church, North published the journal, *Heathen Woman's Friend* (Boston, 1869–1895); the Woman's Foreign Missionary Society of the Presbyterian Church published the journal *Woman's Work for Woman* (Philadelphia and New York, 1871–1885); the Woman's Board of Missions, Congregational published the journal *Life and Light for Heathen Women* (1869–1922); the Woman's Baptist Foreign Mission Society published *Helping Hand* (1872–1914); and the Woman's Union Missionary Society in New York published *Missionary Link* (1861–1893). See Brumberg, "Zenanas and Girlless Villages," p. 352.

53. See Jean Fagan Yellin, *Women & Sisters: The Anti-Slavery Feminists in American Culture* (New Haven: Yale University Press, 1989).

54. See Hazel Carby's discussion of black women's protests at their exclusion from the Woman's Pavilion at the Chicago World's Fair in *Reconstructing Womanhood: The Emergence of the Afro-American Woman Novelist* (New York: Oxford University Press, 1987), pp. 3–7. Also see Paula Giddings, *When and Where I Enter: The Impact of Black Women on Race and Sex in America* (New York: Bantam, 1984).

55. Carby, *Reconstructing Womanhood,* p. 6.

56. Cited without full attribution in Nell Irvin Painter, *Sojourner Truth: A Life, A Symbol* (New York: Norton, 1996), p. 167.

57. Cited without attribution in Painter, *Sojourner Truth,* p. 167. Various versions of this speech also appear in several anthologies, including *Feminism: The Essential Historical Writings,* ed. Miriam Schneir (New York: Vintage Books, 1972), p. 94, and *The Concise History of Woman Suffrage,* ed. Mari Jo Buhle and Paul Buhle (Urbana: University of Illinois Press, 1978).

58. Painter, *Sojourner Truth,* pp. 169–173. Indeed, northerners often expressed shock when they traveled to southern areas of the country, witnessing for the first time the arduous physical labor that enslaved black women (and lower-class white women) were physically capable of and were routinely compelled to do. Frederick Law Olmsted, *A Journey in the Black Country in the Winter of 1853–1854* (New York: Mason, 1860), p. 81; cited in Jacqueline Jones, *Labor of Love, Labor of Sorrow: Black Women, Work and the Family from Slavery to the Present* (New York: Basic Books, 1985), pp. 16–17. Travelers to Europe or to rural areas of New England were often struck by the "robustness" of the women and associated their physical strength with either the invigorating effects of the climate or their lower-class heredity. See, for example, Nathaniel S. Shaler's account of his trip to Western Pennsylvania in "The Summer's Journey of a Naturalist," *Atlantic Monthly* 32 (August 1873): 182–183.

59. See an anonymous review of Edward B. Tyler's classic work *Primitive Culture* (New York: Henry Holt, 1871), Editor's Literary Record, *Harper's New Monthly Magazine* 49 (September 1874): 590–591.

60. Sarah Grand, "The New Aspect of the Woman Question," *North American Review* 158 (March 1894): 274–275.

61. Mary Lowe Dickinson (1839–1914), born in Fitchburg, Massachusetts, and educated at common schools and by private tutors, studied art and literature in Europe for three years before marrying John B. Dickinson, a New York banker. During her lifetime she held prominent offices in the Female Bible Society (secretary), the Women's National Indian Association (president, 1885), the National Council of Women (president), and the International Order of the King's Daughters and Sons (general secretary, 1886–1914). In the 1800s she was active in the Indian reform movement, helping to edit *Lend a Hand.* She also developed a career as an author, publishing two volumes of poetry, six works of fiction, and hundreds of short stories.

62. Mary Lowe Dickinson, *Among the Thorns* (New York: G. W. Carleton, and London: S. Low, 1880). *Among the Thorns* received two brief reviews published anonymously in the New York *Independent: Independent* 32 (July 1, 1880): 10, and 32 (September 23, 1880): 12. Lydia Maria Child, *A Romance of the Republic* (Boston: Ticknor and Fields, 1867). The best discussion of *A Romance of the Republic* is in Carolyn L. Karcher, *The First Woman in the Republic: A Cultural Biography of Lydia Maria Child* (Durham: Duke University Press, 1994), pp. 510–527.

63. Stepan and Gilman, "Appropriating the Idioms of Science," p. 80.

64. See Rosalind Rosenberg, *Beyond Separate Spheres: Intellectual Roots of Modern Feminism* (New Haven: Yale University Press, 1982).

65. Blackwell, *Sexes throughout Nature,* pp. 11, 33–34.

66. Lizzie M. Holmes, "Woman's Future Position in the World," *Arena* 20 (September 1898): 342.

67. Other examples of this position include Wishard, "Sex Nature or Human Nature?" pp. 748–750, and "Statement of Mrs. Charlotte Perkins Stetson, of California," in *Hearing of the National American Woman Suffrage Association,* Committee on the Judiciary, House of Representatives, January 28, 1896 (Washington: Government Printing Office, 1896), pp. 5–6. Copy available in microfilm reel 5, Elizabeth Cady Stanton Papers, Library of Congress.

68. Wishard, "Sex Nature or Human Nature?" p. 749.

69. Ora Brashere, *Science and Suffrage: An Inquiry into the Causes of Sex Differences* (Salt Lake City: n.p., 1909), pp. 8, 10. Copy available in *Gerritsen Collection of Women's History,* (Glen Rock, N.J.: Microfilming Corp. of America, 1975).

70. Eliza Gamble, *The Sexes in Science and History: An Inquiry into the Dogma of Woman's Inferiority to Man* (New York: Putnam, 1916), pp. v, vii–viii; my emphasis.

71. "While it is doubtless true, in a certain sense, that 'that which has been is that which shall be,'" White declared, "nevertheless, [since] *change (in accordance with law) underlies the very idea of evolution,* . . . the sphere of woman will be determined by the kind and degree of development to which she shall attain." "Woman's Place in Nature," *Popular Science Monthly* (January 1875): 301; my emphasis.

72. This argument is further elaborated in chapter 3.

73. This ambivalence became most evident in White's discussion of "woman" participating in "man's" work: "When we look around upon the great industries of [civilized] life, mining, engineering, manufacturing, commerce, and the rest and consider how little direct agency woman has had in bringing them to their present state of progress, we are compelled to believe that she must not look toward direct competition with man for the best unfolding of her powers, but rather, while continuing to *supplement* him, as he does her, in the varied interests of their common life, *that her future progress, as in the past, will consist mainly in the development of a higher character of womanhood through the selection and consequent intension* [sic] *of those traits peculiar to her own sex."* White, "Woman's Place in Nature," p. 301; my emphasis.

74. Stocking, *Victorian Anthropology,* p. 145.

75. John Bascom, "The Gist of the Labor Question," *Forum* 4 (September 1887): 94.

76. See President Garfield's inaugural message of 1881, in *Southern Workman* 10 (March 1881): 29. See also "The Education of the American Indians," *Indian's Friend* 2 (November 1889): 1.

77. See J. Coleman Adams, "Is America Europeanizing?" *Forum* 4 (September 1887): 190–200, especially 192.

78. Roger Daniels, *Asian America: Chinese and Japanese in the United States Since 1850* (Seattle: University of Washington Press, 1988), pp. 67–91.

79. See Thomas Gossett, *Race: The History of an Idea in America* (New York: Schocken, 1969) pp. 253–286, especially p. 281. Shaler's views on racial difference can be found in his "Ex-Southerner in South Carolina," *Atlantic Monthly* 26 (July 1870): 53–61; "Mixed Populations of North Carolina," *North American Review* (January 1873): 150–166; "The Negro Problem," *Atlantic Monthly* 54 (November 1884): 697–706; "The African Element in America," *Arena* 2 (November 1890): 660–673, and "The Nature of the Negro," *Arena* 3 (December 1890): 25. For biographical information on Shaler, see Thomas G. Dyer, *Theodore Roosevelt and the Idea of Race* (Baton Rouge: Louisiana State University Press, 1980), p. 6; David N. Livingston, *Nathaniel Southgate Shaler and the Culture of American Science* (Tuscaloosa: University of Alabama Press, 1987); and Stephen Jay Gould, "In a Jumbled Drawer," *Natural History* 97 (August 1988): 12.

80. Ward's most important monographs, in order of publication, are: *Dynamic Sociology, Or Applied Social Science, as Based upon Sociology and the Less Complex Sciences,* 2 vols. (New York: Appleton, 1883 [2nd ed. 1897]); *The Psychic Factors of Civilization* (Boston: Ginn, 1893); *Pure Sociology: A Treatise on the Origin and Spontaneous Development of Society* (New York: Macmillan, 1903 [2nd ed., 1909]) and

Applied Sociology: A Treatise on the Conscious Improvement of Society by Society (Boston: Ginn, 1906). Also see Gossett, *Race*, p. 166.

81. Shaler, "An Ex-Southerner in South Carolina," p. 60.

82. Shaler, "An Ex-Southerner in South Carolina," p. 60.

83. Shaler, "Mixed Populations of North Carolina," pp. 161–162.

84. Shaler, "Mixed Populations of North Carolina," p. 162.

85. Shaler, "Mixed Populations of North Carolina," p. 163. Similar arguments were made to demonstrate the evolutionary inferiority of (white) women in comparison to (white) men: being less variable, white women's potential for intellectual advancement was also assumed to be more limited than white men's. See Shields, "The Variability Hypothesis," pp. 769–797.

86. Ward, *Pure Sociology*, pp. 210–211; my emphasis.

87. Ward, *Pure Sociology*, pp. 202, 204, 209–210. Also see Gossett's summary of Ward's theory in *Race*, p. 165.

88. In *Pure Sociology*, Ward writes, "[T]he process of race mixture that has always gone on and is still going on through the union of men of superior [races] with women of inferior races is at least in the nature of a leveling *up*, and not a leveling *down*" (360; emphasis in original).

89. "When a woman of a superior race rejects and spurns the man of an inferior race," Ward explained, "it is from a profound though unreasoned feeling that to accept him would do something more than disgrace her, *that it would . . . lower the race to which she belongs*. And when the man of an inferior race strives to perpetuate his existence through a woman of a superior race, it is something more than mere bestial lust that drives him to such a dangerous act. It is the same unheard but imperious voice of nature commanding him at the risk of 'lynch law' to raise his race to a little higher level." *Pure Sociology*, p. 359; my emphasis.

90. Ward, *Pure Sociology*, p. 359.

91. Ward, "Our Better Halves," *Forum* 6 (November 1888): 274.

92. Ward, *Psychic Factors of Civilization*, p. 175.

93. Ward, "Our Better Halves," p. 275; my emphasis.

94. Ward first began to develop his "gynaecocentric" theory—or what might more accurately be called his theory of white racial conservation—through an exchange with a British writer, Grant Allen, published in the *Forum* from 1888 through 1890, although Ward did not use the term "gynaecocentric theory" until 1903. The exchange began with Ward's "Our Better Halves," to which Allen responded with "Woman's Place in Nature," *Forum* 7 (May 1889): 258–263. A year later the debate continued with Allen's "Woman's Intuition," *Forum* 9 (May 1890): 333–340, in response to which Ward wrote "Genius and Woman's Intuition," *Forum* 9 (June 1890): 401–408. The origin of this concept can be found in Johann Jakob Bachofen, *Das Mutterrecht* (Stuttgart: Krais and Hoffmann, 1861), of which Ward read the second edition, published in Basel in 1897. See *Pure Sociology*, p. 336. Ward and Allen's exchange was to prove extremely influential on future feminist thought. See chapter 7 for a discussion of Gilman's response to and use of Ward's gynaecocentric theories.

95. Ward did not specify how women lost the power of sexual selection, but he located it in a very early phase of human history, at a time when extant races were all situated in primitive stages of development, even lower stages than those occupied by the "lowest races" alive in Ward's day. See *Pure Sociology*, p. 337.

96. Charlotte Perkins Gilman, "Feminism," typescript, n.d., c. 1908, folder 175, Charlotte Perkins Gilman Papers, Schlesinger Library, Harvard University.

97. See Anna Julia Cooper, *A Voice from the South, by a Black Women of the South* (Xenia, Oh.: Aldine, 1892; reprint, New York: Negro Universities Press, 1969; New York: Oxford University Press, 1988).

98. "Scope and Content Note accompanying the Otis Tufton Mason Collection," National Anthropological Archives, Smithsonian Institution. Also see Neil M. Judd, *The Bureau of American Ethnology: A Partial History* (Norman: University of Oklahoma Press, 1967), pp. 3, 10, 11.

99. Nancy Oestreich Lurie, "Women in Early American Anthropology," in *Pioneers of American Anthropology*, ed. June Helm (Seattle: University of Washington Press, 1966), pp. 36, 38. Mason's interest in the woman question can be seen in both the opening and closing statements of his book. His first paragraph reads: "Of the billion and a half human beings on the earth, one half, or about seven hundred million are females. What this vast multitude are doing in the world's activities and what share their mothers and grandmothers, to the remotest generation backward, have had in originating culture, is a question which concerns the whole race. The answer to this inquiry will benefit the living in many ways, especially if it can be shown that the achievements of women have been in the past worthy of honor and imitation" *Woman's Share in Primitive Culture* (New York: D. Appleton, 1898), p. 1. At the end of this book, Mason concludes, "It is not here avowed that women may not pursue any path in life they chose. . . . But before it is decided to do that there is no harm in looking backward over the honourable achievements of the sex. All this is stored capital, accumulated experience and energy. . . . All this beneficent labour is the birthright of women, and much of it of women alone. Past glory therein is secure, and it only remains to be seen how far the future will add to its lustre in the preservation of holy ideals" (286).

100. Mason first presented the main themes of his book in a talk he gave at an annual meeting of the American Association for the Advancement of Science held in Cleveland in 1888. See Otis T. Mason, "Woman's Share in Primitive Culture," *American Antiquarian* 11 (January 1889): 3–13. Mason's book was published by D. Appleton, as the first in a series designed to introduce some aspects of recent anthropology to a lay audience.

101. Mason, *Woman's Share in Primitive Culture*, p. 238.

102. See Kevin K. Gaines, *Uplifting The Race: Black Leadership, Politics, and Culture in the Twentieth Century* (Chapel Hill: University of North Carolina Press, 1996).

103. I am indebted to Gail Bederman for clarification of this point. Also see Joan Jacobs Blumberg, *Mission for Life: The Story of the Family of Adoniram Judson, the Dramatic Events of the First American Foreign Mission, and the Course of Evangelical Religion in the Nineteenth Century* (New York: Free Press, 1980), pp. 79–106.

104. Elizabeth Cady Stanton, "Educated Suffrage," *Independent* (February 14, 1895): 2.

105. Mrs. J. B. [Mary Lowe] Dickinson, "Address of the President, at the Annual Meeting of the Women's National Indian Association, November 17, 1885" (Philadelphia, 1885), p. 2.

106. For an overview of white women's activities as foreign missionaries, see Jane Hunter, *The Gospel of Gentility: American Women Missionaries in Turn-of-the-Century China* (New Haven: Yale University Press, 1984); Hill, *The World Their Household*; Brumberg, *Mission for Life*, pp. 79–106; Welter, "She Hath Done What She Could," 624–638; and Marion Kilson, *Mary Jane Forbes Greene (1845–1910), Mother of the Japan Mission: An Anthropological Portrait* (Lewiston, N.Y.: Edwin Mellen Press, 1991), pp. 1–8. See Hill, *The World Their Household*, p. 8, for the size of the foreign mission movement.

107. "What Woman Will Do in War and after War," *Woman's Protest* 9 (1916): 8, cited in Susan E. Marshall, "In Defense of Separate Spheres: Class and Status Politics in the Antisuffrage Movement," *Social Forces* 65 (December 1986): 341.

108. This situation partially explains why African Americans were so hesitant to discuss gender conflicts in public and why so much of the existing discourse on Indian rights, for example, begins with testimonies of Indians who begin their arguments by assuring whites that they as individuals have accepted whites' civilization. See, for example, "Two Indian Speeches," *In-*

dian's Friend 1 (March 1889): 4; Chas. W. Hoffman, "Compulsory Education from an Indian's Standpoint," *Southern Workman* 30 (November 1901): 622–624; and Zallie Rulo, letter published in *Southern Workman* 14 (June 1885): 62.

109. E. D. Cope, "What is the Object of Life?" *Forum* 4 (September 1887): 53.

110. William Graham Sumner, *What Social Classes Owe to Each Other* (New York: Harper, 1883; reprint, Caldwell, Idaho: Caxton Printers, 1982), p. 56.

111. Kevin Gaines' *Uplifting the Race* discusses attempts by the black middle classes to insert class distinctions into a civilization discourse that downplayed the salience and significance of class difference.

112. See Nicole Hahn Rafter, *White Trash: The Eugenic Family Studies, 1877–1919* (Boston: Northeastern University Press, 1989), for the influence of eugenics discourse on the branding of poor whites with the stigma of moral deviance and mental deficiency.

2. The Making of a White Female Citizenry

1. Kristi Andersen, *After Suffrage: Women in Partisan and Electoral Politics before the New Deal* (Chicago: University of Chicago Press, 1996), pp. 1–20.

2. Elizabeth Cady Stanton, article published in *Revolution* (January 14, 1869): 24–25, reprinted as Document 8 in *The Elizabeth Cady Stanton–Susan B. Anthony Reader: Correspondence, Writings, Speeches,* ed. Ellen Carol DuBois (Boston: Northeastern University Press, 1992), pp. 122–123.

3. Andersen, *After Suffrage,* p. 13.

4. Margaret J. Evans, "The Woman Citizen a Woman First of All," in *The Woman Citizen's Library,* ed. Shailer Mathews, vol. 12 (Chicago: Civics Society, 1914), p. 2987.

5. Elizabeth Cady Stanton, "Where Social Progress Must Begin," letter to the editor, *New York Sun* (November 25, 1901). Copy in microfilm reel 2, Elizabeth Cady Stanton Papers, Library of Congress.

6. See Stanton's article in *Revolution* (January 11, 1869); reprinted as Document 8 in DuBois, *Stanton-Anthony Reader,* pp. 119–124.

7. Elizabeth Cady Stanton, "Address of Mrs. Elizabeth Cady Stanton, Delivered at Seneca Falls & Rochester, N.Y., July 19th & August 2nd, 1848," Susan B. Anthony Scrapbook no. 1, microfilm reel 5, Elizabeth Cady Stanton Papers; my emphasis.

8. Cited without attribution in Elizabeth Cady Stanton, Susan B. Anthony, and Matilda Joslyn Gage, eds., *History of Woman Suffrage,* vol. 1 (Rochester: Susan B. Anthony, 1889), p. 551. Also see pp. 699, 712, 874.

9. "Biology and 'Woman's Rights,'" *Popular Science Monthly* 14 (December 1878): 213, 214; emphasis in original. Also see Caroline Corbin, *Letters from a Chimney-Corner: A Plea for Pure Hopes and Sincere Relations between Men and Women* (Chicago: Fergus, 1886).

10. National Woman Suffrage Association, *How Woman Won It* (New York: Wilson, 1940), pp. 161–164.

11. National Woman Suffrage Association, *How Woman Won It,* pp. 161–164.

12. Mary Martha Thomas, *The New Woman in Alabama: Social Reforms and Suffrage, 1890–1920* (Tuscaloosa: University of Alabama Press, 1992).

13. In the case *Minor v. Happersett,* 88 U.S. 627 (1875), Virginia Minor, a white woman, with her husband acting as her attorney, brought suit against the state of Missouri, arguing that the state, by denying her permission to register to vote, had abridged one of the "privileges" of citizenship, to which she was entitled as a native-born resident of the United States. The Supreme Court agreed that Virginia Minor was a citizen, with all the privileges and immunities of citizenship, but specified that suffrage was not one of those privileges or immunities. The result of this

ruling was to sanction two sexually differentiated constructions of citizenship: one for men, in which the franchise was guaranteed by the Constitution, and another for women, in which it was left up to the states to decide whether the franchise would be granted or not.

14. Mary Poovey, *Uneven Developments: The Ideological Work of Gender in Mid-Victorian England* (Chicago: University of Chicago Press, 1988), p. 10.

15. See Elizabeth Cady Stanton, "Address to the National Woman Suffrage Convention," Washington, D.C., January 19, 1869, reprinted in *The Concise History of Woman Suffrage,* ed. Mari Jo Buhle and Paul Buhle (Urbana: University of Illinois Press), pp. 252–256.

16. First quotation: "Address to the National Woman Suffrage Convention," p. 252; second quotation: Stanton's article in *Revolution* (January 14, 1869), reprinted as Document 8 in *Stanton-Anthony Reader,* p. 121.

17. Elizabeth Cady Stanton, "What Woman Suffrage Means," *Woman's Tribune* (August 30, 1890); copy available in microfilm reel 2, Elizabeth Cady Stanton Papers.

18. For example, in 1843 abolitionist Lydia Maria Child stated, "[I]n comparison with the Caucasian race, I have often said that they [Negroes] are what woman is in comparison with man. The comparison between [white] women and the colored race *as classes* is striking. Both are exceedingly adhesive in their attachments; both, comparatively speaking, have a tendency to submission, and hence, both have been kept in subjection by physical force, and considered rather in the light of property, than individuals." "The African Race," *National Anti-Slavery Standard* 3 (April 27, 1843), n.p., cited in Jean Fagan Yellin, *Women & Sisters: The Anti-Slavery Feminists in American Culture* (New Haven: Yale University Press, 1989), p. 58; emphasis in Yellin.

19. See Yellin, *Women & Sisters,* pp. 19 and 22, and the reproductions of abolitionist iconography on pp. 11, 16, 18, 20.

20. Yellin, *Women & Sisters,* p. 19.

21. See Dorothy Sterling, ed., *We Are Your Sisters: Black Women in the Nineteenth Century* (New York: Norton, 1984), and Deborah Gray White, *Arn't I a Woman? Female Slaves in the Plantation South* (New York: Norton, 1985), pp. 27–61.

22. Elizabeth Margaret Chandler, "Kneeling Slave," *Genius,* 3rd series, 1 (May 1830): 41, 44; cited in Yellin, *Women & Sisters,* p. 14.

23. Section 2 of the Fourteenth Amendment reads in part: "But when the right to vote at any election . . . is denied to any of the male inhabitants . . . being twenty-one years of age, and citizens of the United States, or in any way abridged, except for participation in rebellion, or other crime, the basis of representation therein shall be reduced in the proportion which the number of such male citizens shall bear to the whole number of male citizens twenty-one years of age in such State." The Fifteenth Amendment affirms that "the right of citizens of the United States to vote shall not be denied or abridged . . . on account of race, color, or previous condition of servitude."

24. Elizabeth Cady Stanton to Gerrit Smith, January 1, 1866 Gerrit Smith Collection, George Arents Research Library for Special Collections, Syracuse University; cited in Ellen Carol DuBois, *Feminism and Suffrage: The Emergence of an Independent Women's Movement in America, 1848–1869* (Ithaca: Cornell University Press, 1978), p. 61.

25. Cited without clear documentation in Dorothy Sterling, *Ahead of Her Time: Abby Kelley and the Politics of Antislavery* (New York: Norton, 1991), p. 348. Also see Stanton "Address to the National Woman's Suffrage Convention," and Stanton's article in *Revolution* (January 14, 1869), reprinted as Document 8 in *Stanton/Anthony Reader,* pp. 122–123. Within the black community, Stanton's remarks about black racial inferiority seem to have been either not known or not mentioned in public.

26. Cited without clear documentation in Sterling, *Ahead of Her Time,* p. 348. For an ex-

change between Lucy Stone and Abby Kelley on this issue, see Sterling, *Ahead of Her Time*, pp. 347–348.

27. Rosalyn Terborg-Penn, "Nineteenth-Century Black Women and Woman Suffrage," *Potomac Review* 7 (Spring–Summer 1977): 15.

28. Josephine St. Pierre Ruffin, "Trust the Women!" *Crisis* (August 1915): 188. Mary Church Terrell, president of the National Association of Colored Women, claimed that opposition to woman suffrage rarely occurred among "intelligent" black men. Mary Church Terrell, "The Justice of Woman Suffrage," *Crisis* (September 1912): 243. Among a more conservative element of black suffragists there was some concern about whether enfranchisement would mean that women and men would be brought into closer association. One black woman, Mrs. M. E. Lee, proposed that a separate "woman's division" be established at the polls, similar to the "ladies' delivery" at the post office, so that all women could cast their vote "without exposure." Mrs. M. E. Lee, "The Home-Maker," *AME Church Review* 8 (July 1891): 64.

29. N. H. Burroughs, "Black Women and Reform," *Crisis* 10 (August 1915): 187. This opinion was shared by black writer Frances Watkins Harper and Mary McCurdy, a black temperance leader and suffragist; see Terborg-Penn, "Nineteenth-Century Black Women and Woman Suffrage," pp. 19–20.

30. Mary Church Terrell, cited in Terborg-Penn, "Nineteenth-Century Black Women," p. 20.

31. Mary Putnam-Jacobi, *"Common Sense" Applied to Woman Suffrage* (New York: Putnam, 1894), p. 65.

32. Stanton, "Address to the National Woman Suffrage Convention," p. 254.

33. Rochester Ladies' Anti-Slavery Society and Freedmen's Aid, *Fifteenth Annual Report* (Rochester: William S. Falls, 1866), p. 16; cited in Lori D. Ginzberg, *Women and the Work of Benevolence: Morality, Politics, and Class in the Nineteenth-Century United States* (New Haven: Yale University Press, 1990), p. 180.

34. Putnam-Jacobi, *"Common Sense" Applied to Woman Suffrage*, p. 27.

35. Susan B. Anthony, *Autobiography*; cited without full attribution in Mary Roberts Coolidge, *Why Women Are So* (New York: Henry Holt, 1912), pp. 258–259.

36. Coolidge, *Why Women Are So*, pp. 259, 268.

37. Ellen Carol DuBois, "Taking the Law into Our Own Hands: *Bradwell, Minor*, and Suffrage Militance in the 1870s," in *Visible Women: New Essays on American Activism*, ed. Nancy A. Hewitt and Suzanne Lebsock (Urbana: University of Illinois Press, 1993), p. 35 n. 4.

38. Yellin, *Woman & Sisters*.

39. Lydia Maria Child, *An Appeal in Favor of that Class of Americans Called Africans* (New York: John S. Taylor, 1836), pp. 148, 171, 176.

40. Elizabeth Cady Stanton, "Educated Suffrage," *Independent* (February 14, 1895): 198; Elizabeth Cady Stanton Papers, microfilm reel 2.

41. Elizabeth Cady Stanton, Address delivered to the Twenty-third Annual Convention of the National American Woman Suffrage Association, published as "The Degradation of Disfranchisement," *Woman's Tribune* (February 7, 1891); copy available in microfilm reel 4, Elizabeth Cady Stanton Papers.

42. Stanton, "Educated Suffrage," p. 198; my emphasis.

43. R. F. Dibble, *Strenuous Americans* (New York: Boni and Liveright, 1923), p. 185.

44. *Union Signal* (May 14, 1891), p. 11; cited in Ian Tyrell, *Woman's World, Women's Empire: The Woman's Christian Temperance Union in International Perspective, 1880–1930* (Chapel Hill: University of North Carolina Press, 1991), p. 103.

45. Frances E. Willard, *A White Life For Two* (Chicago: Woman's Temperance Publishing Asso-

ciation: 1890); reprinted in *Man Cannot Speak for Her,* ed. Karlyn Kohrs Campbell, vol. 2 (Westport, Conn.: Greenwood Press, 1989), pp. 317–319.

46. Frances E. Willard, "President's Address," *Minutes of the National Woman's Christian Temperance Union at the Nineteenth Annual Meeting* (Chicago: Woman's Temperance Publishing Association, 1892), p. 128.

47. Willard, "President's Address," p. 128.

48. Ware, *Beyond the Pale,* pp. 200, 202.

49. For historiographic treatments of Willard's conflict with Wells, see Ware, *Beyond the Pale,* pp. 200–205, and Gail Bederman, *Manliness & Civilization: A Cultural History of Gender and Race in the United States* (Chicago: University of Chicago Press, 1995), pp. 66–67. Primary-source accounts of this confrontation are contained in Ida B. Wells-Barnett, *On Lynchings: "Southern Horrors," "A Red Record," "Mob Rule in New Orleans"* (Salem, N.H.: Ayer, 1987), pp. 80–90, and Ida B. Wells, *Crusade for Justice: The Autobiography of Ida B. Wells,* ed. Alfreda M. Duster (Chicago: University of Chicago Press, 1970), pp. 201–211. Quotation appears in Wells, *A Red Record,* p. 84, and is cited in Bederman, *Manliness & Civilization,* p. 65.

50. Ida B. Wells, *Southern Horrors: Lynch Law in All Its Phases* (New York: Age, 1892), p. 6.

51. Ida B. Wells, *"A Red Record,"* in *On Lynchings: "Southern Horrors," "A Red Record," "Mob Rule in New Orleans,"* pp. 80, 81.

52. Frances Willard, "Draw no Color Line," *Chicago Daily Inter Ocean* 17 (November 1894): 5, cited in Bedermen, *Manliness & Civilization,* p. 66.

53. See Ware, *Beyond the Pale.*

54. Bederman, *Manliness & Civilization,* p. 66.

55. Published scholarship on antisuffragism includes Eleanor Flexner, *Century of Struggle: The Woman's Rights Movement in the United States* (Cambridge: Belknap, 1959), pp. 294–305; Aileen Kraditor, *The Ideas of the Woman Suffrage Movement, 1890–1920* (New York: Columbia University Press, 1965 [2nd ed., New York: Norton, 1981]), pp. 14–42; Carl N. Degler, *At Odds: Women and the Family in America from the Revolution to the Present* (New York: Oxford University Press, 1980), pp. 328–361; Louise L. Stevenson, "Women Anti-suffragists in the 1915 Massachusetts Campaign," *New England Quarterly* 52 (1979): 80–93; Susan E. Marshall, "In Defense of Separate Spheres: Class and Status Politics in the Antisuffrage Movement," *Social Forces* 65 (December 1986); Manuela Thurner, "'Better Citizens without the Ballot': American Antisuffrage Women and Their Rationale during the Progressive Era," *Journal of Women's History* 5 (Spring 1993): 33–60; Jane Jerome Camhi, "Women against Women: American Anti-suffragism, 1880–1920" (Ph.D. diss., Tufts University, 1973); Thomas James Jablonsky, "Duty, Nature and Stability: The Female Anti-suffragists in the United States, 1894–1920" (Ph.D. diss., University of Southern California, 1978); and James J. Kenneally, "The Opposition to Woman Suffrage in Massachusetts, 1868–1920" (Ph.D. diss., Boston College, 1963). For a collective portrait of female antisuffragists, see Jablonsky, "Duty, Nature and Stability," pp. 278–301.

56. Paul Giddings, *When and Where I Enter: The Impact of Black Women on Race and Sex in America* (New York: Bantam Books, 1984), pp. 119–120.

57. Edith Melvin, "A Business Woman's View of Suffrage," in *Anti-Suffrage Essays by Massachusetts Women* (Boston: Forum, 1916), p. 41.

58. Mary A. M. M'Intire, *Of No Benefit to Woman: She Is a Far Greater Power without Suffrage* (Boston: Massachusetts Association Opposed to the Further Extension of Suffrage to Women, n.d.), pp. 7, 8.

59. Caroline F. Corbin, "The Antisuffrage Movement," *Chicago Daily News* (November 24, 1908), reprint (pamphlet), *The Antisuffrage Movement* (Illinois Association Opposed to the Extension of Suffrage to Women, n.d.), p. 2.

60. Marshall, "In Defense of Separate Spheres," p. 330.

61. Kate Gannett Wells, *An Argument against Woman Suffrage,* delivered before the Special Legislative committee (of the Massachusetts Legislature) (Boston, n.p., 1889), p. 3.

62. Ruth Lyman, "The Anti-Suffrage Ideal," in *Anti-Suffrage Essays,* p. 118.

63. Lyman, "The Anti-Suffrage Ideal," p. 118.

64. See Stevenson, "Women Anti-suffragists in the 1915 Massachusetts Campaign," p. 8. Also see Kenneally, "The Opposition to Woman Suffrage in Massachusetts, 1868–1920," p. 342, and William L. O'Neill, *Everyone Was Brave: The Rise and Fall of Feminism in America* (Chicago: Quadrangle Books, 1969), p. 57. For an incisive reflection on the problem, see Allen, "Woman Suffrage vs. Womanliness," in *Anti-Suffrage Essays,* pp. 77–78.

65. Alice George, "Suffrage Fallacies," in *Anti-Suffrage Essays,* pp. 27; Annie Nathan Meyer, "Woman's Assumption of Sex Superiority," *North American Review* 178 (January 1904), reprinted in *Why Women Do Not Want the Ballot,* vol. 3. (Boston: Massachusetts Association opposed to the Further Extension of Suffrage to Women, n.d.), pp. 3–4; Jeanette Gilder, "Why I Am Opposed to Woman Suffrage," *Harper's Bazaar* (May 19, 1894, reprint (pamphlet), Massachusetts Association Opposed to the Further Extension of Suffrage to Women, n.d.).

66. For examples of male-authored evolutionary analyses of the physical and mental inferiority of women, see Edward D. Cope, "The Relations of the Sexes to Government," *Popular Science Monthly* 33 (October 1888): 721–730, and George F. Talbot, "The Political Rights and Duties of Women," *Popular Science Monthly* 49 (May 1896): 80–97; both reprinted in *Men's Ideas/Women's Realities: Popular Science, 1870–1920,* ed. Louise Michele Newman (New York: Pergamon Press, 1985) pp. 210–216, 220–228.

67. Lyman, "The Anti-Suffrage Ideal," p. 120; emphasis in original.

68. For evidence that antisuffrage women clearly saw themselves as participants within the woman's movement, see Wells, *An Argument against Woman Suffrage,* p. 3; Minnie Bronson, *The Wage Earning Woman and the State,* (Boston: Massachusetts Association Opposed to the Further Extension of Suffrage to Women, 1910); and Mrs. A. J. George, "Suffrage Fallacies;" Mrs. Henry Preston White, "The Ballot and the Woman in Industry"; Monica Foley, "How Massachusetts Fosters Public Welfare"; and Catherine Robinson, "Massachusetts Compared with Suffrage States," all in *Anti-Suffrage Essays,* pp. 24, 31–37, 53–61, 62–66.

69. Annie Nathan Meyer, "Woman's Assumption of Sex Superiority," reprinted in *Why Women Do Not Want the Ballot* vol. 3, p. 2; my emphasis.

70. Grace Duffield Goodwin, *Anti-Suffrage: Ten Good Reasons* (New York: Duffield, 1913), pp. 4–5.

71. Catherine [*sic*] E. Beecher, *Educational Reminiscences and Suggestions* (New York: J. B. Ford, 1874), p. 201. Margaret Deland, "The Third Way," cited in Kenneally, "The Opposition to Woman Suffrage in Massachusetts, 1868–1920," pp. 200–203. Also see Melvin, "A Business Woman's View of Suffrage," p. 42.

72. In reference to immigrants, Goodwin added: "the majority toil incessantly, learn very little, are exploited by the boss of the ward, know little and care less about the government of their adopted country. . . . How will it help to add the foreign woman? All workers among these peoples recognize how much more backward is the foreign woman than the foreign man. . . . The . . . foreign women . . . would add greatly to the danger of the naturalized foreign vote." Goodwin, *Anti-Suffrage,* pp. 43–46.

73. See Mary Kelley, *Private Woman, Public Stage: Literary Domesticity in Nineteenth-Century America* (New York: Oxford University Press, 1984), for an account of how white women writers of the 1830s through the 1850s dealt with their feelings about public visibility and financial independence.

74. Katharine Kish Sklar, *Catharine Beecher: A Study in American Domesticity* (New York: Norton, 1973), p. 134.

75. Catharine E. Beecher, *An Essay on Slavery and Abolitionism* (Philadelphia: Henry Perkins, 1837), p. 28; my emphasis.

76. For example, see Lydia Maria Child's *An Appeal in Favor of That Class of Americans Called Africans* (New York: John S. Taylor, 1833); Elizabeth Margaret Chandler, "The Ladies Repository", a column in Lundy's abolitionist newspaper *The Genius of Universal Emancipation,* 3rd series, 1 (May 1830): 41, 44 and 1 (February 1831): 171, and Sarah and Angelina Grimké, in William Lloyd Garrison's abolitionist newspaper *The Liberator,* in the late 1830s.

77. Beecher, *Educational Reminiscences and Suggestions,* pp. 62–65.

78. Richard C. Wade, *The Urban Frontier: Pioneer Life in Early Pittsburgh, Cincinnati, Lexington, Louisville, and St. Louis* (Chicago: University of Chicago Press, 1959).

79. By 1828, 2,258 blacks lived in Cincinnati, a significant increase from 1810, when there had been less than 100, or less than 2 percent of the city's population at that time. Wade, *Urban Frontier,* pp. 124, 221.

80. Wade, *Urban Frontier,* pp. 224–228. Wade estimates that the number of blacks who left was certainly no less than 1,100 and probably more. Lawrence Thomas Lesnick notes that the black population had declined to less than 3 percent of the total population by the early 1830s. Lawrence Thomas Lesnick, *The Lane Rebels: Evangelicalism and Antislavery in Antebellum America* (Metuchen, N.J.: Scarecrow Press, 1980), p. 20.

81. Lesnick, *Lane Rebels,* pp. 77–82; Gerda Lerner, *The Grimké Sisters from South Carolina: Pioneers for Woman's Rights and Abolition* (New York: Schocken Books, 1967 [2nd ed. 1978)], pp. 117–118.

82. See Harriet Beecher Stowe's account of this incident as reported in Charles Edward Stowe, *The Life of Harriet Beecher Stowe Compiled from Her Letters and Journals* (Boston: Houghton Mifflin, 1889), pp. 83–88. My discussion is drawn from this account and Sklar, *Catharine Beecher,* pp. 132–134.

83. Sklar, *Catharine Beecher,* p. 134.

84. Harriet Beecher Stowe is quoted without attribution in Stowe, *Life of Harriet Beecher Stowe,* pp. 83–84.

85. Stowe, *Life of Harriet Beecher Stowe,* p. 87.

86. Catharine Beecher to "My dear Brethren and Sisteren," January 24–February 18, 1838 Stowe-Day Foundation, Hartford, Conn., reprinted in Jeanne Boydston, May Kelley, and Anne Margolis, *The Limits of Sisterhood: The Beecher Sisters on Women's Rights and Woman's Sphere* (Chapel Hill: University of North Carolina press, 1988), p. 336.

87. Lerner, *Grimké Sisters,* p. 124.

88. The Grimké sisters moved to New York in October 1836 and underwent two weeks of intensive training at the Agents' Convention of the American Anti-Slavery Society in November. The Female Anti-Slavery Society of New York was organized the same month, and Angelina spoke under its auspices. See entry for Sarah and Angelina Grimké in *Notable American Women: A Biographical Dictionary, 1607–1950,* ed. Edward T. James, vol. 2, (Cambridge: Belknap Press, 1971), pp. 97–99; and Lerner, *Grimké Sisters,* pp. 147–148.

89. Beecher, *Essay on Slavery and Abolitionism,* p. 3.

90. Beecher, *Essay on Slavery and Abolitionism,* cited in Boydston et al., *Limits of Sisterhood,* pp. 126, 127.

91. Beecher, *Essay on Slavery and Abolitionism,* p. 24; my emphasis.

92. Catharine E. Beecher, *The True Remedy for the Wrongs of Woman; With a History of an Enterprise Having That for its Object* (Boston: Phillips, Sampson, 1851), pp. 235–236.

93. Beecher, *True Remedy,* pp. 235–236; my emphasis.

94. Beecher, *True Remedy*, pp. 240–241; emphasis in original.

95. Beecher, *Educational Reminiscences and Suggestions.*

96. Beecher, *True Remedy*, p. 241.

97. See Joan Burstyn, "Catharine Beecher and the Education of American Women," *New England Quarterly* 47 (September 1974): 389.

98. These politicians included Rufus King, a senator from New York; James Doolittle of Wisconsin; Owen Lovejoy of Illinois; Anson Burlingame of Massachusetts; Ezra Clark of Connecticut; Galusha Grow of Pennsylvania; and Joshua Giddings of Ohio. Stanley Harrold, *Gamaliel Bailey and Antislavery Union* (Kent, Ohio: Kent State University Press, 1986), pp. 195–196.

99. Susan Coultrap-McQuinn, Introduction to *Gail Hamilton: Selected Writings* (New Brunswick: Rutgers University Press, 1992), p. xvi.

100. Henry C. Vedder, *American Writers of Today* (New York: Silver, Burdett, 1894), p. 196, cited in Coultrap-McQuinn, *Gail Hamilton*, p. xii.

101. Dodge was at the height of her power in the 1880s, when men and women routinely wrote to her asking her for favors. See for example, a letter from Kate Field, a reformer from New York, who wrote to Mary Dodge on April 21, 1880, to ask her to arrange a meeting with President Hayes in order to enlist his support for her Dress Association. Kate Field to Miss Dodge, April 21, 1880, folder 8, Dodge Papers, Essex Institute. Also see Charles E. Smith to Miss Dodge, March 22, 1881; Benjamin J. Butler to M. A. Dodge, Jan. 29, 1883; and J. W. Manley to Miss Dodge, November 9, 1881, all in folder no. 8, and Julian Hawthorne to Miss Dodge, November 27, 1886, folder 9, Dodge Papers, Essex Institute.

102. Dodge's support of Blaine never wavered, not even when suspicion that Blaine had wrongly profited from his office as Speaker of the House cost him his party's presidential nomination in 1876. In the 1880s, Dodge helped Blaine write his memoirs, and after his death she wrote a biography of him. Gail Hamilton, *Biography of James G. Blaine* (Norwich: Henry Bill, 1895).

103. Harriet Prescott Spofford, *A Little Book of Friends* (Boston: Little Brown, 1916).

104. In 1865, Dodge joked with Wood: "You, Mr. Wood, as I have often told you, are clean given up to the pomps and vanities of this world. You use fine-sounding phrases in your letters, but you know you would give every cent of your twenty thousand dollars, this minute, to have me, a handsome woman, at the head of a marble Fifth Avenue sort of house-ruling society, and you a witness and worshipper!" Miss Dodge to Mr. Wood, March 26, 1865 in *Gail Hamilton's Life and Letters*, ed. H. Augusta Dodge, vol. 1 (Boston: Lee and Shepard, 1901), p. 489.

105. Miss Dodge to Mr. French, December 19, 1864, in Dodge, *Gail Hamilton's Life and Letters*, vol. 1, p. 472. Elsewhere Dodge wrote, "Marriage contracted to subserve material ends . . . is legalized prostitution." *A New Atmosphere* (Boston: Ticknor and Fields, 1865), p. 21.

106. Dodge, *A New Atmosphere*, especially pp. 5–22.

107. Gail Hamilton, "A Spasm of Sense," *Atlantic Monthly* 11 (April 1863): 407.

108. As reported by Spofford, *A Little Book of Friends*, p. 95.

109. "Letter from Gail Hamilton," February 9, 1886, Mary Abigail Dodge Papers, Smith College Archives.

110. Susan B. Anthony to Mary Abigail Dodge, 1869, folder 5, Dodge papers, Essex Institute.

111. Reference to the misrepresentation by the *Woman's Journal* is discussed by Mary Dodge in "Letter from Gail Hamilton," February 9, 1886.

112. Mary Roberts [Smith] Coolidge, *Why Women Are So* (New York: Henry Holt, 1912), pp. 278–279.

113. Gail Hamilton, *Woman's Wrongs: A Counter-Irritant* (Boston: Ticknor and Fields, 1868), pp. 6–7.

114. Hamilton, *Woman's Wrongs*, p. 93.

115. Hamilton, *Woman's Wrongs*, p. 87–88.

116. Hamilton, *Woman's Wrongs*, p. 104.

117. Hamilton, *Woman's Wrongs*, pp. 94–95, 104.

118. Hamilton, *Woman's Wrongs*, pp. 101–102.

119. See Gail Hamilton, "Race Prejudice," *North American Review* 141 (October 1885): 475–479, and a response by Charlotte Forten, "One Phase of the Race Distinction," *Boston Commonwealth* 24 (January 16, 1886): 1. Forten began her criticism by saying that she would have been "surprised that so brilliant and acute a writer [as Gail Hamilton] could be so illogical, were it not that so many even more brilliant minds are beguiled into making the same mistakes when dealing with this vexed race question."

120. Hamilton, "Race Prejudice," p. 477.

121. Hamilton, "Race Prejudice," p. 477.

122. Although Dodge believed that "for the same work women ought be paid the same wages as men," she went on to qualify that statement so as not to contradict her arguments in support of laissez-faire economics: "But it is a commercial ought, not a moral ought. . . . Women ought to receive the same wages for the same work as men, if they can get it." Hamilton, *Woman's Worth and Worthlessness: The Complement to "A New Atmosphere"* (New York: Harper, 1872), pp. 105–106.

123. Mrs. Arthur M. Dodge, "Woman Suffrage Opposed to Woman's Rights," *Annals of the American Academy of Political and Social Science* 5 (November 1914): 99.

124. Dodge, "Woman Suffrage Opposed to Woman's Rights," p. 101; my emphasis.

125. Dodge, "Woman Suffrage Opposed to Woman's Rights," p. 99; emphasis in original.

3. The Politics of Patriarchal Protection

1. Azel Ames, Jr., *Sex in Industry: A Plea for the Working-Girl* (Boston: James R. Osgood, 1875), p. 11, and Caroline H. Dall, *"Woman's Right to Labor": Or, Low Wages and Hard Work: In Three Lectures, Delivered in Boston, November 1859* (Boston: Walker, Wise, 1860), p. 57. Helen Campbell believed that some women worked in the trades because they were bored and wanted to earn a little extra pocket or "pin" money. Campbell, *Prisoners of Poverty: Women Wage-Workers, Their Trades and Their Lives* (Boston: Roberts, 1887; reprint, Westport, Conn.: Greenwood Press, 1970), p. 17.

2. Accounts of this debate are contained in Mary Roth Walsh, *"Doctors Wanted: No Women Need Apply": Sexual Barriers in the Medical Profession, 1835–1975* (New Haven: Yale University Press, 1977), pp. 119–124; Rosalind Rosenberg, *Beyond Separate Spheres: Intellectual Roots of Modern Feminism* (New Haven: Yale University Press, 1982), pp. 5–27; Regina Morantz-Sanchez, *Sympathy and Science: Women Physicians in American Medicine* (New York: Oxford University Press, 1985), pp. 54–56; and Barbara Miller Solomon, *In the Company of Educated Women: A History of Women and Higher Education in America* (New Haven: Yale University Press, 1985), pp. 56–57.

3. These details about his Boston address are taken from Rosenberg, *Beyond Separate Spheres*, p. 5.

4. Edward H. Clarke, *Sex in Education; Or, A Fair Chance for the Girls* (Boston: James R. Osgood, 1873 [2nd ed., 1873]), p. 19.

5. For an overview of this debate, see "The 'Sex in Education' Controversy" (Editorial), *Scribner's Monthly* 9 (March 1875): 633–635.

6. Caroline H. Dall, untitled article in *Sex and Education: A Reply to Dr. E. H. Clarke's "Sex in Education"* ed. Julia Ward Howe (Boston: Roberts, 1874), pp. 87–88.

7. Eliza Duffey, untitled article in Howe, *Sex and Education*, p. 117. Duffey had already published a treatise on the woman question, *What Women Should Know: A Woman's Book about Women*

(Cincinnati: Stoddard, 1873); she wrote two more books, *No Sex in Education: Or, An Equal Chance for Both Boys and Girls: A Review of Dr. E. H. Clarke's "Sex in Education"* (Philadelphia: J. Stoddard, 1874), and *The Relations of the Sexes* (New York: Wood and Holbrook, 1876, 1886).

8. Many all-male state universities and some private schools were opening their doors to women, including M.I.T. (1865), Wisconsin (1867), Indiana (1868), Boston University (1869), Northwestern (1869), Kansas (1869), Minnesota (1869), Missouri (1870), Michigan (1870), California (1870), Illinois (1870), Syracuse (1871), Wesleyan (1872), Maine (1872), Cornell (1872), and Ohio (1873), to name a few. Dates given in Louise Michele Newman, ed., *Men's Ideas/Women's Realities: Popular Science, 1870–1920* (New York: Pergamon Press, 1985), p. 64, and Solomon, *In the Company of Educated Women*, p. 53.

9. On the significance of education in creating "a large and influential middle class [of men]," see "Education" (Editorial), *Atlantic Monthly* 32 (September 1874): 379–380.

10. Newman, *Men's Ideas/Women's Realities*, p. 107.

11. Newman, *Men's Ideas/Women's Realities*, pp. 106–118.

12. Walker wrote, "The access of foreigners at the time and under the circumstances, constituted a shock to the principle of population among the native element. . . . [F]oreign immigration into this country has, from the time it first assumed large proportions, amounted not to a re-enforcement of our population, but to a replacement of native by foreign stock." Francis A. Walker, "Immigration and Degradation," reprinted in Francis A. Walker, *Discussions in Economics and Statistics*, vol. 2 ed. Davis R. Dewey (New York: Henry Holt, 1899), pp. 422–425; cited in Newman, *Men's Ideas/Women's Realities*, p. 108.

13. *Universal Suffrage: Female Suffrage* (Philadelphia: J. B. Lippincott, 1867), pp. 103–104; cited in Newman, *Men's Ideas/Women's Realities*, p. 117.

14. Oliver Wendell Holmes, "The Americanized European," *Atlantic Monthly* 35 (January 1875): 85.

15. Clarke, *Sex in Education*, pp. 129, 13–14; my emphasis.

16. Thomas Wentworth Higginson, untitled article in Howe, *Sex and Education*, p. 32.

17. Clarke, *Sex in Education*, p. 13.

18. Rosenberg, *Beyond Separate Spheres*, p. 5.

19. Rosenberg, *Beyond Separate Spheres*, p. 12.

20. Holmes, "The Americanized European," p. 75. Some newspaper reviews were collected and reprinted in Howe, *Sex and Education*. Also see "Dr. Clarke's 'Sex in Education,'" *North American Review* 119 (January 1874): 140–152; "Education" (Editorial), *Atlantic Monthly* 35 (January 1875): 125–128; "Clarke's Building of a Brain," *North American Review* 120 (January 1875): 185–188; Oliver Wendell Holmes, "The Americanized European," pp. 75–86; Rev. J. R. Herrick, "A Fair Chance for Girls; or, A Word for American Women," *New England Journal of Education* 1 (March 20, 1875): 133–135, and "The 'Sex in Education' Controversy," pp. 633–635.

21. "The 'Sex in Education' Controversy," p. 634. Clarke, preface to the 2nd edition of *Sex in Education*, p. 7.

22. M. Carey Thomas, "Present Tendencies in Women's College and University Education," *Educational Review* 24 (1908): 68, cited in Rosenberg, *Beyond Separate Spheres*, p. 12.

23. G. Stanley Hall, *Adolescence* 2 (New York: Appleton, 1904), pp. 569–570, and Walsh, *"Doctors Wanted: No Women Need Apply,"* pp. 119, 124. Also see Maxine Seller, "G. Stanley Hall and Edward Thorndike on the Education of Women: Theory and Policy in the Progressive Era," *Educational Studies* 11 (Winter 1981): 365–374.

24. Clarke, *Sex in Education*, pp. 12–13, cited in Rosenberg, *Beyond Separate Spheres*, p. 7.

25. Clarke, *Sex in Education*, pp. 11–12.

26. Clarke, *Sex in Education*, pp. 36–38.

27. Clarke was careful to point out that he did not think that educational methods alone were the sole cause of (white middle-class) women's reproductive troubles. He also faulted women's diets ("perpetual pie and doughnut"), dress ("as much to the omission of clothing where it is needed as to excess where the body does not require it"), and inadequate exercise. However, he thought these other factors were "indirect" causes and not nearly as important as those arising from inattention to the "peculiarities of a woman's organization." See Clarke, *Sex in Education,* p. 23. In coeducation, specifically, the "problem" as Clarke formulated it was that the "periodicity" of women's reproductive systems meant that they should not be subjected to sustained intellectual work, as was required in men's colleges. Women needed periodic remission of their studies to correspond with the onset of their periods, so as not to overtax and harm their reproductive systems. "A careless management of this function [menstruation], at any period of life during its existence, is apt to be followed by consequences that may be serious; but a neglect of it during the epoch of development, that is, from the age of fourteen to eighteen or twenty, not only produces great evil at the time of the neglect, but leaves a large legacy of evil to the future. The system is then peculiarly susceptible; and disturbances of the delicate mechanism we are considering, induced during the catamenial weeks of that critical age by constrained positions [sitting at tight desks], muscular effort [standing during recitations], brain work, and all forms of mental and physical excitement, germinate a host of ills. . . . The host of ills thus induced are known to physicians and to the sufferers as amenorrhoea, menorrhagia, dysmenorrhoea, hysteria, anemia, chorea, and the like. Some of these fasten themselves on their victim for a lifetime, and some are shaken off. Now and then they lead to an abortion of the function, and consequent sterility. . . . The more completely any such school or college succeeds, while adopting every detail and method of a boy's school, in ignoring and neglecting the physiological conditions of sexual development [of women], the larger will be the number of these pathological cases among its graduates." Clarke, *Sex in Education,* pp. 48–49.

28. Howe, *Sex and Education;* Duffey, *No Sex in Education;* George Fish Comfort and Anna Manning Comfort, *Woman's Education and Woman's Health* (Syracuse: Durston, 1874); Anna Callender Brackett, ed., *The Education of American Girls* (New York: Putnam, 1874). Also see "The 'Sex in Education' Controversy," pp. 633–635.

29. Mary Putnam Jacobi, *The Question of Rest for Women during Menstruation* (New York: Putnam, 1877) as cited in Morantz-Sanchez, *Women Physicians in American Medicine,* p. 55.

30. Solomon, *In the Company of Educated Women,* p. 57; Rosenberg, *Beyond Separate Spheres,* pp. 20–22. Some college presidents spoke out in defense of coeducational systems, including John Bascom, president of the University of Wisconsin. See Bascom, "Coeducation," *Independent* 30 (January 17, 1878): 1. Every decade from the 1870s through the 1920s produced its own gloss on the issues that Clarke first brought to national attention in 1873. In the 1880s, George J. Romanes and William Hammond, physicians widely known for their work on insanity and nervous diseases, followed up on Clarke's arguments about "sex in brains." Hammond argued that girls ought to be educated differently from boys because boys had heavier and more developed brains and could withstand more "brain work." Debates ensued as to whether women's smaller brains accounted for their supposedly inferior mental abilities. See George J. Romanes, "Mental Differences for Men and Women," *Popular Science Monthly* 32 (July 1887): 383–401, William A. Hammond, "Woman in Politics," *North American Review* 137 (August 1883): 137–146; and a response by Nina Morais, "Dr. Hammond's Estimate of Woman," *North American Review* 137 (November 1883): 501–507. In the 1890s, sexual differences were identified with a variety of different aspects of (white) men's and women's physical person: not just in reproductive organs or brains but also in metabolism, bone structure, and so forth. For an excellent overview of sexual difference from the perspective of the early twentieth century, see Willystine Goodsell, *The Education of Women: Its Social Background and Its*

Problems (New York: Macmillan, 1923). Indeed, Clarke's views remained so influential that as late as the 1920s white middle-class women were still contesting them. See Edna Yost, "The Case for the Co-educated Woman," *Harper's Monthly Magazine* (July 1927): 194–202.

31. Mary R. Smith, "Statistics of College and Non-College Women," *Publications of the American Statistical Association* 7 (March/June 1900): 11; cited in Newman, *Men's Ideas/Women's Realities,* p. 116.

32. M. B. Jackson, untitled article in Howe, *Sex and Education,* pp. 150–151; 161, my emphasis. Also see Elizabeth Garrett Anderson, "Sex in Mind and Education: A Reply," *Fortnightly Review* 15 (May 1874): 582–594; especially 583.

33. Duffey, *What Women Should Know,* pp. 17–18. Duffey is insistent on this point: "The larger class of writers in regard to womanly functions, capabilities and incapabilities, have been men. From Michelet, who regards the normal state of womanhood as one of pretty and useless invalidism, to the unnumbered hosts of English and American authors and essayists, they all set up before us a purely ideal creation, eliminated [sic] from their masculine brains, and differing as widely from the reality as—well, say as man from woman" (18). Also see Julia Ward Howe and Elizabeth Stuart Phelps, untitled articles in Howe, *Sex and Education,* pp. 24, 129.

34. Howe, *Sex and Education,* p. 27.

35. Edward Jarvis, "Immigration," *Atlantic Monthly* 29 (April 1872): 454–468. For additional insight into how evolutionists used these arguments, see Holmes, "The Americanized European," especially pp. 78–80.

36. Howe, *Sex and Education,* p. 27.

37. Ames, *Sex in Industry,* p. 3. This study was begun at the instigation of Carroll D. Wright, head of the Massachusetts State Bureau of Statistics of Labor. The State Bureau published annual reports from 1870 onward, many of which exposed the inhumane working conditions to which women were subjected in Massachusetts. See Mark Aldrich, "State Reports on Women and Child Wage Earners, 1870–1906," *Labor History* 21 (Winter 1979–80): 86–90, for a listing of reports documenting the working conditions of women in the industrial labor force.

38. Susan Levine, "Labor's True Woman: Domesticity and Equal Rights in the Knights of Labor," *Journal of American History* 70 (September 1983): 323–339, and Alice Kessler-Harris, *A Woman's Wage: Historical Meanings and Social Consequences* (Louisville: University Press of Kentucky, 1990), especially p. 19. Although Kessler-Harris focuses on the period from 1900 to 1920, the same assumptions were present in the 1870s and 1880s. See Frances Amasa Walker, *The Wages Question: A Treatise on Wages and the Wages Class* (New York: Henry Holt, 1876).

39. One reformer, Alice Henry, exposed how conservatives used protective labor legislation to reinforce cultural notions of patriarchy in her study, *The Trade Union Woman* (New York: Appleton, 1915). Henry believed that male unionists' advocacy of protective legislation was part of a strategy to prevent women from effectively competing with male workers. As evidence for this assertion, Henry quoted the President's [Strasser's] Report of the International Cigarmakers for 1879: "We cannot drive the females out of the trade but we can restrict this daily quota of labor through factory laws. No girl under eighteen should be employed more than eight hours per day; all overwork should be prohibited; while married women should be kept out of factories at least six weeks before and six weeks after confinement." This position, had it been espoused by Florence Kelley, might have been hailed as a progressive position on labor issues. Coming from a union that excluded women from its ranks, it takes on a very different political cast. According to Henry, male labor unions were willing enough to call for equal pay for equal work, but not at all willing to see a "young girl worker . . . as well trained as the boy, in order that the girl may be able with reason and justice to demand the same wage from an employer" (p. 24). Henry also wrote: "Even under conditions of nominal equality the woman was so often handicapped by her physique, by the difficulty she experienced in obtaining thorough training and by the additional

claims of her home, *that the men must have felt they were likely to keep their hold on the best positions anyhow,* and perhaps all the more readily with the union exacting identical standards of accomplishment from all workers, *while at the same time claiming for all identical standards of wages"* (p. 24; my emphasis). See Kessler-Harris, *A Woman's Wage.*

40. Ames, *Sex in Industry,* p. 30.

41. Ames, *Sex in Industry,* p. 30.

42. Dall, *"Woman's Right to Labor,"* pp. 6–7.

43. Dall, *"Woman's Right to Labor,"* pp. 86, 104–105.

44. William Graham Sumner, *What Social Classes Owe to Each Other* (New York: Harper, 1883; reprint, Caldwell, Idaho: Caxton Printers, 1982), p. 36; my emphasis.

45. In 1886, for example, a Pennsylvania state court struck down a statute that required laborers to be paid in cash at regular intervals (instead of in credit at a company store) on the grounds that the legislation represented an "insulting attempt to put the laborer under a legislature tutelage," and was "degrading to his manhood" and "subversive of his rights." *Godcharles v. Wigeman* 113 Pa. St. (1886): 431, cited in Lawrence M. Friedman, *A History of American Law* (New York: Simon and Schuster, 1973), p. 490.

46. As economic historian Martin Sklar has argued, beginning with the landmark Santa Clara decision of 1886, corporations were granted the legal status of a person within the meaning of the Fifth and Fourteenth Amendments of the Constitution. In a series of decisions from 1886 through the 1890s, courts protected corporations against deprivation by either the federal or state governments of their life, liberty, assets, or earnings, without due process of law. Sklar lists the most important cases of the 1880s and 1890s, including *Santa Clara County v. Southern Pacific Railroad,* 118 U.S. 394 (1886); *Pembina Mining Co. v. Pennsylvania,* 125 U.S. 181 (1888); *Minneapolis & St. Louis Railroad Co. v. Beckwith,* 129 U.S. 26 (1889); *Charlotte, Columbia & Augusta Railroad v. Gibbes,* 142 U.S. 386 (1892); and *Gulf, Colorado & Santa Fe Railway Co. v. Ellis,* 165 U.S. 150 (1897), among others. See Martin J. Sklar, *The Corporate Reconstruction of American Capitalism, 1890–1916: The Market, the Law, and Politics* (Cambridge: Cambridge University Press, 1988), p. 49 and p. 50 n. 7.

47. Nancy S. Erickson, *"Muller V. Oregon* Reconsidered: The Origins of a Sex-Based Doctrine of Liberty of Contract," *Labor History* 30 (Spring 1989): 228–250.

48. Erickson argues that the *Muller v. Oregon* (1908) decision, which some scholars see as embodying an abrupt ideological change from *Lochner v. N.Y.* (1905), was in fact based on a sexually differentiated notion of liberty for women that had its origins in the 1870s. I concur with this interpretation of the legal history behind *Muller v. Oregon,* but this does not negate my other point that sexually distinct notions of liberty were also strongly resisted through the period 1870–1920.

49. *Commonwealth v. Hamilton Mfg. Company,* 120 Mass. 383 (1876): 385. Massachusetts had begun limiting the working hours of children in 1842; in 1874, it added the category "women" to the provisions of the statutes that restricted children's hours to ten per day. Alice Kessler-Harris mentions the case briefly in "Protection for Women: Trade Unions and Labor Laws," in *Double Exposure: Women's Health Hazards on the Job and at Home,* ed. Wendy Chavkin (New York: Monthly Review Press, 1984), p. 143. A more extended discussion is available in Erickson, *"Muller V. Oregon* Reconsidered," pp. 228–250.

50. *Commonwealth v. Hamilton Mfg. Company,* 120 Mass. 383 (1876): 385. Fined for employing a woman, Mary Shirley, in its factory for sixty-four hours per week, Hamilton Manufacturing Company, a textile mill in Lowell, Massachusetts, argued that a Massachusetts statute, which mandated that "no minor under the age of eighteen years, and no woman over that age, shall be employed in laboring by any person, firm or corporation in any manufacturing establishment in this Commonwealth more than ten hours in any one day . . . [or] sixty per week" was un-

constitutional because it violated both its own and Mary Shirley's right to enter freely into a labor contract. The court ruled that the legislation in question was in fact legal and that no infringement of freedom to contract had occurred. Yet the court recognized that the legislation in question treated the employer and employee differently: it construed that the legislation restricted Hamilton Manufacturing from hiring any woman for more than sixty hours per week, but did not prevent the employee, Mary Shirley, from finding additional employment elsewhere should she so desire.

As Erickson has pointed out, the ruling of the Massachusetts State Supreme Court was significant as much for what it did not say as for its finding that no infringement of the individual's right to contract had occurred. First, it did not adopt the arguments proposed by labor reformers such as Ames, even though it ended up upholding the type of legislation Ames was advocating. Second, it skirted the question of whether the state could single out women workers as a "special class" of workers. The ruling merely explained that the statute in question had not violated Mary Shirley's right to decide "in accordance with her own judgment as to the number of hours she shall work," because "the law does not limit her right to labor as many hours per day or per week as she may desire. . . . [I]t merely prohibits her being employed continuously in the same service [of Hamilton Manufacturing company] more than a certain number of hours per day or week." Erickson, *"Muller V. Oregon* Reconsidered," pp. 228–250.

51. *Ritchie v. People,* 40 N.E. 454 (1895): 459. The case is discussed in Erickson, "Muller V. Oregon Reconsidered," pp. 228–250.

52. The Illinois State Supreme Court was asked to assess the constitutionality of a maximum-hour statute passed in 1893, which limited women's hours of work in factories to eight per day. The Illinois court wrote a long opinion in which it carefully analyzed whether there were any legitimate grounds upon which it might be argued that the female individual's right to contract might be abridged. It did not need to do this in order to reach its ruling. The court could have resolved the case on quite other grounds. The Illinois court ruled first that the statute was unconstitutional because it singled out owners and employers of labor of a particular class—that is, manufacturers—rather than all owners and employers of labor. On these grounds alone, the Illinois court could have declared the 1893 statute invalid and ended its discussion. But it went on to ask whether a revised version of the statute—one that did apply equally to all employers and owners of labor—would be constitutional. This question, the court argued, required analyzing more fully whether the state's abridgment of individuals' right to make contracts was warranted on any grounds. In deciding this question, the court first acknowledged that "police power" gave the state a legitimate right to pass ordinances that promoted the "health, comfort, safety, and welfare of society." The court then argued that it was a recognized legal principle that "woman is entitled to the same rights, under the constitution, to make contracts with reference to her labor, as are secured thereby to men." It cited *Minor v. Happersett,* the case cited in Chapter 2, n. 13 involving Virginia Minor's argument that her Fourteenth Amendment rights were violated when she was denied the right to vote. The Illinois court also affirmed woman's right to acquire and possess property, a right that, the court argued, guaranteed her the right to make and enforce contracts. The law, the Illinois court summed up, "accords to her [woman], as to every other citizen, the right to gain a livelihood by intelligence, honesty, and industry in the arts, the sciences, the professions, or other vocations." Thus, the Illinois court argued, the mere fact of woman's sex was not enough to justify the legislature's invocation of the police power of the state. However, the Illinois Court continued its analysis still further: "the question is whether . . . she shall be deprived of the right to determine for herself how many hours she can and may work during each day." And the court ar-

gued that women could not be so deprived unless the court could be convinced that the statute under question "has at least in fact some relation to the *public health,* that the *public health* is the end actually aimed at, and that it [the legislation] is appropriate and adapted to that end." The Illinois court could not see any connection between limiting women's hours and promoting public health (that is, protecting the individual's or a group of individuals' health), and so it pronounced Illinois's statute unconstitutional and void. *Ritchie v. People,* 40 N.E. 454 (1895): 457–460.

53. Female antisuffragists were among those who supported protective labor legislation in this period, and they frequently pointed out that suffragist arguments encompassed an ideology that threatened the labor legislation already on the books.

54. Louis D. Brandeis and Josephine Goldmark, *The Case against Nightwork for Women, Revised with New Introduction to March 1, 1918* (New York: National Consumers' League, 1918).

55. In *Muller v. Oregon,* the Supreme Court stated: "As minors, though not to the same extent, [woman] has been looked upon in the courts as needing especial care that her rights may be preserved. . . . Differentiated by these matters from the other sex, she is properly placed in a class by herself, and legislation designed for her protection may be sustained, even when like legislation is not necessary for men, and could not be sustained." *Muller v. Oregon* 208 U.S. 412. Maximum-hour legislation could not be easily enforced, however, if women were allowed to assume a second job working during the night. Soon after the ruling in *Muller v. Oregon,* laws restricting women from working at night also proliferated, and were again justified on the grounds that they were essential to protect women's health and preserve women's morals in order to ensure the well-being of children as yet unborn. Legislation barring women from working at night was upheld by the United States Supreme Court in 1924, when it sustained a New York State statute that prohibited women from working in restaurants between the hours of 10 P.M. and 6 A.M. See Kessler-Harris, *Out to Work,* p. 195.

Limiting the number of daytime hours women were permitted to work during the week and barring them altogether from night work created an even greater need for minimum wage laws, since women could no longer increase their incomes by working longer hours. Massachusetts passed the first minimum-wage law in 1912, and eight other states followed in 1913. For the most part, state courts upheld these laws on the grounds that "women and minors should be protected from conditions of labor which have a pernicious effect on their health and morals and inadequate wages have a pernicious effect." But this time the United States Supreme Court did not agree. In another landmark decision, *Adkins v. Children's Hospital* (1923), the Court struck down the minimum-wage law for women in the District of Columbia. Justice Sutherland again wrote the majority opinion: "It is quite simply and exclusively a price-fixing law, confined to adult women . . . who are legally as capable of contracting for themselves as men." Chief Justice Taft, seeing a contradiction between this case and *Muller v. Oregon,* wrote a separate dissent: "a sweating wage has as great and as direct a tendency to bring about an injury to the health and morals of workers, as . . . long hours." *Adkins v. Children's Hospital,* 261 U.S. 525; quoted in Elizabeth Faulkner Baker, *Protective Labor Legislation with Special Reference to Women in the State of New York* (New York: AMS Press, 1969 [1st ed. 1925]), pp. 91, 92; also cited by Kessler-Harris, *Out to Work,* p. 198.

56. Leslie Woodcock Tentler, *Wage Earning Women: Industrial Work and Family Life in the United States, 1900–1930* (New York: Oxford University Press, 1979); Harris, *Out to Work;* Susan Lehrer, *Origins of Protective Labor Legislation for Women, 1905–1925* (Albany: State University of New York Press, 1987); and Judith A. Baer, *The Chains of Protection: The Judicial Response to Protective Labor Legislation* (Westport, Conn.: Greenwood Press, 1978).

57. Lizzie M. Holmes, "Woman's Future Position in the World," *Arena* 20 (September 1898): 339.

4. A Feminist Explores Africa

1. The best published secondary account on May French-Sheldon is T. J. Boisseau, "'They Called Me *Bebe Bwana*': A Cultural Study of an Imperial Feminist," *Signs* 21 (Autumn 1995): 116–146; also see Dea Birkett, *Spinsters Abroad: Victorian Lady Explorers* (Oxford: Basil Blackwell, 1989), p. 282, 117–119; Jeanne Madeline Moore, "Bebe Bwana," *American History Illustrated* 21 (October 1986): 36–42; Julie English Early, "Unescorted in Africa: Victorian Women Ethnographers Toiling in the Fields of Sensational Science," *Journal of American Culture* 18 (Winter 1995): 69–70; and brief biographical sketches in Jane Robinson, *Wayward Women: A Guide to Women Travellers* (New York: Oxford University Press, 1990), p. 27; Daniel B. Baker, ed., *Explorers & Discovers of the World* (Detroit: Gale Research, 1993), p. 508; and Rita Volmer Louis, ed., *Biography Index: A Cumulative Index to Biographical Material in Books and Magazines* (New York: Wilson, 1968), p. 608.

2. Fannie C. Williams, "A 'White Queen' in Africa," *Chautauquan* 18 (December 1893): 342.

3. "A White Lady Visits the Masai" (review of *Sultan to Sultan), New York Times* (December 11, 1892): 19.

4. Williams, "A 'White Queen' in Africa," pp. 342–343.

5. Williams, "A 'White Queen' in Africa," p. 342.

6. Award for "African Collection of Garments, Ornaments, Etc." box 10, Mary [*sic*] French Sheldon Papers, Library of Congress.

7. For a discussion of French-Sheldon's reception in England, see Early, "Unescorted in Africa," pp. 69–70.

8. Scrapbook of newspaper clippings, Box 7, Sheldon Papers.

9. Williams, "A 'White Queen' in Africa," p. 343.

10. Ladelle Rice, "Lions, Savages, White Eagles, Nothing before Woman Who Faces African Trials Alone," *Daily Lariat* (February 6, 1925); cited in Boisseau, "'They Called Me *Bebe Bwana*,'" pp. 116–117.

11. M[ay] French-Sheldon, *Sultan to Sultan: Adventures among the Masai and Other Tribes of East Africa* (Boston: Arena, 1892), n. p.

12. Obituary of May French-Sheldon, *New York Times* (February 11, 1936), Scrapbook of newspaper clippings, box 7, Sheldon Papers.

13. French-Sheldon, *Sultan to Sultan,* p. 85.

14. Quoted in "With Gayest Parisian Clothes She Travelled Alone through African Jungles," *Evening Sun* (February 15, 1915), Scrapbook of newspaper clippings, box 7, Sheldon Papers.

15. Quoted in "With Gayest Parisian Clothes She Travelled Alone through African Jungles."

16. Boisseau, "'They Called Me *Bebe Bwana*,'" p. 121.

17. "A White Lady Visits the Masai." According to historian Julie English Early, the British press scorned and ridiculed French-Sheldon as a vulgar American. Early, "Unescorted in Africa," p. 69.

18. Scrapbook of newspaper clippings, box 7, Sheldon Papers.

19. Scrapbook of newspaper clippings, box 7, Sheldon Papers, and Boisseau, "'They Called Me *Bebe Bwana*,'" p. 129.

20. Mrs. French-Sheldon, *Customs among the Natives of East Africa, from Teita to Kilimegalia, with Special Reference to their Women and Children* (London: Harrison, 1892); "England's Commercial and Industrial Future in Central Africa," *Journal of the Tyneside Geographical Society* 3 (May 1897): 415–418.

21. According to Boisseau, the Society admitted fourteen women in 1892 and then offered memberships to seven more women in 1893, before reversing its decision and barring any additional women from membership until 1913. Boisseau, "'They Called Me *Bebe Bwana*,'" p. 128.

22. According to Jeanne Madeline Moore, May French was married and divorced at a young

age before her second marriage to Sheldon. Moore, "Bebe Bwana," p. 37. I have not yet found any other sources that corroborate a prior marriage.

23. Henry Morton Stanley to May French-Sheldon, January 15, 1891, Correspondence, box 1, Sheldon Papers.

24. French-Sheldon, *Sultan to Sultan*, p. 66.

25. French-Sheldon, *Sultan to Sultan*, p. 105.

26. For a list of these people, see French-Sheldon, *Sultan to Sultan*, pp. 387–390.

27. French-Sheldon, *Sultan to Sultan*, p. 170.

28. French-Sheldon, *Sultan to Sultan*, pp. 165–166. Boisseau writes that French-Sheldon was also accompanied by a Swiss maid, whom she brought with her from Europe. Boisseau, "'They Called Me *Bebe Bwana*,'" p. 117.

29. French-Sheldon, *Sultan to Sultan*, pp. 170, 351.

30. French-Sheldon, *Sultan to Sultan*, pp. 112–113.

31. French-Sheldon, *Sultan to Sultan*, pp. 114–115.

32. French-Sheldon, *Sultan to Sultan*, pp. 115–116.

33. French-Sheldon, *Sultan to Sultan*, p. 105.

34. French-Sheldon, *Sultan to Sultan*, p. 136; emphasis in original. In the most serious cases, French-Sheldon used corporeal punishment, flogging two men who threatened a revolt and another who "came very near embroiling me with the natives" when he "brutally hurled to the ground the daughter of a chief, for no greater offence than that she persistently offered some sweet corn for sale, after he had ordered her to quit the encampment." French-Sheldon, *Sultan to Sultan*, pp. 174–176, 135.

35. There are at least two such incidents, one when Kara, a favorite porter, whom she admired for his extraordinary strength, lifted her up bodily to prevent her stepping on a mound of vicious ants (French-Sheldon, *Sultan to Sultan*, p. 145); and a second when her night attendant called on twelve porters to kill a deadly python that had wrapped itself around her palanquin (pp. 311–312).

36. See List of Lectures, typescript, box 7, Sheldon Papers.

37. French-Sheldon, *Sultan to Sultan*, pp. 347–348.

38. French-Sheldon, *Sultan to Sultan*, pp. 380, 381.

39. French-Sheldon, *Sultan to Sultan*, p. 366.

40. French-Sheldon, *Sultan to Sultan*, p. 373.

41. L. H. Gann and Peter Duignan, *The Rulers of Belgian Africa, 1884–1914* (Princeton: Princeton University Press, 1979), p. viii.

42. William Stead to French-Sheldon, September 23 and September 26, 1903, box 1, Correspondence, Sheldon Papers.

43. Boisseau, "'They Called Me *Bebe Bwana*,'" p. 130.

44. French-Sheldon's husband died some time during 1892, while she was writing her account of her safari, and she never remarried. Her most significant emotional relationship afterward was with Miss Nellie Butler, a British woman who was her personal assistant and companion and with whom she lived for over two decades. This woman's existence is only indirectly documentable through existing primary sources. French-Sheldon seems to have destroyed all of her personal papers that touched upon this crucial relationship.

45. "Woman Explorer Finds Sex Has Achieved Economic Independence in Africa Jungle," *New York Press* (April 4, 1915), n.p.; cited in Boisseau, "'They Called Me *Bebe Bwana*,'" p. 132.

46. Correspondence, box 1, and Scrapbook of newspaper clippings, box 7, Sheldon Papers, and Boisseau, "'They Called Me *Bebe Bwana*,'" p. 132.

47. Scrapbook of newspaper clippings, box 7, Sheldon Papers.

48. M. French-Sheldon, "Congratulatory Message of Mme. M. French-Sheldon," *Baylor Towers* 2 (1925): 3–4; cited in Boisseau, "'They Called Me *Bebe Bwana,*'" p. 135.

49. Boisseau, "'They Called Me *Bebe Bwana,*'" pp. 134–135.

50. "Feminine Views, Reviews and Interviews of Interest to Men and Women," *New York Press,* April 4, 1915, Scrapbook of newspaper clippings, box 7, Sheldon Papers.

51. French-Sheldon, *Sultan to Sultan,* p. 94.

52. French-Sheldon, *Sultan to Sultan,* pp. 246–247.

53. Obituary of May French-Sheldon, *London Evening News,* Lunch Edition, February 1, 1936, Scrapbook of newspaper clippings, box 7, Sheldon Papers. Another paper reported: "close on half-a-century ago, just at the time when the world was being thrilled by the chronicles of Stanley's adventurous exploits in Darkest Africa, news of the journey of Mrs. French Sheldon . . . unaccompanied by any white companion, came as an astonishing feat of intrepid courage and daring." Obituary of May French-Sheldon, *West London Observer,* February 21, 1936, Scrapbook of newspaper clippings, box 7, Sheldon Papers.

54. Obituary of May French-Sheldon, *New York Times,* February 11, 1936, Scrapbook of newspaper clippings, box 7, Sheldon Papers.

5. Assimilating Primitives

1. The Women's National Indian Association chose not to take part in this conference. See Helen M. Wanken, "Woman's Sphere and Indian Reform: The Women's National Indian Association" (Ph.D. diss., Marquette University, 1981), pp. 5–6.

2. Frances E. Willard, "Address to the National Council of Women, 1888," in National Council of Women, *Transactions of the National Council of Women of the United States Assembled in Washington, D.C., February 22 to 25, 1891,* ed. Rachel Foster Avery (Philadelphia: J. B. Lippincott, 1891), p. 39.

3. Willard, "Address to the National Council of Women, 1888," p. 39; emphasis in original.

4. David D. Smits, "The 'Squaw Drudge': A Prime Index of Savagism," *Ethnohistory* 29 (1982): 281–306.

5. A. S. Quinton, untitled article, *Indian's Friend* (March 1888): 1, cited in Deborah A. Kallina, "'There's Nothing a Woman Can't Do If She Undertakes To Do It': The Women's National Indian Association, 1879–1951" (B.A. thesis, Brown University, 1986), p. 57. Biographical information on Quinton is available in *Lamb's Biographical Dictionary of the United States,* vol. 7 (Boston: Federal Book Company of Boston, 1903), p. 389, and *Notable American Women, 1607–1950,* ed. Edward T. James (Cambridge: Belknap Press, 1971), pp. 108–110.

6. According to Fletcher, this was a dominant view, but not one she shared. See Alice C. Fletcher, "The Indian Woman and Her Problems," *Woman's Journal* (November 10, 1900): 354.

7. Quinton, "The Annual Address of the President, Mrs. A. S. Quinton," *Indian's Friend* 1 (January 1889): 3.

8. Joan Mark, *A Stranger in Her Native Land: Alice Fletcher and the American Indians* (Lincoln: University of Nebraska Press, 1988), p. 105.

9. Sara Kinney, *Home Building Report* (1890), p. 7, cited in Kallina, "'There's Nothing a Woman Can't Do If She Undertakes To Do It,'" p. 56; my emphasis.

10. "Incidents of Indian life at Hampton," *Southern Workman* 10 (January 1881): 7.

11. Otis T. Mason, *Woman's Share in Primitive Culture* (New York: Appleton), p. 274. Also see chapter 1 of this book.

12. "Incidents of Indian Life at Hampton," p. 7.

13. "Letter from Alice C. Fletcher," *Seventh Annual Lake Mohonk Conference of the Friends of the Indian* (1889), p. 14.

14. I have chosen to focus on Alice Fletcher, rather than Elaine Goodale Eastman or Helen Hunt Jackson, for several reasons. First, Fletcher had much more power and visibility in her culture than did Eastman. Jackson had tremendous visibility, as a result of the publication of *A Century of Dishonor* (1881) and *Ramona* (1884), but she died (for my purposes) early, in 1885, before the Dawes legislation was passed. Fletcher, on the other hand, was influential into the first decade of the twentieth century. For biographical work on Eastman, see Ruth Ann Alexandedr, "Finding Oneself through a Cause: Elaine Goodale Eastman and Indian Reform in the 1880s," *South Dakota History* 22 (Spring 1992): 1–37, Eastman's memoirs, *Sister to the Sioux: The Memoirs of Elaine Goodale Eastman, 1885–91,* ed. Kay Graber (Lincoln: University of Nebraska Press, 1978); and Elaine Goodale Eastman, "All the Days of My Life," *South Dakota Historical Review* 2 (July 1937): 174–177. For biographical treatment of Jackson, see Valerie Sherer Mathes, *Helen Hunt Jackson and Her Indian Reform Legacy* (Austin: University of Texas Press, 1990); Ruth Odell, *Helen Hunt Jackson* (New York: Appleton-Century, 1939); and Thurman Wilkins's entry in *Notable American Women,* vol. 2, pp. 259–261.

15. Robert M. Utley, *The Indian Frontier of the American West, 1846–1890* (Albuquerque: University of New Mexico Press, 1984), pp. 157–201; Mathes, *Helen Hunt Jackson,* pp. 4–5, 23–25.

16. See, for example, Alice C. Fletcher, "Economy of Justice," *Lend a Hand* 1 (July 1886): 528–530.

17. See Alice C. Fletcher, "Tribute to Helen Hunt Jackson," *Third Annual Lake Mohonk Conference of the Friends of the Indian* (1885), p. 71.

18. Historians have referred to these policies collectively as Grant's peace policy, a phrase that can only be understood ironically, since the period immediately following the implementation of these policies was characterized by coercion, violence, and unofficial but bloody wars. In the late 1860s, Congress passed the Indian Appropriations Act of April 10, 1869, which empowered the president to appoint ten people "eminent for their intelligence and philanthropy" to a Board of Indian Commissioners, who, together with the Secretary of the Interior, were to oversee the treatment of Indian tribes. Congress also outlawed the appointment of army officers to civil posts, putting an end to the assignment of military officers as Indian agents on reservations. These positions were now divvied up among the nation's principal religious denominations, who recommended individuals for the jobs, who were then formally nominated by the president and ratified by the Senate. Utley, *The Indian Frontier,* pp. 129–133. Details of the new procedure in the appointment of Indian agents can be found in Alice Fletcher, *Civilization and Education* (Washington, D.C.: Government Printing Office, 1888).

19. As far as I know, no published monographs on the WNIA exist. In my view, the best unpublished sources are Helen Marie Bannan, "Reformers and the 'Indian Problem,' 1878–1887 and 1922–1934" (Ph.D. diss., Syracuse University, 1976), Wanken, "'Woman's Sphere' and Indian Reform." Also see Kallina, "'There's Nothing a Woman Can't Do If She Undertakes To Do It.'" The best primary source on the history of the WNIA that I have found is Amelia Stone Quinton, "The Indian," in *The Literature of Philanthropy,* ed. Frances A. Goodale (New York: Harper, 1893), pp. 116–140.

20. Irene Joanne Westing, entry for Amelia Stone Quinton, *Notable American Women,* vol. 3, p. 108.

21. Irene Joanne Westing, entry for Mary Lucinda Bonney, *Notable American Women,* vol. 1, p. 197.

22. Alice S. Fletcher, "Standing Bear," *Southern Workman* 38 (1909): 75–78.

23. Westing, entry for Quinton, p. 108.

24. Much of the following discussion is drawn from Joan Mark's superb biography *A Stranger in Her Native Land.* Also see Wilkins, entry on Fletcher, pp. 630–632. According to Mark, Fletcher,

more than any other single person, bears ultimate responsibility for the final form that the Dawes Act of 1887 eventually assumed. Henry Dawes himself alluded to Fletcher's importance with the quip, "I stand in reference to that [legislation] very much as Americus Vespuscious [sic] stands to Columbus." Mark, *A Stranger in Her Native Land*, p. 119.

25. Fletcher, "Standing Bear," p. 78.

26. Mark, *A Stranger in Her Native Land*, pp. 13, 18, 28–29. For an example of her views on class differences among women at this time, see Alice C. Fletcher, "Feminine Idleness," *Woman's Journal* 4 (September 13, 1873): 291.

27. Mark, *A Stranger in Her Native Land*, pp. 39, 42, 45. Alice Fletcher to Lucian Carr, August 3, 1881, Peabody Museum Papers, cited in Mark, *A Stranger in Her Native Land*, p. 42.

28. Mark, *Stranger in Her Native Land*, p. 63.

29. See for example, Alice C. Fletcher, "Between the Lines," *Lend a Hand* 1 (July 1886): 429–431, especially 431.

30. Alice C. Fletcher, "Among the Omahas," *Woman's Journal* 13 (February 11, 1882): 46.

31. Fletcher, "Among the Omahas," p. 46; also cited in Mark, *Stranger in Her Native Land*, p. 62.

32. Mark, *A Stranger in Her Native Land*, pp. 89, 91.

33. Mark, *A Stranger in Her Native Land*, p. 93.

34. Mark, *A Stranger in Her Native Land*, p. 93.

35. Mark, *A Stranger in Her Native Land*, p. 93.

36. Philip Garrett, *18th Annual Report*, 1886 (Washington, D.C., Board of Indian Commissioners, 1887), p. 51, as cited in Mark, *A Stranger in Her Native Land*, p. 105.

37. A. C. Fletcher, "On Indian Education and Self-Support," *Century* 26 (May 1883): 314; Fletcher, "Between the Lines," p. 430.

38. Alice C. Fletcher, *On the Lawlessness of the Indian Reservation System* (Boston: Frank Wood, 1884), p. 33. The same passage also appears in Alice C. Fletcher, "Land, Law, Education—The Three Things Needed by the Indian," *Southern Workman* 14 (March 1885): 33.

39. Mark, *A Stranger in Her Native Land*, p. 106.

40. Senator Richard Coke of Texas, chairman of the Indian Affairs Committee (Dawes's predecessor) had introduced the first general allotment bill in the Senate, which passed the Senate floor during the winter of 1880–1881. Over the next seven years, several different versions of the Coke-Dawes bill were debated in Congress. Some versions of the bill did not make the severalty policy mandatory but permitted tribes to choose whether they wanted to continue to hold their land in common or receive individual allotments. Other versions of the bill created a tribal patent for those Indians within a tribe who did not wish to accept individual allotments. The Dawes Act was implemented on a case-by-case basis, beginning with tribes who appeared to whites to be more eager for individual land ownership. See Frederick E. Hoxie and Joan T. Mark, introduction to E. Jane Gay, *With the Nez Perces: Alice Fletcher in the Field, 1889–92* (Lincoln: University of Nebraska Press, 1981), pp. xiv–xvi.

41. "The Cherokee Protest," *Independent* 30 (February 1878): 16.

42. Fletcher, "Between the Lines," p. 430. Also see Fletcher, "Land, Law, Education," p. 33.

43. Alice Fletcher, "The Crowning Act," *Morning Star* 7 (March 1887): 1.

44. Fletcher, *On the Lawlessness of the Indian Reservation System*, p. 33; my emphasis.

45. Fletcher, *On the Lawlessness of the Indian Reservation System*, p. 33.

46. Mark, *A Stranger in Her Native Land*, pp. 293–295, 307–308.

47. Fletcher, *On the Lawlessness of the Indian Reservation System*, pp. 10–11.

48. Mark, *A Stranger in her Native Land*, pp. 265–268.

49. Alice C. Fletcher, "Flotsam and Jetsam from Aboriginal America," *Southern Workman* 28 (January 1899): 13.

50. Fletcher, "Flotsam and Jetsam from Aboriginal America," p. 13.

51. Fletcher, "Flotsam and Jetsam from Aboriginal America," p. 13.

52. Alice C. Fletcher, "The Indian Woman and Her Problems," *Southern Workman* 28 (May 1899): 175. This anecdote reverberated for white women at the turn of the twentieth century. The incident was fairly well known—another account of it appears in Josephine E. Richards, "The Training of the Indian Girl as the Uplifter of the Home," *Southern Workman* 29 (September 1900): 507.

53. Fletcher, "The Indian Woman and Her Problems, p. 354.

54. Mary C. Collins, "The Dependence of the Indian," *Southern Workman* 29 (July 1900): 427.

55. Collins, "The Dependence of the Indian," pp. 427–429. Also see Alice Rollins Crane, "Why the Indians Break Out," *Arena* 20 (October 1898): 491–498; Mary E. Dewey, *Historical Sketch of the Formation and Achievements of the Women's National Indian Association in the United States* (n.p., 1900).

56. Crane, "Why the Indians Break Out," pp. 496, 497.

57. Fletcher, "The Indian Woman and Her Problems," p. 354.

58. Fletcher, "The Indian Woman and Her Problems," p. 354.

6. Eliminating Sex Distinctions from Civilization

1. Charlotte Perkins Stetson, "Masculine, Feminine, and Human," *Kate Field's Washington* (July 6, 1892): 7.

2. Charlotte Perkins Gilman, "A Suggestion on the Negro Problem," *American Journal of Sociology* 14 (July 1908): 78–85. This article is reprinted within an anonymous response, entitled "To Make the Negro Work," *Literary Digest* 37 (October 10, 1908): 499–500.

3. Gilman, "Suggestion on the Negro Problem," p. 83; cited in Gail Bederman, *Manliness & Civilization: A Cultural History of Gender and Race in the United States, 1880–1917* (Chicago: University of Chicago Press, 1995), p. 123.

4. Gilman, "Suggestion on the Negro Problem," p. 83.

5. "To Make the Negro Work," pp. 499–500.

6. Bederman, *Manliness & Civilization,* p. 122.

7. Charlotte Perkins Gilman, "The Biological Anti-Feminist" (written in response to an interview by William B. Sedgwick in the *New York Times*), *Forerunner* 5 (March 1914): 65.

8. Mary Roberts Coolidge, *Why Women Are So* (New York: Henry Holt, 1912), p. 311; my emphasis. Copy available in *Gerristen Collection of Women's History* (Glen Rock, N.J.: Microfilming Corporation of America, 1975).

9. Charlotte Perkins Stetson, "Masculine, Feminine and Human," p. 7.

10. Coolidge, *Why Women Are So,* p. 300.

11. Gilman, "Suggestion on the Negro Problem," p. 80.

12. Charlotte Perkins Gilman, *The Home* (New York: McClure, Phillips, 1903; reprint, Urbana: University of Illinois Press, 1972), p. 217.

13. Coolidge, *Why Woman Are So,* p. 300.

14. "Personal Problems," *Forerunner* 1 (July 1910): 23–24, cited in Susan S. Lanser, "Feminist Criticism, 'The Yellow Wallpaper,' and the Politics of Color in America," *Feminist Studies* 15 (Fall 1989): 433.

15. Lanser, "Feminist Criticism," p. 433.

16. Charlotte Perkins Gilman, *The Man-Made World, or, Our Androcentric Culture* (New York: Charlton, 1911), p. 31; my emphasis.

17. Coolidge, *Why Women Are So,* p. 24.

18. Charlotte Perkins Stetson, "Masculine, Feminine, and Human," p. 7.

19. Gordon argues that "the emotional significance of this usage lay in the fact that it connoted both meanings simultaneously encouraging a tendency to identify the human race with the white race." Linda Gordon, *Woman's Body, Woman's Right: A Social History of Birth Control in America* (New York: Penguin, 1976), p. 142.

20. Coolidge, *Why Woman Are So,* p. 316; my emphasis. For similar expressions, see Mary Putnam-Jacobi, *"Common Sense" Applied to Woman Suffrage* (New York: Putnam 1894), pp. 26, 65, 75.

21. The best biographical treatments include Bederman, *Manliness & Civilization,* pp. 121–169; Ann J. Lane, *To "Herland" and Beyond: The Life and Work of Charlotte Perkins Gilman* (New York: Pantheon Books, 1990), and Mary A. Hill, *Charlotte Perkins Gilman: The Making of a Radical Feminist, 1860–1896* (Philadelphia: Temple University Press, 1980).

22. Bederman, *Manliness & Civilization,* p. 124.

23. Bederman, *Manliness & Civilization,* p. 125.

24. *The Living of Charlotte Perkins Gilman, An Autobiography* (New York: Appleton-Century, 1935), p. 37 and Bederman, *Manliness & Civilization,* p. 126.

25. Bederman, *Manliness & Civilization,* pp. 126–127.

26. See *Living,* p. 39, and Bederman, *Manliness & Civilization,* p. 128.

27. Bederman, *Manliness & Civilization,* p. 128.

28. Gilman, *The Living of Charlotte Perkins Gilman,* p. 83; cited in Bederman, *Manliness & Civilization,* p. 129.

29. See Charlotte Perkins Gilman, "Why I Wrote the Yellow Wallpaper," *Forerunner* 4 (October 1913): 271, and Lane, *To "Herland" and Beyond,* pp. 110–111.

30. Bederman, *Manliness & Civilization,* pp. 128–134.

31. Bederman, *Manliness & Civilization,* pp. 122, 135.

32. Bederman, *Manliness & Civilization,* p. 122.

33. Bederman, *Manliness & Civilization,* p. 135.

34. Charlotte Perkins Gilman, *Women and Economics* (Boston: Small, Maynard, 1898; reprint, New York: Harper, 1966), p. 8.

35. Gilman, *Women and Economics,* pp. 8–9, 11.

36. Gilman, *Women and Economics,* p. 29.

37. Gilman, *Women and Economics,* p. 38.

38. Gilman, *Women and Economics,* p. 46.

39. Gilman, *Women and Economics,* p. 46.

40. See Lester Ward, "Our Better Halves," *Forum* 6 (November 1888): 266–275, and "Genius and Woman's Intuition," *Forum* 9 (June 1890): 401–408; Edward Alsworth Ross, "The Causes of Race Superiority," *Annals of the American Academy of Political and Social Science* 18 (July 1901): 67–89; *Social Control: A Survey of the Foundations of Order* (New York: Macmillan, 1901); and *The Old World in the New* (New York: Century, 1914); Thorstein Veblen, "The Barbarian Status of Women," *American Journal of Sociology* 4 (January 1899): 503–514, and *The Theory of the Leisure Class,* 1st ed. (New York: Macmillan 1899; reprint, New York: New American Library, 1953).

Many other people were members of this intellectual community, including the sociologist William I. Thomas at Columbia University; the historian George E. Howard at Stanford University; and the economist Richard Ely. Ely trained Ross when the latter was a graduate student at Johns Hopkins in 1890–1891, and he also taught Helen Campbell, a close friend and mentor of Gilman, at the University of Wisconsin in 1893. Gilman met Ely around 1895 through her connection with Jane Addams. The philosopher John Dewey and the sociologist Albion Small at the University of Chicago were also part of these intellectual circles, and Gilman met both men in Chicago in 1895 while she was staying at Hull House.

Other women of Coolidge and Gilman's generation who had similar views include Anna

Garlin Spencer, a leader in the American Purity movement, an active member in the temperance movement, and author of *Woman's Share in Social Culture* (New York: Mitchell Kennerley, 1913); Beatrice Forbes-Robertson Hale, author of *What Women Want: An Interpretation of the Feminist Movement* (New York: Frederick A. Stokes, 1914); and Jane Addams, founder of Hull House and author of *Democracy and Social Ethics* (New York: Macmillan, 1902), and *A New Conscience and an Ancient Evil* (New York: Macmillan, 1912). Two younger feminist women, Winnifred Harper Cooley and Elsie Clews Parsons, also discussed the relation of the civilized to the primitive in ways that were similar to Gilman and Coolidge.

41. Lane, *To "Herland" and Beyond,* p. 186. My discussion of Gilman's life draws heavily on Lane and, to a lesser extent, Gilman's autobiography *The Living of Charlotte Perkins Gilman,* published posthumously in 1935. Gilman's papers are housed on microfilm at the Schlesinger Library at Harvard University.

42. See Ward, "Our Better Halves," pp. 266–275; "Genius and Woman's Intuition," pp. 401–408; *The Psychic Factors of Civilization* (Boston: Ginn, 1893), especially chapters 14 and 26; "The Course of Biologic Evolution," *Proceedings of the Biological Society of Washington* 5 (c. 1893): 23–55; and *Pure Sociology: A Treatise on the Origin and Spontaneous Development of Society* (New York: Macmillan, 1909), especially pp. 290–377.

43. See also chapter 1 for a discussion of Ward's gynaecocentric theories of racial conservation.

44. Gilman, preface to *Man-Made World,* n.p. The other evolution theorist who had an enormous impact on Gilman was Sir Edward Burnett Tylor, a British anthropologist and historian whose *Primitive Culture, Researches into the Development of Mythology, Philosophy, Religion, Language, Art, and Custom* (1871 [2nd ed., New York: Henry Holt, 1881]) was probably the source of Gilman's notion of primitive survivals.

45. Gilman, *Man-Made World,* preface, n.p., and p. 255.

46. Gilman, *Man-Made World,* pp. 38–39.

47. Gilman, *The Home,* p. 275.

48. From the mid-1890s on, Gilman wrote regularly to both Ward and Ross. Her correspondence suggests that she revered Ward and, as he was thirteen years her senior, maintained some deferential formality in her relationship with him. There was also some tension in this relationship; Gilman once chastised Ward for not appreciating how much she had done to popularize his work. See Mary A. Hill, *Charlotte Perkins Gilman: The Making of a Radical Feminist, 1860–1896* (Philadelphia: Temple University Press, 1980), pp. 266–267.

49. Ward and Ross remained close intellectual associates and friends throughout Ward's life. See Julius Weinberg, *Edward Alsworth Ross and the Sociology of Progressivism* (Madison: State Historical Society of Wisconsin, 1972), p. 31, and Edward Alsworth Ross, *Seventy Years of It: An Autobiography* (New York: Appleton, 1936).

50. See Mary O. Furner, *Advocacy and Objectivity: A Crisis in the Professionalization of American Social Science, 1865–1905* (Lexington: University Press of Kentucky, 1975), pp. 233–253.

51. Charlotte Perkins Gilman to E. A. Ross, November, 28, 1900, microfilm reel 17, E. A. Ross Papers, State Historical Society of Wisconsin, Madison.

52. Charlotte Perkins Gilman to E. A. Ross, November 28, 1900, reel 17, Edward A. Ross Papers.

53. Over the years, deep feelings of love and respect developed between Gilman and Ross. After Gilman's suicide (at seventy-six) in 1936, Ross wrote of the friendship that had lasted over forty years: "Charlotte Perkins Gilman, niece of Henry Ward Beecher, was a dear intimate of ours. She was the most brilliant woman I have known and had the most beautiful woman's head I ever laid eyes on." Two days before she killed herself, Gilman sent Ross a last letter, which he cherished, reprinting a portion of it in his memoirs. Ross, *Seventy Years of It,* p. 60.

54. Gilman to E. A. Ross, November 28, 1900 and February 1, 1900, reel 17, Edward A. Ross Papers. For the influence of Veblen on Gilman's discussion of women and labor, see *The Home,* pp. 106–109, 119, 220; *Human Work* (New York: McClure, Phillips, 1904), p. 179; and *Man-Made World,* pp. 36–37, 234.

55. See Gilman's correspondence with Edward A. Ross, especially her letters to him of February 1, 1900, March 15, 1906, October 17, 1907, and October 17, 1915, reel 17, Edward A. Ross Papers

56. Mrs. Jane Lathrop Stanford demanded Ross's dismissal on the grounds that his expression of his political views (about free silver in the 1890s) jeopardized his production of objective scholarship, but David Starr Jordan (1851–1931), president of the university, prevailed on her to give Ross a sabbatical leave in 1898–1899 so that he could look for another position. Ross agreed to resign at the end of that academic year, 1898–1899, if Stanford still demanded his dismissal at that time. However, as Jordan had hoped would happen, tensions abated between Ross and Stanford, and Ross was reappointed for the following academic term, 1899–1990. During 1900, however, Ross continued to express political opinions that Stanford continued to find objectionable—this time his support of legislation restricting Chinese immigration so as to protect "American" labor. For an account of the events leading to Ross's dismissal from Stanford University, see Furner, *Advocacy and Objectivity,* pp. 233–253.

57. President Theodore Roosevelt gave national currency to the term "race suicide" in speeches delivered in 1905. See Gordon, *Woman's Body, Woman's Right,* p. 142.

58. Weinberg, *Edward Alsworth Ross,* pp. 88–89.

59. Veblen, *Theory of the Leisure Class,* pp. 150.

60. Gilman to E. A. Ross, November 28, 1900, February 1, 1900, reel 17, Edward A. Ross Papers.

61. Veblen, *Theory of the Leisure Class,* p. 168.

62. Ross, *Social Control,* p. 21.

63. Roosevelt, "The Strenuous Life: Address delivered to the Appomattox Day Banquet of the Hamilton Club, April 10th, 1899" in *The Strenuous Life: Essays and Addresses* (New York: Century, 1918), pp. 6–7, 9. Also see T. J. Jackson Lears, *No Place of Grace: Antimodernism and the Transformation of American Culture, 1880–1920* (New York: Pantheon Books, 1981), and Gail Bederman, "Manly Civilization/Primitive Masculinity: Race, Gender and the Evolution of Middle-Class American Manhood, 1880–1915" (Ph.D. diss., Brown University, 1993).

64. See discussion of Ward, "Our Better Halves" in chapter 1.

65. Ross, "The Causes of Race Superiority," pp. 67–89, especially p. 75. Some anti-imperialists of this period exposed the fallacy of the claim that the United States needed more land to continue its own racial evolution. See for example, James L. Blair, *Imperialism: Our National Policy. An Address Delivered before the Monday Evening Club, January 9, 1899* (St. Louis: Gottschalk, 1899), p. 6.

66. Gilman, *Man-Made World,* p. 216.

67. Gilman, *Man-Made World,* p. 216.

68. Gilman, *Man-Made World,* p. 217.

69. Charlotte Perkins Gilman, "Men's Babies," Gilman mss., Schlesinger Library; cited in Linda Gordon, *Woman's Body, Woman's Right,* p. 145.

70. Gilman, *Man-Made World,* p. 217.

71. Charlotte Perkins Stetson, "The Labor Movement," a prize essay read before the trades and labor unions of Alameda County, September 5, 1892 (Oakland, Ca.: Alameda County Federation of Trades, 1893), p. 7.

72. Gilman exempted one occupation and one set of character traits, which she believed were distinctively masculine: fighting and aggression. "The business of slaughter," Gilman

wrote, "belongs by inherent sex-distinction to the male; and there has never been any danger of women's 'competing with man' in this field." Charlotte Perkins Gilman, "Competing with Men," *Woman's Journal* 35 (February 6, 1904): 42.

73. Gilman, *The Home*, p. 89.

74. Mary Roberts Smith Coolidge to Edward A. Ross, August 16, 1912, reel 6, Edward A. Ross Papers. My discussion of Coolidge's life is pieced together from Rosalind Rosenberg, *Beyond Separate Spheres: Intellectual Roots of Modern Feminism* (New Haven: Yale University Press, 1982), pp. 179–189, 194–196; James McKeen Cattell, ed., *Leaders in Education: A Biographical Dictionary* (New York: Science Press, 1932); and some of my own research, part of which is contained in *Men's Ideas/Women's Realities: Popular Science, 1870–1920*, ed. Louise Michele Newman (New York: Pergamon Press, 1985), pp. 116, 170. Documents pertaining to Coolidge's life are sparse and scattered. Some of her personal papers are at the Bancroft Library at the University of California at Berkeley, filed under her husband Dane Coolidge's name, and there are some newspaper clippings about her life in the archives at Cornell University in New York and Mills College in California.

75. Mary Roberts Coolidge, *Chinese Immigration* (New York: Holt, 1909). Gilman mentioned Coolidge's book *Why Women Are So* in her "Comment and Review" column for *Forerunner* 13 (March 1913): 82, but it is not possible to tell from the context whether Gilman had actually read the book.

76. Coolidge, *Chinese Immigration*, p. 446.

77. Coolidge, *Chinese Immigration*, pp. 436–440, 454–458.

78. Coolidge, *Chinese Immigration*, pp. 446, 437

79. Coolidge, *Chinese Immigration*, pp. 419–420.

80. Another early example is Hale, *What Women Want*. Coolidge dedicated her book to "D.C. [Dane Coolidge] and other new men who set Human quality above femininity in women," and she offered an account of the nineteenth-century woman's movement from the perspective of a woman who identified herself as a "feminist." Although Coolidge did not list other "new men" by name, she was probably also thinking of men like Edward Ross and Floyd Dell. Ross explained his attitudes toward women in his autobiography: "I laugh at the notion that the other sex is 'inscrutable.' . . . I . . . have no difficulty in quickly getting on a sympathetic basis with them. . . . Once they realize that I am quite free from the silly notion that the male sex is 'superior' or that the female is 'of finer clay,' they feel no call to fence with me but allow the riches of their heart to appear." Ross, *Seventy Years of It*, p. 20.

81. The only commentary I could locate on *Why Women Are So* was a brief discussion in Rosenberg, *Beyond Separate Spheres*, pp. 194–95.

82. For Coolidge, temperance women were forerunners of the modern muckrakers in journalism. See *Why Women Are So*, p. 204. Quotations are from p. 206.

83. Rosenberg, *Beyond Separate Spheres*, p. 184.

84. Coolidge in an appendix, c. 1910, to the Mosher sex survey she initially filled out in 1892, Mosher Survey, case no. 2; cited in Rosenberg, *Beyond Separate Spheres*, pp. 195–96. A letter from Coolidge to Edward Ross in 1912, thanking him for his help in securing a publisher for *Why Women Are So*, reiterates this view of her second marriage. Coolidge to E. A. Ross, August 10, 1912, reel 17, Edward A. Ross Papers.

85. Coolidge, *Why Woman Are So*, p. 24; my emphasis.

86. Coolidge, *Why Woman Are So*, p. 107.

87. See Mary Roberts Smith [Coolidge], "Recent Tendencies in the Education of Women," *Popular Science Monthly* 48 (November 1895): 27–33.

88. Coolidge, *Why Women Are So*, pp. 63–64.

89. Coolidge, *Why Women Are So*, p. 58.

90. Coolidge, like Gilman, was willing to acknowledge that there had existed a "few primitive peoples where men and women were approximately equal in status." *Why Women Are So,* p. 91.

7. Coming of Age, but Not in Samoa

1. Margaret Mead, Preface to the 1973 edition of *Coming to Age: A Psychological Study of Primitive Youth for Western Civilisation* (1st ed., New York, W. Morrow, 1928; Morrow Quill, 1973), n. p. All future citations from *Coming of Age* are from the 1973 edition. This book was reissued with at least five new prefaces—in 1939, 1949, 1953, 1961, and 1973.

2. In the 1930s, in the midst of the Depression, Mead gave advice about homemaking and childrearing. During World War II, she became an expert on "national character" and argued that the United States could defeat totalitarian regimes without jeopardizing its own democratic institutions. After the war, with the nation's attention focused on domesticity, Mead lectured on marriage and the family. At the height of the civil rights and women's movements in the 1960s, Mead spoke and published on racial and gender issues. Mead discusses her publishing venues and decisions in the introduction to a bibliography of her corpus; see Joan Gordan, ed., *Margaret Mead: The Complete Bibliography, 1925–1975* (The Hague: Mouton, 1976), pp. 1–21.

3. As other historians have pointed out, Mead's work coincided with an ongoing social movement in the 1920s to overcome the Victorian prudery and repression endemic in middle-class Anglo (hetero)sexual relations. See Stephen O. Murray, "On Boasians and Margaret Mead: Reply to Freeman," *Current Anthropology* 32 (August–October 1991): 488; Paula S. Fass, *The Damned and the Beautiful: American Youth in the 1920's* (New York: Oxford University Press, 1977); and James R. McGovern, "The American Woman's Pre–World War I Freedom in Manners and Morals," *Journal of American History* 55 (September 1968): 315–333.

4. The best treatment of evolutionist anthropology is George W. Stocking, Jr.'s classic works, *Victorian Anthropology* (New York: Free Press, 1987), and *Race, Culture, and Evolution: Essays in the History of Anthropology* (Chicago: University of Chicago Press, 1968, 1982).

5. For an account of how Elsie Clews Parsons challenged evolutionist paradigms in anthropology, see Rosalind Rosenberg, *Beyond Separate Spheres: Intellectual Roots of Modern Feminism* (New Haven: Yale University Press, 1982), pp. 147–177.

6. Margaret Mead, *Blackberry Winter: My Earlier Years* (New York: William Morrow, 1972; reprint, New York: Pocket Books, 1975), pp. 151–152.

7. For over one hundred years, Westerners had presumed that primitive women were overworked, sexually abused, or otherwise badly treated by the men of their cultures. As historian Nicholas Thomas has pointed out, "the degradation of women was a measure for the degradation of a society and enabled it to be mapped against others in a region. Gender was thus central to the evolutionary ranking of societies." *Colonialism's Culture: Anthropology, Travel, and Government* (Princeton: Princeton University Press, 1994), p. 102.

8. Margaret Mead, *Sex and Temperament in Three Primitive Societies* (New York: William Morrow, 1935; reprint, Morrow Quill Paperbacks, 1963), p. 310. All citations of this work hereafter are from this edition unless otherwise indicated.

9. I thank Todd Gernes for suggesting the term "cultural comparativism" as a substitute for "cultural relativism."

10. Mead, *Coming of Age,* p. 4; my emphasis.

11. See Charlotte Perkins Gilman, *The Home: Its Work and Influence* (New York: McClure Phillips, 1903), and *The Man-Made World, or, Our Androcentric Culture* (New York: Charlton, 1911); Mary Roberts Coolidge, *Why Women Are So* (New York: Henry Holt, 1912); and Elsie Clews Parsons, "Facing Race Suicide," *Masses* 6 (June 1915): 15, and *The Family* (New York: Putnam, 1906).

12. By the early 1900s, Hall had achieved prominent status as one of the founding fathers and current leaders of American psychology, having taught first at Johns Hopkins and then at Clark University, a graduate institution in Worcester, Massachusetts, where he served both as a professor of psychology and as its first president, from its inception in 1888 until 1920. Dorothy Ross, *G. Stanley Hall: The Psychologist as Prophet* (Chicago: University of Chicago Press, 1972); Cynthia Eagle Russett, *Sexual Science: The Victorian Construction of Womanhood* (Cambridge: Harvard University Press, 1989), p. 57.

13. Mead, *Coming of Age,* p. 5.

14. Mead, *Coming of Age,* p. 201.

15. "This acceptance of a wider range as 'normal' provides a cultural atmosphere in which frigidity and psychic impotence do not occur and in which a satisfactory sex adjustment in marriage can always be established. The acceptance of such an attitude without in any way accepting promiscuity would go a long way towards solving many marital impasses and emptying our park benches and our houses of prostitution." Mead, *Coming of Age,* p. 223.

16. Mead, *Coming of Age,* p. 206.

17. According to historian Nicholas Thomas, gender relations was "a crucial dimension of difference that often encode[d] or valorize[d] other differences such as those based in 'race' or geographic location." Thomas, *Colonialism's Culture,* p. 100.

18. Mead, *Coming of Age,* pp. 236–237.

19. This book drew many readers for over four decades. As late as the 1960s, *Sex and Temperament* was still routinely being taught in introductory psychology and anthropology courses in U.S. colleges.

20. Mead, *Sex and Temperament,* p. 279; cited in Jane Howard, *Margaret Mead: A Life* (New York: Simon and Schuster, 1984), p. 162.

21. Mead, *Sex and Temperament,* p. 313. Numerous reviewers read this book avidly, accepted most of its conclusions, and strongly recommended that others read it because "of its theoretic importance to the subject of the relations of the sexes." C. H. Wedgwood, review of *Sex and Temperament, Oceania* 6 (September 1935): 113.

22. Mead, *Sex and Temperament,* pp. 280–281.

23. For example, Freda Kirchwey's review was published under the headline "Sex in the South Seas," *Nation* 127 (October 24, 1928), p. 427.

24. Mead, preface to the 1950 edition of *Sex and Temperament in Three Primitive Societies* (New York: New American Library 1950), n.p.

25. Hortense Powdermaker, review of *Sex and Temperament, Annals of the American Academy of Political and Social Science* 181 (September 1935): 221–222.

26. Mead, preface to the 1950 edition of *Sex and Temperament,* n.p.

27. Readers in the 1930s understood and embraced this point. Jeannette Mirsky, a reviewer for the *Survey,* wrote: "the author concludes that by assigning definite and different traits to the sexes or by setting a single pattern for men and women, we get misfits, persons of either sex who cannot fit into their defined roles. Her plea is for a variety of roles open to both men and women so that everyone will have institutionalized backing to express his temperament and talents." Jeanette Mirsky, "Review of *Sex and Temperament, Survey* 71 (October 1935): 315.

28. Mead, *Coming of Age,* p. 248.

29. The clearest presentation of these ideas can be found in Otis T. Mason, "Woman's Share in Primitive Culture," *American Antiquarian* 11 (January 1889): 3–13, and *Woman's Share in Primitive Culture* (New York: Appleton, 1898); and Lester Ward, "Our Better Halves," *Forum* 6 (November 1888): 266–275, and *The Psychic Factors of Civilization,* 1st ed. (Boston: Ginn, 1893; reprint, New York: Johnson, 1970).

30. Mrs. M. F. Armstrong, "Sketches of Mission Life, No. IV," *Southern Workman* 10 (April 1881): 44.

31. Armstrong, "Sketches of Mission Life, No. IV," p. 44.

32. Frances Drewry McMullen, "'Going Native' for Science," *Woman's Journal* 15 (July 1930): 8, and *American Magazine* 120 (September 1935): 42. The *New York Times* reported on a dinner held to honor Dr. Mead in 1934 with the headline "Women Explorers Held Equal to Men." The lead to this article began, "Whether in the steaming jungles of Central Africa or atop the frozen summits of some of the world's highest peaks, the modern woman explorer 'can more than hold her own.'" *New York Times,* March 14, 1934, p. 9.

33. Margaret Mead, *Male and Female: A Study of the Sexes in a Changing World* (New York: William Morrow, 1949), p. 39.

34. Mead to unidentified recipient, January 15, 1932, reprinted in Margaret Mead, *Letters from the Field, 1925–1975* (New York: Harper and Row, 1977), p. 103.

35. Howard, *Margaret Mead,* p. 398. Although Howard is not clear on this point, it appears that this quotation comes from an interview that she held with Leonora Foerstel, who it seems was an eyewitness to the event.

36. Margaret Mead, "The Comparative Study of Cultures and the Purposive Cultivation of Democratic Values, 1941–1949," in *Perspectives on a Troubled Decade: Science, Philosophy, and Religion, 1939–1949* (New York: Harper, 1950), p. 91.

37. Margaret Mead and James Baldwin, *A Rap on Race* (New York: Laurel Books, 1971), pp. 27–28.

38. Mead and Baldwin, *A Rap on Race,* p. 28.

39. Mead was aware that many would find this an oversimplified and inadequate analysis, and to ward off criticism, she wrote, "You perhaps think that I am constantly bringing this back to simple family points and not facing the major issues, but the big differences that exist in any society, like . . . between the three races, are all originally worked out in the home." Mead, "Race Majority—Race Minority," in *The People in Your Life: Psychiatry and Personal Relations by Ten Leading Authorities,* ed. Margaret M. Hughes, 1st ed. (New York: Knopf, 1951; reprint, Freeport, N.Y.: Books for Libraries Press, 1971), p. 132.

40. Mead, "Race Majority—Race Minority," p. 147.

41. John Dollard, *Caste and Class in a Southern Town* (New York: Harper, 1949), p. 168.

42. An excellent and early example of this complex and ambivalent position can be found in Margaret Mead, "Americanization in Samoa," *American Mercury* 16 (March 1929): 264–270.

43. Margaret Mead, "Human Differences and World Order," in *World Order: Its Intellectual and Cultural Foundation,* ed. Ernest Johnson (New York: Harper, 1945), pp. 42–43.

44. There is an excellent, burgeoning scholarship historicizing and critiquing anthropology, including James Clifford and George E. Marcus, eds., *Writing Culture: The Poetics and Politics of Ethnography* (Berkeley: University of California Press, 1986); George E. Marcus and Michael M. J. Fischer, *Anthropology as Cultural Critique: An Experimental Moment in the Human Sciences* (Chicago: University of Chicago Press, 1986); Stocking, *Victorian Anthropology;* James Clifford, *The Predicament of Culture: Twentieth-Century Ethnography, Literature, and Art* (Cambridge: Harvard University Press, 1988); Marc Manganaro, ed., *Modernist Anthropology: From Fieldwork to Text* (Princeton: Princeton University Press, 1990); Micaela di Leonardo, ed., *Gender at the Crossroads of Knowledge: Feminist Anthropology in the Postmodern Era* (Berkeley: University of California Press, 1991); Arnold Krupat, *Ethnocriticism: Ethnography, History, Literature* (Berkeley: University of California Press, 1992); and Thomas, *Colonialism's Culture.*

A feminist historiography on the history of social science is just beginning to emerge. See Rosenberg, *Beyond Separate Spheres,* and Dorothy Ross, *The Origins of American Social Science* (Cambridge: Cambridge University Press, 1991). Practicing feminist anthropologists are currently engaged in specifying the theoretical contributions of their feminist predecessors; see Micaela di

Leonardo, Introduction to *Gender at the Crossroads of Knowledge,* pp. 1–50, and Louise Lamphere, "Feminist Anthropology: The Legacy of Elsie Clews Parsons," *American Ethnologist* 16 (August 1989): 518–533.

45. Betty Friedan, *The Feminine Mystique* (New York: Norton, 1963), pp. 145, 135. Activist-scholars who produced the first round of histories of the so-called second wave of feminism scarcely took notice of Mead's presence. For example, Aileen Kraditor, who edited one of the earliest collections of second wave feminist writings, *Up From the Pedestal: Selected Writings in the History of American Feminism* (Chicago: Quadrangle Books, 1968), included entries for Charlotte Perkins Gilman (1912), Mary Bunting (1960), and the National Organization for Women's statement of purpose (1966), along with several less well-known figures. Miriam Schneir ended her anthology, *Feminism: The Essential Historical Writings* (New York: Random House, 1972), with selections from Margaret Sanger (1920), Clara Zetkin (1925), and Virginia Woolf (1929). Only sociologist Alice Rossi recognized that there was "much in the work of Margaret Mead that can contribute new qualities to the thinking of contemporary feminists" and saw fit to place Mead in the company of Virginia Woolf and Simone de Beauvoir in her collection, *The Feminist Papers: from Adams to de Beauvoir* (New York: Columbia University Press 1973). Margaret Rossiter, in *Women Scientists in America: Struggles and Strategies to 1940* (Baltimore: Johns Hopkins University Press, 1982), dealt peripherally with Mead, largely because her career, along with Ruth Benedict's, presented counterevidence to Rossiter's central and valid purpose, which was to demonstrate the marginalization of women in science from 1920 to 1940. Even Michelle Rosaldo and Louise Lamphere's pathbreaking collection *Woman, Culture and Society* (Stanford: Stanford University Press, 1974), which arrayed the most promising work in feminist anthropology up until that time, makes only slight mention of Mead, although Rosaldo points out that Mead was among the first to use crosscultural analysis to argue that Westerners' conceptions of "natural" sexual differences were not in fact natural, necessary, or universal. My quick perusal of the most prominent journals—*Feminist Studies, Signs,* the *Journal of Women's History, Gender and Society,* and *Gender and History*—turned up no articles on Mead. Prominent secondary-source collections, such as Mary S. Hartman and Lois Banner, eds., *Clio's Consciousness Raised: New Perspectives on the History of Women* (New York: Row, 1974); Nancy Cott and Elizabeth Pleck, eds., *A Heritage of Her Own; Toward a New Social History of American Women* (New York: Simon and Schuster, 1979), and Ellen Carol DuBois and Vicki L. Ruiz, eds., *Unequal Sisters: A Multi-cultural Reader in U.S. Women's History* (New York: Routledge, 1990), contain no articles on Mead. The major exception is Rosalind Rosenberg, who in *Beyond Separate Spheres* identifies Mead as part of a generation that, in distinguishing itself from those politics of its suffragist mothers, "rejected the public side of feminism, with its ideology of female uniqueness and its organizational focus on female interests" (p. 209).

46. Derek Freeman, *Margaret Mead and Samoa: The Making and Unmaking of an Anthropological Myth* (Cambridge: Harvard University Press, 1983).

47. Jane Howard gives a list of some of these articles in her bibliography in *Margaret Mead,* pp. 505–506. A good review of this scholarly debate can be found in Ray A. Rappaport, "Desecrating the Holy Woman: Derek Freeman's Attack on Margaret Mead," *American Scholar* 55 (Summer 1986): 313–347.

48. For example, feminist theorist Jean Bethke Elshtain accepts Freeman's charge that Mead's study of Samoa was fundamentally shaped by her own cultural preoccupations. Elshtain writes, "It should neither surprise nor shock us that [Mead's] perspective and politics helped gear her expectations and color her interpretations. . . . Science provides no corrective lens that adjusts automatically for the 'distortions' inherent in the fact that the researcher is, after all, from another culture." Jean Bethke Elshtain, "Coming of Age in America: Why the Attack on Margaret Mead?" *Progressive* (October 1983): 33–35. Despite Elshtain's caution that the

issue of scientific accuracy takes us down an unproductive line of inquiry, some scholars continue to tread this path. See Eleanor Leacock, "Anthropologists in Search of Culture: Margaret Mead, Derek Freeman, and All the Rest of Us," in *Confronting the Margaret Mead Legacy: Scholarship, Empire and the South Pacific,* ed. Leonora Foerstel and Angela Gilliam (Philadelphia: Temple University Press, 1992), pp. 3–30.

49. Micaela di Leonardo, introduction to *Gender at the Crossroads of Knowledge,* p. 27.

50. I use the ambiguous term "author-reader" purposefully to suggest a double meaning: first, that anthropological researchers read their subjects before they author accounts, and second, that all subsequent readers of ethnography are just as actively involved and implicated in the act of anthropological interpretation. Ethnographies are always contested political acts. This is true regardless of the cultural origin or affiliation of the author-reader. Native anthropologists (cultural insiders) are no more advantageously positioned to produce "objective," "true," or "authentic" narratives than nonnative ones (cultural outsiders), although one might want to consider whether one should grant indigenous or insider accounts greater claims to authority on moral grounds as a sort of anthropological corollary to the political right to self-determination. In short, ethnography, like history, is always already an interpretative act that imposes on its subject and thus always requires further interpretations (impositions). These interpretations are in response to and derive their meanings from the past and help direct the meanings of the future. The subsequent rereadings and reinterpretations are as important as the original anthropologist's—indeed more so, for it is through these rereadings, reinterpretations, and rewritings that the relationship between feminism and imperialism might be changed. So the sooner Western feminists begin to try to understand how our feminism, as well as our ethnographies, derive from and are connected to the history of imperialism, the sooner we may be able to envision a nonimperialistic feminist ethnography. Joan Scott makes a similar argument in relation to the category of "experience" for feminist historiography. See Joan Scott, "Experience," in *Feminists Theorize the Political,* ed. Judith Butler and Joan W. Scott (New York: Routledge, 1992), pp. 22–40. Also see Pauline Marie Rosenau, *Post-Modernism and the Social Sciences: Insights, Inroads and Intrusions* (Princeton: Princeton University Press, 1992), pp. 40, 88, and especially 105–106. For an interesting discussion of the problem of the native anthropologist see Indira Karamcheti, review of Nita Kumar, *Friends, Brothers and Informants, Women's Review of Books* 9 (September 1992): 16–17.

51. Susan Chira, "Nursing becomes a Feminist Battlefield" (op. ed.), *New York Times* (October 10, 1993).

52. I am singling out Chira's article because it represents a compact example of a tendency I find common in contemporary feminist discourse. For other examples, see Mary Daly, *Gyn/ecology: The Metaethics of Radical Feminism* (Boston: Beacon Press, 1978) and Marilyn French, *The War against Women* (New York: Summit Books, 1992).

53. See, for example, Nadine R. Peacock, "Rethinking the Sexual Division of Labor: Reproduction and Women's Work among the Efe," in di Leonardo, *Gender at the Crossroads of Knowledge,* pp. 339–360.

54. Ann duCille, *Skin Trade* (Cambridge: Harvard University Press, 1996).

Conclusion

1. Harriet B. Bradbury, "War as a Necessity of Evolution," *Arena* 21 (January 1899): 94–96.

2. Rev. Wallace Radcliff, "Presbyterian Imperialism," *Assembly Herald* 1 (1899): 5–6; quoted in Stuart Creighton Miller, *"Benevolent Assimilation": The American Conquest of the Philippines, 1899–1903* (New Haven: Yale University Press, 1982), p. 18.

3. Beatrice Forbes-Robertson Hale, *What Women Want: An Interpretation of the Feminist Movement* (New York: Frederick A. Stokes, 1914), p. 34.

4. Elsie Clews Parsons, *Social Rule: A Study of the Will to Power* (New York: Putnam, 1916), p. 54.

5. The statement was originally made on *Nightline* in 1995, but I am drawing my account from media reporting of the incident afterwards, in particular from an interview with Patricia Ireland by Teresa Moore, "Taking NOW into the Future," *San Francisco Chronicle* (April 21, 1996): n.p. (Lexis/Nexis).

6. As cited in Patricia J. Williams, "American Kabuki," *Birth of a Nation'hood: Gaze, Script, and Spectacle in the O.J. Simpson Case,* ed. Toni Morrison and Claudia Brodsky Lacour (New York: Pantheon Books, 1997), pp. 273–274.

7. Cited in Kathleen Barry, *Susan B. Anthony: A Biography of a Singular Feminist* (New York: New York University Press, 1988), pp. 318–319.

8. Moore, "Taking NOW into the Future."

9. Searching Lexis/Nexis turned up hundreds of articles on these issues, in which these types of constructions were rampant.

Selected Bibliography

Manuscript Collections

Mary Abigail Dodge [Gail Hamilton] Papers, Essex Institute, Salem, Mass.
Mary Abigail Dodge [Gail Hamilton] Papers, Women's Rights Biography, Smith College Archives, Northampton, Mass.
Charlotte Perkins Gilman Papers, Schlesinger Library, Harvard University, Cambridge, Mass.
Otis Tufton Mason Collection, National Anthropological Archives, Smithsonian Institution, Washington, D.C.
Mary [sic] French Sheldon Papers, Manuscript Division, Library of Congress, Washington, D.C.
Lester Ward Papers, John Hay Library, Brown University, Providence, R.I.

Manuscript Collections on Microfilm

Gerritsen Collection of Women's History. Glen Rock, N.J.: Microfilming Corporation of America, 1975.
History of Women Microfilm Collection.
National Woman's Party Papers Microfilm Collection.
The Papers of Elizabeth Cady Stanton and Susan B. Anthony. Ed. Patricia G. Holland and Ann D. Gordon. Wilmington: Scholarly Resources, 1991.
Elizabeth Cady Stanton Papers. Manuscript Division, Library of Congress.
Wisconsin Progressives: The Edward A. Ross Papers: Guide to a Microfilm Edition. Ed. Harold L. Miller and Lynn Buckley Aber. Madison: State Historical Society of Wisconsin, 1986.

Published Primary Sources

Allen, Grant. "Plain Words on the Woman Question." *Popular Science Monthly* 36 (December 1889): 170–181. Rpt. from *Fortnightly Review* (October 1889).
————. "The Romance of Race." *Popular Science Monthly* 53 (August 1898): 511–521.

————. "Spencer and Darwin." *Popular Science Monthly* 50 (April 1897): 815–827.

————. "Woman's Place in Nature." *Forum* 7 (May 1889): 258–263.

————. "Woman's Intuition." *Forum* 9 (May 1890): 333–340.

Ames, Azel, Jr. *Sex in Industry: A Plea for the Working-Girl.* Boston: J. R. Osgood, 1875.

Anderson, Elizabeth Garrett. "Sex in Mind and Education: A Reply." *Fortnightly Review* 15 (May 1874): 582–594.

Anthony, Susan B. "The Status of Woman, Past, Present, and Future." *Arena* 17 (May 1897): 901–908.

Anti-Suffrage Essays by Massachusetts Women. Ed. J. A. Haien. Boston: Forum, 1916.

Armstrong, Mrs. M. F. "The Negro Problem in Virginia." *Nation* 16 (February 20, 1873): 131–132.

————. *On Habits and Manners.* Hampton: Normal School Press, 1888.

————. "Sketches of Mission Life, No. IV." *Southern Workman* 10 (April 1881): 44.

Armstrong, Mrs. M. F., and Helen W. Ludlow. *Hampton and Its Students.* New York: Putnam, 1874.

Association for the Advancement of Women. *Historical Account of the Association for the Advancement of Women, 1873–1893.* Dedham: Association for the Advancement of Women, 1893.

————. *Reports.* Syracuse, 1873–1893. Copies of the reports for 1878–1893 available in *Gerritsen Collection of Women's History Microfilm Collection.*

Association of Collegiate Alumnae. *Health Statistics of Women College Graduates.* Boston: Wright and Potter, 1885.

Beecher, Catharine E. *Educational Reminiscences and Suggestions.* New York: J. B. Ford, 1874.

————. *An Essay on Slavery and Abolitionism.* Philadelphia: Henry Perkins, 1837.

————. *The True Remedy for the Wrongs of Woman.* Boston, 1851.

————. *Woman's Profession as Mother and Educator, With Views in Opposition to Woman Suffrage.* Philadelphia: George MacLean, 1872.

————. *Woman Suffrage and Woman's Profession.* Hartford, 1871.

Blackwell, Antoinette Brown. "The Alleged Antagonism Between Growth and Reproduction." *Popular Science Monthly* 5 (September 1874): 606–610.

————. "Comparative Mental Power of the Sexes Physiologically Considered." Paper read before the Woman's Congress, 1877. Rpt. in *Victoria Magazine* 28 (March 1877): 405–416.

————. "The Relation of Woman's Work in the Household to the Work Outside." In *Papers and Letters Presented at the First Woman's Congress of the Association for the Advancement of Woman.* New York, 1874. Rpt. in *Up From the Pedestal: Selected Writings in the History of American Feminism.* Ed. Aileen S. Kraditor. Chicago: Quadrangle, 1970. 150–159.

————. *The Sexes Throughout Nature.* New York: Putnam, 1875.

Blair, James L. *Imperialism: Our National Policy. An Address Delivered Before the Monday Evening Club, January 9, 1899.* St. Louis: Gottschalk, 1899.

Boas, Franz. "The Methods of Ethnology." *American Anthropologist* 22 (1920): 311–321.

————. *The Mind of Primitive Man.* 1st. ed., 1911; rev. ed., New York: Macmillan, 1938.

Brackett, Anna Callender, ed. *The Education of American Girls.* New York: Putnam, 1874, 1886.

Brandeis, Louis D., and Josephine Goldmark. *The Case Against Nightwork for Women, Revised with New Introduction to March 1, 1918.* New York: National Consumers' League, 1918.

Brashere, Ora M. *Science and Suffrage: An Inquiry into the Causes of Sex Differences.* Salt Lake City, 1909.

Bronson, Minnie. *The Wage Earning Woman and The State.* Boston: Massachusetts Association Opposed to the Further Extension of Suffrage to Women, 1910.

Buchanan, Joseph. "The Cosmic Sphere of Woman." *Arena* 1 (May 1890): 666–681.

Buhle, Mari Jo and Paul, eds. *The Concise History of Woman Suffrage: Selections from the Classic Work of Stanton, Anthony, Gage and Harper.* Urbana: University of Illinois Press, 1978.

Bushnell, Horace. *Women's Suffrage: The Reform Against Nature.* New York: Scribner, 1869.

Calverton, V. F., and S. D. Schalhausen. *Sex in Civilization*. New York: Macaulay, 1929; Garden City, NY: Garden City, 1929.

Campbell, Helen. *Household Economics: A Course of Lectures in the School of Economics of the University of Wisconsin*. 1st. ed., 1896; 2nd ed., New York: Putnam, 1898.

————. *Prisoners of Poverty: Women Wage Workers, Their Trades and Their Lives*. Boston: Roberts, 1887. Rpt. Westport, Conn.: Greenwood Press, 1970.

————. *Women Wage Workers: Their Past, Their Present, and Their Future*. Introduction by Richard T. Ely. Boston: Roberts, 1893.

Campbell, Karlyn Kohrs, ed. *Man Cannot Speak For Her*. 2 vols. Westport, Conn.: Greenwood Press, 1989.

Ceplair, Larry, ed. *The Public Years of Sarah and Angelina Grimké: Selected Writings, 1835–1839*. New York: Columbia University Press, 1989.

Chandler, Lucinda B. "The Woman Movement." *Arena* 4 (November 1891): 704–711.

Child, Lydia Maria. *An Appeal in Favor of that Class of Americans called Africans*. New York: John S. Taylor, 1833.

————. *A Romance of the Republic*. Boston: Ticknor and Fields, 1867.

Claflin, Tennie C. *Constitutional Equality: A Right of Women*. New York: Woodhull, Claflin, 1871.

Clarke, Edward H. *Sex in Education; Or, A Fair Chance for the Girls*. Boston: James R. Osgood, 1873.

"Clarke's Building of a Brain." *North American Review* 120 (January 1875): 185–188.

Cobbe, Frances Power. *The Duties of Women*. Boston: G. H. Ellis, 1881.

Collins, May L. *A Plea for the New Woman. An Address Delivered Before the Ohio Liberal Society*. New York: Truth Seeker, 1896.

Collins, Mary C. "The Dependence of the Indian." *Southern Workman* 29 (July 1900): 427–429.

Coman, Katharine. "The College Settlement." *Southern Workman* 29 (November 1900): 650–653.

Cooley, Winnifred Harper. "The Eternal Feminine." *Arena* 27 (April 1902): 375–380.

————. *The New Womanhood*. New York: Broadway, 1904.

————. "The Younger Suffragists." *Harper's Weekly* 58 (September 27, 1913): 7–8.

[Coolidge,] Mary Roberts Smith. *Almshouse Women: A Study of 228 Women in the City and County Almshouse of San Francisco*. Stanford: Stanford University Press, 1896.

Coolidge, Mary Roberts Smith. *Chinese Immigration*. New York: Holt, 1909.

[Coolidge,] Mary Roberts Smith. "Education for Domestic Life." *Popular Science Monthly* 53 (August 1898): 521–525.

————. "Recent Tendencies in the Education of Women." *Popular Science Monthly* 48 (November 1895): 27–33.

————. "Statistics of College and Non-College Women." *Publications of the American Statistical Association* 7 (March–June 1900): 1–26.

Coolidge, Mary Roberts Smith. *Why Women Are So*. New York: Henry Holt, 1912. Copy available on *Gerristen Collection of Women's History Microfilm Collection*.

Cooper, Anna Julia. *A Voice From the South, by a Black Women of the South*. 1st ed., Aldine Publishing Co, 1892. Rpt. New York: Negro Universities Press, 1969; New York: Oxford University Press, 1988.

Cope, Edward D. "The Relations of the Sexes to Government." *Popular Science Monthly* 33 (October 1888): 721–730.

Corbin, Caroline F. "The Antisuffrage Movement." *Chicago Daily News*. November 24, 1908. Rpt. as a pamphlet by the Illinois Association Opposed to the Extension of Suffrage to Women, n.d.

————. *Letters from a Chimney-Corner: A Plea for Pure Hopes and Sincere Relations Between Men and Women*. Chicago: Fergus, 1886.

Crane, Alice Rollins. "Why the Indians Break Out." *Arena* 20 (October 1898): 491–498.

Dall, Caroline Wells Healey. *The College, The Market and the Court; Or, Woman's Relation to Education, Labor, and Law.* 1st ed., 1867. Rpt: Boston: Memorial Edition, 1914.

———. *'Woman's Right to Labor'; or, Low Wages and Hard Work. In Three Lectures, Delivered in Boston, November 1859.* Boston: Walker, Wise, 1860.

Darwin, Charles. *On the Origin of Species by Means of Natural Selection, Or the Preservation of the Favoured Races in the Struggle for Life.* 1st ed., 1859; 5th ed., London: John Murray, 1869.

———. *The Descent of Man and Selection In Relation to Sex.* 1st ed., 1871; 2nd ed., New York: Appleton, 1906.

Davis, Mrs. Jefferson. "The White Man's Problem." *Arena* 23 (January 1900): 1–4.

Davis, Paulina Wright. *A History of the National Women's Rights Movement.* 1st. ed., 1871. Rpt. New York: Kraus Reprint, 1971.

Deland, Margaret. "The Change in the Feminine Ideal." *Atlantic Monthly* 105 (March 1910): 289–302.

Delauney, G. "Equality and Inequality in Sex." *Popular Science Monthly* 20 (December 1881): 184–192.

Dewey, Mary E. *Historical Sketch of the Formation and Achievements of the Women's National Indian Association in the United States.* N.p., 1900.

Dickinson, Mary Lowe. "A Half Century of Progress." *Arena* 15 (February 1896): 361–370.

———. Mrs. J. B. "Address of the President, at the Annual Meeting of the Women's National Indian Association, November 17, 1885." Philadelphia: Women's National Indian Association, 1885.

———. *Among the Thorns.* New York: G. W. Carleton, and London: S. Low, 1880.

———. "The National Council of Women." *Arena* 17 (February 1897): 478–493.

Dodge, Mary Abigail [pseud. Gail Hamilton]. *A Battle of the Books.* Cambridge: Riverside Press, 1870.

———. *A New Atmosphere.* Boston: Ticknor and Fields, 1865.

———. *Biography of James G. Blaine.* Norwich, Conn.: Henry Bill, 1895.

———. *Country Living and Country Thinking.* Boston: Ticknor and Fields, 1862.

———. *Gala-Days.* Boston: Ticknor and Fields, 1863.

———. *The Insuppressible Book.* Boston, 1885.

———. "Race Prejudice." *North American Review* 141 (October 1885): 475–479.

———. *Skirmishes and Sketches.* Boston: Ticknor and Fields, 1866.

———. "A Spasm of Sense." *Atlantic Monthly* 11 (April 1863): 407.

———. *Stumbling Blocks.* Boston: Ticknor and Fields, 1864.

———. *Summer Rest.* Boston: Ticknor and Fields, 1866.

———. *Woman's Worth and Worthlessness: The Complement to "A New Atmosphere."* New York: Harper, 1872.

———. *Woman's Wrongs: A Counter-Irritant.* Boston: Ticknor and Fields, 1868.

Dodge, H. Augusta, ed. *Gail Hamilton's Life in Letters.* 2 vols. Boston: Lee and Shepard, 1901.

Dodge, Mrs. Arthur M. "Woman Suffrage Opposed to Woman's Rights." *Annals of the American Academy of Political and Social Science* 5 (November 1914).

"Dr. Clarke's 'Sex in Education.'" *North American Review* 119 (January 1874): 140–152.

DuBois, Ellen Carol, ed. *Elizabeth Cady Stanton–Susan B. Anthony Reader: Correspondence, Writings, Speeches.* Boston: Northeastern University Press, 1992.

Duffey, Eliza Bisbee. *No Sex in Education: Or, An Equal Chance for Both Boys and Girls. A Review of Dr. E. H. Clarke's "Sex in Education."* Philadelphia: J. Stoddard, 1874.

———. *The Relations of the Sexes.* New York: Wood and Holbrook, 1876, 1886.

———. *What Women Should Know: A Woman's Book About Women.* Cincinnati: Stoddard, 1873.

Eastman, Elaine Goodale. "How to Americanize the Indians." *New Englander and Yale Review* 52 (May 1890): 452–455.

———. "The Indian—A Woman Among the Indians." *The Literature of Philanthropy.* Ed. Frances A. Goodale. New York: Harper, 1893. 129–140.

———. *Sister to the Sioux: The Memoirs of Elaine Goodale Eastman, 1885–91.* Ed. Kay Graber. Lincoln: University of Nebraska Press, 1978.

———. "The Waste of Life." *Popular Science Monthly* 87 (August 1915): 187–194.

———. "Wives and Property." *Indian's Friend* 4 (December 1891): 1.

Ellis, Havelock. "The Changing Status of Women." In *The Woman Question by Ellen Key, Dickinson and Others.* Ed. T. R. Smith. New York: Boni and Liveright, 1918. 219–229.

———. *Man and Woman: A Study of Human Secondary Sexual Characters.* London: Walter Scott, 1894; 6th ed., London: A. & C. Black, 1930.

———. "Mind of Woman." *Atlantic Monthly* 118 (September 1916): 366–374.

———. "Variation in Man and Woman." *Popular Science Monthly* 62 (January 1903): 237–253.

Fletcher, Alice C. "Among the Omahas." *Woman's Journal* 13 (February 11, 1882): 46–47.

———. "Between the Lines." *Lend a Hand* 1 (July 1886): 429–431.

———. *Civilization and Education.* Washington, D.C.: Government Printing Office, 1888.

———. "The Crowning Act." *The Morning Star* 7 (March 1887): 1.

———. "Economy of Justice." *Lend a Hand* 1 (July 1886): 528–530.

———. "Flotsam and Jetsam from Aboriginal America." *Southern Workman* 28 (January 1899): 12–14.

———. "Indian Characteristics." *Southern Workman* 29 (1900): 202–205.

———. *Indian Education and Civilization.* Washington, D.C.: Government Printing Office, 1888.

———. "The Indian Woman and Her Problems." *Southern Workman* 28 (May 1899): 172–176. Another version is published in *Woman's Journal* 31 (November 10, 1900): 353–354.

———. "Land and Education for the Indian." *Southern Workman* 14 (1885): 6.

———. "Land, Law, Education—The Three Things Needed by the Indian." *Southern Workman* 14 (March 1885): 33.

———. "Land, Law, Education—The Three Things Needed by the Indian. Indians Ready for Land in Severalty." *Southern Workman* 14 (April 1885): 45.

———. "The New Orleans Exposition." *Southern Workman* 14 (July 1885): 79.

———. "On Indian Education and Self-Support." *Century* 26 (May 1883): 312–315.

———. *On the Lawlessness of the Indian Reservation System.* Boston: Frank Wood, 1884.

———. "The Preparation of the Indian for Citizenship." *Lend a Hand* 9 (1892): 190–198.

———. "Standing Bear." *Southern Workman* 38 (1909): 75–78.

———. "Tribal Life Among the Omahas." *Century Magazine* 51 (January 1896): 450–461.

[Flower, E. O.] "The Era of Woman" [editorial]. *Arena* 4 (August 1891): 382–385.

Forten, Charlotte, "One Phase of the Race Distinction." *Boston Commonwealth* 24 (January 16, 1886): 1.

French-Sheldon, M[ay]. *Sultan to Sultan: Adventures among the Masai and other Tribes of East Africa.* Boston: Arena, 1892.

French-Sheldon, Mrs. *Customs among the Natives of East Africa, from Teita to Kilimegalia, with Special Reference to their Women and Children.* London: Harrison, 1892.

———. "England's Commercial and Industrial Future in Central Africa." *Journal of the Tyneside Geographical Society* 3 (May 1897): 415–418.

Frothingham, Octavius B., et al. *Woman Suffrage Unnatural and Inexpedient.* Boston, 1886.

Gage, Matilda Josyln. *Woman, Church and State: A Historical Account of the Status of Woman Through the Christian Ages: With Reminiscences of the Matriarchate.* 2nd ed., New York: Truth Seeker, 1893. Rpt. Salem, N.H.: Ayer, 1985.

Galton, Francis. "Eugenics: Its Definition, Scope and Aims [Address Read Before the Sociological Society, at a Meeting in the School of Economics, London University, May 16, 1904]." *American Journal of Sociology* 10 (July 1904): 1904–05.

Gamble, Eliza B. *The Sexes in Science and History: An Inquiry Into the Dogma of Woman's Inferiority to Man.* New York: Putnam, 1916. Copy available on *Gerritsen Collection of Women's History Microfilm Collection.*

Gay, E. Jane. *With the Nez Perces: Alice Fletcher in the Field, 1889–1892.* Ed. Frederick E. Hoxie and Joan T. Mark. Lincoln: University of Nebraska Press, 1981.

Geddes, Patrick, and J. Arthur Thomson. *The Evolution of Sex.* 1st ed., London: Scott, 1889; New York: Humboldt, 1890, and New York: Scribner, 1897.

Gilder, Jeanette. "Why I Am Opposed to Woman Suffrage." *Harper's Bazaar* (May 19, 1894). Rpt. as a pamphlet by Massachusetts Association Opposed to the Further Extension of Suffrage to Women, n.d.

Gilman, Charlotte Perkins. "Are Women Human Beings? A Consideration of the Major Error in the Discussion of Woman Suffrage." *Harper's Weekly* 56 (May 25, 1912): 11.

———. "The Biological Anti-Feminist [written in response to an interview by William B. Sedgwick in *New York Times*]." *Forerunner* 5 (March 1914): 65.

———. "Comment and Review." *Forerunner* 13 (March 1913): 82.

———. "Competing With Men." [Vital Issues] *Woman's Journal* 35 (February 6, 1904): 42.

———. *Concerning Children.* Boston: Small, Maynard, 1901.

———. *The Diaries of Charlotte Perkins Gilman.* Ed. Denise D. Knight. Charlottesville: University Press of Virginia, 1994.

———. *Herland.* First published serially in *Forerunner,* 1915. Rpt. New York: Pantheon, 1979.

———. *The Home: Its Work and Influence.* 1st. ed., New York: McClure, Phillips, 1903; New York: Charlton, 1910. Rpt. University of Illinois Press, 1973.

———. *Human Work.* New York: McClure, Phillips, 1904.

———. *In This Our World and Other Poems.* 1st ed., San Francisco: J. H. Barry, 1893; Boston: Small Maynard, 1898, 1899. Rpt. New York: Arno Press, 1974.

———. *The Living of Charlotte Perkins Gilman, An Autobiography.* New York: Appleton-Century, 1935.

———. *The Man-Made World, or, Our Androcentric Culture.* New York: Charlton, 1911.

———. "Masculine, Feminine and Human." *Woman's Journal* 35 (January 16, 1904): 18.

———. "Suggestion on the Negro Problem." *American Journal of Sociology* 14 (July 1908): 78–85.

———. "Why I Wrote the Yellow Wallpaper." *Forerunner* 4 (October 1913): 271.

———. *Women and Economics.* Boston: Small, Maynard, 1898. Rpt. New York: Harper, 1966.

———. *Women and Social Service.* Warren, Ohio: National American Woman Suffrage Association, c. 1907. Copy available on *Gerritsen Collection of Women's History Microfilm Collection.*

———. "The Yellow Wallpaper." *New England Magazine* (May 1891): Rpt. Old Westbury, Conn.: Feminist Press, 1973.

[Godkin, E. L.] "A Neglected Side of the Woman's Rights Question." *Nation* 7 (November 26, 1868): 434–436.

———. "Another Delicate Subject." *Nation* 11 (July 14, 1870): 21–23.

———. "The Feud in the Woman's Rights Camp." *Nation* 11 (November 24, 1870): 346–347.

———. "Sex in Politics." *Nation* 12 (April 20, 1871): 270–272.

Goodale, Frances A., ed. *The Literature of Philanthropy.* New York: Harper, 1893.

Goodwin, Grace Duffield. *Anti-Suffrage: Ten Good Reasons.* New York: Duffield, 1913.

Grand, Sarah. "The New Aspect of the Woman Question." *North American Review* 158 (March 1894): 270–276.

Grimké, Angelina. *An Appeal to the Women of the Nominally Free States.* Issued by an Anti-Slavery Convention of American Women. New York: W. S. Dorr, 1837.

————. *Appeal to the Christian Women of the South.* New York: n.p., 1836. Rpt. New York: Arno Press and *New York Times,* 1969.

Grimké, Sarah. *Letters on the Equality of the Sexes and the Condition of Woman. Addressed to Mary S. Parker, President of the Boston Female Anti-Slavery Society.* Boston: Isaac Knapp, 1838.

Gruening, Martha. "Two Suffrage Movements." *Crisis* 4 (September 1912): 245–246.

Hale, Beatrice Forbes-Robertson. *What Women Want: An Interpretation of the Feminist Movement.* New York: Stokes, 1914.

Hall, Florence Howe, ed. *Julia Ward Howe and the Woman Suffrage Movement: A Selection From Her Speeches and Essays, with Introduction and Notes by her Daughter.* Boston: Dana Estes, 1913. Rpt. New York: Arno Press, 1969.

Hall, G. Stanley. *Adolescence: Its Psychology and Its Relations to Physiology, Anthropology, Sociology, Sex, Crime, Religion and Education.* 2 vols. New York: Appleton, 1904.

Hamilton, Gail. See Dodge, Mary Abigail.

Hanaford, Phebe A. *Women of the Century.* Boston: B. B. Russell, 1877.

Hanson, J. W., ed. *The World's Congress of Religions: The Addresses and Papers Delivered Before the Parliament . . . held in the Art Institute, Chicago Illinois, August 25 to October 15, 1893 under the Auspices of the World' Columbian Exposition.* Chicago: International Publishing, 1894.

Harper, Frances E. W. "Duty to Dependent Races." In *Transactions of the National Council of Women of the United States.* Ed. Rachel Foster Avery. Philadelphia: Lippincott, 1891. 86–91.

————. "Woman's Political Future" in *World's Congress of Representative Women.* Ed. May Wright Sewell. Chicago: Rand McNally, 1894. 433–37.

Higginson, Thomas Wentworth. *Common Sense About Women.* Boston: Lee and Shepard, 1881.

————. *Higher Education of Woman: A Paper Read Before the Social Science Convention, Boston, May 14, 1873.* Boston: Woman's Journal, 1873.

Holmes, Lizzie M. "Woman's Future Position in the World." *Arena* 20 (September 1898): 333–343.

Holmes, Oliver Wendell. "The Americanized European." *Atlantic Monthly* 35 (January 1875): 75–86.

Howe, Julia Ward. *A Trip to Cuba.* Serialized in *Atlantic Monthly,* 1859. Ticknor and Fields, 1860. Rpt. New York: Negro Universities Press, 1969.

————. *Reminiscences, 1819–1899.* Boston: Houghton Mifflin, 1899.

————. "Shall the Frontier of Christendom be Maintained?" *Forum* 22 (November 1896): 321–326.

Howe, Julia Ward, ed. *Sex and Education: A Reply to Dr. E. H. Clarke's "Sex in Education."* Boston: Roberts, 1874.

Howe, Julia Ward, et al. "The Other Side to the Woman Question." *North American Review* 129 (November 1879): 413–446.

Illinois Association Opposed to Woman Suffrage: *A Protest Against the Granting of Municipal Suffrage to Women in the City of Chicago.* Chicago, 1906.

Illinois Association Opposed to the Extension of Suffrage to Women. *Publications.* 1886–1913. Copies available in *Gerritsen Collection of Women's History Microfilm Collection.*

International Council of Women. *Report of the International Council of Women Assembled by the National Woman Suffrage Association, March 25–April 1, 1888.* Washington, D.C.: Rufus H. Darby, 1888.

Jacobi, Mary Putnam. *"Common Sense" Applied to Woman Suffrage.* New York: Putnam, 1894.

————. *The Question of Rest for Women During Menstruation.* New York: Putnam, 1877.

————. "Status and Future of the Woman Suffrage Movement." *Forum* 18 (December 1894): 406–414.

————. "Women in Medicine." In *Woman's Work in America.* Ed. Annie Nathan Meyer. New York, 1891. 139–205.

Jarvis, Edward. "Immigration." *Atlantic Monthly* 29 (April 1872): 454–468.

Jordan, David Starr. *The Blood of the Nation: A Study of the Decay of Races Through the Survival of the Unfit.* Boston: American Unitarian Association, 1902.

———. "Evolution: What It is and What it is Not." *Arena* 18 (August 1897): 145–159.

Kraditor, Aileen S., ed. *Up From the Pedestal: Selected Writings in the History of American Feminism.* Chicago: Quadrangle, 1968, 1970.

Lee, Mrs. M. E. "The Home-Maker." *AME Church Review* 8 (July 1891): 63–66.

Loewenberg, Bert James, and Ruth Bogin, eds. *Black Women in Nineteenth Century American Life: Their Words, Their Thoughts, Their Feelings.* University Park: Pennsylvania State University Press, 1976.

Man-Suffrage Association Opposed to Political Suffrage for Women. *Publications 1–22.* New York: 1914–1916. Copy available in *Gerritsen Collection of Women's History Microfilm Collection.*

Martin, Wendy, ed. *The American Sisterhood: Writings of the Feminist Movement From Colonial Times to the Present.* New York: Harper & Row, 1972.

Mason, Otis T. *The Origins of Invention: A Study of Industry Among Primitive Peoples.* New York: Scribner, and London: Walter Scott, 1915.

———. "Woman's Share in Primitive Culture." *American Antiquarian* 11 (January 1889): 3–13.

———. *Woman's Share in Primitive Culture.* New York: Appleton, 1894, 1898.

Mathews, Shailer, ed. *The Woman Citizen's Library: A Systematic Course of Reading in Preparation for the Larger Citizenship.* 12 vols. Chicago: Civics Society, 1913–1914.

Maudsley, Henry. "Sex in Mind and in Education." *Popular Science Monthly* 5 (June 1875): 198–215. Rpt. from *Fortnightly Review* 15 (April 1874): 466–483.

McMullen, Frances Drewry. "'Going Native' for Science." *Woman's Journal* 15 (July 1930): 8.

Mead, Margaret. "Americanization in Samoa." *American Mercury* 16 (March 1929): 264–270.

———. *Blackberry Winter: My Earlier Years.* New York: William Morrow, 1972. Rpt. New York: Pocket Books, 1975.

———. *Coming of Age: A Psychological Study of Primitive Youth for Western Civilisation.* 1st. ed., 1928; Morrow Quill Paperbacks, 1928, 1955, 1961, 1973.

———. "The Comparative Study of Cultures and the Purposive Cultivation of Democratic Values, 1941–1949." In *Perspectives on a Troubled Decade: Science, Philosophy, and Religion, 1939–1949.* New York: Harper, 1950. 87–108.

———. "Human Differences and World Order." In *World Order: Its Intellectual and Cultural Foundation.* Ed. Ernest Johnson. New York: Harper, 1945. 42–43.

———. *Letters from The Field, 1925–1975.* New York: Harper & Row, 1977.

———. *Male and Female: A Study of the Sexes in a Changing World.* New York: William Morrow, 1949.

———. "Race Majority—Race Minority." In *The People in Your Life: Psychiatry and Personal Relations by Ten Leading Authorities.* Ed. Margaret M. Hughes. 1st ed. Knopf, 1951. Rpt. Freeport, New York: Books for Libraries Press, 1971, 120–157.

———. *Sex and Temperament in Three Primitive Societies.* New York: William Morrow, 1935. Rpt. Morrow Quill Paperbacks, 1963.

Mead, Margaret, and James Baldwin. *A Rap on Race.* New York: Laurel, 1971.

Meyer, Annie Nathan. "Woman's Assumption of Sex Superiority." *North American Review* 178 (January 1904): 103–109. Rpt. as a pamphlet in *Why Women Do Not Want the Ballot.* Vol. 3. Boston: Massachusetts Association Opposed to the Further Extension of Suffrage to Women, n.d.

Mirsky, Jeannette. "Review of *Sex and Temperament.*" *Survey* 71 (Oct. 1935): 315.

Montgomery, Helen Barrett. *Western Women in Eastern Lands: An Outline Study of Fifty Years of Woman's Work in Foreign Missions.* New York: Macmillan, 1911.

Morgan, John T. "The Race Question in the United States." *Arena* 12 (September 1890): 385–398.

Mott, Lucretia. *Discourse on Woman.* Philadelphia: T. B. Peterson, 1850. Copy available in *National Woman's Party Papers Microfilm Collection.*

National Association of Colored Women. *Lifting as They Climb.* Ed. Elizabeth Lindsay Davis. Washington, D.C.: National Association of Colored Women, n.d.

National Association Opposed to Woman Suffrage. *The Case Against Woman Suffrage.* Boston: National Anti-Suffrage Association, 1916.

National Council of Women. *History and Minutes of the National Council of Women of the United States.* Organized in Washington, D.C., March 31, 1888. Ed. Louise Barnum Robbins. Boston: E. P. Stillings, 1898.

———. *Transactions of the National Council of Women in the United States.* Assembled in Washington, D.C., February 22–25, 1891. Ed. Rachel Roster Avery. Philadelphia: Lippincott, 1891.

Nearing, Scott and Nellie M. S. *Woman and Social Progress: A Discussion of the Biologic, Domestic, Industrial, and Social Possibilities of American Women.* New York: Macmillan, 1912.

"New Woman Under Fire." *Review of Reviews* 10 (December 1894): 656–657.

Newman, Louise Michele, ed. *Men's Ideas/Women's Realities: Popular Science, 1870–1915.* New York: Pergamon Press, 1985.

Noble, Margaret W. "What Next in Women's Societies." *Chautauquan* 14 (February 1892): 600–602.

Olmsted, Frederick Law. *A Journey in the Back Country in the Winter of 1853–1854.* New York: Mason, 1860.

Parkman, Francis. "The Failure of Universal Suffrage." *North American Review* 127 (July–August 1878): 7.

———. *Some of the Reasons Against Woman Suffrage.* New York, n.p., c. 1896.

———. "The Woman Question." *North American Review* 129 (October 1879): 303–321.

———. "The Woman Question Again." *North American Review* 130 (January 1880): 16–30.

Parsons, Elsie Clews. "The Aversion to Anomalies." *Journal of Philosophy, Psychology and Scientific Methods* 12 (April 1915): 212–219.

———. "Circumventing Darwin." *Journal of Philosophy, Psychology and Scientific Methods* 12 (October 1915): 610–612.

———. "Facing Race Suicide." *Masses* 6 (June 1915): 15.

———. *The Family.* New York: Putnam, 1906.

———. "Feminism and Sex Ethics." *International Journal of Ethics* 26 (July 1915): 462–465.

———. "When Mating and Parenthood are Theoretically Distinguished." *International Journal of Ethics* 26 (January 1916): 207–216.

Powdermaker, Hortense. "Review of *Sex and Temperament.*" *Annals of the American Academy of Political and Social Science* 181 (September 1935): 221–222.

Prucha, Francis Paul, ed. *Americanizing the American Indians: Writings by the 'Friends of the Indian' 1880–1900.* Cambridge: Harvard University Press, 1973.

Quinton, Amelia Stone. "Care of the Indian." In *Woman's Work in America.* Ed. Annie Nathan Meyer. New York: Henry Holt, 1891.

Robinson, Helen Ring. *Preparing Women for Citizenship.* New York: Macmillan, 1918.

Romanes, George J. *Darwin and After Darwin.* 4th ed. Chicago: Open Court Publishing, 1910. Originally given as lectures from 1888 through early 1890s.

———. "Mental Differences of Men and Women." *Popular Science Monthly* 31 (July 1887): 383–401.

Roosevelt, Theodore. *The Strenuous Life: Essays and Addresses.* New York: Century, 1902.

Ross, Edward Alsworth. "The Causes of Race Superiority." *Annals of the American Academy of Political and Social Science* 18 (July 1901): 67–89. Rpt. in *Foundations of Sociology,* New York, 1905, 353–385.

————. *Changing America: Studies in Contemporary Society*. New York: Century, 1912.

————. *The Changing Chinese: The Conflict of Oriental and Western Cultures in China*. 1st ed., 1911; New York: Century, 1914.

————. *Foundations of Sociology*. New York: Century, 1905.

————. *The Old World in the New*. New York: Century, 1914.

————. *The Principles of Sociology*. New York: Century, 1920.

————. *Sin and Society: An Analysis of Latter-Day Iniquity. With a Letter from President Roosevelt*. 1st. ed., 1907. Rpt. Gloucester: Peter Smith, 1965.

————. *Seventy Years of It: An Autobiography*. New York: Appleton-Century, 1936.

————. *Social Control: A Survey of the Foundations of Order*. New York: Macmillan, 1901.

————. *Social Psychology: An Outline and Source Book*. New York: Macmillan, 1908.

Rossi, Alice S., ed. *The Feminist Papers: From Adams to de Beauvoir*. New York: Bantam, 1976.

Scharlieb, Mary. *Womanhood and Race-Regeneration*. New York: Moffat, Yard, 1912.

Schreiner, Olive. "The Woman Question." *Cosmopolitan* 28 (November 1899): 45–54, 182–192.

Schurz, Carl. *American Imperialism: The Convocation Address Delivered on the Occasion of the Twenty-Seventh Convocation of the University of Chicago, January 4, 1899*. Boston: Dana Estes, 1899.

Sewall, May Wright, ed. *The World's Congress of Representative Women*. 2 vols. Chicago: Rand, McNally, 1894.

"The 'Sex in Education' Controversy" [editorial]. *Scribner's Monthly* 9 (March 1875): 633–635.

Shaler, N. S. "The African Element in America." *Arena* 2 (November 1890): 660–673.

————. "An Ex-Southerner in South Carolina." *Atlantic Monthly* 26 (July 1870): 53–61.

————. "Mixed Populations of North Carolina." *North American Review* 116 (January 1873): 150–166.

————. "The Nature of the Negro." *Arena* 3 (December 1890): 23–35.

————. "The Negro Problem." *Atlantic Monthly* 54 (November 1884): 696–709.

————. "The Summer's Journey of a Naturalist, Part I." *Atlantic Monthly* 32 (August 1873): 181–183.

————. "The Summer's Journey of a Naturalist, Part II." *Atlantic Monthly* 32 (August 1873): 349–357.

Smith, Goldwin. "Female Suffrage." *Popular Science Monthly* 5 (August 1874): 427–443.

————. "Woman's Place in the State." *Forum* 9 (January 1890): 515–530.

————. *Woman Suffrage*. New York: Macmillan, 1894.

Smith, Mary Roberts. See Coolidge, Mary Roberts Smith.

Spencer, Anna Garlin. "Is the Declaration of Independence Outgrown?" *Woman's Journal* (January 14, 1899): 12.

————. *Woman's Share in Social Culture*. New York: Mitchell Kennerley, 1912, 1913.

Spencer, Herbert. *Education: Intellectual, Moral, and Physical*. New York: Appleton, 1860.

————. *The Principles of Biology*. 2 vols. New York: Appleton, 1864.

————. *The Principles of Ethics*. 2 vols. New York: Appleton, 1892, 1893.

————. *The Principles of Psychology*. London: Williams and Norgate, 1855.

————. *The Principles of Sociology*. 3 vols. New York: Appleton, 1898.

————. "Psychology of the Sexes." *Popular Science Monthly* 4 (November 1873): 30–38.

————. *Social Statics: Or, the Conditions Essential to Human Happiness Specified, and the First of Them Developed*. New York: Appleton, 1865.

————. *Social Statics, Abridged and Revised: Together with The Man Versus the State*. New York: Appleton, 1892.

————. "The Status of Women and Children." *Popular Science Monthly* 8 (January 1876): 433–455.

————. *The Study of Sociology*. New York: Appleton, 1896.

————. "A Theory of Population Deduced From the General Law of Animal Fertility." *Westminster Review* 57 (April 1852): 468–501.

Stanton, Elizabeth Cady. "Divorce Versus Domestic Warfare." *Arena* 1 (April 1890): 560–569.

————. "Educated Suffrage." *Independent* (February 14, 1895): 2.

————. *Eighty Years and More: Reminiscences 1815–1897.* Fischer Unwin, 1898. Rpt. New York: Schocken, 1975.

————. "Nursery Names Unfit for Women." *Woman's Journal* 29 (October 22, 1898): 342–343.

————. *Suffrage A Natural Right.* Chicago: Open Court, 1894.

————. *The Woman's Bible: Part I.* New York: European, 1895.

————. *The Woman's Bible: Part II.* New York: European, 1898.

Stanton, Elizabeth Cady, et al. eds. *The History of Woman Suffrage.* 6 vols. Rochester: Susan B. Anthony, 1881–1922.

Stanton, Theodore, and Harriot Stanton Blatch, eds. *Elizabeth Cady Stanton As Revealed in Her Letters, Diary and Reminiscences.* 2 vols. New York: Harper, 1922. Rpt. New York: Arno Press, 1969.

Sterling, Dorothy, ed. *Turning the World Upside Down: The Anti-Slavery Convention of American Women Held in New York City, May 9–12, 1837.* New York: Feminist Press, 1987.

————. *We Are Your Sisters: Black Women in the Nineteenth Century.* New York: Norton, 1984.

Stowe, Charles Edward. *The Life of Harriet Beecher Stowe Compiled From Her Letters and Journals.* Boston: Houghton Mifflin, 1889.

Sumner, William Graham. *Folkways: A Study of the Sociological Importance of Usages, Manners, Customs, Mores, and Morals.* Boston: Ginn, 1906.

————. *What Social Classes Owe to Each Other.* 1st ed., 1883. Rpt. New York: Arno Press, 1979, and Caldwell, Idaho: Caxton, 1982.

Taft, Jessie. *The Woman Movement From the Point of View of Social Consciousness.* Chicago: University of Chicago Press, 1915.

Tarbell, Ida. *The Business of Being A Woman.* New York: Macmillan, 1912.

Terrell, Mary Church. *A Colored Woman in a White World.* Washington, D.C.: Randsell, 1940.

————. "Club Work of Colored Women." *Southern Workman* 30 (1901): 435–438.

————. "The International Congress of Women." *Voice of the Negro* 2 (October 1904): 454–461.

————. "The Justice of Woman Suffrage." *Crisis* 4 (September 1912): 243–245.

————. "Progress and Problems of Colored Women." *Home Mission College Review* 2 (March 1929): 41–48.

————. "The Progress of Colored Women." *Voice of the Negro* 1 (July 1904): 291–294.

————. *The Progress of Colored Women . . . An Address Delivered before the National American Women's Suffrage Association at the Columbia Theater, Washington, D.C., February 18, 1898.* Washington, D.C.: Smith, 1898.

————. "Society Among the Colored People of Washington." *Voice of the Negro* 1 (April 1904): 150–52.

————. "Susan B. Anthony, The Abolitionist," *Voice of the Negro* 3 (June 1906): 411–416.

————. "Votes for All: A Symposium." *Crisis* 15 (November 1917): 19–21.

————. "Votes for Women." *Crisis* 4 (September 1912): 234.

Terrell, Robert H. "Our Debt to Suffragists." *Crisis* 10 (August 1915): 181.

Thomas, William Isaac. "Is the Human Brain Stationary." *Forum* 36 (October 1904): 305–320.

————. "On a Difference in the Metabolism of the Sexes." *American Journal of Sociology* 3 (July 1897): 31–63.

————. "The Mind of Woman and the Lower Races." *American Journal of Sociology* 12 (January 1907): 435–469.

———. "Race Psychology: Standpoint and Questionnaire with Particular Reference to the Immigrant and Negro." *American Journal of Sociology* 17 (1912): 726.

———. *Sex and Society: Studies in the Social Psychology of Sex.* Chicago: University of Chicago Press, 1907.

———. Sex in Primitive Morality." *American Journal of Sociology* 4 (May 1899): 774–787.

———. "The Significance of the Orient for the Occident." *American Journal of Sociology* 13 (May 1908): 729–755.

———. *Votes for Women.* Boston: Massachusetts Woman Suffrage Association, n.d. Copy available in *History of Women Microfilm Collection,* #9229.

Tiedeman, Christopher. *A Treatise on the Limitations of Police Power in the United States.* Boston: 1886.

"Twenty-five Answers to Antis." Reports of speeches delivered on March 11, 1912, New York. Copy available in *National Woman's Party Papers Microfilm Collection.*

Tylor, Edward B. *Primitive Culture: Researches Into the Development of Mythology, Philosophy, Religion, Language, Art and Custom.* 2 vols. 1st ed., 1871; New York: Henry Holt, 1881.

Veblen, Thorstein. "The Barbarian Status of Women." *American Journal of Sociology* 4 (January 1899): 503–514.

———. "The Economic Theory of Woman's Dress." *Popular Science Monthly* 46 (December 1894): 198–205.

———. *The Theory of the Leisure Class.* 1st ed., New York: Macmillan 1899; New York: New American Library, 1953.

Walker, Francis Amasa. *The Indian Question.* Boston: J. R. Osgood, 1874.

———. *The Wages Question: A Treatise on Wages and the Wages Class.* New York: Henry Holt, 1876.

Ward, Lester F. *Applied Sociology: A Treatise on the Conscious Improvement of Society by Society.* Boston: Ginn, 1906.

———. "The Career of Herbert Spencer." *Popular Science Monthly* 74 (January 1909): 5–18.

———. "The Course of Biologic Evolution." *Proceedings of the Biological Society of Washington* 5 (c. 1893): 23–55.

———. *Dynamic Sociology, or Applied Social Science as Based Upon Statistical Sociology and the Less Complex Sciences.* 2 vols. 1st ed., 1883; 2nd ed., New York: Appleton, 1907.

———. "Genius and Woman's Intuition." *Forum* 9 (June 1890): 401–408.

———. "Individual Telesis," *American Journal of Sociology* 2 (March 1897): 699–717.

———. "Our Better Halves." *Forum* 6 (November 1888): 266–275.

———. *Pure Sociology: A Treatise on the Origin and Spontaneous Development of Society.* 1st ed., 1903; New York: Macmillan, 1909.

———. *The Psychic Factors of Civilization.* Boston: Ginn, 1893.

Wells, Kate Gannett. *An Argument Against Woman Suffrage.* Boston, 1889.

———. "The Transitional American Woman." *Atlantic Monthly* 46 (December 1880): 817–823.

Wells-Barnett, Ida B. *Crusade for Justice: The Autobiography of Ida B. Wells.* Ed. Alfreda M. Duster. University of Chicago Press, 1970.

———. *On Lynchings: "Southern Horrors," "A Red Record," "Mob Rule in New Orleans."* New York: Arno Press and the *New York Times,* 1969.

"White Woman's Burden." *Nation* (February 16, 1921): 257.

White, Carlos. *Ecce Femina: An Attempt to Solve the Woman Question.* Boston: Lee & Shepard, 1870.

White, Frances Emily. "Dr. Van de Warker on 'The Relations of Women to the Professions and Skilled Labor.'" *Penn Monthly* 6 (July 1875): 514–528.

———. "Woman's Place in Nature." *Popular Science Monthly* 6 (January 1875): 292–301.

Why Women Do Not Want the Ballot. Boston: Massachusetts Association Opposed to the Further Extension of Suffrage to Women, n.d.

Willard, Frances E. *A White Life For Two.* Chicago: Woman's Temperance Publishing Association, 1890. Rpt. in *Man Cannot Speak For Her: Key Texts of the Early Feminists.* Vol. 2. Ed. Karlyn Kohrs Campbell. Westport: Greenwood Press, 1989. 317–338.

———. "Arousing the Public Conscience." *Arena* 11 (December 1894): 198–201.

———. "The Coming Brotherhood." *Arena* 6 (August 1892): 317–324.

———. *Glimpses of Fifty Years: The Autobiography of an American Woman.* Chicago: Woman's Temperance Publication Association, 1889.

———. "President's Address." *Minutes of the National Woman's Christian Temperance Union at the Nineteenth Annual Meeting.* Chicago: Woman's Temperance Publishing Association, 1892. 128.

———. "Scientific Temperance Instruction in the Public Schools." *Arena* 12 (March 1895): 10–16.

———. *Woman and Temperance, or, The Work and Workers of the Woman's Christian Temperance Union.* Hartford: Park, 1888.

———. "The Woman's Cause is Man's." *Arena* 5 (May 1892): 712–725.

Williams, Fannie Barrier. "The Club Movement Among Colored Women." *Voice of the Negro* 1 (March 1904): 99–102.

———. "The Club Movement Among Colored Women of America." In *A New Negro for a New Century.* Ed. Booker T. Washington, N. B. Wood, and F. B. Williams. 1st ed., 1900. Rpt. New York: Arno Press, 1969. 379–405.

———. "The Colored Girl." *Voice of the Negro* 2 (June 1905): 400–403.

———. *Present Status and Intellectual Progress of Colored Women. Address Before the Congress of Representative Women.* World's Congress Auxiliary of the World's Columbian Exposition. Chicago: n.p., 1898.

———. "The Woman's Part in a Man's Business." *Voice of the Negro* 1 (November 1904): 543–547.

———. "Work Attempted and Missed in Organized Club Work." *Colored American Magazine* 14 (May 1908): 281–285.

Woolson, Abba Goold. *Woman in American Society.* Boston: Roberts, 1873.

Wright, Carroll Davidson, *The Working Girls of Boston.* Boston: Wright and Potter, 1889. Rpt. New York: Arno Press, 1969.

Secondary Sources

Alonso, Harriet Hyman. *Peace as a Woman's Issue: A History of the U.S. Movement for World Peace and Women's Rights.* Syracuse: Syracuse University Press, 1993.

Andersen, Kristi. *After Suffrage: Women in Partisan and Electoral Politics before the New Deal.* Chicago: University of Chicago Press, 1996.

Andolsen, Barbara Hilkert. *"Daughters of Jefferson, Daughters of Bootblacks": Racism and American Feminism.* Macon, Ga: Mercer University Press, 1986.

Anthony, Katharine. *Susan B. Anthony: Her Personal History and Her Era.* New York: Doubleday, 1954.

Baker, Paula. "The Domestification of Politics: Women and American Political Society, 1780–1920," *American Historical Review* (June 1984): 620–647.

Bannan, Helen, M. "The Idea of Civilization and American Indian Policy Reformers in the 1880s." *Journal of American Culture* 1 (1979): 787–799.

———. "Reformers and the 'Indian Problem' 1878–1887 and 1922–1934." Ph.D. dissertation, Syracuse University, 1976.

———. "True Womanhood' and Indian Assimilation." In *Selected Proceedings of the Third Annual Conference on Minority Studies.* Vol. 2. Ed. George Carter and James R. Parker. LaCrosse, Wis: Institute for Minority Studies, 1976. 187–194.

Banner, Lois. *Elizabeth Cady Stanton: A Radical for Woman's Rights.* Boston: Little, Brown, 1980.

Barry, Kathleen. *Susan B. Anthony: A Biography of a Singular Feminist.* New York: Ballantine Books, 1988.

Baum, Dale. "Woman Suffrage and the 'Chinese Question': The Limits of Radical Republicanism in Massachusetts, 1865–1876." *New England Quarterly* 56 (March 1983): 60–77.

Beasley, Maurine. "Mary Abigail Dodge: 'Gail Hamilton' and the Process of Social Change." *Essex Institute Historical Collections* 116 (1980): 82–100.

Beaver, R. Pierce. *All Loves Excelling: American Protestant Women in World Mission.* Grand Rapids: William B. Eerdmans, 1968.

Becker, Susan D. *The Origins of the Equal Rights Amendment: American Feminism Between the Wars.* Westport, Conn.: Greenwood Press, 1981.

Bederman, Gail. "'Civilization,' the Decline of Middle-Class Manliness, and Ida B. Wells's Antilynching Campaign (1892–94)." *Radical History Review* 52 (Winter 1992): 5–30.

———. *Manliness & Civilization: A Cultural History of Gender and Race in the United States, 1880–1917.* Chicago: University of Chicago Press, 1995.

———. "Manly Civilization/Primitive Masculinity: Race, Gender and the Evolution of Middle-Class American Manhood, 1880–1915." Ph.D. dissertation, Brown University, 1993.

Beisner, Robert. *Twelve Against Empire: The Anti-Imperialists, 1898–1900.* New York: McGraw Hill, 1968.

Berg, Barbara J. *The Remembered Gate: Origins of American Feminism: The Woman and the City, 1800–1860.* New York: Oxford University Press, 1978.

Birkett, Dea. *Spinsters Abroad: Victorian Lady Explorers.* Oxford: Blackwell, 1989.

Blair, Karen J. *The Club Woman as Feminist: True Womanhood Redefined, 1868–1914.* New York: Holmes and Meier, 1979.

Blocker, Jack S., Jr. "Separate Paths: Suffragists and the Women's Temperance Crusade." *Signs* 10 (Spring 1985): 460–476.

Boisseau, T. J. "'They Called Me *Bebe Bwana*': A Cultural Study of an Imperial Feminist." *Signs* 21 (Autumn 1995): 116–146.

Boller, Paul F., Jr. *American Thought in Transition: The Impact of Evolutionary Naturalism, 1865–1900.* Chicago: Rand McNally, 1971, 1969.

Bolt, Christine. *American Indian Policy and American Reform: Case Studies of the Campaign to Assimilate the American Indians.* Boston: Allen and Unwin, 1987.

———. *Victorian Attitudes to Race.* London: Routledge and Kegan Paul, 1971.

Bordin, Ruth. *Frances Willard: A Biography.* Chapel Hill: University of North Carolina Press, 1986.

———. *Woman and Temperance: The Quest for Power and Liberty, 1873–1900.* Philadelphia: Temple University Press, 1981.

Boydston, Jeanne, Mary Kelley, and Anne Margolis. *The Limits of Sisterhood: The Beecher Sisters on Women's Rights and Woman's Sphere.* Chapel Hill: University of North Carolina Press, 1988.

Brown, Wendy. "Finding the Man in the State." *Feminist Studies* 18 (Spring 1992): 7–34.

Brumberg, Joan Jacobs. *Mission for Life: The Story of the Family of Adoniram Judson.* New York: Free Press, 1980.

———. "Zenanas and Girlless Villages: The Ethnology of American Evangelical Women, 1870–1910." *Journal of American History* 69 (September 1982): 347–371.

Buechler, Steven M. *The Transformation of the Woman Suffrage Movement: The Case of Illinois, 1850–1920.* New Brunswick: Rutgers University Press, 1986.

———. *Women's Movements in the United States.* New Brunswick: Rutgers University Press, 1990.

Buhle, Mari Jo. "Gender and Labor History." In *Perspectives on American Labor History: The Problem of Synthesis.* Ed. J. Carroll Moody and Alice Kessler-Harris. Dekalb: Northern Illinois University Press, 1989. 55–79.

————. *Women and American Socialism, 1870–1920.* Urbana: University of Illinois Press, 1981, 1983.

Burstyn, Joan. "Catharine Beecher and the Education of American Women." *New England Quarterly* 47 (September 1974): 386–403.

Butler, Judith, and Joan W. Scott, eds. *Feminists Theorize the Political.* New York: Routledge, 1992.

Camhi, Jane Jerome. "Women Against Women: American Anti-Suffragism, 1880–1920." Ph.D. dissertation, Tufts University, 1973.

Campbell, Helen. *Prisoners of Poverty: Women Wage-Workers, Their Trades and Their Lives.* Boston: Roberts, 1887. Rpt. Greenwood Press, 1970.

Carby, Hazel V. "'On the Threshold of Woman's Era': Lynching, Empire and Sexuality in Black Feminist Theory." *Critical Inquiry* 12 (Autumn 1985). Rpt. in *"Race" Writing and Difference.* Ed. Henry Louis Gates. Chicago: University of Chicago Press, 1986. 301–316.

————. *Reconstructing Womanhood: The Emergence of the Afro-American Woman Novelist.* New York: Oxford University Press, 1987.

Chambers-Schiller, Lee Virginia. *Liberty, A Better Husband.* New Haven: Yale University Press, 1984.

Clifford, Deborah Pickman. *Mine Eyes Have Seen the Glory: A Biography of Julia Ward Howe.* Boston: Little, Brown, 1978, 1979.

Clifford, James. *The Predicament of Culture: Twentieth-Century Ethnography, Literature and Art.* Cambridge: Harvard University Press, 1988.

Clifford, James, and George E. Marcus, eds. *Writing Culture: The Poetics and Politics of Ethnography.* Berkeley: University of California Press, 1986.

Clinton, Catherine. *The Other Civil War: American Women in the Nineteenth Century.* New York: Hill and Wang, 1984.

Coleman, Willie Mae. *Keeping the Faith and Disturbing the Peace: Black Women from Anti-Slavery to Women's Suffrage.* Ph.D. dissertation, University of California-Irvine, 1981.

Conway, Jill. "Women Reformers and American Culture, 1870–1930." *Journal of Social History* 5 (Winter 1971–1972): 164–177.

Cott, Nancy F. *The Bonds of Womanhood.* New Haven: Yale University Press, 1977.

————. "Feminist Politics in the 1920s: The National Woman's Party." *Journal of American History* 71 (June 1984): 43–68.

————. *The Grounding of Modern Feminism.* New Haven: Yale University Press, 1987.

————. "What's In a Name? The Limits of 'Social Feminism'; or, Expanding the Vocabulary of Women's History." *Journal of American History* 76 (December 1989): 809–829.

Cott, Nancy, and Elizabeth Pleck. *A Heritage of Her Own: Toward a New Social History of American Women.* New York: Simon and Schuster, 1979.

Coultrap-McQuin, Susan. *Doing Literary Business: American Women Writers in the Nineteenth Century.* Chapel Hill: University of North Carolina Press, 1990.

————. "Legacy Profile: Gail Hamilton (1833–1896)." *Legacy* 4 (Fall 1987): 53–58.

Coultrap-McQuin, Susan, ed. *Gail Hamilton: Selected Writings.* New Brunswick: Rutgers University Press, 1992.

Curtis, Bruce. *William Graham Sumner.* Boston: Twayne, 1981.

Daniels, Roger. *Asian America: Chinese and Japanese in the United States Since 1850.* Seattle: University of Washington Press, 1988.

Davis, Angela. *Women, Race and Class.* New York: Vintage, 1983.

Degler, Carl N. *At Odds: Women and the Family in America from the Revolution to the Present.* New York: Oxford University Press, 1980.

di Leonardo, Micaela, ed., *Gender at the Crossroads of Knowledge: Feminist Anthropology in the Postmodern Era.* Berkeley: University of California Press, 1991.

Dorr, Rheta Childe. *Susan B. Anthony: The Woman Who Changed the Mind of a Nation.* New York: Stokes, 1928.

DuBois, Ellen Carol. *Feminism and Suffrage: The Emergence of an Independent Women's Movement in America, 1848–1869.* Ithaca: Cornell University Press, 1978.

———. "Making Women's History: Activist Historians of Women's Rights, 1880–1940." *Radical History Review* 49 (Winter 1991): 61–85.

———. "The Radicalism of the Woman Suffrage Movement: Notes Toward the Reconstruction of Nineteenth-Century Feminism." *Feminist Studies* 3 (Fall 1975): 63–71.

———. "Women's Rights and Abolition: The Nature of the Connection," in *Antislavery Reconsidered: New Perspectives on the Abolitionists.* Ed. Lewis Perry and Michael Fellman. Baton Rouge, La: Louisiana State University Press, 1979. 238–251.

———. "Working Women, Class Relations, and Suffrage Militance: Harriot Stanton Blatch and the New York Woman Suffrage Movement, 1894–1909." *Journal of American History* 74 (June 1987): 34–58.

DuBois, Ellen Carol, and Vicki L. Ruiz, eds. *Unequal Sisters: A Multicultural Reader in U.S. Women's History.* New York: Routledge, 1990.

duCille, Ann. *Skin Trade.* Cambridge: Harvard University Press, 1996.

Dyer, Thomas G. *Theodore Roosevelt and the Idea of Race.* Baton Rouge: Louisiana State University Press, 1980.

Earhart, Mary. *Frances Willard: From Prayers to Politics.* Chicago: University of Chicago Press, 1944.

Early, Julie English. "Unescorted in Africa: Victorian Women Ethnographers Toiling in the Fields of Sensational Science." *Journal of American Culture* 18 (Winter 1995): 67–75.

Elshtain, Jean Bethke. "Coming of Age in America: Why the Attack on Margaret Mead?" *Progressive* (October 1983): 33–35.

———. "The Feminist Movement and the Question of Equality." *Polity* 7 (Summer 1975): 452–477.

Emmerich, Lisa E. "'Right in the Midst of My Own People': Native American Women and the Field Matron Program." *American Indian Quarterly* 15 (Spring 1991): 201–216.

———. "'To Respect and Love and Seek the Ways of White Women': Field Matrons, the Office of Indian Affairs, and Civilization Policy, 1890–1938." Ph.D. dissertation, University of Maryland, 1987.

Epstein, Barbara Leslie. *The Politics of Domesticity: Women, Evangelism and Temperance in Nineteenth-Century America.* Middletown: Wesleyan University Press, 1981.

Erickson, Nancy S. "Muller V. Oregon Reconsidered: The Origins of a Sex-Based Doctrine of Liberty of Contract." *Labor History* 30 (Spring 1989): 228–250.

Fass, Paula S. *The Damned and the Beautiful: American Youth in the 1920's.* New York: Oxford University Press, 1977.

Fields, Barbara J. "Ideology and Race in American History." In *Region, Race and Reconstruction: Essays in Honor of C. Vann Woodward.* Ed. J. Morgan Kousser and James M. McPherson. New York: Oxford University Press, 1982. 143–75.

Fitzpatrick, Ellen. *Endless Crusade: Women Social Scientists and Progressive Reform.* New York: Oxford University Press, 1990.

Flexner, Eleanor. *Century of Struggle: The Woman's Rights Movement in the United States.* Cambridge: Belknap, 1959.

Foerstel, Leonora, and Angela Gilliam, eds. *Confronting the Margaret Mead Legacy: Scholarship, Empire and the South Pacific.* Philadelphia: Temple University Press, 1992.

Frankfort, Roberta. *Collegiate Women: Domesticity and Career in Turn-of-the-Century America.* New York: New York University Press, 1977.

Freedman, Estelle B. "The New Woman: Changing Views of Women in the 1920s." *Journal of American History* 61 (September 1974): 372–393.

————. "Separatism as Strategy: Female Institution Building and American Feminism, 1870–1930." *Feminist Studies* 5 (Fall 1979): 512–529.

————. *Their Sisters' Keepers: Women's Prison Reform in America, 1830–1930.* Ann Arbor: University of Michigan Press, 1981.

Freeman, Derek. *Margaret Mead and Samoa: The Making and Unmaking of an Anthropological Myth.* Cambridge: Harvard University Press, 1983.

Friedan, Betty. *The Feminine Mystique.* New York: Norton, 1963.

French, Marilyn. *The War against Women.* New York: Summit, 1992.

Furner, Mary O. *Advocacy and Objectivity: A Crisis in the Professionalization of American Social Science, 1865–1905.* Lexington: University Press of Kentucky, 1975.

Gabel, Leona C. *From Slavery to the Sorbonne and Beyond: The Life and Writings of Anna J. Cooper.* Northampton: Smith College, 1982.

Gaines, Kevin Kelly. *Uplifting the Race: Black Leadership, Politics, and Culture in the Twentieth Century.* Chapel Hill: University of North Carolina Press, 1996.

Gann, L. H., and Peter Duignan. *The Rulers of Belgian Africa, 1884–1914.* Princeton: Princeton University Press, 1979.

Giddings, Paula. *When and Where I Enter: The Impact of Black Women on Race and Sex in America.* New York: Bantam, 1984.

Gifford, Carolyn DeSwarte. "Home Protection: The WCTU's Conversion to Woman Suffrage." In *Gender, Ideology and Action: Historical Perspectives in Women's Public Lives.* Ed. Janet Sharistanian. Westport, Conn.: Greenwood Press, 1986. 95–120.

Ginzberg, Lori. *Women and the Work of Benevolence: Morality, Class, and Politics in the Nineteenth-Century United States.* New Haven: Yale University Press, 1990.

Gordan, Joan, ed., *Margaret Mead: The Complete Bibliography, 1925–1975.* The Hague: Mouton, 1976.

Gordon, Linda. *Woman's Body, Woman's Right: A Social History of Birth Control in America.* New York: Penguin, 1974, 1976.

Gossett, Thomas. *Race: The History of an Idea in America.* New York: Schocken, 1969.

Gould, Stephen Jay. *The Mismeasure of Man.* New York: Norton, 1981.

Green, Rayna. "The Pocahontas Perplex: The Image of Indian Women in American Culture." *Massachusetts Review* 16 (1976): 698–714.

Greenwald, Maurine Weiner. "Working-Class Feminism and the Family Wage Ideal: The Seattle Debate on Married Women's Right to Work, 1914–1920." *Journal of American History* 76 (June 1989): 118–149.

Griffith, Elisabeth. *In Her Own Right: The Life of Elizabeth Cady Stanton.* New York: Oxford University Press, 1984.

Grimes, Alan P. *The Puritan Ethic and Woman Suffrage.* New York: Oxford University Press, 1967.

Grimshaw, Patricia. *Paths of Duty: American Missionary Wives in Nineteenth-Century Hawaii.* Honolulu: University of Hawaii Press, 1989.

Haller, John S., Jr. *Outcasts from Evolution: Scientific Attitudes of Racial Inferiority, 1859–1900.* Urbana: University of Illinois Press, 1971.

Haller, Mark. *Eugenics: Hereditarian Attitudes in American Thought.* New Brunswick: Rutgers University Press, 1963.

Haraway, Donna J. *Simians, Cyborgs, and Women: The Reinvention of Nature.* New York: Routledge, 1991.

————. "Teddy Bear Patriarchy: Taxidermy in the Garden of Eden, New York City, 1908–36." *Social Text,* no. 11 (Winter 1984–1985): 20–64. Rpt in Donna J. Haraway. *Primate Visions: Gender, Race and Nature in the World of Modern Science.* New York: Routledge, 1989. 26–58.

Hardesty, Nancy A. *Women Called to Witness: Evangelical Feminism in the Nineteenth Century.* Nashville: Abingdon Press, 1984.

Harding, Sandra. *The Science Question in Feminism.* Ithaca: Cornell University Press, 1986.

Harley, Sharon. "Anna Julia Cooper: A Voice For Black Women," in *The Afro-American Woman: Struggles and Images.* Ed. Sharon Harley and Rosalyn Terborg-Penn. Port Washington, N.Y.: Kennikat Press, 1978. 87–96.

Harper, Ida. *The Life and Work of Susan B. Anthony.* 2 vols. Indianapolis: Bowen-Merrill, 1899.

Harrison, Cynthia. *On Account of Sex: The Politics of Women's Issues, 1945–1968.* Berkeley: University of California Press, 1988.

Harrold, Stanley. *Gamaliel Bailey and Antislavery Union.* Kent: Kent State University Press, 1986.

Hartman, Mary, and Lois W. Banner, eds. *Clio's Consciousness Raised: New Perspectives on the History of Women.* New York: Harper and Row, 1974.

Helm, June, ed. *Pioneers of American Anthropology.* Seattle: University of Washington Press, 1966.

Hersh, Blanche Glassman. *The Slavery of Sex: Feminist-Abolitionists in America.* Urbana: University of Illinois Press, 1978.

———. "The 'True Woman' and the 'New Woman' in Nineteenth-Century America: Feminist-Abolitionists and a New Concept of True Womanhood." In *Woman's Being, Woman's Place: Female Identity and Vocation in American History.* Ed. Mary Kelley. Boston: Hall, 1979. 271–282.

Hewitt, Nancy A. *Women's Activism and Social Change: Rochester New York, 1822–1872.* Ithaca: Cornell University Press, 1984.

Hewitt, Nancy A., and Suzanne Lebsock, eds. *Visible Women: New Essays on American Activism.* Urbana: University of Illinois Press, 1993.

Higham, John. *Strangers in the Land: Patterns of American Nativism, 1860–1925.* New York: Atheneum, 1970.

Hill, Mary A. *Charlotte Perkins Gilman: The Making of a Radical Feminist, 1860–1896.* Philadelphia: Temple University Press, 1980.

Hill, Patricia R. *The World Their Household: The American Woman's Foreign Mission Movement and Cultural Transformation, 1870–1920.* Ann Arbor: University of Michigan Press, 1985.

Hobsbawm, Eric. *The Age of Empire, 1875–1914.* New York: Vintage, 1989.

Hodes, Martha. "Wartime Dialogues on Illicit Sex: White Women and Black Men." In *Divided Houses: Gender and the Civil War.* Ed. Catherine Clinton and Nina Silber. New York: Oxford University Press, 1992.

Hoff-Wilson, Joan, ed. *Rights of Passage: The Past and Future of the ERA.* Bloomington: Indiana University Press, 1986.

Hofstadter, Richard. *Social Darwinism in American Thought.* Boston: Beacon Press, 1955.

Howard, Jean. *Margaret Mead: A Life.* New York: Simon and Schuster, 1984.

Hoxie, Frederick E. *A Final Promise: The Campaign to Assimilate the Indians, 1880–1920.* Lincoln: University of Nebraska Press, 1984.

Hunter, Jane. *The Gospel of Gentility: American Women Missionaries in Turn-of-the-Century China.* New Haven: Yale University Press, 1984.

Hutchinson, Louise D. *Anna Julia Cooper: A Voice From the South.* Washington, D.C.: Smithsonian Institution Press, 1981, 1982.

Ignatiev, Noel. *How the Irish Became White.* New York: Routledge, 1995.

Jablonsky, Thomas James. "Duty, Nature and Stability: The Female Anti-Suffragists in the United States, 1894–1920." Ph.D. dissertation, University of Southern California, 1978.

Jacobson, Matthew. *Special Sorrows: The Diasporic Imagination of Irish, Polish and Jewish Immigrants in the United States.* Cambridge: Harvard University Press, 1995.

Jones, Beverly W. "Mary Church Terrell and the National Association of Colored Women, 1896–1901." *Journal of Negro History* 67 (Spring 1982): 20–33.

Jones, Jacqueline. *Soldiers of Light and Love: Northern Teachers and Georgia Blacks, 1865–1873.* Chapel Hill: University of North Carolina Press, 1980.

————. *Labor of Love, Labor of Sorrow: Black Women, Work, and the Family from Slavery to the Present.* New York: Basic, 1985.

Judd, Neil M. *The Bureau of American Ethnology: A Partial History.* Norman: University of Oklahoma Press, 1967.

Kallina, Deborah A. "'There's Nothing a Woman Can't Do If She Undertakes To Do It': The Women's National Indian Association, 1879–1951." B.A. thesis, Brown University, 1986.

Kaplan, Amy. "Romancing the Empire: The Embodiment of American Masculinity in the Popular Historical Novel of the 1890s." *American Literary History* 2 (December 1990): 659–690.

————. *The Social Construction of American Realism.* Chicago: University of Chicago Press, 1988.

Karcher, Carolyn L. *The First Woman in the Republic: A Cultural Biography of Lydia Maria Child.* Duke University Press, 1994.

Keasy, W. R. "The Lane Seminary Rebellion." *Bulletin of the Historical and Philosophical Society of Ohio* 9 (April 1951): 141–160.

Keller, Rosemary Skinner, Louise L. Queen, and Hilah F. Thomas, eds. *Women in New Worlds.* 2 vols. Nashville: Abingdon, 1982.

Kelley, Mary. *Private Woman, Public Stage: Literary Domesticity in Nineteenth-Century America.* New York: Oxford University Press, 1984.

Kenneally, James J. "The Opposition to Woman Suffrage in Massachusetts, 1868–1920." Ph.D. dissertation, Boston College, 1963.

————. "Women and Trade Unions, 1870–1920: The Quandary of the Reformer." *Labor History* 14 (Winter 1973): 83–91.

Kessler-Harris, Alice. *A Woman's Wage: Historical Meanings and Social Consequences.* Louisville: University Press of Kentucky, 1990.

————. "The Just Price, The Free Market, and the Value of Women." *Feminist Studies* 14 (Summer 1988): 235–250.

————. *Out To Work: A History of Wage-Earning Women in the United States.* New York: Oxford University Press, 1982.

————. "Women's Wage Work as Myth and History." *Labor History* 19 (Spring 1978): 287–301.

Kilson, Marion. *Mary Jane Forbes Greene (1845–1910), Mother of the Japan Mission: An Anthropological Portrait.* Lewiston, N.Y.: Edwin Mellen Press, 1991.

Kraditor, Aileen S. *The Ideas of the Woman Suffrage Movement, 1890–1920.* New York: Columbia University Press, 1965; 2nd ed., New York: Norton, 1981.

————. "Tactical Problems of the Woman Suffrage Movement in the South." *Louisiana Studies* 5 (1966): 289–305.

Krichmar, Albert. *The Woman's Rights Movement in the United States, 1848–1970: A Bibliography and Sourcebook.* Metuchen, N.J.: Scarecrow Press, 1972.

Kugler, Israel. *From Ladies to Women: The Organized Struggle for Woman's Rights in the Reconstruction Era.* Westport, Conn.: Greenwood Press, 1987.

Lamphere, Louise. "Feminist Anthropology: The Legacy of Elsie Clews Parsons." *American Ethnologist* 16 (August 1989): 518–533.

Lane, Ann J. *To 'Herland' and Beyond: The Life and Work of Charlotte Perkins Gilman.* New York: Pantheon, 1990.

Lanser, Susan S. "Feminist Criticism, 'The Yellow Wallpaper,' and the Politics of Color in America." *Feminist Studies* 15 (Fall 1989): 415–442.

Leach, William. *True Love and Perfect Union: The Feminist Reform of Sex and Society.* New York: Basic, 1980.

Lears, T. J. Jackson. *No Place of Grace: Antimodernism and the Transformation of American Culture, 1880–1920.* New York: Pantheon Books, 1981.

Lerner, Gerda. *The Grimké Sisters from South Carolina: Pioneers for Woman's Rights and Abolition.* 1st ed., 1967; New York: Schocken Books, 1978.

Lesnick, Lawrence Thomas. *The Lane Rebels: Evangelicalism and Antislavery in Antebellum America.* Metuchen, N.J.: Scarecrow Press, 1980.

Liestman, Daniel. "To Win Redeemed Souls from Heathen Darkness: Protestant Response to the Chinese of the Pacific Northwest in the Late Nineteenth Century." *Western Historical Quarterly* 24 (1993): 179–201.

Livingston, David N. *Nathaniel Southgate Shaler and the Culture of American Science.* Tuscaloosa: University of Alabama Press, 1987.

Lubove, Roy. *The Professional Altruist: The Emergence of Social Work as a Career, 1880–1930.* New York: Atheneum, 1983.

Lumpkin, Katharine Du Pre. *The Emancipation of Angelina Grimké.* Chapel Hill: University of North Carolina Press, 1974.

Lunardini, Christine A. *From Equal Suffrage to Equal Rights: Alice Paul and the National Woman's Party, 1910–1928.* New York: New York University Press, 1986.

Lutz, Alma. *Created Equal: A Biography of Elizabeth Cady Stanton, 1815–1902.* New York: John Day, 1940.

———. *Crusade for Freedom: Women of the Antislavery Movement.* Boston: Beacon Press, 1968.

———. *Susan B. Anthony: Rebel, Crusader, Humanitarian.* Boston: Beacon Press, 1959.

Manganaro, Marc, ed. *Modernist Anthropology: From Fieldwork to Text.* Princeton: Princeton University Press, 1990.

Marcus, George E., and Michael M. J. Fischer. *Anthropology as Cultural Critique: An Experimental Moment in the Human Sciences.* Chicago: University of Chicago Press, 1986.

Mardock, Robert Winston. *The Reformers and the American Indian.* Columbia: University of Missouri Press, 1971.

Mark, Joan. *A Stranger in Her Native Land: Alice Fletcher and the American Indians.* Lincoln: University of Nebraska Press, 1988.

Marshall, Susan E. "In Defense of Separate Spheres: Class and Status Politics in the Antisuffrage Movement." *Social Forces* 65 (December 1986): 327–351.

Mathes, Valerie Sherer. *Helen Hunt Jackson and Her Indian Reform Legacy.* Austin: University of Texas Press, 1990.

———. "Nineteenth Century Women and Reform: The Women's National Indian Association." *American Indian Quarterly* 14 (1990): 1–18.

McClintock, Anne. *Imperial Leather: Race Gender and Sexuality in the Colonial Contest.* New York: Routledge, 1995.

McPherson, James M. "Abolitionists, Woman Suffrage, and the Negro, 1865–1869." *Mid-America: An Historical Review* 47 (January 1965): 40–47.

———. *Ordeal by Fire: The Civil War and Reconstruction.* New York: Knopf, 1982.

Melder, Keith E. *Beginnings of Sisterhood: The American Woman's Rights Movement, 1800–1850.* New York: Schocken, 1977.

Miller, Stuart C. *Benevolent Assimilation: The American Conquest of the Philippines, 1899–1903.* New Haven: Yale University Press, 1982.

Mohanty, Chandra Talpade, Ann Russo, and Lourdes Torres, eds. *Third World Women and the Politics of Feminism.* Bloomington: Indiana University Press, 1991.

Moore, Jenane Madeline. "Bebe Bwana." *American History Illustrated* 21 (October 1986): 36–42.

Morantz-Sanchez, Regina. "Feminism, Professionalism, and Germs: The Thought of Mary Putnam Jacobi and Elizabeth Blackwell." *American Quarterly* 34 (Winter 1982): 459–478.

———. *Sympathy and Science: Women Physicians in American Medicine.* New York: Oxford University Press, 1985.

Morgan, David. *Suffragists and Democrats: The Politics of Woman Suffrage in America.* East Lansing: Michigan State University Press, 1972.

Morrison, Toni, and Claudia Brodsky Lacour, eds. *Birth of a Nation'hood: Gaze, Script and Spectacle in the O.J. Simpson Case.* New York: Pantheon, 1997.

Mosedale, Susan. "Science Corrupted: Victorian Biologists Consider the Woman Question." *Journal of the History of Biology* 11 (Spring 1978): 1–55.

Murray, Stephen O. "On Boasians and Margaret Mead: Reply to Freeman." *Current Anthropology* 32 (August–October 1991): 488.

The National Woman Suffrage Association. *How Woman Won It.* New York: Wilson, 1940.

Newcomer, Mabel. *A Century of Higher Education for American Woman.* New York: Harper, 1959.

Noun, Louise R. *Strong Minded Women: The Emergence of the Woman Suffrage Movement in Iowa.* Ames: Iowa State University Press, 1969.

Oakley, Mary Ann B. *Elizabeth Cady Stanton.* Old Westbury Conn.: Feminist Press, 1972.

O'Neill, William L. *Everyone Was Brave: The Rise and Fall of Feminism in America.* Chicago: Quadrangle, 1969.

Painter, Nell Irvin. *Sojourner Truth: A Life, a Symbol.* New York: Norton, 1996.

————. *Standing at Armageddon: The United States, 1877–1919.* New York: Norton, 1987.

Papachristou, Judith. "Woman's Suffrage Movement: New Research and New Perspectives." *OAH Newsletter* (August 1986): 5–8.

Pascoe, Peggy. *Relations of Rescue: The Search For Female Authority in the American West, 1874–1939.* New York: Oxford University Press, 1990.

Pearce, Roy Harvey, *Savagism and Civilization: A Study of the Indian and the American Mind.* Baltimore: Johns Hopkins University Press, 1953, 1965.

Pomerantz, Linda. "The Chinese Bourgeoisie and the Anti-Chinese Movement in the United States, 1850–1905." *Amerasia Journal* 11 (1984): 1–34.

Poovey, Mary. *Uneven Developments: The Ideological Work of Gender in Mid-Victorian England.* Chicago: University of Chicago Press, 1988.

Prucha, Francis Paul. *American Indian Policy in Crisis: Christian Reformers and the Indian, 1865–1900.* Norman: University of Oklahoma Press, 1976.

Quarles, Benjamin. "Frederick Douglass and the Women's Rights Movement." *Journal of Negro History* 25 (January 1940): 35–44.

Rabkin, Peggy. *Fathers to Daughters: The Legal Foundations of Female Emancipation.* New York: Greenwood Press, 1980.

Rafter, Nicole Hahn. *White Trash: The Eugenic Family Studies, 1877–1919.* Boston: Northeastern University Press, 1989.

Rappaport, Ray A. "Desecrating the Holy Woman: Derek Freeman's Attack on Margaret Mead." *American Scholar* 55 (Summer 1986): 313–347.

Reuther, Rosemary Radford, and Rosemary Skinner Keller, eds. *Women and Religion in America.* Vol. 1. San Francisco: Harper & Row, 1981.

Riley, Glenda. *Women & Indians on the Frontier, 1825–1915.* Albuquerque: University of New Mexico Press, 1984.

Robinson, Jane. *Wayward Women: A Guide to Women Travellers.* New York: Oxford University Press, 1990.

Roediger, David, *The Wages of Whiteness: Race and the Making of the American Working Class.* New York: Verso, 1991.

————. *Towards the Abolition of Whiteness: Essays on Race, Politics and Working-Class History.* London: Verso, 1994.

Rosaldo, Michelle Zimbalist, and Louise Lamphere. *Woman, Culture and Society.* Stanford: Stanford University Press, 1974.

Rosenberg, Rosalind. *Beyond Separate Spheres: Intellectual Roots of Modern Feminism.* New Haven: Yale University Press, 1982.

———. "The Dissent from Darwin, 1890–1930: A New View of Woman Among American Social Scientists." Ph.D. dissertation, Stanford University, 1974.

Ross, Dorothy. *G. Stanley Hall: The Psychologist as Prophet.* Chicago: University of Chicago Press, 1972.

———. *The Origins of American Social Science.* Cambridge: Cambridge University Press, 1991.

Russett, Cynthia Eagle. *Sexual Science: The Victorian Construction of Womanhood.* Cambridge: Harvard University Press, 1989.

Ryan, Mary P. *Women in Public: Between Banners and Ballots, 1825–1880.* Baltimore: Johns Hopkins University Press, 1990.

Rydell, Robert W. *All the World's a Fair: Visions of Empire at American International Expositions, 1876–1916.* Chicago: University of Chicago Press, 1984.

Sánchez-Eppler, Karen. "Bodily Bonds: The Intersecting Rhetorics of Feminism and Abolition." *Representations* n. 24 (Fall 1988): 28–59.

Saxton, Alexander. *The Rise and Fall of the White Republic: Class Politics and Mass Culture in Nineteenth-Century America.* London: Verso Books, 1990.

Sayers, Janet. *Biological Politics: Feminist and Anti-Feminist Perspectives.* London: Tavistock, 1982.

Scharnhorst, Gary. *Charlotte Perkins Gilman: A Bibliography.* Metuchen, N.J.: Scarecrow Press, 1985.

———. "Making Her Fame: Charlotte Perkins Gilman in California." *California History* 64 (1985): 192–201.

Scott, Anne and Andrew. *One Half the People: The Fight for Woman Suffrage.* New York: Lippincott, 1975.

Seidman, Steven. "Sexual Attitudes of Victorian and Post-Victorian Women: Another Look at the Mosher Survey." *Journal of American Studies* 23 (April 1989): 68–72.

Seller, Maxine. "G. Stanley Hall and Edward Thorndike on the Education of Women: Theory and Policy in the Progressive Era." *Educational Studies* 11 (Winter 1981): 365–374.

Shields, Stephanie. "The Variability Hypothesis: The History of a Biological Model of Sex Differences in Intelligence." *Signs* 7 (Summer 1982): 769–797.

Sklar, Kathryn Kish. *Catharine Beecher: A Study in American Domesticity.* New York: Norton, 1973.

———. "'Women Who Speak for an Entire Nation': American and British Women Compared at the World Anti-Slavery Convention, London, 1840." *Pacific Historical Review* 59 (1990): 453–499.

Smith-Rosenberg, Carroll. *Disorderly Conduct: Visions of Gender in Victorian America.* New York: Oxford University Press, 1985.

Smits, David. "The 'Squaw Drudge': A Prime Index of Savagism." *Ethnohistory* 29 (Fall 1982): 281–306.

Solomon, Barbara Miller. *In the Company of Educated Women: A History of Women and Higher Education in America.* New Haven: Yale University Press, 1985.

Spelman, Elizabeth V. *Inessential Woman: Problems of Exclusion in Feminist Thought.* Boston: Beacon Press, 1988.

Spivak, Gayatri Chakravorty. *In Other Worlds: Essays in Cultural Politics.* New York: Methuen, 1987.

Sterling, Dorothy. *Ahead of Her Time: Abby Kelley and the Politics of Antislavery.* New York: Norton, 1991.

Stevenson, Louise L. "Women Anti-Suffragists in the 1915 Massachusetts Campaign." *New England Quarterly* 52 (1979): 80–93.

Strachey, Ray. *Frances Willard: Her Life and Work.* New York: Revell, 1913.

Stocking, Jr., George W. *Race, Culture and Evolution.* New York: Free Press, 1968.

———. *Victorian Anthropology.* New York: Free Press, 1987.

Strom, Sharon Hartman. "Leadership and Tactics in the American Woman Suffrage Movement: A New Perspective from Massachusetts." *Journal of American History* 62 (September 1975): 296–315.

Takaki, Ronald. *Iron Cages: Race and Culture in Nineteenth-Century America.* New York: Knopf, 1979.

Tax, Meredith. *The Rising of the Women: Feminist Solidarity and Class Conflict, 1880–1917.* New York: Monthly Review Press, 1980.

Terborg-Penn, Rosalyn. "Afro-Americans in the Struggle for Woman Suffrage." Ph.D. dissertation, Howard University, 1977.

———. "Discontented Black Feminists: Prelude and Postscript to the Passage of the Nineteenth Amendment." In *Decades of Discontent: The Women's Movement, 1920–1940.* Ed. Lois Scharf and Joan M. Jensen. Westport, Conn.: Greenwood Press, 1983. 267–278.

———. "Discrimination Against Afro-American Women in the Women's Movement, 1830–1920." In *The Afro-American Woman: Struggles and Images.* Ed. Sharon Harley and Rosalyn Terborg-Penn. Port Washington, N.Y.: Kennikat Press, 1978.

———. "The Historical Treatment of Afro-Americans in the Women's Movement, 1900–1920." *A Current Bibliography of African Affairs* 7 (Summer 1974): 245–259.

———. "Nineteenth Century Black Women and Woman Suffrage." *Potomac Review* 7 (Spring–Summer 1977): 13–24.

Thomas, Mary Martha. *The New Woman in Alabama: Social Reforms and Suffrage, 1890–1920.* Tuscaloosa: University of Alabama Press, 1992.

Thomas, Nicholas. *Colonialism's Culture: Anthropology, Travel and Government.* Princeton: Princeton University Press, 1994.

Thurner, Manuela. "'Better Citizens Without the Ballot': American Antisuffrage Women and Their Rationale During the Progressive Era." *Journal of Women's History* 5 (Spring 1993): 33–60.

Torgovnick, Marianna. *Gone Primitive: Savage Intellects, Modern Lives.* Chicago: University of Chicago Press, 1990.

Trowbridge, Lydia Jones. *Frances Willard of Evanston.* Chicago: Willett, Clark, 1938.

Tyrrell, Ian. *Woman's World, Woman's Empire: The Woman's Christian Temperance Union in International Perspective, 1880–1930.* Chapel Hill: University of North Carolina Press, 1991.

Utley, Robert M. *The Indian Frontier of the American West 1846–1890.* University of New Mexico Press, 1984.

Wade, Richard C. *The Urban Frontier: Pioneer Life in Early Pittsburgh, Cincinnati, Lexington, Louisville, and St. Louis.* Chicago: University of Chicago Press, 1959.

Wagner, Sally Roesch. *A Time of Protest: Suffragists Challenge the Republic, 1870–1887.* Sacramento: Spectrum, 1987.

Walsh, Mary Roth. *"Doctors Wanted: No Women Need Apply": Sexual Barriers in the Medical Profession, 1835–1975.* New Haven: Yale University Press, 1977.

Wang, L. Ling-Chi. "The Structure of Dual Domination: Toward a Paradigm for the Study of the Chinese Diaspora in the United States." *Amerasia* 31 (1995): 149–169.

Wanken, Helen M. "'Woman's Sphere' and Indian Reform: The Women's National Indian Association, 1879–1901." Ph.D. dissertation, Marquette University, 1981.

Ware, Vron. *Beyond the Pale: White Women, Racism and History.* London: Verso Routledge, Chapman and Hall, 1992.

Washington, Mary Helen. "A. J. Cooper—The Black Feminist Voice of the 1890s." *Legacy* 4 (1987): 3–15.

———. Introduction. *A Voice From the South, by a Black Women of the South.* By Anna Julia Cooper. New York: Oxford University Press, 1988.

Weinberg, Julius. *Edward Alsworth Ross and the Sociology of Progressivism.* Madison: State Historical Society of Wisconsin, 1972.

Welter, Barbara. "The Cult of True Womanhood: 1820–1860." *American Quarterly* 18 (Summer 1966): 151–174.

252 • SELECTED BIBLIOGRAPHY

————. "She Hath Done What She Could: Protestant Women's Missionary Careers in Nineteenth-Century America." In *Women in American Religion.* Ed. Janet James. Philadelphia: University of Pennsylvania Press, 1980. 111–125.

Welter, Barbara, ed. *The Woman Question in American History.* Hinsdale, Ill.: Dryden Press, 1973.

White, Deborah Gray. *Ar'n't I A Woman?: Female Slaves in the Plantation South.* New York: Norton, 1985.

Williams, Walter L. "United States Indian Policy and the Debate Over Philippine Annexation: Implications for the Origins of American Imperialism." *Journal of American History* 66 (March 1979): 810–831.

Williamson, Joel. *New People: Miscegenation and Mulattoes in the United States.* New York: New York University Press, 1984.

Wolgast, Elizabeth H. *Equality and the Rights of Women.* Ithaca: Cornell University Press, 1980.

Yellin, Jean Fagan. *Women & Sisters: The Anti-Slavery Feminists in American Culture.* New Haven: Yale University Press, 1989.

Index